International Cookb

5 Books In 1: Over 500 ʀ͏ͼ͏ͼͺ͏
Chinese, Indian, Thai, Mexican And Japu͏ͷ͏ͼ͏   d
At Home

By

Adele Tyler

Indian Home Cooking

The ultimate cookbook to prepare over 100 delicious, traditional and modern Indian recipes to spice up your meals

By

Adele Tyler

Table of Contents

Introduction

India, South Asia's great area of land, is host to one of the largest and most powerful civilizations in the world. We are all quite mindful of the fact that the Indians are quite foodie. We always wish to speak about cooking, to eat and to try various recipes. Certainly, each and every single household in India has its own formula which they elevate from generation to generation. Yet, how much are we really conscious of Indian food history? Thus, the Indian Food Heritage journey will be discussed in this topic.

India has received a multitude of immigrants with a number of religious traditions through more than 4,000 years of recorded history.

To understand the dynamics of India's native food culture, one has to know that this nation is far from culturally homogeneous.

Regions and sects make up a great deal of the food. "Indian food" was invented a term that a native will probably chuckle at because such a word would be like saying "North American wine" to a wine expert.

There are many places in India that have their own special cooking methods, seasonings, and fresh ingredients. Tipping its population-scale to over a billion, its food diversity is as diverse as its inhabitants.

Muslims and Hindu are the two dominant sects that most affected Indian food culture and food choices. They took out their own food practices with each movement of natives. There is the widespread practice of the vegetarian Hindu culture. In comparison, Muslim culture is the most common in meat cooking. Mughlai cuisine, kababs, nargisi kaftas, biryani and favorite dishes served in the tandoor are great benefits provided by Muslim natives in India. The food in South India is mostly rice related, with a thin porridge accent named Rasam. In all South Indian cuisine, coconut is an essential component. Dosa and idli are very common foods among vegetarian from Hindu culture. Also, the Portuguese, Persians, and British contributed a great deal too Indian food. The British brought tea to India, and it is nowadays the favorite drink of many Indians.

The four main geographic types of Indian cooking are the North, East, South, and West. North India was impacted by the Mughal dynasty which held power for 300 years until they were substituted by the British in the 18th century. Naan bread, produced in a tandoor, is not native. It is the Afghani people's daily meal. Naan is not Indians' baked daily bread, but it has been a common misconception of Indian food outside the region for decades.

Among Southern Indians, specified steamed rice cakes are favorite. Rice is consumed in all meals, and lunch mostly consists of all meal courses, each filled with rice again. The Hindus are categorized into vegetarians and non-vegetarians. Their common thread in Kerala's Southern Region is coconut, which is the state's culinary mascot.

The Gujarat, Maharashtra and Goa western states all have unique experiences of health. Gujarat has predominantly Muslims, Hindus, Parsis and Jains who have their own cooking methods. Parsis have a rich diet of poultry and seafood. Gujaratis are primarily veggie eaters, and Gujarat is known as one of the best places for consuming vegetarian food. Maharashtra is a large state with its Mumbai city of fame. East states are very distinct. Bengali cuisine, with fish and rice at the core of the diet, can be characterized as delicate and subtle. The order of a Bengali meal starts with a mixed vegetable dish with a bitter taste and finishes with a rich sweet dessert based on milk for which Bengali is popular. Orissa is popular for squash blossoms rolled in rice and deep-fried paste or turned into patties. Cod and other fish are in the diet too. It is very rare that chicken will be eaten here, and poultry plays a small culinary role in general. Bihar and Jharkhand love their vegetables and beans, but with their diet, they do have Western overtones like beef, pork, goat and poultry. Indian cuisine tends to be unified only by its locality from East to West, but its taste is evidently boundless.

Brief History of Traditional Indian Dishes

The past of Indian food is the background of innovation from various societies in periods of need and succession. Such dishes were created for general populous sake, while others have been imported from all over the geographies. Many of those fascinating Indian food tales are now unaware of. Some of the Traditional Indian is explained as below:

- Petha is older than Taj Mahal

Petha in Agra is the best choice to consume. The innovation is relevant to the development of the Taj Mahal in the Mughals. When the monumental shrine was under a building, the daily meal containing just dal and roti bored some 20,000 employees. Then Mughal Emperor Shah Jahan expressed his worry with the master architect Ustad Isa Effendi who demanded a response to the Emperor's problems from Pir Naqshbandi Sahib. It is claimed that one day, during prayers, the Pir formed a trance and gave Petha's formula to Mughal. About 500 cooks then rendered Petha for the staff.

- **Dal Bati Was a Tool of Survival in Wars**

This is Rajasthan's best food to eat. The recipe of Dal Bati is a tale worth sharing with. This Rajasthani food has its roots in the popular Mewar Chittorgarh Fort. Bati is wheat dough fried in oil, a food that the Mewar Rajput kings needed to live in unfavorable wartime circumstances. Bati could be produced in the desert lands of Rajasthan with the few supplies and a little water available.

- **Mysore Went from Monarchy to Common**

It is South India's, iconic sweetmeat. The past of Mysore is related to the Mysore Palace kitchen of the early 20th century. In the Mysore Palace, the royal cook used to impress the King with numerous dishes. He rendered a new sweet dish one day with the mixture of chickpea flour, oil and sugar. The cook coined the word 'Mysore Paka' in a split second on being questioned the word of the sauce. 'Paka' is a Kannada word which signifies a sweet mixture.

- **Khaja is Generational of the Mauryan and Gupta Realms**

While the cooking art of creating Khaja is a moment of honor for the Orissa citizens, it is claimed that the technique was borrowed from Bihar's central highlands around 2200 years ago. Khaja's roots go back to antique Indian Gupta empires. Rajgir's Khaja in Bihar is famed for its swelling, while Kakinada's Khaja in Andhra Pradesh is popular for its dry outside but savory within.

- **Jalebi's Culture is Not Necessarily Indian**

One of India's most famous sweet dishes, Jalebi owes its roots to West Asia. Jalebi was introduced to India in mediaeval times by the Persian-speaking invaders. This sweetmeat was called 'Kundalika' in India in the 14th century, and 'Jalavallika'. During Ramadan in Iran, the poor were given platefuls of Jalebi.

- **Dum Biryani Provided Meals in Awadh for the Needy**

According to numerous historical records, the root of biryani is the provincial capital of Hyderabad in the Nawab period. Some discussions show that biryani was initiated in the early mediaeval era during Timur's invasion of India. While biryani's origin is being discussed, Dum Biryani or Awadh's Biryani emerged in Lucknow. The Nawab of Awadh directed all the poor folks of his area to cook a meal in big handis (round-shaped brass pots) when food was scarce. A large volume of food was cooked in covered and sealed pans, with limited energy. This cooking craft has been popular as 'dum'.

Indian Food and Its Popularity in the US

Indian food is becoming increasingly common in the US. It is like a highly specialized food right now.

Apart from Chinese cuisine, which is almost part of the American environment, the food network shows even more references of Indian cuisine and Indian ingredients are showing up everywhere in the US. Thanks to their wonderful taste, Indian dishes have earned popularity around the world. Several tasty Indian meals are cooked in different dining spots around the country. Various fans on a global scale have noticed the vast range of salads, appetizers, sweets, side dishes and desserts, as Indian restaurants have been expanded at an unprecedented pace, with immense popularity in every imaginable community and in every imaginable corner of the Globe.

India is the world's largest grocer of fruit. India has tremendous science and engineering potential that is rapidly being used to produce modern, popular food goods in the US. New products are still in demand, so there is tremendous potential for new products, especially in the US, where people love to eat Indian food. The success of American Indian food has also enabled a movement for Indian businesses to sell more food products to the US.

Indian cuisine is known in the world for its spices and aromatic taste. The numerous Indian restaurants in Washington DC prepare mouth-watering dishes and serve it to both the visitors and the local people in the region. Every place has unique culinary art, which is completely different from each other. These techniques were introduced to western countries and acquired enormous prominence among citizens. For special occasions, the special dish is cooked. Many international buyers have been fascinated by the spices and the different products used to cook such dishes.

It is very important to remember that there is a therapeutic benefit in most Indian spices. The most widely used herbs are turmeric, ginger and cardamom since they have therapeutic properties.

This is one of the key explanations, why citizens in the US are sincerely willing to consume Indian food, claiming that the Indian food would not affect their body in any way as the spices used, have medicinal properties. In this book, you will learn the Indian Cuisine, spices often used in them, and 100 recipes, in detail.

Chapter 01: Learning the Basics of Indian Cuisine

Indian cuisine is comprised of a number of modern and conventional Indian subcontinent cuisines. Owing to the variety of land, climate, history, ethnic groups, and professions, these foods differ considerably and use herbs, vegetables, and fruits available locally. Also, Indian food is highly related to religion, particularly Hinduism, social decisions and rituals.

1.1 Indian Regional Foods - at a Glance

While presenting dishes as part of a standardized, nationalized cuisine is popular for Indian restaurants. India's food is actually as regionally unique and diverse as its people. These foods are hugely affected by the past of India, it is trading relations, and it is cultural and religious traditions. A little context on the commonalities and variations between the regional cuisines of India will transform your next Indian meal into an entertaining, and profoundly gratifying.

While Indian food is highly local unique, there are some popular ties that connect the numerous cuisine practices. Indian cuisine across the nation is highly reliant on sauces, which are sauce-like sauce or soup-like meat, potato, or cheese dishes. However, the unique spice mixtures, liquidity amount, and ingredients are decided by regional choice. In general, Indian cuisine is also highly dependent upon agriculture, while Southern Indian areas use rice more strongly than other places. Both regional foods depend on legumes or "pulses." Indian cuisine can use a wider range of peas than any other menu selections: Red lentils, black gram, peas or yellow gramme, black gramme, and green gramme are used in a variety of Indian dishes as a whole, broken, or ground in flour. Add tartness to meals that do not use eggs, legumes, and nutrition to vegan diets.

The rich usage of spices is probably the most distinguishing feature of Indian food. Indian spice blends mostly use up to five separate spices, occasionally adding ten or more. Garam masala is a common mixture of spices, cardamom, cinnamon, and clove, with the specific spices differing by area and personal recipe.

⊥ Observations Indicated: Commerce and Invasion

In India's cuisine, the cultural effect of trade is clear, with unique areas and dishes carrying the sign of international influence. Arab and Canadian traders strongly desired India's spices; in return, India obtained several commodities that profoundly shaped its food heritage. Portuguese merchants carried in New World products such as onions, peppers, and chilies, which were profoundly incorporated into Indian dishes. Coffee was carried by Arab merchants.

India's occupation times have also significantly influenced the nature of its delicacies. Mughal conquerors, who ruled India between both the early 1500s and late 1600s, introduced Persian spices and traditions in India's culinary culture.

The influence is noticeable in the use of cheese and milk in sauces, the use of meat and nuts in salads, and in particular in salads.

Although the arrival of the British in India exposed the nation to soup and tea; it had no effect on its food. However, the imperial incorporation of local food into British society has profoundly influenced Indian food translation abroad. Tikka Masala, a flavorful sauce on many Indian menus, is originally an Anglo-Indian invention and is widely called as "Britain's true national dish". Even European conceptions of Indian "curry"-the term applies to a myriad of garlicky and stew-like meals-are inferred from British understanding of Indian cuisine.

⊹ India: Large Community

The population of India is incredibly complex, with cultural traditions deeply shaped by ethnic and religious specificities. Ayurvedic traditions also exercised control on Indian cuisine in particular by trying to dictate spice combinations and cooking methods, stressing the balance between brain, body, and spirit. This theory is a popular influence in Indian cuisine, as per religion and cultural characteristics. Around one-third of the population in India is vegetarian, determined by its Hindu, Jain or Buddhist values. Consequently, a large portion of the countrywide Indian dishes is without beef. In addition, religious traditions influence other dietary prohibitions that form India's cuisine: Hindu believers abstain from meat, since cattle are holy in this religion, whereas Muslims claim that pork is impure and they never eat it. Depending on a region's prevailing religious beliefs, cooking in a given area can exclude those ingredients to conform to religious rules.

⊥ Northern Indian Kitchen

Northern Indian cuisine, possibly the most widespread cuisine form found from outside India, demonstrates a clear Mughal influence. It is distinguished by strong dairy consumption: milk, paneer (a mild Indian cheese), butter, and yoghurt are all commonly used in Northern dishes. A famous Northern treat is samosas and sometimes beef. Clay ovens identified as tandoors are common in the North, offering their distinct barbecue flavor to dishes such as naan. A considerable number of Northern foods appear daily on Indian menus. Dal or Paneer Makhani is common vegetarian dishes, comprising of dal or paneer fried in a creamy tomato sauce, oignons, mango dust, and curry powder. Korma, another Northern Indian staple meal, is a smooth curry with coconut milk or yoghurt, cumin, cilantro and tiny quantities of cashews or walnuts. It can be eaten with numerous meats, typically poultry or lamb, but often beef and a vegan dish with paneer.

⊥ West Indian Kitchen

Western local food is characterized by its region's political and cultural particularities. The coastal area of Maharashtra is known for their milk-dominant seafood and coconut cuisine. Gujarati food is mainly vegetarian, and due to strong influences, has an inherent sweetness to most of its dishes. Since this region's dry climate reported to be low veggies, this region is well renowned for its chutneys, common Indian condiments which use fried, fresh, or marinated fruits and vegetables with sweet, sour, or spicy flavors. Goa served as a large port and colony of commerce for Portugal, culminating in a rare mix of Indian and Portuguese cuisine features. Goa cuisine utilizes more commonly than other different foods in India, utilizing beef and pork. Vinegar is also a distinctive component in Goa cuisine. Its coastal presence results in the proliferation of coconut milk, coconut powder and fish in Goa cuisine.

ⵜ East Indian Kitchen

Eastern local food is renowned mainly for their sweets. Not only are these desserts preferred by other states of India, but they are also found in restaurants. Their delicate sweet is rendering an outstanding finale to dinner. Rasgulla is a common sweet treat, consisting of balls of semolina and cheese curd, boiled in light sugar syrup. Eastern dishes prefer mustard seeds and mustard oil, bringing a pleasant smell to the dishes. In Eastern cuisine rice and seafood are also prominent. Eastern foods, on the whole, are spiced more strongly than from certain countries.

ⵜ Indian Southern Food

Southern Indian food is not usually seen on many menus of restaurants and is somewhat distinct from other areas. Their "curries" vary greatly in their appearance and may usually be classified as per the drier quality, or those preferring a more stew-like or soupy appearance. Poriyals, dried curries made up of a mixture of veggies and seasoning, complement the rice food. Sambars are basically pea and vegetable stews with a tamarind taste, which are soupier than curries from many other countries, but smoother than rasams. Rasams in their quality is somewhat comparable to soups, and comprise mostly of tomatoes, tamarind, and a variety of spices. Kootus is more comparable to curries seen in other regions, but instead of being fluffy like the North's dairy-based curries, kootus gets its strength from drained lentils.

Southern Indian food is renowned for its exquisite fried or griddle-cooked sweets, in addition to curry-style dishes. Dosas consist of a broad crepe. They are normally packed with curries of veggies, curries, or seasonings. Idli is fried delicacy identical to savory doughnuts, which are eaten as sambar and rasam side dishes.

Apart from restaurants directly serving Southern Indian cuisine, pappadams, fried crispy rice cookies commonly spiced with black peppercorns, are the only South Indian food that are often seen in Indian restaurants.

1.2 Features of Indian Food

Indian food has penetrated all territorial frontiers and entered the international territory. Everyone seems to recognize and love the Tandoori chicken or the Pav bhaji or the Kesar kulfi today. Foodies worldwide are massive fans of both vegetarian and non-vegetarian Indian delicacies.

+ The Pattern Present

More and more customers are visiting the world's prestigious Indian restaurants and eating famous Indian culinary delights. In the food chain, Indian food is growing rapidly by the day. Tandoori is strongly in request all over the world. North Indian food is extremely delicious. The wonderful Tandoori snacks like the Tandoori Chicken Chicken Reshmi Kebabs and much more you will never get over.

+ Astonishing Richness

Owing to its exceptional variety Indian food is becoming famous over the years. Indian food has plenty for any form of taste bud to satisfy. Some citizens are interested in South Indian delicacies; some are intrigued by Punjabi delights, some are obsessed with Rajasthani or Goa food, Parsi food or mouth-watering Bengali foods. A new life has been granted to Indian street food by adding a few fusion variants.

+ Food the Unstoppable Ratio

Most Indian foods are cooked in such a way that the nutritious content of all the products is preserved and is not compromised due to the cooking method.

Indian cuisine gets its true experience and tastes owing to a number of spices. These spices are good for the skin. It offers pickles and greens in various parts of India. Their flavors are special to the area, but they can activate your taste buds.

1.3 Essentials of Indian Foods in your Diet and Its Benefits

Taking into account considerations, we have arranged an important Indian food that must be part of every diet. Remember that if you are struggling from any health condition, please ask your doctor what you can take from this chart and cannot.

⁜ Fruits

Many typical fruits of Indian heritage are perfect for you. They include all sorts of essential vitamins and minerals which are important to us. You can consume daily seasonal and annual fruits, such as strawberries, bananas, pomegranates, pineapples, etc. People with such health problems ought to avoid certain fruits but, for the normal citizen, these are the ideal healthy food that can supplement the fried chip bag. Health advantages Fruits provides:

> ➤ Fruits are suppliers of various under-consumed vital nutrients, including calcium, dietary fiber and vitamin C.

> ➤ Typically most fruits are poor in sugar, salt and energy.

> ➤ As you consume fruit, the energy production rises in no time; it is one of the fruit's main advantages that we can include in our hectic schedules.

> ➤ Not only does the fiber content in the fruit have a genius relaxing effect, but it also helps you feel complete when incorporating bulk protein to your diet.

↓ Chilies

New chilies, even more than other vegetables, are an outstanding rich in vitamin C. If you want spicy cuisine, you are here for luck. There are plenty of less "hard" chilies accessible for those averse to intense spicy recipes that can have the same advantages without the burning feeling. Even chilies are improving metabolism. Chilies wellness advantages:

➢ Chili provides up to 7 times the amount of orange vitamin C, which has a variety of health benefits like combating sinus inflammation, improving metabolism, which relieving migraines and heart, joint and nerve discomfort.

➢ Chili has traditionally been used to minimize bio-contamination of food and is often considered a possible weight reduction metabolic accelerator.

➢ It can also play a part in managing leukemia and removing lung cancer.

↓ Beans

They provide a fantastic source of protein, calcium, magnesium, and folic acid. They are flexible too, helping you to prepare loads of Indian dishes. They also go along for other community's cuisines-from Asian to the USA. Beans Benefits:

➢ Beans are "heart safe" since they produce reduce cholesterol levels of soluble fiber.

➢ The bulk of beans are around 2 to 3% fat and do not produce cholesterol unless cooked or packed with other products.

➢ Beans packed with fiber, avoiding acid reflux will foster regularity.

➢ The daily intake of beans will reduce the likelihood of cardiovascular disease.

ⵌ Garlic

Not only is garlic savory, but it is also often known for its numerous medicinal powers. It is a key natural source of antimicrobial agents. For garlic's nutritional benefits:

➢ Garlic produces a Labeled Allicin compound with strong healing uses.

➢ Frequent application of garlic (in diet or raw) tends to reduce total cholesterol because of Allicin's antioxidant property.

➢ The exhilarating properties of garlic safeguard the body from free radicals and slow down collagen depletion leading to loss of conductivity in ageing skin.

ⵌ Spices

Since ancient times Indian spices have become world-renowned. In addition to their amazing flavor and tastes, several spices are good for you too. Haldi or turmeric has soothing powers, helps to lower cholesterol, and avoids blood clots which may contribute to heart attacks. Cardamom improves metabolism while garam masala ingredients comprise various levels of nutrients, thus facilitating digestion as well. Spices Nutritional advantages:

➢ Many herbs and spices often provide more antioxidants to suppress the disease than vegetables and fruits.

➢ Cinnamon has a potent anti-diabetic activity and reduces blood sugar levels.

➢ Turmeric consists of curcumin, a material with significant antioxidant effects

➢ Ginger has anti-inflammatory action and may relieve nausea.

ⵌ Paneer

It is a big part of the vegetarian diet, but it is frequently eaten also by non-vegetarians. Paneer is a flexible meal that lends itself well to several various types of dishes. You can also stop the muscle mass-heavy variety produced from whole milk. Home-made breadcrumbs made of milk produce fewer fatty acids and cholesterol and are much better for you. But can also maintain the large amino and calcium concentrations. Paneer Advantages:

➢ Up to now, maybe popular knowledge, but paneer is a rich source of protein, particularly for vegetarian diets that do not get their meat intake.

➢ Since paneer is composed of protein, it steadily absorbs energy into the bloodstream, ensuring that it does not induce a spike in one's blood sugar levels, nor does it provide an immediate rise that will soon decrease.

➢ Besides being high in protein, paneer is a fantastic source of linoleic — a fatty acid that helps to shed weight by growing the mechanism of burning fat in the body.

➢ Avoids numerous disorders of the body, such as osteoporosis, knee discomfort and dental issues such as rotting of the teeth and gums.

✦ Flour and Rice

White rice is the most widely-eaten grain in India. You can, though, aim to turn to brown rice, since it incorporates more protein, making it a safer option. The switch to whole wheat flour has become more popular. Even for other wheat items like bread, you should suggest doing the same. Health advantages, which Rice and Flour provide:

➢ Our bodies require insoluble fibers to help them get rid of waste, so if constipation is an issue, rice and flour — particularly brown rice flour — will help alongside nuts, beans and vegetables such as cabbage— all foods that provide most of the fiber.

➢ Rice and flour are high in protein, with an advanced rank of B vitamins.

➢ Dietary fiber is an integral portion of every diet. Rice contains dietary fiber and helps to transfer waste products via the digestive tract.

✦ Pulses

The Indian diet is incredibly high in grains. The main instances are rice and pasta but note that pulses are an important part of our staple. Luckily, there are so many varieties of pulses accessible that diversity can always be preserved in your diet. Pulses are abundant in nutritious fibers and nutrients A, B, C and E. Even they produce minerals such as calcium and iron. Over everything, they are the primary source of nutrition in a vegetarian diet. Pulses health advantages:

➢ The use of more pulses in your eating habits can reduce your risk of heart disease.

➢ Pulses are the item with a lot of sugar. The sugar content lists the diet in terms of how it influences blood sugar.

➢ Pulses often render the protein a safe and cheap source.

✦ Leafy Vegetables

In the Indian diet, green leafy vegetables already are common. Yet they can be placed to further use. During the whole year Spinach is found throughout the region.

Cabbages are also available in several areas throughout the year, too. Furthermore, hundreds of different types of leafy greens are just ready to include in your diet, depending on where in the world you reside. Leafy Vegetation has health advantages:

> Mustard and Kale greens aid reduce cholesterol.

> Leafy greens maintain good vision and reduce the likelihood of cataracts and improve the clarity you can see.

> They help to feed the body and create electricity.

> They have a mildly acidic taste: It represents their elevated calcium levels.

🞥 Eggs Proceed

Although they are not necessarily a choice for vegetarian diets, they are excellent protein sources. The yolk does produce cholesterol – even if you are careful about eating the whole thing, the egg-white will help the body get the necessary minerals and nutrients. You can add eggs to almost every plate. Health advantages that Eggs provide:

> Eggs provide a very great method of free, high-quality protein.

> Feeding small kid's just one egg per day for six months, coupled with a decreased sugar-sweetened diet, can help them reach a healthy height.

> Eggs are rich in cholesterol but do not negatively impact cholesterol throughout the tissue.

> Eggs are high in some nutrients which support cardiac protection.

1.4 Health Benefits of Consuming Indian Food

The use of spices like onion, turmeric, ginger and garlic in the recipe contributes to several health advantages such as better cholesterol, lower risk of cancer and better kidney function. While we know that Indian food has several medical advantages, including spices and vegetables, you may be shocked that Indian food is not always safe. Most Indian cuisine is plant-based. Research shows there are several positive effects of consuming a plant-based diet. Some of these advantages are listed below:

- **A healthy Vegetarian Diet**

Indian dishes are perfect nutritious recipes, using a wide range of vegetables, legumes, and grains. The mixture of rice that helps you to get full protein. Since Indian ingredients use a variety of foods every day, all the minerals and vitamins found in different plants are more likely to be collected.

There are several nutrients and antioxidants in the vegetables in these dishes that are good for health, liver and brain. The Sulphur compounds present in garlic, cauliflower, and cabbage, for example, help detoxify the body from mycotoxins and toxic toxins.

- **Anti-Inflammatory Effect**

Turmeric and other spices give anti-inflammatory properties and reduce the likelihood of several chronic disorders. They frequently help relieve inflammation.

Other spices minimize inflammation, improve metabolism, aid weight control and aid detoxify the body. Often, cinnamon tends to control blood sugar levels. If you want your Indian dish to be hot and spicy, the chili is your buddy not just for your taste sense but also for your general health. Chilies are accessed of vitamin C and vitamin A.

Higher Concentrations of Fiber

Good sources of both soluble and insoluble fibers are chickpeas, green vegetables, corn, grains, lentils, green beans etc. When immersed in water, soluble fibers from the peas and beans form a gel-like material. It plays a significant role in reducing your cholesterol levels and regulating your blood sugar levels. Insoluble dietary fiber facilitates regularity in the intestines and avoids indigestion.

Ghee Wellness Facilities

In reality, ghee is nutritious, and if used correctly in balance, it has healing characteristics. Pure cow ghee is a key product in Indian and Ayurvedic medicinal cooking. You will use ghee as an alternative technique to butter, palm oil and hydrolyzed fat on the market. The explanation is because ghee's chemical composition is more robust than olive oil, and it does not quickly flame or get rancid. The concern for much on the market vegetable oil is that the molecular structure starts to break down during the process of heating. They quickly get oxidized and create several complications in the body by growing the number of free radicals. And you actually even know yourself how awful saturated fat is. Clarified butter or ghee, on the other side, helps guard against the toxins and supplies important fatty acids for the hormone development in the body. Ghee decreases inflammation, facilitates nutrition and improves metabolism as per Ayurveda.

1.5 How is Home Cooked Indian Food Different from Restaurant Food?

South Asian cuisine is salty, fatty, wholesome and absolutely delicious cuisine. Indian cuisine is a significant feature of U.S.-Asian life, whether in the warmth of their own homes or at a local restaurant.

Eating out, however, was not a practice among the prior eras of South Asians who were settling in the US. Many saw it as something they did not do back home, an unnecessary privilege, distrusting the recipes or culinary style of 'outside' cuisine, believing the cuisine was designed for the English palate and classifying it as an elite practice. It was the custom to prepare at home, only rarely did US-Asian family go out to dinner. Many stayed as extended families in the same home for up to three families and dining out was not even a choice.

Today, in Indian restaurants, young people of USA-Asians are dining out more, bringing families out for dinner, getting take-outs and not preparing as much at home as in the past. The notion of dining out in Asian Americans is, therefore, a question of preference and culture, not hindered by disparities between generations.

And What Might be better? Home Eating or Out?

Many USA Asians also love home-made food as they feel that it is unique because of the raw vegetables and the freedom to put something you like into your own oven. Others say going out to eat makes a night more fun, sociable and calming. Although all have their positive and bad points, Asians in the USA love a hot curry and enjoy it more when there is a choice to choose from. This is where restaurant cuisine comes in handy, as it offers various meals for all of you who want to eat. So if you are with your mates, you may select from a list and eat whatever you want, but if you are at home, let's just agree it is easier to consume everything.

However, food can always be roasted at restaurants to accommodate the crowd, rather than the person. Chicken Tikka Masala, for example, is a very common restaurant recipe, and maybe never named it in an Asian home when made.

Personalized ingredients are used at home to create such a dish centered on relatives or previously acquired recipes. Ingredients like unique herbs, achaar, or yoghurt are used to create such a recipe that fits your own palate.

Asians enjoy the food but most especially eat it as quickly as possible on our tables. Eating in does not necessarily mean you are going to eat on time, since preparing Asian meals at home will take time utilizing established fresh produce and recipes. It is giving love and attention to your home, always cooking pays-off, particularly if it's something unique for someone!

You have a starter at restaurants, a main dish meal as well as a cake, but this is not that much for those of you with a huge appetite. You can feel like you do not get your money worth as the sizes of the section are rather limited. A Lamb Balti bowl, for instance, can cost around $6-8. If cooking at home, this quantity may suffice for you and your guests, with larger serving sizes and the opportunity, if needed, to incorporate more. All of us, Asians, are now victims to the fast-food community as Britain gets more urbanized. This is because of the hectic lives that we all live through. While most of the old people enjoy a good home-cooked dinner, the new ones consider it more convenient to eat out.

Chapter 02: Common Spices Used in Indian Cuisine and their Properties

Indian food includes the use of a large range of spices. They are mixed and used extensively in different recipes The same spice flavor may be rendered completely different with a slight change in the style of cooking. To discover these amazing products, we have identified several of India's most frequently used spices.

⊥ Red Powder Chili

Red chili is produced of red chili seeds. It is extremely solid, being the strongest component of the chili, only used in limited amounts. The Americans and the Portuguese brought this substance to India, which has became an important part of Indian cuisine. Even the chili is used in numerous Southern Indian curries. The key feature of chili is hotness, probably due to its capsaicin portion, but there are types that also have a lot of fragrance and flavor.

♣ Mustard Seeds

Brown mustard seeds are more widely used in Indian cuisine than any other mustard seeds. These seeds may be roasted whole for flavoring oil which is then used for cooking raw food. Even this favourite oil may be used as a dipping sauce. Although the seeds are local in Rome, the closest approximation to their usage is in Buddha literature, where he uses certain seeds to save the life of a child.

♣ Coriander

Coriander is a part of the Parsley Genus, and when they mature, the seeds are round, ridged, and change its color from dark green to bright orange. This spice looks tangy and pleasant, with a mild citrusy aroma. This invisible spice is undoubtedly the world's oldest and is commonly cultivated in Rajasthan States.

♣ Cinnamon

Cinnamon is a sweet-flavored spice with a soft and woody fragrance. It is a perfect product for use in sweets and cakes. Cinnamon also has numerous benefits, including bringing spice to the food. Also it helps to reduce leukaemia and lower cholesterol. It is cultivated primarily along the Kerela and Tamil Nadu Western Ghats.

♣ Asafoetida

This is the cured resin emerging from a plant's base. It is particularly pungent in its natural state with a garlic like sulphur scent. However, the scent dies down when cooked in oil, and the flavour significantly improves.

Typically, asafoetida is added to boiling oil before some other component. It is prized for its truffle-like taste and roasted garlic scent and it is used in Indian food as a seasoning blend and flavoring agent. Asafoetida, grown primarily in Kashmir and some parts of Punjab. It is very beneficial for its bashing flatulence properties.

⥥ Cumin

Cumin is extracted from the Parsley group and is used in most Indian sauces and veggies to give a smoky flavor and a strong fragrance. Cumin seeds are fried in its dry shape and cooked before use. It is typically the very first spice to be added while preparing Indian foods. It is often roasted dry and reduced to dust before adding to dishes such as pancakes and heavy cream. It is also used for flavoring meat, stuffed onions and tonnes of Indian cooking. It is used carefully since it burns quickly and may become intoxicating.

⥥ Saffron

Saffron is the world's costly spice. Actually originated in Kashmir and originating from the prejudice of Cocus Bulbs. It is considered that saffron is more precious than money. Its most notable thing is its musky, honey-like scent. It is commonly used after soaking in water or milk, which eases its intense fragrance and taste.

⥥ Tumeric

Another spice that belongs to the ginger tribe is tumeric. It is possibly the spice used mostly in India. Turmeric has been used primarily as a pigment, and for hundreds of years in traditional Ayurvedic. Generated from the roots of the Indian born leafy plant Curcuma Longa.

It has an oaky quality and mild smell and flavour. It is used in items intended for cooking and skincare products. It has a wide variety of medical applications. It aids in coping with skin issues. Its powder could be used to heal open wounds. It also allows to deal with diabetes.

⁜ Cardamom

It is the world's third most costly spice, primarily since it needs a lot of physical work. While it has a moderate and soft eucalyptus colour on the green cardamom, the black cardamom is coarse, smoky and usually mostly used for its seeds. The most popular usage for cardamom is to improve tea and pudding taste.

It is used to provide a strong taste and scent in most Indian and other sweet dishes. It is commonly used in the drug industry . It helps protect against poor smell and stomach disease. Whole chewed cardamom is ideal for dealing with diabetes.

⁜ Indian Bay Leaf

Indian Bay Leaf is quite distinct from European Bay Leaf even though both belong to the Lauraceae tribe. They are the leaves of a cinnamon tree parent and are distinctive from their white shelves streaks that extend through the root. They are extremely light but have a heavy spice taste.

It grows in northern India, Himalayan slopes and Nepal. Sikkim State is the biggest producer in India, but it is most frequently formed from raw or wild plants. It is a critical element in Mughal food and produced in popular dishes like Korma and biryani.

⁜ Ginger

Ginger is one of India's most valuable crops, with more than one thousand tonnes growth per year.

Mostly the fresh ginger is used. Dry ginger is used only in certain states in India, such as Goa and Kashmir.

There are two major ginger types, called after the port they were transported from "Cochin" in the south of Kerala, and "Calicut" in the north of Kerala. Both are strongly aromatic with about 4 percent essential oil content and low fibre content. Owing to its milder and more nuanced taste, it is found to be superior to ginger grown in many other countries. Dried ginger is not as common as fresh ginger in Indian dishes.

⊹ Leaves Curry

The curry leaves, which have little to do with spice, are the leaf of a bush in the Rutaceae family, which is local to India and Sri Lanka. This vegetation is very smelly and friendly. The curry tree is now cultivated in all parts of India but it is more cultivated in the Southern India. So many households have a plant in their greenhouse because it is simple to cultivate. The leaves are often used in the north (for example combined with potato and peas samosa stuffing). They are used in sauces of beef and poultry.

⊹ Kalonji / Nigella

This plant has black triangular seeds, sometimes mistakenly referred to as black cumin, have a mild and somewhat bitter taste, with earthy tones and an onion-like pungent flavour. India is the leading supplier of Kalonji. Egypt and Morocco are the other production countries.

These seeds are also a potent antioxidant and are associated with several medicinal effects, against asthma, fever, pneumonia and other fall diseases.

⊥ Ajowan

Another seed spice from a member of the family Umbelliferae is Ajowan. It has a faint bitter earthy flavour, and a fragrance identical to thyme but more strong. The process of cooking (especially baking) smooths the tendency to influence Ajowan, thus producing a rather peculiar nutty taste.

Rajasthan is India's leading Ajowan manufacturer, responsible for 90 percent of total production. Sometimes used for savoury snacks and baked goods in Indian cuisine, it gives a savoury feel to many vegetable meals. Its therapeutic properties vary from assisting with digestion to curing colds and eliminating bloating.

⊥ Dark Brown Mustard

It is one of the few seasonings that is as popular in the states having the most flavor consuming nations such as Indonesia and India. In Europe and America, mustard seeds are almost solely used for producing the sauce of the very same name originating from the Roman mixture of mustard seeds with their distinctive sourness.

There are three mustard types that are the light, the brown and the black. The light one is the gentler, whereas the other two are pungent. It is also part of the North-East traditional spice blend. In this area, there is an Indian variant of mustard sauce produced from a mixture of mustard seeds that are soaked for a few days.

Mustard seeds only produce their pungency when grounded or compressed and combined with a fluid using the sourness and stabilise it with an acidic fluid.

⊥ Fenugreek

Fenugreek is a herb of the Legumes family. Its plants are used in fresh, dry, and seed forms.

The Hindi word is Methi. Its flavour is whacky and sour (toasting the seeds decreases the bitterness) and its usage is as common as a medicinal treatment in the kitchen. The seeds as a spice are mainly used in India, Turkey, but India is the main source and purchaser of it.

It is an essential component of curry in the kitchen. In Punjab, it is used to complement the flavour of vegetables such as pumpkin, and in the Southern India it is applied to dosa. Batter-dosa includes tasty Indian rice and dal pancakes (split lentils). It is also a component of the Bengali five-spice blend.

According to conventional medicine, it improves absorption and decreases the amount of sugar. It is often used to manage colitis and is recommended for mothers who are breastfeeding since it has a material that enhances the supply of milk.

⁜ Clove

This tasty spice is the crisped unlabeled bud of a Myrtle family vine, indigenous to the island chains of Moluccas. The production of cloves extended beyond the Moluccas only towards the end of the XVIII century and the dominance was established. Now mostly in Indonesia, as well as in Tanzania, clove is still produced. South India production began in 1800 but mostly the clove now eaten is transported from Sri Lanka. The usage of clove in Indian cooking is restricted to mixes and masala. It is very high in fragrance and flavour. It is also used in many rice dishes.

Clove has one of the largest proportion of volatile oil relative to other spices, and a tiny quantity goes a long way for this. Clove is also the seasoning with the strongest antioxidant potential.

✦ Black Pepper

Pepper is the spice produced from the Piper nigrum plant berries. We do have three most popular varieties of pepper as per the period of harvest and the post-harvest process: white pepper, black pepper and green pepper.

In India, it is native in the southern area of Malabar and now Black Pepper also grows in Kerala, which is obtained by extracting the green drupes only as they are ripe and begin to turn red, and then by processing them under the sunlight or in a furnace until the humidity content is below a certain level. A process of oxidation occurs during the drying period. Black pepper can be used in many spice mixtures, meat and chicken dishes in the north.

✦ Amchur Powder

This is a sweet and malty spice which acts as a thickening agent and it is used as a dipping sauce. It gives a sour fruity taste to curries, sauces and chutneys.

Chapter 03: Indian Breakfast Recipes

The Indian Breakfast Recipes can be cooked in less time and can be useful for every one of you. Both Northern India breakfast dishes and Southern India breakfast dishes which can be cooked in a matter of minutes, are scattered throughout this chapter. Look at these Indian Recipes for the breakfast and brunch. You will now make them at home in the mornings easily by following given recipes.

⊥ Vegetable Rava Upma

Cooking time: 20 minutes

Serving meals: 2

❖ Ingredients

- 1 cup of Rava
- 1 sliced onion

- ¼ cup peas
- 1 cup of combined, diced vegetables
- 3 green, sliced chilies
- 1 tablespoon of ginger, sliced
- Just a couple leaves of curry
- ½ teaspoon urad dal
- ¼ teaspoon of mustard seeds
- Leaves of coriander, sliced, to marinade
- Oil 1 tablespoon
- Salt as per your liking

❖ **Method**

1) Take a big saucepan and add vegetable oil and heat it over medium-high heat.

2) Add all seeds that are finely chopped, red chilies and ginger. With a wooden skewer, blend the products together properly.

3) In a pan, add peas and dal in order to combine the products properly, flip the pan tightly.

4) Stir fry for a few moments then add curry leaves. Meanwhile, grab a cutting board and individually cut all the vegetables. Now in the pan put chopped vegetables and mix it all well.

5) Add ample water to the pan and sprinkle very well salt. Use a lid to cover the pan and cook it over medium-high heat.

6) Cook until a deep mixture is created. Now, for a couple of minutes, take a non-stick pan and add 1 tablespoon of oil and cook semolina in it over medium-high heat.

7) When vegetables are fried, add cooked semolina in small amount steadily, stirring constantly. Keep continuously stirring, and check that no chunks are created.

8) Cook on a low flame for 5 minutes and then move it to a serving bowl. Garnish it with cashews and mint leaves.

9) Serve immediately.

⬇ Upma Sooji with Coconut

Cooking time: 30 minutes

Servings: 4 persons

❖ Ingredients

- 1 cup sooji (semolina)
- 2 teaspoons of ghee
- 1 ½ teaspoon mustard seed
- Asafetida as much you like
- 10 split organic cashews
- 1 teaspoon of Chana dal and urad dal immersed in a bath at least for 10 minutes.
- 1 diced ginger tablespoon
- 1 tiny sliced red onion
- 1 diced green chili
- 10 leaves of curry
- 4 tablespoons of green peas
- 2.5 cups of water
- Salt as much you like
- 2 teaspoons of cilantro minced

- 1 teaspoon of ghee

❖ **Method**

1) Roast the sooji over a moderate flame until moist, continue to stir for around 5 minute. Take sooji off the pan and move it to some other dish.

2) This phase of frying sooji can be completed before and you can save time for packed mornings.

3) Now add two tablespoons of oil at medium heat to the same pan.

4) Then add seeds, hing, cashews, dal ginger and stir fry for 1 minute before they begin to change color.

5) Add carrot, green chili pepper and curry leaves. Once the onions are added, cook for an additional minute.

6) Then after sometime add the peas and stir. Heat till the fresh scent of peas falls out.

7) Add 3 cups of water. Then squeezed lemon zest into it and add cilantro and then, blend properly. If you want a little sweetness in your Upma, you can also add honey or sugar.

8) Put the water in it to a boil now. Until the water has boiled, start adding the cooked sooji little by little at the moment.

9) With a dough scraper, blend sooji in one way after each inclusion.

10) Then cover it with a lid over the pot and adjust heat to normal. Let it stay this way for some time.

11) Remove the cover and add ghee 2 teaspoon. That is voluntary, but it is encouraged. Switch the heat off.

12) Upma is served warm with coconut chutney.

🍴 Puffed Upma Rice

Serving to 1–2 persons

Cooking time: 15 minutes

❖ Ingredients

- 3 puffed rice cups
- 1 tiny onion
- 1 tiny tomato
- 1-2 chilies
- ½ teaspoon powder of turmeric
- Seeds with ½ teaspoon mustard
- 1 sliced dry red chili
- Just a couple leaves of curry
- 2 teaspoon of oil
- Salt as per your liking

❖ Methods

1) Chop everything.
2) Heat a skillet with one tablespoon of oil. Add seeds in it.
3) Insert dry red chili and urad dal in the frying seeds. Fry until dal turns into brown color.
4) And add all chopped stuff in it.
5) Also, salt as per your liking and turmeric in it.
6) Cover for a minute and let it cook for a while.

7) Take the puffed rice and add running water via the puffed rice to literally wash it. Try squeezing the water out and quickly return it to the plate.

8) Add it in a pan. And cook over high heat for a moment.

9) Remove it from the heat.

10) Immediately serve puffed Upma rice.

❖ **Things to be Noted**

- Do not wash the puffed rice in water, as it gets soggy.

- Upma-puffed rice is better eaten when wet.

✦ **Tamarind and Rava Upma Rice**

Cooking time: 20-30 min

Serves 6-8 people

❖ **Ingredients**

- 2 cups Rava rice

- 1 onion thinly chopped

- 3-4 green chili with a cut

- ½ roughly chopped ginger

- 1 cup of minced vegetables

- 1 ½ teaspoons ghee

- 9 cashew-nuts (optional)

- 4 cups of water

- Salt

For Seasoning Purposes:

- 1 teaspoon of mustard seeds

- 1 curry sprig leaves

- 1 teaspoon seeds of cumin
- 1 teaspoon gram of Bengal
- 1 teaspoon black dal

❖ **Method**

1) In a pan, heat the oil, add cumin and seeds in it.
2) Insert curry leaves, onion and green chilies and then let the color change with the leaves.
3) Add the dal in it and fry until the dal is finely baked in oil.
4) Add water in it and let it to boil. Put salt as per your liking.
5) Add rice rava constantly when cooking.
6) Stir well, cover the lid and cook over medium-high heat until all of the humidity is consumed.
7) Lower the flame and steam until they are cooked.
8) Turn the heat off and serve it.

➕ **Ragi Rava Idli**

It helps to protect the integrity of the bones and avoids osteoporosis for those with low haemoglobin concentrations. It is a decent source of natural fiber and is gluten free as well. Ragi idli is a really nutritious meal which is ideal for children and the elderly. These idlis are soft, healthy and spongy.

Servings: 4 persons

❖ **Ingredients**

- Idli rice 1 cup
- Flour 2 cups
- 1 cup dal
- ½ teaspoon seeds of fenugreek

- Salt if required

❖ **Steps to Follow**

1) Wash and soak seeds, urad dal and fenugreek for 4 hours. For 5 hours, clean and rinse the rice independently.

2) Crush dal and seeds until it become sleek and creamy. Remove in a container, and set it aside.

3) Crush the rice to make it flour and add water in it to prepare a visibly rough mixture or batter.

4) Now add rice batter into a dal seeds mixture. Add salt and other spices all together until combined properly.

5) The strength of the batter should be close to the Idli batter.

6) Take the wet blender out of it and blend really well with your fingertips.

7) Allow it to settle for some time. To keep it from spilling, use a wide vessel since it can double during fermentation.

8) Our batter Ragi Idli is set.

❖ **How to Cook Ragi Idli**

1) Hot the water in an idle or steamer vessel. Mix well the soaked ragi idli batter and pour a spoonful of idli batter in the oiled moulds and put it into the broiler pan.

2) Heat to cook for 20 minutes or a toothpick placed in the idli core comes out clean.

3) After 5 minutes, extract it from the mould using a teaspoon submerged in water.

4) Serve the hot Ragi Idli with your option of chutney.

Rava Idli Sabbakki

Cook Time: 12 minutes

Servings: 15

❖ Ingredients

- 1 Sooji cup
- 1 tablespoon mustard seeds
- Cumin seeds with one teaspoon
- 1 tablespoon Chana dal
- 1 tablespoon Black Dal (Split)
- Cashew nuts 1/3 cup, sliced
- 1 sprig of shredded curry leaves
- Ginger 1 tablespoon
- Asafoetida as per your liking
- 2 chilies, chopped
- Oil as per your use
- 2 tablespoons of coriander thinly sliced
- Salt
- ¼ cup Tapioca Perls
- 1 cup Curd, battered
- Oil for greasing

❖ Method

1) Firstly, simmer tapioca perls in enough water for two hours. Filter this and squeeze out the extra water using your fingertips, do not panic if it partially crumbles or loses its form.

2) In a moderate-flame pan, heat oil. Add seeds and let it vibrate. After some time add cumin seeds and dal mixture. Mix in a low flame until it becomes golden

3) Add hinges, curry, ginger and chilies at this point and cook for 5 minutes, ensure that the products are cooked perfectly.

4) This helps the Rava idli mix to be processed for potential usage in an airtight bag. Add the Rava and roast, then switch off the flame after 5 minutes.

5) Heat water in idli steamer. Lubricate the moulds of Idli.

6) Add Rava idli mixture, strained tapioca perls, coriander leaves, salt as per your liking and yoghurt in a bowl and mix and give it a nice blend.

7) Change the batter's reliability to a thick consistency.

8) Force the batter into the idli mould and heat for 15 minutes.

9) Sprinkle with some oil and serve it.

⊥ Rava Idli: Foxtail Millet

Cooking time: 10 minutes

Servings: 3

❖ **Ingredients**

- Millet Foxtail-3 cups
- Dal: 1 cup
- Fenugreek Seed – ¼ tablespoon
- Oil as required
- Water as required
- Salt as per your liking

❖ Method

1) Clean and simmer the millet and Urad Dal in different bowl of water for 6 hours. Along with the Dal, you can immerse Fenugreek seeds in water.

2) Crush your millet and Dal individually.

3) Move the soaked dal and Fenugreek beans in a processor and grind them to a fine paste. Drop it into a bowl. Next, grind the submerged millet in the same blender. Shift it and the Dal batter to the bowl.

4) Balance well the batter and all that for overnight to ferment. Mix well after fermenting.

5) Add salt and blend properly before frying. Add the necessary water to the batter to prepare Idli and get to the consistency of the idli batter. Lubricate the idli plate with butter, then steam for 10 mins in medium-low heat.

6) Enable it to cool down a bit, then sprinkle with little water and extract the hot Idli.

7) Add water to prepare the dosa and change the batter to the consistency required. Heat a dosa tawa and pour a spoonful of batter and distribute evenly. Cook and sprinkle oil around the rim.

8) Flip the other side and fry and then serve it.

⊥ Dosa Rava Onion

Cooking time: 15 minutes

Servings to 3 persons

❖ **Ingredients**

- Half cup of semolina (sooji)
- 2 teaspoons sliced coriander
- 1 sprig Stripped curry
- Half cup flour of rice
- 1 tablespoon roughly minced ginger
- 1 sliced chili
- ¼ cup of Maida
- One teaspoon cumin seeds
- 1 thinly sliced onion
- Ghee-where appropriate

❖ **Method**

1) Get all of the products in a cup except onions and add water. For fast mixing use a whisker.

2) Hold aside the onions. The batter must be really thin.

3) Preferably, heat a non-stick dosa plate. It should be heated. Drizzle and spill the soupy batter with some grease, first making a larger ring and then filling in the middle.

4) Instantly scatter over the sliced onions on it. Add a teaspoon of oil/ghee to it. Let the moderate flame cook till the dosa turns to a golden hue.

5) Then serve it.

✦ **Dosa Buckwheat**

It is simple to prepare this nutritious and safe dosa and it is a perfect replacement for bread. Buckwheat has a robust and mildly nutty taste that goes well with a number of fillings.

This recipe allows the batter to rest for at least overnight to enable the flours to be mixed with water. We schedule this and make it stand over time so that the next day it is able to be used. The batter can be kept for up to 2 days in the fridge.

Servings: 10 persons

Cooking time: 10 min

❖ **Ingredients**

- 1 cup of flour for Buckwheat
- ½ cup Oat flour
- ½ cup almond flour
- Water as your liking
- ½ tsp of salt

❖ **Method**

1) To prepare a softer batter: whisk Buckwheat, oat, and salted almond flours. Cover and allow to remain in the refrigerator at room temperature for at overnight.

2) Add water and mix it well.

3) Set a temperature for Dosa maker machine to setting 1.

4) To the upper and bottom cooking racks, grease it with a thin layer of oil. Pour spoonful of batter in.

5) Cook for 3 minutes. Open to inspect the dosa, and cook for 1 minute if necessary.

6) Serve it.

+ **Dosa Dhania Palak**

Cooking Time 10 min

For 5 Individuals

❖ **Ingredients**

- 2 ½ cups rice, has to be soaked overnight
- 1 cup Dal, has to be soaked overnight
- One tablespoon Fenugreek Seeds
- Salt as per your liking
- Leaves of Spinach and Coriander, finely sliced
- Oil to use

❖ **Method**

1) For the preparation of dosa, wash the rice, spinach and coriander in water. Let the rice completely submerged in water. Let it simmer for about six hours.

2) Drench the dal and fenugreek in water, so that the whole dal is fully submerged in water. Let them simmer for about six hours.

3) When saturated, grind the dal into a fluffy batter. Only add sufficient water when grinding to turn it into a really softer batter. The batter is going to appear fluffy. Put this batter into a bowl.

4) Crush the rice into a somewhat smooth batter, add only the amount of water needed to process. Using a lot of water would make it too watery for the dosa mixture. The rice batter can be a little bit softer, but it must be extremely soft for the dal batter.

5) Merge the dal and the rice batter, add salt as per your liking and settle it down for the batter fermentation process for at least overnight. You will note that the amount of the batter will have gone up. That is why you can position the batter in a wide jar.

6) In a blender grinder, blend spinach leaves and coriander to create a perfect paste and hold aside.

7) Stir rapidly with a spatula until the batter gets its thickness, and add the salt as per the flavor.

8) Now add the paste and combine the vegetable mixture, so that all is well absorbed.

9) Steam a dosa, and apply a few drops of oil. Lubricate the tawa(pan) with a limited quantity of oil.

10) Take a batter handful and drop back down in the tawa middle. Spread it uniformly in a clockwise direction into the outside.

11) Apply a few drops of oil from the edges and even in the middle. Fry the dosa till it gets brown at the bottom. And then serve it.

✦ Dosa Aval

Cooking time: 20 mins

Servings to 4 persons

❖ **Ingredients**

- 3 cups of rice
- 1 cup dal
- 2 tsp fenugreek seeds
- Salt
- Ghee or oil, as per your liking
- Water according to requirements

❖ **Method**

1) Rinse rice in the water and dal in running water individually, and simmer it in containers with just enough salted water.

2) Let the rice and dal simmer in the bath for a minimum of 6 hours before overnight.

3) Wash aval and add it to the washed rice bowl with water.

4) Grind the dal, rice mixture and fenugreek seeds in a grinder until it becomes smooth batter.

5) Set the oven for 15 minutes to 180 degrees and then switch it off.

6) Hold the overnight batter in an oven.

7) Add salt in the batter the next day.

8) Heat a Dosa Tawa and pour a ladle of dosa batter.

9) Range uniformly with the aid of a slotted spoon. Sprinkle the sides with some oil.

10) Cook until it turns out to be golden.

⊥ Dadpe Pohe

Servings to 3 persons

Cooking time 30 minutes

❖ Ingredients

- 1 ½ cups Small Flattened Rice
- 1 cup of onion thinly Sliced
- ¾ Cup coconut grated
- Powdered Sugar 2 tablespoon
- Lemon zest 2-3 teaspoons
- Fresh Peanuts 3 teaspoons
- Two tablespoon Leaves of Coriander
- Salt as per your liking or taste
- Oil 3 teaspoons

- Asafetida ¼ teaspoon

❖ **Method**

1) Mix the finely sliced onions, coconut grated, cinnamon, sugar and lemon zest.

2) Scatter smooth flattened rice in a bowl and mix at the rim.

3) Heat a pan and add cooking oil to it. Insert the fresh peanuts and fried before they shift hue. Remove and set aside.

4) Now add the mustard seeds to the same hot oil and add the asafetida, chopped chilies and leaves of curry. Turn off the flame and add the turmeric powder. Mix it well.

5) Put this mixture over the ready pohe.

6) Offer a quick flip of the whole mix.

7) Shield and hold aside for around 10 to 15 minutes to merge and relax all the tastes.

8) Serve this tasty Dadpae Pohe for brunch or snack at any time.

⊥ **Pohe Tomato with Peas**

Cooking time: 50 mins

Serving to 3 persons

❖ **Ingredients**

- Two teaspoons of olive oil
- 1 Big, minced onion

- 1 Clove of garlic, thinly minced
- 3 Small-sized tomatoes, thinly sliced
- ½ cup of sugar
- One spoonful of new oregano
- 1 of a cup of water or as you required
- One teaspoon of tomato
- 1 Small diced zucchini,
- 1 cup of peas
- Salt

❖ **Method**

1) Refresh to fill poha with only enough water and keep away for 10 minutes.

2) After 10 minutes, absolutely drain the water, release the poha and separate the lumps, if any.

3) Add salt, turmeric powder, lime zest and red chili powder in it.

4) Use a ladle and blend properly.

5) Heat oil in a large frying pan or large base pan.

6) Add the seeds of mustard and cumin.

7) Let them split.

8) Stir-fry light brown on medium-low flame before the onions transform. Add the vegetables and combine well.

9) After some time add the nuts and poha. Cook it for 5 minutes and blend properly.

10) Move to a bowl for serving.

11) Garnish it with coriander and serve right away.

Rotli's Vaghareli

Serving to 2 persons

Cooking time: 30 minutes

❖ Ingredients

- 4 or 5 chapattis left over
- One cup of yoghurt-a good chance to use the extra natural yoghurt in the refrigerator.
- 2 teaspoons of garlic
- 1 spoonful of mustard seeds.
- Two smashed green chilies
- 1 tablespoon of turmeric
- 1 spoonful of cooking oil
- Salt with flavor
- A tiny collection of cilantro
- One lemon tablespoon

❖ Method

1) Break the chappatis into bits.
2) In a saucepan heat the oil. Add the seeds and switch the heat to medium.
3) Add bits of chappati and swirl them in oil.
4) Mix the mustard, turmeric, garlic, chilies in it.
5) Add a cup and a half of water and yoghurt in it and also mix it well.
6) Add the chapattis to this and let it cook in normal heat.
7) Allow the mixture to cook for 5 minutes, then include sugar and lemon in it.

8) To the mixture, add coriander and stir well. They will soak up the liquids while the chapattis cook. If the mixture begins to cling to the bottom of the saucepan, you may need to add more hot water.

9) With a touch of sweet and sour, the flavor of this dish should be mild, so change the taste to your preference. Serve it.

⊥ Bengali Vegetable Form Pohe

Cooking time: 40 minutes

❖ Ingredients

For batter you need:

- Maida ½ cup
- ½ semolina cup (sooji)
- 1 tablespoon of sugar
- 1 tablespoon of shredded fennel seeds
- Evaporated milk 350ml
- Oil as per you needs for frying.

For sugar syrup you need:

- 1 Cup of drinking water
- Four green cardamom
- 1 cup of sugar

❖ Method

1) Get all the items specified for a batter in a medium bowl and blend them properly, so that no chunks are there. Add just a little milk if you like it is too dense. Let it rest for some time.

2) Put the ingredients for sugar sauce in a saucepan and cook them together until you have syrup of one string.

3) Hot enough oil in a pan to deep fry.

4) To shape a tiny pancake of 2 diameters, pour a spoon of flour in the liquid.

5) Fry on medium fire. Cook and turn one side over.

6) Suppose all sides turn brown remove with a spatula and indulge in sugar syrup instantly. Leave for 1 minute to full.

7) Remove hot, and serve it.

+ The Sesame and Beetroot Thepla

Cooking Time: 25 min

Serving to 2 persons

❖ **Ingredients**

- 1 Grated Beetroot
- ½ cup of Ground wheat
- ½ cup of besan
- ½ teaspoon cumin powder
- ½ Amchur teaspoon
- ½ teaspoon powder of Garam masala
- 1 teaspoon mixture of Red Chili
- Oil as per you need
- Salt as per your taste

❖ **Directions**

1) Add all the herbs, salt and ghee with the diced beetroot.

2) Also add wheat and besan flour and squeeze a soft mixture with water.

3) Take a small portion and shape it into a thepla.

4) Heat up the Tawa and put a thepla on it.

5) Heat it for about a minutes and then turn it and heat about a minute but at the other side.

6) Serve it with curd.

⊥ Dhokla Buckwheat Corn

Servings to 5 persons

Cooking time: 35 minutes

❖ **Ingredients**

- Two minced Green Chilies
- Chopped 1 Ginger
- ½ teaspoon soda for frying
- 2 teaspoon of fruit salt
- ½ teaspoon Turmeric powder
- 2 tablespoons Sunflower Oil
- 1/3 cup of Water
- 2 cups Gram (besan) flour
- 1 cup water, or more where possible
- 2 teaspoons of salt to taste

❖ **Method**

1) Start preparing all the items to start cooking the Dhokla.

2) Grease and leave aside a cake tray or a dhokla plate. Get a steamer prepared with water and have it loaded.

3) Next, create a combination of chili and ginger. Add this combination and water into a shallow blender mixer jar and combine to create a puree. Hold this away.

4) Put all the items along with the above paste into a large bowl and hold aside.

5) Whisk well to mix, add lemon zest and soda will froth up the Dhokla batter.

6) Into the lubricated plate, put the Dhokla batter and put it in the steamer ready.

7) Wrap the steamer and switch the heat on and steam it for 15 minutes.

8) If you stick a knife in the middle and along the sides and it falls out dry, you will recognize when it is finished.

9) Remove from the steamer the Khaman Dhokla, and leave it to cool fully.

The next move is to prepare the water in the sugar lemon:

10) Heat a skillet over medium heat with oil. Add the mustard seeds and cumin seeds, and let it crack. Apply the green chilies and curry leaves and mix for about a minute until it crackles.

11) If done, add the water, lemon zest, salt and sugar. Remove it before the sugar dissolves, then switch off the fire. Let the tadka cool off a little.

12) From over Khaman Dhokla, sponge the tadka so that it gets well saturated.

13) Remove it from the pan and serve it.

ⵏ Paneer Crepes and Green Peas

Cooking time: 45 minutes

Servings to 4 persons

❖ **Ingredients**

- 1 cup Green peas
- 2 cup of Paneer (Homemade Cheese Cottage)
- Chopped two tablespoon Ginger
- 2 Green Chili, sliced
- 2 teaspoon Turmeric powder
- 4 teaspoons of Powder Red Chili
- 2 Amchur teaspoon
- 2 teaspoon of Powdered Coriander
- 1 cup wheat flour
- For kneading, olive oil

❖ **Method**

1) Put the sifted flour in a broad mixing cup. Add water a few times to make a moist to the fluffy dough by kneading.

2) When all the dough has become round, drizzle the top of the dough with a teaspoon of oil and knead for another few minutes. Wrap the dough, but we are going to prepare the filling.

3) Heat a skillet with some oil over medium flame. Add cumin seeds in it and allow it to splutter for a couple of seconds. Add all spices, and cook it well. Add peas in it. Cook them until they are half done.

4) Add crushed paneer and cook them well over medium heat before the raw flavor of the spice fades. Hold it to cool away.

5) Divide parts of the dough into medium sized lemon balls.

6) Pat the dough section and sprinkle it with flour. Roll the dough out into a coil 5 inches in diameter. In the middle of the dough, spoon a good part of the filling.

7) Wrap the ends by pulling the ends close. Lightly brush the paratha back into the flour and roll gently to clear any pockets of air.

8) Roll the paratha such that the filling remains within and therefore does not seep out, creating very little strain.

9) The next move is to cook the paratha. Heat up the skillet and put the paratha on it.

10) Switch and cook from both surfaces before external brown stains emerge. Drizzle the paratha with ghee or oil and cook at low to medium heat until both sides have the paratha cooked through it and golden brown.

11) Move the paratha to a plate until finished, and prepare the rest of the Paneer and Green Peas Packed Parathas the same way.

12) Serve it.

✦ Oats Cheela with Paneer Stuffed Palak

Cooking time: 40 minutes

Serving to 4 persons

❖ **Ingredients**

- 1 cup of gram flour
- Oil from 2 to 3 teaspoon
- Ginger-1 teaspoon paste
- Seeds for the carom ¼ teaspoon
- Chilly red powder- ¼ teaspoon
- Spinach-1 cup (cut thinly)

- Salt as per you need

❖ **Method**

1) First of all, make a batter again with the besan chilla and take a spoonful of batter.

2) Pour batter over hot Tawa.

3) Spread carefully to ensure a moderately dense chilla.

4) A teaspoon of oil is scattered across the edges.

5) Enable cooking for a minute on low to medium flame, or until the underside is completely cooked.

6) Now softly turn over the chilla without splitting.

7) Make sure all sides of the chilla are prepared.

8) Now spread out part of the chilla with 2 teaspoon of cooked paneer stuffing.

9) Serve it.

Chapter 04: Indian Lunch and Dinner Recipes

The main course meals are taken for lunch and dinner. We may have a light dinner, too, but you can still have a nice breakfast and a better lunch. A list of such recipes has been shared in this chapter which can be served for lunch or dinner. The purpose is not only to share the recipes, but you can also get the collection-based ideas and can seek or make any other dishes not listed here.

⬇ **Madras Curry Chicken**

Serves to 4 persons

Time to cook: 2 hours

❖ **Ingredients**

- Ghee
- Onion
- Coriander
- Garlic
- Clean ginger
- Salt as per your taste
- Boneless chicken thighs without skin
- Citrus zest
- Finely sliced tomatoes
- Curry Powder
- Coconut milk

❖ **Steps to Follow**

1) Firstly, over medium heat, set up a big pot. Add the sliced onion, chopped garlic, and smashed ginger to the oil. Stir for 10 minutes until the onions become very tender.

2) Then include curry powder, salt and chili powder. Mix and cook it all for some time until it becomes aromatic.

3) Boost the flame to normal, and add the coconut milk and tomatoes in it. Cook it for some time.

4) Then mix the sliced pieces of chicken into the gravy — cover and cook. Frequently stir, for 25 minutes.

5) Finally, in order to finish the sauce, add chopped coriander in it. Just before eating, sprinkle the lemon zest for garnishing.

⊕ Casserole Chicken Tikka Masala

Serving to 4 persons

Cooking time: 3 hours

❖ Ingredients

- Eight chicken bone-in thighs
- 1 tablespoon lime zest

For a marinate

- Ginger-pieces, mashed
- Ten cloves of garlic, mashed
- Yoghurt as per your need
- Chili powder- a pinch
- 1 teaspoon of coriander
- 1 teaspoon cumin
- 1 teaspoon masala garam
- 1 teaspoon of turmeric
- 1 tiny chili

For of the sauce

- 1 ½ tablespoon butter
- 1 big, coarsely diced onion
- 1 tablespoon of cumin seeds
- 1 tablespoon mustard
- ½ teaspoon fenugreek crushed
- ½ teaspoon of paprika
- 3 of cardamom
- 1 big slice of cinnamon

- 1 tablespoon of purée tomato
- 40 g of almonds, chopped
- 1 teaspoon of vinegar
- Milk as per your need.
- Passata as you per your need.

❖ **Steps to Follow**

1) Cut the chicken skin and slice single thigh 2 to 3 times. Put the chicken pieces, lemon juice and salt in a plastic jar and mix it well. Leave aside while the seasoning is being made.

2) Grind the ginger and garlic in a tiny spice grinder to produce a sauce, add a drop of water if necessary. For the gravy, cast aside a quarter of the paste. In the spice grinder, add the necessary marinade components, then grind to a fine paste.

3) Load the mixture over the chicken in a jar and let it marinate for minimum of 4 hours.

4) On medium flame, heat 2 tablespoons of the ghee in a deep pan to render the sauce. Cook the onions over medium heat for 20 minutes before they start browning.

5) Add the spices and the remaining paste of garlic and ginger, and cook for 5 minutes. Add a sauce of tomatoes, almonds and vinegar in it. Heat it for some time.

6) Put in the passata, then refill the container with water up high. Put it to a moderate flame, then boil for 2-3 hours until a deep sauce is present. It can be kept frozen in the refrigerator for 24 hours while the chicken is marinated.

7) Set the barbecue to its full level.

8) Take a chicken and arrange it on a big, cut-side-up baking sheet. Set 10-15 mins under the grill before charred and start blackening. Take the sheet from the oven.

9) Reheat the sauce, apply the retained marinate and curry sauce in the chicken. Cook until the chicken is fully ready. Leave the curry to stay for a few minutes.

10) Garnish it with cilantro and almonds, then serve it.

⊥ Beef Kofta with Saag Aloo

Serves to 4 persons

Cooking time: 1 hour

❖ Ingredients

- •1 onion
- •1 garlic
- •2 small-medium potatoes
- •½ pile of coriander
- •½ teaspoon cumin
- •½ teaspoon turmeric
- •½ teaspoon mustard
- •1 pot of chicken reserve
- •300 g of minced beef
- •Coconut Milk as per your need
- •½ teaspoon of lemon zest
- •Water

❖ **Steps to Follow**

1) Firstly, cut and slice into bits of onion. Slice the garlic and grind it. Slice the potato into cubes. Cut the coriander loosely.

2) On moderate fire, heat oil in a big frying pan. Add the garlic and onion in it and cook for 5 mins or until it becomes tender. Keep half of this substance out and put it away in a tray.

3) Put the rest onion in the frying pan with the cumin, turmeric, and mustard and mix and cook it for 3 minutes.

4) Add the potato cubes and water as per your need and half a pot of chicken supply. Mix it so that it will dissolve. Cover with a lid, switch the heat to low and boil for around 15-20 mins.

5) In the meanwhile, place the beef in a bowl and mix with salt as per your taste, a decent black pepper and grind.

6) Form the mixture of beef into four small balls per individual. In a frying pan, heat oil on moderate flame and fry until golden brown everywhere.

7) Remove the koftas from the pan.

8) Put the koftas in boiling mixture and boil gently.

9) Add the spinach, then remove the pan from the flame, place the lid on, and keep on the side for 10 minutes. Mix it in the spinach. Put over a little lemon zest and stir it straight. Serve it.

⁌ **Chicken Curry Mango**

Serves to 4 persons

Cooking time: 2 hours

❖ **Ingredients**

- 2 teaspoons of coconut oil
- 1 large sliced onion
- 4 cloves of garlic
- 8 teaspoons of chopped ginger
- 4 teaspoons of curry powder
- Salt and pepper, as per your taste
- 3 sliced, diced and split mangos
- Coconut milk as per your need
- 2-4 Chicken thighs, sliced

❖ **Steps to Follow**

1) Heat the coconut oil over a moderate flame in a wide and deep fryer. Add the onion, garlic, and ginger and cook it until they turn out to be brown.

2) Then add the curry powder, salt, pepper, 1 cup of the fresh mangoes, and the coconut milk to the bowl and mix it well.

3) Then add the above sauce to the frying pan and put the chicken and ½ cup of water in it. Cover with a lid and let it cook for 20 minutes. Turn the heat down if the edge of the frying pan starts to cling to the sauce.

4) Add the leftover mango to the plate when the chicken parts are completely cooked and eat.

✦ **Tandoori Curry Sandwich**

Serves to 4 persons

Cooking time: 1 hour

❖ Ingredients

- 1 entire chicken, cut into pieces.
- 1 cup Greek simple yoghurt
- ½ yellow, diced onion
- 1 peeled, freshly grated ginger
- 2 Garlic Cloves
- 2 tablespoons healthy citrus juice
- ½ teaspoon of cumin
- ½ teaspoon of ground cilantro
- 1 tablespoon olive oil
- Salt and potatoes

For making Sandwiches

- big, half warmed, entire wheat bread
- Regular Greek yoghurt
- ½ teaspoon of cumin field
- ½ teaspoon of ground cilantro
- ¼ teaspoon garlic powder
- Salt and tomatoes
- Lettuce

❖ Steps to Follow

1) Put chicken pieces in a big zip-lock bag.

2) Mix milk, onion, ginger, garlic, lemon juice, cumin, coriander, and oil in a food processor, until it becomes creamy. Season with salt and pepper as per your taste.

3) Put the sauce with the chicken into the zip-lock bag and shake to cover it. Just let the chicken marinate in the fridge for a minimum of 4 hours.

4) Preheat the oven up to 500 degrees. Put the chicken into the rack, skin downside. Roast, approximately 35 minutes, before burnt spots begin to emerge on the bird, tossing once. Reduce heat to 450 and proceed to cook, about 10 minutes more, before the chicken is cooked completely.

5) Dice the remaining chicken into pieces of bite-size if you wanted.

6) In a shallow bowl, mix yoghurt and spices. Open each half of the pita to shape a pocket and fill with meat, lettuce, tomato sauce and yoghurt.

ⵜ Veggie Filled Butter Curry Chicken

Serves to 3 persons

Cooking time 2 hours

❖ Ingredients

- Two tablespoons butter
- One huge white onion, tiny dice
- 2 big garlic cloves
- One teaspoon clean ginger
- One tablespoon Garam Masala
- One tablespoon curry powder
- One tablespoon cilantro powder
- ½ teaspoon paprika
- ¼ tablespoon cinnamon
- Chili flakes about ¼ tablespoon

- Two tomatoes
- 1 400 ml coconut milk bottle

❖ **Steps to Follow**

1) Heat coconut oil or butter in a wide skillet or pot over moderate-low heat until it is melted. Add onion in it and cook for around 6 minutes or until it is translucent.

2) Garlic and ginger are added and sautéed for 5 minutes until it turns out to be aromatic, then add garam masala, curry powder, cilantro, paprika and cinnamon. Let it cook for around 1 minute, thus swirling periodically.

3) Add the chili flakes and tomatoes to the jar. For around 15 minutes, let all the sauce boil until the sauce thickness increases and it will become a strong and dark red-brown shade.

4) Remove it from flame and put it into a mixer and add salt as per your taste. Then add up to quarter a cup of water in it if the mixture is too heavy to incorporate. Blend in batches if you have a small blender.

5) Put back the sauce into the tub. Add coconut milk and sugar in it. You would insert your cooked lentils, tomatoes, chickpeas and vegan chicken at this stage and cook it for 10-15 minutes.

6) Represent it with corn and coriander.

✚ **Paneer Pulao**

Serves to 4 persons

Cooking time: 2 hours

❖ **Ingredients**

- One cup of Rice Basmati
- One and half of Paneer cubes

- Half cup of Peas & carrot
- One large Onion
- 2 Green Chilies
- One teaspoon Ginger Garlic Paste
- Leaves of coriander, diced-as desired
- Salt-As required
- Oil or Ghee

❖ **Steps to Follow**

1) For about 30 mins, rinse and soak the rice. On moderate flame, put ghee in a saucepan and let it heat for 3 minutes. Add soaked rice well-drained in it and cook for a while until it becomes dry.

2) Add oil in a pan over moderate flame. Add onion, green chili and fry until the onion is only translucent, without altering its hue.

3) Add the paste of ginger and garlic, fried it and then add the vegetables. Fry them to half-finished vegetables.

4) Add 1 cup water and salt in it and let it cook. Add the rice which is already cooked. Cover with a lid, and cook in moderate flame.

5) Prepare the paneer cubes. For better taste, let the paneer cubes be small. Paneer cubes (previously thawed or immersed in hot water) are typically toasted in a non-stick skillet until it turns out to be golden.

6) Once the pulao is accomplished, the paneer is drained and added to the pulao. Before adding, ensure the water is depleted from the paneer.

⊥ Makhni Dal

Serves to 4 persons

Cooking time: 2 hours

❖ Ingredients

- 2 teaspoons of red beans drenched overnight
- 1 spoonful of red chili powder
- 8 teaspoons of butter
- 1 tall, chopped onion
- Half cup of puree tomato
- One-half cup new milk
- Half teaspoon of paste with ginger
- Salt as needed
- Sliced two ginger
- 2 large diced chili
- ½ cup of dal, immersed in water whole night
- Garlic paste of 1/2 teaspoon

❖ Steps to Follow

1) Soak dal overnight in two cups of water. Drain it, then cook in pressure cooker with salt and 3 cups of water. This allows the dal and rajma to become tender.

2) Put a pan on a moderate heat and add the cumin seeds in it. You should slowly add the ginger and garlic paste until the cumin seeds rasp and swirl after some time. You should then add some carrots, sliced green chilies and puree of tomatoes.

3) Fry before it becomes golden mixture. If you are somebody who enjoys Dal Makhani's authentic look, then we recommend that you use ghee rather than oil.

4) When the masala is fit to your liking, you can add the Rajma and dal in it and let it to steam.

5) Then, as per your preference, add garam masala and salt. Carry to a cook and stir well, if you think the dal is too dense, you may add more water.

6) Then add some fresh cream in it and combine well. That will render your creamy and tasty Dal Makhani.

Chicken Lemon

Serves to 4 persons

Cooking time: 2 hours

❖ Ingredients

- Four chicken breasts that are skinned
- One tablespoon of lemon zest
- 1 tablespoon of honey
- 1 cup oil
- 2 cloves of garlic, minced
- 1 teaspoon of oregano crushed
- Fresh, green salad and potatoes to eat

❖ Steps to Follow

1) Warm the gas furnace to 170C. In a deep oven tray, place the chicken into a layer.

2) Add all the available ingredients in a pan and heat it for 1 min in the oven or tiny skillet. Remove all together, then spill over the chicken.

3) Grill the chicken for 45 minutes and roast every 10 minutes. Progressively, the juice thickens to offer the chicken a glossy covering.

4) Allow the chicken to rest for 5 minutes before adding with a green salad and fresh potatoes.

✠ Fry Chittenad Trout

Serves to 2 persons

Cooking time: 2 hours

❖ Ingredients

- Fish 400g
- Powder with turmeric-1 tablespoon
- Salt as per preference
- Lemon juice one tablespoon
- 3 onions
- 2 Garlic cloves
- 2 tablespoons of ginger
- 2 teaspoons of Cumin seeds
- 2 teaspoons of rice flour
- Oil as per your need
- 1 tablespoon of red chili powder
- Coriander powder -1 tablespoon

❖ Steps to Follow

1) Carve the fish into bits and wash them with water.

2) Add some turmeric powder, salt, one lemon juice and cover the cod, then set aside.

3) Time to take the blender jar and add the cumin seeds, garlic, ginger and onion in it. And blend to make a paste.

4) To create a dense paste, move the masala paste to a pan and add the red chili powder, coriander powder, and rice flour, salt and add two tablespoons of oil.

5) Remove parts of fish now and cover the masala with even paste on the fish.

6) Let the fish marinate for 2 hours.

7) Then, Heat oil on a grill pan or skillet.

8) When the oil is hot sufficient, add the pieces of fish one by one and fry until they are cooked on one side and then turn to the next hand.

9) Switch the fish to a clean cloth until finished to extract excess fat.

10) Serve it with a cup of freshly boiled rice.

✦ Mutton Do Pyaaza

Serves to 2 persons

Cooking time: 1 hour

❖ Ingredients

- A half kilogram of Mutton
- Half cup of yogurt
- 3 Cardamom
- 5 Chilies or as per your taste
- Half teaspoon of Cinnamon powder
- Half teaspoon of cumin
- 1 tablespoon of garlic pulp
- Salt for flavor

- 1 teaspoon of powdered red chili
- ½ tablespoon of turmeric
- Half cup of Oil
- 3 diced onion
- One teaspoon poppy seeds
- One teaspoon Coconut soil

❖ **Steps to Follow**

1) Clean the beef and hold the strainer in place.

2) Mix yoghurt, cardamom, cinnamon powder, chilies, cumin, a paste of garlic, salt, powder of red chili and turmeric.

3) Add this mixture to the meat and let it rest for 1 hour.

4) In a skillet, heat the oil and fry the onion until it is lightly brown in color. Remove onion in a pan and cook the meat in the same pan.

5) When water from yoghurt dries out, substitute enough liquid to prepare the beef. Cover until tender and cook.

6) Mix in coconut and poppy seeds.

7) Add the fried onion and cook for 2 minutes. And serve it.

⊥ **Makhmali Kofte**

Serves to 3 persons

Cooking time: 2 hours

❖ **Ingredients**

For the preparation of the Koftas:

- 400g. Indian Cottage Cheese (Paneer), sliced

- 2 big, baked and mashed potatoes
- 2 chopped Green Chilies
- ¼ teaspoon of white pepper powder
- Two broad tablespoons of corn flour
- 4 tablespoons of oil to prepare
- Salt, for taste

For the preparation of the gravy:

- A quarter cup of oil
- 2 moderate sliced onions
- 1 tablespoon of ginger
- Half a garlic plant, sliced
- 20 cashews, 10 minutes immersed in water
- 1 cup puree tomatoes
- 1 cardamom dark
- 3 Cardamom Gray
- 1 Bay leaf
- 1 pinch of cinnamon
- Half teaspoon of powder chili
- 2 teaspoons of milk
- One teaspoon Kasuri methi also called fenugreek.
- Salt, for taste

❖ **Steps to Follow**

1) Combine all the ingredients well and form them into balls (excluding the oil).

2) In a deep pan, heat the oil and cook the Koftas until both sides are golden brown.

3) Keep half of the chopped onion

4) In a hot oil, fried them until it turns out to be nicely brown.

5) In a processor, mix the leftover onions, ginger, garlic and cashews and blend them into a fine paste.

6) In a shallow pan, heat the oil and add all of the garam masala, black and green cardamom, garlic, bay leaf and cinnamon.

7) Add the paste as the spices shift color. Heat up on the high heat for 3 minutes

8) Add the fried onion and stir fry for 5 minutes.

9) Place in a puree of tomato, red Kashmiri chili and salt. Add a glass of water and cook on a moderate flame for 20 minutes.

10) Gently add the cream and methi when the mixture cools down a little.

11) Pour the sauce into a bowl that is big and deep. One by one, lower the koftas in the sauce, taking caution not to layer them on top of one another.

12) Apply a little cream sprinkling over the end. Serve mild.

Pasta Masala

Serves to 3 persons

Cooking time 1 hour

❖ Ingredients

- 1 cup of pasta to pick as per your liking
- 1 tablespoon of olive oil

- 1 teaspoon of seed cumin
- 3 sliced garlic cloves
- 1 tiny sliced onion
- 3 thin, diced tomatoes
- 1 tablespoon powder of turmeric
- 1 teaspoon of option curry powder
- 1 tablespoon powder of coriander
- Ground red chili as per your taste
- Salt as per your taste
- 1 cup of water or, as needed

❖ **Step to Follow**

1) Place an electric pot in high stir fry mode. Add oil, then let it get warm.

2) Add garlic, onions and cumin seed and cook for a while.

3) Now add the tomatoes and cook them until they are tender. Include all the dried spices and salt.

4) Fry for one or two minutes.

5) Add pasta and water. Mix properly, then turn off stir fry mode.

6) Set it to mode high for 7 minutes, holding the ventilation to sealing spot. After 10 minutes, unlock it.

7) Serve it as per your liking.

⬇ **Garlic Mushrooms**

Serves to 3 persons

Cooking time: 1 hour

❖ Ingredients

- 2 tablespoons of butter
- Oil: 2 tablespoons
- Quarter cup of finely sliced onion
- 1 cup of Mushrooms Button
- 2 tablespoons of finely ground garlic
- 2 tablespoons Parsley Fresh, Split, thinly sliced
- ½ teaspoon thyme, finely minced
- Oregano New, ½ tablespoon, Finely chopped
- Red chili flakes as per your taste

❖ Steps to Follow

1) In a non-stick skillet, add oil and butter and cook over low or moderate heat.

2) Add onions in it and stir fry for 3 minutes.

3) Include the mushrooms and fry until it turns out to be light brown.

4) Add all the spices and stir and cook it well.

5) Cook until it is flavor-some with garlic. Be alert not to let the garlic burn.

6) Add the rest parsley and turn off the heat easily and enjoy it.

Chapter 05: Indian Dessert Recipes

Dessert is the icing on a plate. There is no doubt saying that desserts offer every meal a satisfactory ending. No wonder, people have a weakness for sweets and deserts. Not only are deserts part of our staple food, but they are also even served in many worship areas. By and wide, sugar, milk and khoya are used as staple ingredients in all Indian desserts.

+ **Shahi Falooda**

❖ **Ingredients**

- Two bottles of milk

- 2 tablespoon of rice

- Two tablespoons of Honey

- Two teaspoons of syrup of flavor

- Two tablespoons of dry fruits as per your choice and preference, minced finely

❖ **Steps to Follow**

1) Cook the rice in water for 15 minutes or so — strain to cool it down and set it aside.

2) In a mixer, add the milk, sugar, and dry fruit and blend until it turns out to be creamy.

3) Place two glasses and put the rice in each of them.

4) Add half of the milk now in them. Blend it well each of them after putting syrup in it and then, cool in the fridge.

5) If you like to use ice cream, add an ice cream scoop to this and seasoning with dried berries. Attach a long-handled serve.

✦ **Gulab Jamun**

❖ **Ingredients**

For the balls of dough:

- 1 cup of condensed milk
- Plain flour 110 g
- One and half of teaspoon of baking powder
- Half teaspoon of soda
- One and a half cup of milk
- 25g of sugar, warmed
- Oil for frying

For the preparation of a syrup:

- 1 cup of caster sugar
- Water 100ml

- Saffron as per your preference

For garnishing:

- 1 tablespoon pistachio nuts sliced

- 1 tablespoon of almonds, toasted in a skillet

❖ **Steps to follow**

1) Blend all the components together in any bowl for the dough balls, adding sufficiently extra water to shape a smooth, sticky dough. Cover and put aside for 20 minutes. Form the dough into tiny, round pieces.

2) Heat oil in a deep fryer with thick sides. Fry the balls thoroughly in it until they turn out to be light brown, then scrape the oil with a serving dish and put aside to drain.

3) Prepare a sugar syrup by boiling the sugar and water along with the saffron.

4) When the balls of dough are cooked, add to the sugar fluid and enable to soak for around 1 hour.

5) Garnish it with nuts and almonds and serve it.

✦ **Kulfi**

❖ **Ingredients**

- 1 liter of whole milk

- Half cup of heavy cream

- 1/3 cup of crushed khoya

- 1 tablespoon dry milk powder, for the flavor

- 3 tablespoons of a combination of cashews and pistachios

- 10 teaspoons of sugar

- Skin separated & smashed by five green cardamom

❖ **Steps to follow**

1) Add entire milk to a heavy middle pan and put it over low or medium flame.

2) Add cream to it after around 10 minutes, as it heats up a bit.

3) Let the solution simmer and then let the heat down to low.

4) Let the milk boil for around 25 minutes at low heat, constantly stir it in between.

5) The milk will look very thick after about 25-30 minutes, then add crushed khoya and blend at this point. Keep stirring this; it will take 10 minutes to melt the khoya.

6) If the khoya has melted, add the sugar in it and cook until it melts.

7) And also add the nuts which were chopped before. The finely chopped nuts offer more texture to the kulfi.

8) Add the condensed milk and mix. Boil for an extra 5 minutes. At the end of it, it should get very thick, and it will begin to thicken as it cools off.

9) Remove the pan from heat and add cardamom powder in the pan and mix it well. Let it cool off.

10) Until the milk has completely cooled, pour it into kulfi moulds or some other jar of your liking. Cover and freeze it until fully developed.

11) Place the kulfi mould under warm, clean water once it has been frozen and then tap the mould on the counter. The kulfi will quickly fall out. Enjoy the tasty Kulfi malai.

Mishti Doi

❖ Ingredients

- 1 liter of cream milk
- 8 Cardamom
- Curd as per your taste
- 1 cup of sugar or as per your taste

❖ Steps to Follow

1) Heat one liter of cream milk in a deep non-stick saucepan.

2) Stir it continuously while heating the milk.

3) Add a cup of sugar and mix well.

4) Boil the milk over a moderate flame until it becomes dense. Stir periodically, until the milk becomes half of the amount. Meanwhile, put two tablespoon brown sugar in a saucepan. Add the water in it, then blend properly. Stir until the sugar melts, holding fire on low.

5) Transferring caramel sugar to boiling milk.

6) Stir well enough and carry the milk to the next simmer. Now let it cool to the maximum. Move to a clay pot or other jar after the milk is chilled and still slightly wet.

7) Place a teaspoon of curd in and combine well.

8) Shield and allow it to settle for 8 hours in a warm position or until it is completely set.

9) To get a good creamy texture, refrigerate for 2 hours. Sweeten it with sliced nuts as well.

10) Finally, serve chilled mishti doi.

Indian Cham Cham Desert

Ingredients

- Four cups of cream milk
- Paneer as you have prepared this earlier or you take it readymade
- Two cups sugar
- 5 cups of water
- 1/8 tsp powder of cardamom

Steps to Follow

1) Prepare paneer first. Take a small piece of paneer in your hand and rub with your fingertips to verify whether adequate water has been extracted from the paneer or not. After 30 seconds of pressing, to create a strong yet smooth surface.

2) Put the soaked paneer on a flat, smooth edge and knead until it forms into a smooth, soft dough for 3 to 4 minutes. Fill in a teaspoon of water if the paneer is too mushy.

3) Divide the dough of the paneer into eight equal portions and form each into a flat oval face disc.

4) For the syrup: Put 5 cups of water in a large saucepan to boil. Add sugar, then whisk to completely dissolve. Using a wide pan as the Chum Chum doubles in volume as they cook in the syrup.

5) Add the balls of the paneer to the syrup and stir to combine again. Then lower the flame to a medium level and cover with foil. Cook 15 minutes.

6) Open the cover of the pan, turn over the chum chums and cook for a further 15 minutes. Check to see how

the chum chums look solid yet sponge-like. Switch the flame off and leave it to stay for a full 10 minutes.

7) Keep the chum chums off the water. Represent it after chilling.

+ **Sitaphal**

❖ **Ingredients**

- 1 cup of fresh custard apple pulp (eliminated seeds)
- 2 White Eggs
- Cream milk 400 ml, cooled
- 1/3 cup powdered sugar
- 1/3 teaspoon of Vanilla extract

❖ **Steps to Follow**

1) Using a blade, grind the custard apple to a gritty pulp in a large dish.

2) While the Sitaphal is freezing, take a dry container stir the two egg whites in it until they get fuzzy and soft tips are produced in them with a hand beater. The trick is to carefully distinguish the egg white. And the slightest amount of yolk stops the whites from being soft.

3) Mix together all the water, butter, and extract into a small dish. Do not whisk as hard as the cream will transform to butter.

4) Now add the pulp of the custard apple to the milk mixture and blend the two together with a spoon.

5) Add this combination carefully into the egg whites. The aim is to hold as many of the air as possible in the egg whites to get silky, smooth, delicious ice cream. When thoroughly prepared, place in a freezer bowl.

6) Freeze to stand for 3 hours. Erase and stir again from the refrigerator until it becomes smooth.

7) Put it back in the fridge and keep it again. Scroll out into and feed single pots.

✦ Till Ladu Classical

❖ Ingredients

- 500 gram of flour
- 1 liter of milk or drink
- 750 gram ghee
- 750 grams sugar
- 3 cups of water
- 5-10 drops Color Orange
- 10 to 12 flakes of Saffron, saturated
- 50 cashew, sliced
- Raisins as per you need
- 12 Cardamoms

❖ Steps to Follow

1) Prepare a thin mixture of water and gram flour or milk. Heat ghee in a saucepan.

2) Fill the frying pan or strainer with up to half the batter.

3) Place it in hot ghee over the pan and drain boondis by striking the strainer on the side of the tub, picking up and hitting again. The phase should be done quite easily.

4) Fry them to the color of gold. Using the batter all around.

5) By heating sugar and water, prepare sugar syrup with a one and a half threaded thickness.

6) Add saffron water and color in the syrup. Add the boondis, cardamom, dried fruits and honey. And mix it well.

7) Sprinkle on a little hot water after 10 minutes, cover and retain for 1 ½ hours.

8) Make it in circular spheres by using wet hands.

 ⵜ **The Peanut Indian Brittle**

 ❖ **Ingredients**

- One cup-roasted peanut (skin free).
- One cup-of sugar.

 ❖ **Steps to Follow**

1) Place the peanuts in the blender and grind them into a smooth paste. On a moderate flame, put a pan with the sugar and 2 spoons of water in it. Continue stirring. The sugar transforms steadily into the caramel.

2) As all the lumps melt, turn the heat off, add the peanut powder, blend it properly, shift the paste easily onto a grated tray and spread uniformly.

3) Draw lines with a knife when the paste is hot and allow it to chill.

4) When chilled, divide to create squares along with the outlines.

 ⵜ **Indian Barfi**

 ❖ **Ingredients**

- 2 cups of granules of creamy milk
- Hard cream about 300ml
- 400 g Condensed milk that can be sweetened
- Half cup of pistachios finely sliced

❖ **Steps to Follow**

1) Collect all the ingredients.

2) Mix together all milk and cream and whisk it until creamy.

3) Cover the pan and put it in the microwave and set the time for about 8 minutes.

4) Carefully monitor the dish, and if the solution seems like it could boil over, avoid automatically by stopping microwave for 8 to 10 seconds. Start again and work until the duration of 8 minutes has elapsed. Take it out and mix it well.

5) Return the pan to the microwave and put it high again for 8 minutes. Monitor the first minute carefully and then allow the cooking to begin.

6) Scatter the sliced pistachios over the barfi's surface whenever the time is up while still in the microwave and let stay for 10 minutes.

7) Remove the barfi from the microwave after 10 minutes and cut it into 2- inch squares. Cool it down, and then serve it.

➕ **Indian Rice Pudding**

❖ **Ingredients**

- Half cup of rice
- 3 cups of full-fat milk
- 1 cup of coconut milk
- Half cup of sugar
- Half teaspoon of green cardamom
- One tablespoon oil
- One spoonful of cashews

- One spoonful of pistachios
- One tablespoon of almonds, all nuts should be chopped
- One teaspoon of saffron

❖ **Steps to Follow**

1) Gather all of your ingredients.

2) Soak the rice that you are using it for 30 minutes if you want to reduce the cooking period. Not only does this reduce the boiling period, however, up to half less milk would be used.

3) If you use entire pods of cardamom, smash them coarsely with a pestle and mortar. Add nuts in it and crush it to a fine paste.

4) Add the milk, coconut milk, and the rice into a deep saucepan and carry it to a boil. To steam, reduce the heat and insert the sugar and cardamom. To heat the butter. Stir it continuously.

5) Cook until the rice are smooth, not rubbery, stirring regularly. Based on the rice you have been using, the cooking period would vary around 1 hour. Keep a close eye on the mixture as it heats, and if it is becoming too hot, add some more sugar.

6) Assemble the toppings you want to use and toast the nuts in rice.

7) Let it cool off. And then serve it.

✚ **Jalebi**

❖ **Ingredients**

- 1 cup of flour
- One tablespoon of chickpea starch

- Powder of ¼ teaspoon cardamom
- ½ teaspoon of baking powder
- ¼ teaspoon of soda
- Five teaspoons of yoghurt
- Food color orange, if you want to
- Water as required
- Fry jalebi with oil or ghee

Syrup for dipping the jalebi

- 1 cup of sugar
- ½ cup of water
- Powder of 1/4 teaspoon cardamom,
- ½ teaspoon of lemon extract

❖ **Steps to Follow**

1) Mix all the ingredients.

2) Focus on a sustainable batter, add food color and water in it.

3) This should not be too dense for the batter. Depending on maida and besan consistency, you can need up to 3/4 of the water.

4) Wrap the batter with foil, and allow the batter to ferment for 10 hours.

5) Whisk a little more of the batter later. If the batter is too thick at this stage, you can need to add a little water.

6) In the meanwhile, add water then add sugar to the mixture to let it all simmer.

7) Let it steam until the syrup is thick and sticky. Basically, put a drop of syrup between your thumb and

forefinger, and it should develop a unified thread as you shift your fingers away from one another.

8) Put the batter in a container.

9) In a pan, heat oil or ghee. Keep the heat down to moderate-low.

10) Squeeze the batter in hot oil, allowing the spiral pass. Note to hold the shape at low heat, or you probably would not be able to form it. If the batter disperses in the oil, it is maybe too thin, and you need to add more flour in it. With the batter, after you have rendered the spiral form, lift the heat to moderate to high.

11) Fry until it becomes crispy. Remove from the oil and dip directly in warm sugar syrup, nice enough for a couple of seconds on either side.

12) Strip the sugar syrup from the jalebis and pass it to the serving tray. Enjoy the homemade jalebi with rabri or milk. You should garnish the top with any almonds.

✢ Shakkarpara

❖ Ingredients

- Processed flour-2 tassels
- Ghee -1/4 cup
- Sugar-1 cup
- Ghee

❖ Steps to Follow

1) Begin with grinding the processed flour to make the dough for shakarparas.

2) Take processed flour and a quarter cup of melted ghee in a dish. Mix it all together very nicely. Add water in it. You may use warm water during the winters to knead the flour. We used half a cup of water to knead

the same volume of dough. Cover the dough and leave it aside to settle for a half-hour.

3) Then make the dough again after 20 minutes to make it smoother and fluffy. Break the dough into two separate pieces. To avoid drying, take one part and cover the other one. First, form it into a flat dough disc.

4) Take out the sheet being stored. Second, even out the stretched sheet from the corners. Then break it into pieces which are wide. Break the stripes down into long pieces. As required, you may hold the size large or tiny. Now set the shakarparas apart and placed them on a tray. Repeat the process.

5) Heat the oil in a wok enough to fry those. To verify the ghee, drop one piece of shakarpara. We do not need the very hot ghee to fry the shakarparas it ought to be moderately hot. Keep a moderate-low flame. When the ghee is fully hot, drop the rest of the shakarparas into the ghee, too.

6) When the shakarparas rise on the top, flip the sides and begin to fry till they get light golden from all sides. On a pan, strain out the cooked shakarparas. Keep the skillet on the wok's edge, so excess ghee flows back into the wok.

7) Take a container to make a sugar syrup. Add sugar and water in it. Cook until the sugar decomposes. Take some drops in a bowl to sample, then take it in between your thumb and index finger. Check if a long string is shaped when the fingers are spread apart. The syrup is set. Switching the flame off.

8) Over a net stand, position this vessel so that the syrup condenses down a bit. When the syrup becomes small dense in consistency, drop the shakarparas into the sugar syrup and cover them beautifully — taking out the

shakarparas directly from the syrup in a large bowl after combining them in the syrup. In the same container, pour out the excess syrup. You should reheat it a little if the syrup becomes too dense when covering the shakarparas.

9) Stir a spoon of sugar-coated shakarparas to detach them. Otherwise, they would cling to each other.

Chapter 06: Vegetarian Indian Recipes

These days, more people want to eat only vegetarian food rather than Non-veg because most Non-veg dishes raise fat amount in our body and take a long time to get digested because of certain health issues such as obesity, thyroid, weight gain. In this chapter, you will study about some of the vegetarian dishes, which are both nutritious and tasteful.

⥣ Vegetable Biryani

Serves to 3 persons

Cooking time: 2 hours

❖ **Ingredients**

- 2 teaspoons of oil
- One small cauliflower, separated into tiny parts
- 2 big, peeled and cut into cubes sweet potatoes
- 1 big onion, chopped
- One stock of hot veggies
- One tablespoon of curry paste

- One chili, thinly sliced
- Big pinch of threads of saffron
- One tablespoon of mustard seeds
- 500 g Rice
- 140 g beans
- Two tablespoons of lemon juice
- A couple of leaves of coriander

❖ **Steps to Follow**

1) On moderate flame, heat ghee in a big deep pan. Add the onion, and simmer for around 5 minutes until it softened. Mix the cumin seeds in it; cook it for around 5 minutes, and the cumin seeds start to pop.

2) Add the paste of ginger garlic, onions, and ½ cup sugar in it. Take it to a boil and cook for around 5 minutes until the water is absorbed. Mix the peas, onion, and carrots in it. Also, add all spices in it. Stir carefully, then wrap it with lid and simmer for three minutes.

3) Add 4 cups of water and carry to a cook over medium temperature. Mix rice after boiling, reduce heat to mild, re-heat and cook for 10 minutes. Lower the heat and proceed to cook for another 20 minutes before the rice has softened.

⊹ **Indian Sparkling Dhal**

Serves to 4 persons

Cooking time: 1 hour

❖ **Ingredients**

- One tablespoon of oil
- 1 cup sliced onion

- 2 (delicately sliced) garlic cloves
- 1 tablespoon (coarsely diced) ginger
- 4 cups of water
- 1 cup rinsed dried red lentils
- 1 tablespoon cumin
- 1 tablespoon of coriander
- 1 tablespoon of turmeric
- ¼ teaspoon cardamom
- ¼ teaspoon of Cinnamon
- ¼ teaspoon pepper
- Salt as per your liking
- 2 tablespoons of a paste of tomato

❖ **Steps to Follow**

1) Collect all ingredients.

2) Warm the oil over a moderate flame in a medium-sized soup pan. Add the onion, garlic and ginger in it. Cook and keep stirring regularly, for around 6 minutes.

3) Add water, lentils, vegetables and salt. Keep stirring continuously. Carry the soup to a low boil, then switch the heat down to low, cover and cook for around 20 minutes or until the lentils become very soft.

4) Add the tomato paste when well blended. Cook for some more minutes.

5) Serve it and enjoy.

⚓ **Koora Cabbage**

Serves to 4 persons

Cooking time: 2 hours

❖ Ingredients

- Cooking oil: 3 tablespoons
- 2 chili peppers dried hot, cut into bits
- 1 tablespoon black split skinned lentils
- 1 tablespoon Bengal gram
- 1 teaspoon of mustard seeds
- A few curry leaves
- 1 pinch of powder Asafetida
- 4 peppers of green chili, chopped.
- 1 cabbage head, thinly sliced
- ¼ cup of frozen peas

❖ Steps to Follow

1) Heat the oil over moderate-high flame in a broad skillet; cook the red chili peppers, all types of gram mentioned above, and mustard in the hot oil. If the gram starts browning, add the curry leaves and asafetida powder. Stir it well.

2) Add the green chili peppers and proceed to cook for another 3 minutes.

3) Add the cabbage, peas and lentils to the combination; season it with salt; continue cooking until it starts to wilt, but stays a little crunchy for about 10 minutes.

4) Put the coconut into the combination, and simmer for another 2 minutes.

5) Instantaneously serve and enjoy.

✚ Dhal of Indian with Spinach

Serves to 4 persons

Cooking time: 2 hours

❖ **Ingredients**

- 2 cups of yellow split peas (approximately 14 ounces)

- 8 cups of water

- Freshly squeezed lemon juice for two teaspoons (from around one medium lemon)

- Kosher salt two teaspoons, plus more as required

- Eight teaspoons butter unsalted (1 stick)

- Two teaspoons of cumin seeds

- 1 ½ teaspoons of turmeric

- 5 big, peeled and finely minced garlic cloves

- ¼ cup of fresh ginger peeled and finely chopped

- 1 medium chili serrano stemmed and thinly chopped

- Spinach, 8 ounces, washed and coarsely chopped

❖ **Steps to Follow**

1) In a fine-mesh strainer, position the split peas and rinse them vigorously under cold water. Switch to a wide saucepan, add the water you have weighed and bring to a boil over high heat.

2) Reduce the heat to medium-low and simmer, occasionally stirring and skimming any scum off the surface with a large spoon until the peas are completely soft and the consistency of split pea soup thickens for about 30 minutes.

3) Set aside, remove from the heat and add the lemon juice and the measured salt in it.

4) Heat the butter over medium heat in a frying pan, until it is foamed. Add the cumin seeds and turmeric in it and simmer until the cumin seeds are toasted and fragrant and the butter is very foamy, stirring periodically, for around 3 minutes.

5) Add the garlic, ginger and serrano; season with salt; and simmer for around 2 to 3 minutes, stirring periodically, until the vegetables have softened. Add the spinach in it and simmer until the spinach is fully wilted, stirring periodically, for around 4 minutes.

6) With the split peas, move the spinach mixture to the reserved saucepan and mix to blend. Serve with steamed rice or naan.

⊹ Masoor Daal

Serves to 4 persons

Cooking time: 2 hours

❖ Ingredients

- 2 cups of dry masoor dal, sorted and well rinsed (aka red lentils)
- 8 cups of water
- 1 tablespoon of oil (flavored coconut oil or neutral)
- 1 big, finely diced yellow onion
- 6 cloves of garlic, minced
- 1 tablespoon of minced ginger
- 2 green chilies, minced
- 1 tablespoon of Indian curry powder

- 1 teaspoon of whole seed mustard
- 1 teaspoon of coriander
- ½ teaspoon of cumin
- 1 ½ teaspoon salt or as per your taste
- 1 ½ cups of new chopped tomatoes

❖ **Steps to Follow**

1) In a broad jar, mix the lentils and water. Carry to a boil, then put down the pressure to simmer. Cook it while partly wrapped with lid until the lentils are soft, for about 15-20 minutes normally.

2) Prepare the tadka when the lentils are cooking. Heat a skillet over medium heat and add a pinch of salt, oil and onion, garlic, ginger, chilies. Fry for around 5 minutes until it becomes tender.

3) Add the spices along with the salt, curry powder, mustard, coriander, and cumin. Remove for around 60 seconds to mix and prepare, then add the tomatoes. If frozen, cook the tomatoes for around 7 minutes, or until the tomatoes are soft and saucy.

4) To infuse with spice, add the tadka to the cooked lentils, and simmer over low heat for around 5 minutes.

5) Garnished it with basmati rice and cilantro. And serve.

Conclusion

Indian food can be both thrilling and daunting, with all its exotic products, unfamiliar sauces, and tongue-tingling tastes. It is a complete world of taste. To get a titillating culinary experience, you mix many of the strategies from other cuisines and incorporate mysterious spices. Do not be afraid to start cooking Indian food at home. First, the different dishes and flavors that make up Indian food are important to consider. The food in India is as popular as you can find in Europe. All are entirely new, and the only element that links is a judicious awareness of the usage of spices.

There are 20 to 30 essential spices used in many sauces, such as cumin, coriander, turmeric, and ginger, to name a handful, and there are numerous ways to use them. Spices have cardiovascular advantages, and they also make the meal more tasty and entertaining.

In history, geography and environment, variety can be seen in India's cuisine. Spices are a crucial part of the preparation of food and are used to increase a dish's taste. For the proper preparation of Indian cuisine, accurate usage and combining of the aromatic spices are essential. Also, oil is an essential part of cooking, be it mustard oil in the north or coconut oil in the south. Vegetables differ according to season and area. The vegetables are cooked as a main dish.

Indian Food has an extra advantage for vegetarians. It is one of the most comfortable cuisines around for them. Judicious application of seasoning and sauces bring the taste of potatoes, cauliflower, spinach, and eggplant. Keep things easy at home as you start out.

Chinese Home Cooking

The Easy Cookbook to Prepare Over 100 Tasty, Traditional Wok and Modern Chinese Recipes at Home

By

Adele Tyler

Table of Contents

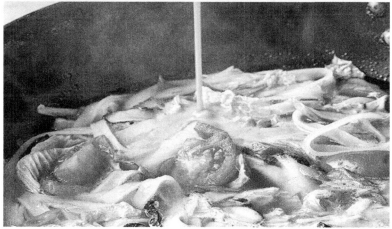

Introduction

Chinese cuisine developed from different areas of China and soon became very popular around the world for its unique cooking style and flavor. There are eight central cuisines in china. Chinese foods are mainly comprised of two components that are grains and meat. Starch and vegetables are essential ingredients of all dishes. The necessary foundation of the most Chinese dishes is garlic, ginger, and sesame. Soy sauce is used in all cuisines for saltiness.

Stir-frying is an essential technique to cook Chinese cuisines. A wok is used to stir-fry vegetables in garlic. Wok dishes are the most common and widespread in America. Chinese cuisine got popular when Chinese immigrants came to America and worked in food shops.

Many traditional Chinese dishes gained popularity in America. Thus, many chefs in the United States made a bit changes in Chinese cooking style, hence Chinese-American dishes emerged.

Chinese cuisine is not only tasty but also healthy and nutritious. Spices used in Chinese cooking are full of nutrients that a human body needs to work the whole day. These are a rich source of carbohydrates, starch, proteins, and fibers. This book "Chinese Home Cooking" will explain Chinese cuisine and its early history. The first chapter will introduce Chinese food and its emergence from the Zhou dynasty to the Ming Dynasty, how it has evolved from time to time, and has become famous in the United States.

The second chapter is a brief discussion about the benefits of the Chinese cuisine. Moreover, it will help you enhance your cooking skills through specific techniques used in Chinese restaurants. This chapter will also tell you the difference between Chinese traditional home cooking and restaurant cooking style. The third chapter is about breakfast and appetizer recipes to make you start your day with delicious and quick recipes. The fourth Chapter is about lunch and snack recipes to regain the energy you have wasted during your work. The fifth chapter includes dinner and dessert recipes to make tasty food for your family meal with some sweet dishes and side dishes.

The last chapter will provide you three different kinds of meals, including traditional wok recipes, famous recipes known worldwide, and, the most importantly, vegetarian recipes. You can choose to make these recipes in your special events or family gatherings.

Finally, a brief conclusion about choosing Chinese cuisine for you and your family are given to help you support your idea of selecting Chinese food.

So, start reading this book and enhance your cooking knowledge and cooking skills with "Chinese Home Cooking".

Chapter 1: Origin and Historical Background of Chinese Food

China is the country with the most prominent citizens and the nation with the highest and most innovative cuisine in the world. The general name for dishes from different regions and ethnicities in China is Chinese cuisine. With excellent infrastructure, rich divisions and institutions, and a distinctive theme, it has a long history. It is the crystallization of the past of thousands of years of Chinese cuisine. A significant aspect of Chinese culture, also known as the Chinese culinary tradition, is Chinese cuisine. Chinese cuisine is one of the triple international cuisines and has a far-reaching influence on the East Asian region. The ingredients are sourced from different areas and cultural dishes.

Chinese Cuisine in the Zhou Dynasty

According to ancient records, China already had a barbecue, fried fish, and other foods more than 5000 years ago.

Food was primarily grains such as peas, buckwheat, corn, and brown rice during the Zhou dynasty in China, although they were not the same as what we have produced in the modern agricultural industry today. In the late Zhou dynasty, people began to get white rice/peeling rice, which was very rare and expensive and affordable for the wealthy class to consume. Similar to other countries, salt was a key factor in cooking and people's everyday life. By then, salt was widely used already. There was a popular cuisine called 'Ba Zheng' in the Zhou Dynasty, which was quite popular for centuries to come.

Chinese Cuisine in the Qin Dynasty

In the Qin dynasty, the sour taste was accepted by the people at a certain time. Bamboo slides recovered from temples, according to historical documents, berries were another hot cooking by then. It was primarily used for extracting fishy unusual from meat or fish inferred by academics. Besides, during the Qin dynasty, cinnamon, spring onions, canola source, and cider were also used in the cooking.

Chinese Cuisine in Han Dynasty

When it came to the Han dynasty, salty taste was preferred. Han was a time when Chinese cuisine took a major move forward. There were many "foreign-made" food and cooking ingredients for people at the period, such as peppers, grapefruit, oranges, hazelnuts, cardamom, pineapple, pomegranate, broccoli, lettuce, thyme, fennel, spinach, garlic, and onion, owing to the opening of the Silk Road in the Han Dynasty, for traders and commercial trade. In the later tang dynasty, this lay a strong cornerstone for the advances of Chinese cuisine. Chinese cuisine quickly evolved during the Han, Wei, northern and Southern Dynasties, and many popular cuisines emerged.

Chinese Cuisine in Tang Dynasty

Chinese cuisine had already grown to a standard of quality by the period of the Tang dynasty. People also had several types of gatherings or cocktail parties to live their time at a certain period.

Chinese Cuisine in the Song Dynasty

The Song Dynasty is among the stars of the history of Chinese cuisine. There were various cold meals, hot meals, soups, and decorative dishes at Bianjing and Linen's menus. The dishes were labeled with North, South, Chuan flavors, and vegetable meals, which indicated that cuisines' institutions started to develop.

Chinese Cuisine in Yuan, Ming, and Qing Dynasty

During the Yuan, Ming, and Qing Dynasty, Chinese cuisine had a huge success. Hundreds of cuisines emerged. During this time, ethnicities believed in Islamism, migrated to all parts of China, and halal certification occupied China's role as a new form of Chinese food. Since the Qing Dynasty was a king ruling under the Manchu people, Manchu style and flavors were introduced to Chinese cuisine. During the Ming Dynasty of this time frame, chilled pepper crops were introduced as an elegant plant in China. It did not take too long until Chinese people learned its high benefit in cooking methods. The spicy flavor soon became popular in Hunan and Sichuan provinces at that period and had since left a massive impact on their cooking style. Chinese cuisine schools were founded. From the late Qing Dynasty and outsiders came to China, Chinese cuisine even added some characteristics of western cuisines. In the world, Chinese cuisine is very popular for its color, scent, flavor, and better style.

1.1 History of Traditional Chinese Dishes

Chinese cooking is commonly seen to represent one of the country's wealthiest and most varied cuisine histories and cultures. It emerged in various areas of China, and it has been spread from Southeast Asia to Western Europe and North America to other regions of the world. In Chinese culture, dinner is usually seen as made up of two specific components: (1) a source of starch or carbohydrate and (2) fruit, seafood, pork, or other things corresponding meals.

Rice is a vital component of much of Chinese food, as it is widely known globally. Wheat-based items like noodles and boiled buns play a large role in comparison to South China, where rice is prevalent. Despite the value of rice in Chinese cuisine, it is always the case that no grain would be provided at all on highly formal events; in such a scenario; rice will be offered only if all other dishes existed, or as a consolation dish at the end of dinner. To relieve one's stomach, soup is usually eaten at the end of dinner. Serving soup at the beginning of a meal is still very common nowadays, owing to Western influences.

Chinese cuisine history dates back to approximately 5000 BC. Chinese people have created their special way of cooking meat over this large period. Their ways of defining ingredients to make ideal combos, their multi-method cooking strategies, and their multidisciplinary flavoring management have all been increasingly improved. There was a very good diet for the ancient Chinese, and from historical records, agriculture in China appears to have begun around 5,000 years ago. Both variations and transitions are marked by Chinese cuisine. Since ancient times, food has been at the heart of social life, and many current-day dishes with their variations of fragrance and flavor can be linked back to ancient Chinese food patterns.

Food and art have often been regarded by the Chinese, emphasizing preparing food and how it is consumed.

Chopsticks are the main dining utensil for real food in Chinese culture, while sauces and other fluids are enjoyed with a large, flat-bottomed (historically stainless) spoon. Due to the recent deforestation deficits in china and other Asian countries, wooden chopsticks are decreasing their supremacy; many Chinese dining facilities are considering switching to a more environmentally friendly eating fork and spoon, such as plastics or bamboo chopsticks. In the past, more luxurious items used included silver and gold. On the other side, in small restaurants, plastic chopsticks crafted of bamboo/wood have all replaced recycled ones.

Vegetables: Soy Bean and Cucumber

There were not many types of veggies in ancient China, but vegetables were an important part of people's diets regardless. They consumed vegetables with their main meal, rice, whenever they were able to afford it. During that time, the main vegetables were cucumber and soybean, and when soybeans had become the main grain in ancient China, soybean production can be dated back to 1000 BC. The word Shu means soybean began appearing on brass artifacts from the early Zhou period. Soybeans were also described in the Analects of Confucius in the 5th century BC.

Wine: Rice and Millet

China is considered to be one of the earliest countries to produce wine in the world. Wine has not only been a beverage since its launch, but has also been provided with moral and cultural importance, representing political and social life and design concepts, and even appearing in modern literature.

People started to drink wine during the Shang dynasty (16th to 12th century) and used it to honor the deities; yellow grain wine is probably the first of this kind.

Since the Han and Tang dynasties, all other types of wine are believed to have been produced. Millet wine was released years later, and it was a major success, much more common than tea.

Sorghum

The "camel of crops" is classified as sorghum since it does not require much moisture and develops in the soil in which other grains do not. Also, the cost of grain and fertilizer for sorghum is smaller than for other crops. Dating back to the Stone Age is the use of sorghum. A significant volume of carbonized sorghum was detected from the feuding State Period in Shijiazhuang. "China is the oldest and greatest Centre for the roots of sorghum," according to the Genomic Resources Center.

Meat: Pork, Chicken, Beef

Pork is China's most widely-eaten meat, including beef, mutton, goat, duck, bird, etc., and other kinds. From 3000 or 4000 BC, the people in china consumed pork, which was indigenous to China, but cattle and sheep were not indigenous, and soon after that they were imported in China from West Asia. Many people used tofu, or bean paste, as a dietary protein source because the beef was too pricey and because Buddhist monks did not consume meat.

Tea

The origin of Chinese tea can be measured to 4,000 years. The Chinese probably drink tea to be an elegant form of art with so many traditions and traditions attached to it. Tea, along with espresso and cocoa, is China's national beverage and is one of the three popular sweet drinks. China firmly considers itself the cradle of tea as China was the first nation to bring its planting strategies, manufacturing, and drinking practices to the rest of the globe.

Tofu

Tofu, or bean paste, is also of Chinese ancestry and is made from soy protein, milk, water, and a coagulating agent. It has been a dietary staple in Chinese and Asian food since prehistoric times, abundant in minerals, low in fat, and full of protein, calcium, and iron. Since it was a great source of vitamins, Chinese doctors considered that meat was an important meal, but only the wealthiest could afford to consume it. A bill was made to remedy this, where any person living in China will get a free cup of tofu each week, which was a combination of sorghum and other stuff like rice to give everyone the same amount of protein as the meat will. It was hard to cook on a massive scale in China at that time, so people might cut their meat into tiny pieces to prepare it. In Western vegetable meals even, tofu has also become a primary ingredient.

Wheat

People began developing and consuming wheat in China about 2500 BC, previously dependent on exports from West Asia, wheat soon became the primary source of carbohydrates. The traditional Chinese people consumed porridge, but they made no bread out of wheat. The key factor for this was that to cook the rolls, the coal they used for the energy was too pricey.

Rice

Rice is indeed a good source of carbohydrates, comparable to millet, grain, and other crops. In China, rice background goes back to the late Stone Age (around 2000 BC). Rice production is believed to have begun in Thailand, but Chinese farmers invented grain rice.

The method of rice cultivation in muddy, natural ponds is called rice paddies.

Rice was used as a commodity in China since prehistoric times, and when we think of Chinese cuisine, rice is most certainly the very first thing you say of. While rice has been growing in China for a long time, that was too cool to grow rice in north china, so wheat and soybeans were farmed anyway. People cooked rice to render it softer by boiling or steaming it, and rice was also used to create a sort of wine called rice wine, which is still drunk in China today.

1.2 Evolution of Chinese Cuisine

The history of Chinese food covers three centuries of recorded history, spanning an unprecedented expansion of food preparations, food preparation methods, and the use of tons of ingredients.

History of Chinese Noodles

One of the important steps of their whole cuisine is Chinese boiling noodles. They can be located within countless recipes in hundreds of combinations, which has sparked the improvements in cooking style over the Chinese country's history and national tastes. The earliest recorded noodles discovered in China date back 4,000 years. They have been found in historical discoveries along China's Yellow River. However, the first definite historical records of noodles are from the period around 25 to 200 AD. when the East Han Dynasty ruled. These early noodles were traditionally made from corn flour, and as years went by, they became even more common. In the Song Dynasty period, noodles could be bought from Chinese restaurants in major cities in China. Noodles are extensively used in China, Korea, the Philippines, Cambodia, Thailand, Vietnam, and others as Chinese presence spread throughout Asia.

One of the three major components is typical noodles made in China: white flour, corn starch, and mung bean flour. They are sliced using one of the five methods until they are baked and used as a component of other foods: Sliced (with the blade from rolled bread sheet), compressed (dough moved by the device into tiny holes), Peel (large bread strips are cut straight into hot water), Pulled (squeezed dough folded to produce thinner layers) and mashed (rolled bread to the shape desired). Without any hesitation, Char kway teow, Cup Noodles Ban mien, Cart noodle, Beef chow fun, Laksa, Lo mien, Zhejiang mien, and Re gan mien are the most common dishes in Chinese food that use noodles.

History of Chinese Sweet Food

Chinese cuisine has become one of the best diverse globally with an amazing array of dairy products invented by Chinese chefs and developed by more than Three thousand years of things change, proximity to trade channels, and local food products availability. China has managed to produce a wide range of desserts, in contrast to thousands of recognizable dishes and a wide range of liquid drinks (both distilled and unsweetened), which can be made on both prepared foods such as fruit and more complex recipes, often requiring preparation that can last many months or years.

Chinese sweets are delicious, but typically with less amount of sugar than Western deserts. They also have a greater proportion of natural fruit products, which can be used as an integral part of the Chinese Ying and Yang custom of consuming "healthy" meals, not only during dinners and with coffee, but also during meal options.

Chinese desserts are typically classified into several major groups, such as pastry products, candy products (including baked wheat goods such as Moon pastries), candies, cookies, rice-based treats, sweet flavorings, desert meringues, caramels, and ice creams.

Traditional Chinese sweets also played a significant role in upholding Chinese lifestyles and the nutrition of many Asian countries, which have established a cultural and economic relationship with China, making Chinese desserts much more popular and broader.

History of Chinese Soups

China has a long tradition of using many kinds of soups in its kitchen, almost always cooked and eaten to provide the meal with nutrition and provide nutrition and be a provider of natural and therapeutic herbs that can improve the vitality and immune function. Although western soups can contain daily products (dairy products or cream) from start to end, Chinese soups are often broth-based, thickened by refined starches of maize or sweet potatoes.

Chinese Pickles History

A big part of the local food is Chinese pickles. In certain variants, fermented veggies or berries are available because Chinese people usually do not consume fresh fruits. They tend to eat them fried, baked, and processed in several other ways, and if food is poorly handled, the processing is better for many reasons, most important. In China, pickled food is processed by soaking and roasting in salt or brine vegetables and fruits instead of fermenting in paste or sauce compounds. Along with a wide range of medicinal herbs and several other components (even beers), it is very popular to dissolve fruits and vegetables in the pickling method. It should be remembered that mainstream medicine and research do not suggest that many marinated foods be used in their everyday diets. Some researchers have found that marinated food can increase cancer risks, and even marinated vegetables have been reported as possible carcinogens by the World Health Organization. Pickled food could also get riddled with different fungi species very quickly, which can increase the carcinogenic potential of certain foods much further.

Chinese Tea History

Tea holds the most significant position in the Chinese cuisine development, having been present in its society for more than 3,000 years and gradually evolving to its present form with each moving century. Chinese heritage holds the evidence of the first tea drinking during the Zhou Dynasty, stretching back to the third century BC, with various reports confirming that they have been used mainly as medicines since the earliest days. The rich noble's use of tea as a treat and community drink helped popularize in the 8th and 9th centuries during the Tang Dynasty. The style of tea preparing, serving, rituals, protocol, procedures, and even cookware used has altered many Chinese imperial dynasties. The Song Dynasty (960-1276, tea pancakes that were ground into flour and combined with warm water) and the Ming Dynasty (1368-1644, Hiqiu tea, song Luo tea, and several others) were the two most important royal dynasties that made popular the dissemination of new varieties of tea throughout Asia. In the late 1700s, new forms of Chinese tea began to grow under the Qing Dynasty.

Chinese tea varieties can be distinguished between trees, regions that have been grown, and processed. Today, beyond any doubt, the most common form of tea is Chinese Green Tea, produced from the "Camellia Sinensis" herb and manufactured with limited oxidation. Not just because of its good taste and body feel, but because of its medicinal qualities that can minimize the risk of cardiovascular disease and certain forms of cancer, improve the metabolism, and this tea was more praised in China.

1.3 Rise of Chinese Food's Popularity in the United States

The first big influx of Asian refugees to America was the "Chinese 49'ers" who settled in the United States a century before the American Revolutionary War and grafted the first Asian food to America. The first multicultural cuisine at the national scale to be heavily commercialized as a form of food specifically cooked and eaten away from family was Chinese food. Food from China started to draw a fast-growing non-Asian customer base of varied different ethnicities in major cities throughout the nation at the turn of the nineteenth century, and Chinese food became the most popular multicultural cuisine throughout the United States by 1980, helped by the resurgence of Chinese immigration to the United States. As one of the two primary sources of jobs for Chinese immigrants and communities for centuries, Chinese cuisine has also been a critical economic lifesaver for Chinese Americans. Hence, its creation is a significant chapter in United States history and a core part of Chinese America's understanding. The numerous and sometimes disparate developments in the United States the Chinese food industry shows that it is currently at an intersection. The future depends on the degree to which Chinese Americans will dramatically shift their impact on the social and political arena and on the willingness of China in its relationship between the two countries to alter the financial system.

The Transplantation of Chinese Food

When the 49'ers entered California through China, Chinese food landed in America in the major gold period, illustrating immigrants' crucial role in implanting regional food to America.

Not because they wished to evangelize their cuisine amongst non-Chinese, but because of its exceptional significance in establishing their culture and identity, Chinese immigrants took their cuisine to the New World.

The implantation of Chinese food coincided with the development of Chinese societies. During this time, food companies represented a critical sector in the ethnic Chinese industry in major California cities, such as San Diego and San Fran. Thirty-three supermarkets, along with seven hotels and five food stores, accounted for almost half of all firms in the developing Chinese settlement of San Francisco in 1857, outstripping all other forms of enterprises. While in the 1870s, laundry stores in San Diego and San Francisco soon outnumbered Chinese food companies, the former were dispersed in numerous parts of their respective localities. By contrast, within Chinatown, the latter was the central component of exchange and established its significance.

Chinese restaurants selling foods became another significant draw for Chinese immigrants in Chinatown and exposed the fundamental importance of food to the Chinese culture. Indeed, the arrival of Chinese restaurants has often marked the start of a society. For instance, in 1849, in San Francisco, four restaurants launched an emerging culture. In the developing Chinese communities in other towns, such as Marysville, restaurants were also present. It was a major Chinese village site, also known as the larger town (san bu) among the Chinese. There were already three restaurants and two Chinese shops in 1853. At inexpensive rates, Chinese restaurants deliver historically recognized cuisine. In the late 1870s, migrants like Ah Quin could buy a meal for as little as 10 cents in San Fran's Chinatown. However, Chinese dining establishments provided a culturally significant room to relax and socialize. The Chicago Post described a respectable Chinese restaurant in the center as "the resort and gathering room of East Asiatic".

The Birth of "Chinese-American Cuisine"

At the beginning of the 20th century, as Chinese restaurants penetrated to non-Chinese neighborhoods, the third stage in Chinese food development and its popularity in America started to establish an omnipotent presence across the country. As a paper published in 1903, "there is scarcely an American city that did not have its Chinese restaurants to which people of all classes want to go." The proliferation of Chinese restaurants beyond Chinatown during this time created a special Chinese cuisine for American customers. The distribution of Chinese food gained from two important interactions that many Chinese Americans had in the service industry: first, their role as household work, which gave them great knowledge of serving food to a non-Chinese customer base; second, their role as laundrymen, from which they knew how to enabled service in non-Chinese neighborhoods.

Not middle-class visitors and affluent enthusiasts, but white people on the fringes of society, such as hippies, African Americans, and refugees like Jews from Eastern Europe, were the customers who helped make Chinese food into the first non-Anglo cuisine to gain national popularity in popular consumption. Unlike the middle-class visitors who, out of interest, dined in Chinatown cafes, these more oppressed Americans became the most loyal customer base, regularly visiting these restaurants inside and outside Chinatown. The latter two parties sponsored Chinese dining institutions in various East Coast cities. "The New York Tribune reported in 1901, describing the importance of Chinese food amongst the less fortunate, "So many who, though having a limited share of the products of this country, still impact 'sportiness' visit the restaurant for its cheapness and rise to enjoy the strongly flavorful dishes. Chinese food gained little intellectual recognition until recently, because of its historical importance and pervasive appearance.

Chapter 2: Cooking Methods and Health Benefits of Chinese Food

Chinese food usually includes those vegetables and spices that are very nutritious and good for health. Although many different and unique techniques to prepare Chinese cuisine at home and restaurants are there. The ingredients used in the Chinese food are rich in carbohydrates, fiber, proteins, and calcium. This chapter will provide you information about different restaurants' techniques to prepare food and the health benefits of the ingredients they use.

2.1 Preparing Chinese Food at Home vs. Eating at Restaurants

The food that is served at home is very close to that served in China's restaurants.

Restaurant food appears to be cooked more intricately than one would usually do at home.

Restaurants often tend to be more creative when making variants on a cooking method, whereas organic cuisine is more conventional and sticks to the standard recipe rigidly. This is only a consequence, though, of one person being a professionally skilled cook, and the other being a distracted wife/husband. China is a large country, and the cuisine has a great deal of variation from region to region.

In comparison, Chinese meals served in restaurants appear to be less nutritious than real Chinese foods available at home. Chefs can do less for the ingredients that their consumers eat, whether it be high sugar or unhealthy fat, which can be seen at any restaurant. Many restaurants buy inexpensive goods to make a full profit while Chinese foods eaten at home are made from the finest and freshest products. Restaurants will usually use an assortment of liquids and herbs to make these dishes taste healthier. While these restaurant dishes may be extremely tasty, they are not as flavorful and delicious as home-cooked meals because they are normally miss-sauced, too much-salted, or sometimes over-rich.

The Chinese food we see in local New York restaurants is somewhat different from the typical Chinese food in Chinese households. The products used are the key contrast between conventional and American Chinese foods. Many American Chinese restaurants replace conventional ingredients for those available in the surrounding areas to cater to the community's citizens. American Chinese diets focus on meats instead of including vegetables such as rice, pasta, and sorghum, including steamed veggies as side dishes.

Thus, restaurants have a huge amount of content to pick from when writing their meals.

On the table, there are sometimes dishes that people don't know how to prepare or have never consumed before only because they are the dishes that are lifted from another part of China.

As many western restaurants modify Chinese and Indian cuisine to fit a western pallet, Chinese restaurants adjust dishes from other regions to meet the local preferences. Thus, if in a style bar, the food you see in the restaurant may be nothing like the typical home-cooked recipe as the chef must have modified it.

One meal that is used in nearly every restaurant is pork over grain. Much as Americans want it, the dish's main emphasis is the pork, using rice to bring variation to the meal. While American Chinese products include corn, they sometimes replace more Western vegetables such as carrot, broccoli, cabbage, tomatoes, and dairy products for the other main vegetables used. The process used in cooking and serving the food is another extremely significant contrast between Chinese domestic cooking and cafeteria cooking. Considering the vast quantities of food that restaurants have to prepare during a normal working day, many restaurants start cooking food the day before delivering it.

Much as restaurant-style and Chinese house style cooking cuisine vary in the products used and in the preparing processes, they also vary in the cooking types overall. Chinese cuisine foods, ranging from simmering to frying, can be cooked in any manner that the person likes. However, most dishes are cooked by frying techniques in Chinese restaurants, using either a wok, a round-bottomed frying container used for stir-frying, or a cooking pot. Even traditional Chinese foods discovered at home commonly use other ways, such as simmering, to cook rice. Usually, Chinese domestic style cooking is much healthy but lacks the taste that can be seen in cooking in the restaurant-style.

2.2 Health Benefits of Chinese Food

Chinese food is very famous, and it contains all the nutrition that a sound metabolism and body require to remain healthy. While Chinese people consume, on average, thirty percent more calories than Americans, and they have the same behavior patterns, they do not have obesity issues. This is because fructose and vitamin free food are avoided in Chinese cuisine.

Vegetables are "add-ons" to other recipes in the West, but vegetables are key in Chinese cuisine. Chinese assume the significant proportion of vegetables can be properly combined with a minor portion of livestock. Meat is important since excess calories are incorporated. Sugar, processed sugars, and high fat ingredients are quite less in Chinese foods, allowing our bodies to know quickly when they are full. This encourages people who consume Chinese food to survive more on sufficient amounts of food and not overfill their bodies with excessive calories. On the other side, the Western diet tricks our bodies into knowing their boundaries even longer than is ideal.

Chinese cuisine also supplements the food consumption by relying much on liquid foods. Western food is mostly dry, making it necessary for customers to drink water during the day. With daily consumption of Chinese food, there is no need for that, and desire would be better managed. You may know that Chinese food is good, but you do not know that it is one of the healthiest foods you can consume, either.

Healthy Carbohydrates

Carbohydrates give the organism the energy it needs to get through the day. They are converted to glycogen by the liver, a readily available resource in the muscles and liver.

Other types of energy resources, including fat, are unreliable. Good carbohydrates, including noodles and rice, are also used in Chinese meals, helping you remain energized without eating too many calories.

Nutritional Balance

It's essential to add carbohydrates, proteins, as well as other nutrients into your meal. Carbs supply the fuel required, while proteins help maintain and build muscle strength. That's why the ideal choice is Chinese food. Vegetables, noodles, or rice are often used in recipes, and any beef, fish, or other protein gives you a nutritious balance. It can be hard to find a meal that combines all these diverse nutritious elements into one dish with other cuisines.

Fiber

Fiber is another vital element, helping the body's digestive process. However, many individuals don't get plenty, so they don't like eating the soft vegetables that supply it. However, Chinese cuisine is remarkable for serving many well-seasoned and fried high-fiber dishes, giving them a more intense flavor.

Nutrition in Spices

Ginger- Ginger has a long history of use in traditional Chinese medicine; it has long been used to relieve vomiting and stimulate the appetite. Newer research has found that ginger can ease morning sickness and provoke pain that comes with osteoarthritis.

Garlic- Pungent garlic was used in traditional medicine to relieve respiratory problems. It has a range of proven health effects, including decreasing cholesterol and the risk of osteoporosis and some cancers, plus these have antibacterial activity.

Sesame Seeds- Sesame seeds are exploding with nutrients, including copper, iron, and calcium, and a heavy amount of fiber, although they are tiny.

Shiitake Mushrooms- Mushrooms add a pleasant aroma and taste to foods and make a perfect substitute for any or all of the meats in some sauces, allowing you to cut calories and maintain taste. A decent source of energy-producing Vitamin B and magnesium and immune-supporting manganese is shiitake mushrooms.

Tofu- Tofu is a perfect source to get a reasonable amount of protein from the vegetable resources. It is also an outstanding source of bone-building calcium and magnesium.

Bok Choy- This part of the cabbage family is rich in immune system-boosting vitamins A and C.

2.3 Specific Cooking Techniques Used in Chinese Restaurants

In China, there have been hundreds of ways of cooking. However, deep-frying, stir-frying, braising, shallow-frying, heating, boiling, and reheating are the most common techniques.

Stir-Frying

The most widely used process is stir-frying. This process cooks the manufactured ingredients for a brief amount of time at high temperatures. As the source of heating, edible oil is being used. Usually, a wok will be used at high temperatures, spices, and seasonings to apply edible oil. Owing to the brief amount of time involved with the process, foods mostly retain their nutrient benefit. Usually, stir-fried meat is moist and crispy, and vegetables are normally soft and crispy.

Deep Frying

Deep-frying requires much more vegetable oil than stir-frying (the component should be entirely immersed in the fat), providing buttery-textured food. The traditional way of making deep-frying dishes is to break the components into medium-sized parts or pieces, soak them in seasoned spices for a while, cover with corn flour and finally fry in warm cooking oil over medium-high heat. The coating thickness will decide the degree of crunchiness and gentleness on the inside and outside of the products used.

Shallow Frying

Shallow-frying is a preparation method requiring fewer oil products than used in deep-frying and less temperature than stir-frying. Shallow-fried foods are typically very delicate inside, becoming golden or mildly burnt externally. The products for shallow-frying are typically split into strips or flat pieces and brushed with herbs and spices. After being processed, the ingredients are also partially brushed with corn flour to make the external skin crispy. When frying, the products should be shallow-fried on one side first and then switched to the other.

Braising

To prepare large-sized foods crumble-in-your-mouth, braising is to add ingredients and flavorings in a wok or a frying pan simultaneously, add in some water, heat it, and then simmer it for an hour more than. The components are usually formed into pieces or stones. To fry dishes by braising, the seasoning mixes, especially the animal products, should be rid of the strange smell in boiling water and washed in clean water first. The sauce is thickened either with corn flour or reduced by simmering eventually.

Steaming

A special form of cooking developed in China is steaming. It is commonly used for steaming tortillas and wontons in northern China, where people survive on wheaten rice. The method involves putting the materials in a steamer basket, which is put over the liquid in a steamer jar. Steamed food provides more nutrients than that which is dissolved into the water for less protein. Quite little edible oil and fewer seasonings are used, so the food's natural taste is preserved and improved.

Roasting

Roasting is to prepare the food over the open fire of coal or in a microwave. Although seasonings are rubbed in from outside, the odor of the food is eliminated. The roast food's surface still gets denser and golden brown, but it preserves and improves flavors. Many products can be fried, like all meat types, just like most root and bulb veggies. To roast poultry, the products must be prepared, processed, and braised with edible oil to avoid moisture in the products during the roasting process.

Chapter 3: Chinese Appetizers and Breakfast Recipes

3.1 Delicious Chinese Appetizer Recipes

Chef John's Shrimp Toast

Cooking Time: 24 minutes

Serving Size: 4

Calories: 212.3

Ingredients:

- 1 tablespoon soy sauce
- 1 egg white
- ½ teaspoon white sugar
- ½ teaspoon paprika
- ½ pound raw shrimp
- ½ cup finely sliced green onions

- 3 garlic cloves

- Salt to taste

- 4 slices white bread

- 1 teaspoon sesame seeds

- 1 tablespoon ginger root

- 1 anchovy filet

- 1 teaspoon sesame oil

- ¼ cup cilantro leaves

- 1 teaspoon Asian fish sauce

- 1 pinch cayenne pepper

- 1 cup of vegetable oil

Method:

1. Blend all ingredients in a food processor and blend until the mixture becomes smooth.

2. Lightly toast slices of bread and paste shrimp mixture over toasts.

3. Cut edges and slice into halves.

4. Add vegetable oil in the skillet and fry until golden brown.

5. Serve hot with green onion.

Pork Dumplings

Cooking Time: 35 minutes

Serving Size: 100 dumplings

Calories: 751.5

Ingredients:

- 5 cups Chinese cabbage

- 100 wonton wrappers
- 1 ¾ pounds pork
- 1 tablespoon fresh ginger root
- 3 tablespoons sesame oil
- 4 cloves garlic
- 2 tablespoons green onion
- 4 tablespoons soy sauce
- 1 egg

Method:

1. In a bowl, combine the soy sauce, pork, sesame oil, green onion, ginger, garlic, egg, and cabbage.

2. Add 1 teaspoon cabbage mixture into each wonton wrapper and form a triangle shape.

3. Steam dumplings for 20 to 25 minutes and serve hot.

Chinese Chicken Wings

Cooking Time: 65 minutes

Serving Size: 12

Calories: 256.1

Ingredients:

- 2 tablespoons garlic powder
- 5 pounds of chicken wings
- 2 cups soy sauce
- 2 cups brown sugar

Method:

1. Mix all ingredients except chicken wings.

2. Heat ingredients until brown sugar melts completely.

3. Pour mixture over chicken wings and wrap the bowl with plastic cover.

4. Marinate chicken for 8 hours in the refrigerator.

5. Heat oven on 365°F.

6. Cover chicken with aluminum foil and bake for 45 minutes in the oven.

7. Remove foil and bake for 15 minutes more.

8. Serve hot with sauce.

Perfect Pot Stickers

Cooking Time: 30 minutes

Serving Size: 6

Calories: 438.5

Ingredients:

- ½ cup green onions

- 1 pinch cayenne pepper

- 1 ½ cups green cabbage

- 3 tablespoons fresh ginger

- 2 tablespoons soy sauce

- 1-pound pork

- 4 cloves garlic

- 1 teaspoon sesame oil

Dipping Sauce:

- ¼ cup of rice vinegar

- ¼ cup of soy sauce

Dough Ingredients:

- ¾ teaspoon kosher salt

- 2 ½ cups all-purpose flour
- 1 cup hot water

Frying:

- 8 tablespoons water for steaming
- 6 tablespoons vegetable oil

Method:

1. Mix green onion, cabbage, pepper, garlic, ginger soy sauce, sesame oil, and pork in a bowl and mix with a fork.
2. Cover with plastic and chill for an hour in the refrigerator.
3. Mix dough ingredients and make the dough.
4. Knead dough until it becomes soft and smooth.
5. Wrap the dough and let it rest for 30 minutes.
6. Cut dough into small pieces and make sticker wrappers.
7. Fill stickers with pork mixture and fold.
8. Mix dipping sauce ingredients to make the dipping sauce.
9. Heat a skillet and put pot stickers in hot oil until golden brown.
10. Drizzle water and steam for 7 minutes or until crispy.
11. Serve with dipping sauce.

Chinese Egg Rolls

Cooking Time: 70 minutes

Serving Size: 20

Calories: 169

Ingredients:

- 8-ounce bamboo shoots
- 1 cup wood ear mushroom
- 4 teaspoons vegetable oil
- 3 large eggs
- 1 teaspoon sugar
- 14-ounce egg roll wrappers
- 1 egg white
- 1-pound roasted pork
- 2 green onions
- 2 ½ teaspoons soy sauce
- 4 cups oil for frying
- 1 medium head cabbage
- ½ carrot
- 1 teaspoon salt

Method:

1. Heat the skillet and add 1 tablespoon oil.
2. Add beaten egg in oil and cook for 2 minutes on low heat.
3. Change side and cook for another 1 minute.
4. Set aside and let it cool and slice into thin strips.
5. Add vegetable oil in skillet and heat remaining ingredients until vegetables are fully cooked.
6. Add sliced egg in vegetables and refrigerate for 1 hour.
7. Take a plastic wrapper and put vegetable mixture.
8. Roll plastic sheet until top corners are sealed.

9. Cover with plastic to avoid drying.

Chinese cabbage Pork Dumplings

Cooking Time: 95 minutes

Serving Size: 10

Calories: 120

Ingredients:

- 1 teaspoon sugar
- 1 teaspoon salt
- 2 ½ cups all-purpose flour
- 1 tablespoon scallions
- ¼ teaspoon salt
- ¾ cup of water
- ½ pound cabbage
- 1 teaspoon rice cooking wine
- 1 tablespoon ginger
- 1-pound pork sirloin

Method:

1. Mix flour and salt.
2. Add water and make an elastic, smooth dough.
3. Rest it for 10 minutes.
4. Divide the dough into small 50 pieces and roll into a thin circle piece.
5. Mix other ingredients and process slowly until well combined.
6. Add the mixture on pieces and make dumplings.
7. Steam for 6 to 7 minutes until cooked.

Chinese-Style Chicken and Mushrooms

Cooking Time: 40 minutes

Serving Size: 4

Calories: 170

Ingredients:

- ½ teaspoon sugar
- 1 garlic clove
- 100 grams of mushrooms
- ½ cup of water
- soy sauce
- olive oil
- 400 grams of chicken
- 3 teaspoons cornstarch
- salt
- black pepper
- 2 teaspoons fresh ginger

Method:

1. Cook mushrooms on low heat in a skillet with olive oil.
2. Cut chicken into pieces and add other ingredients over it.
3. Mix and marinate for 15 minutes.
4. Cook chicken pieces in skillet and add cooked mushrooms.
5. Heat until well cooked.
6. Serve with sauce.

Hand-Pulled Chinese Noodles

Cooking Time: 90 minutes

Serving Size: 4

Calories: 560

Ingredients:

- 2 teaspoons chili oil
- ¼ cup of soy sauce
- black sesame seeds
- 1 Thai Chile
- 3 ½ cups all-purpose flour
- ½ teaspoon kosher salt
- 1 green onion
- 4 teaspoons toasted sesame oil

Method:

1. Mix flour and salt.
2. Add water and make the dough.
3. Rest the dough for 30 minutes and cut into small pieces.
4. Pull these pieces into thin sticks.
5. Boil this for 10 minutes and rest aside.
6. Heat the skillet and add other ingredients to cook.
7. Add hand-pulled noodles and cook for more 2 minutes.
8. Serve with sauces.

Crispy Sesame Tofu and Broccoli

Cooking Time: 55 minutes

Serving Size: 4

Calories: 370

Ingredients:

- ½ teaspoon salt
- ¼ teaspoon pepper
- 2 scallions
- ¾ pound broccoli florets
- 2 teaspoons sesame seeds
- 1 garlic clove
- 3 tablespoons light brown sugar
- 4 teaspoons rice vinegar
- ½ inch fresh ginger
- 1-pound extra-firm tofu
- 1/3 cup water
- 2 teaspoons cornstarch
- 1/3 cup tamari
- 1 tablespoon toasted sesame oil
- 1 tablespoon neutral oil

Method:

1. Take tofu and rinse with water.
2. Add broccoli in a pan and heat with little water until broccoli becomes green and crispy.
3. Make tamari sauce with tamari, garlic, ginger, and seasoning.
4. Mix other ingredients and cook on low heat.
5. Cut tofu into small pieces and put mixture with a spoon.

6. Heat tofu on low heat until crispy.

7. Heat sauce until bubble comes out.

8. Add broccoli and tofu into the bubbling sauce.

9. Mix for 2 minutes and serve with scallions on top.

Cream Cheese Wontons

Cooking Time: 30 minutes

Serving Size: 6

Calories: 228

Ingredients:

- 8 ounces cream cheese
- ½ teaspoon sugar
- 24 wonton wrappers
- 1 egg beaten
- oil for frying
- 2 teaspoons minced chives
- ½ teaspoon onion powder

Method:

1. Combine and mix sugar, cream cheese, and onion powder.

2. Place a wonton wrapper and put a teaspoon on cream cheese over it.

3. Brush edges with egg and wraps into package shape.

4. Heat pan on 350°F with 4 tablespoon oil.

5. Fry wontons for 6 to 7 minutes or until golden brown.

6. Soak into a paper towel and set aside.

7. Fry all wonton wraps and serve with tamari sauce.

Lumpia Shanghai

Cooking Time: 25 minutes

Serving Size: 6

Calories: 230

Ingredients:

- 3 cups cooking oil
- 50 pieces lumpia wrappers

Filling Ingredients:

- ½ teaspoon black pepper
- ½ cup parsley
- 1 ½ lb. ground pork
- 1 tablespoon sesame oil
- 2 eggs
- 2 pieces onion
- 1 ½ teaspoons salt
- 2 pieces of carrots
- 1 ½ teaspoon garlic powder

Method:

1. Mix all filling ingredients in a bowl and stir.
2. Take lumpia wrap and put fillings on it.
3. Beat an egg and brush it to edges.
4. Roll wrappers and set aside.
5. Heat the skillet with oil and put wrappers into the hot oil.
6. Cook until lumpia floats in oil.
7. Soak extra oil and serve with sauce.

3.2 Chinese Breakfast Recipes

Here are some breakfast recipes to start your day with delicious and easy Chinese dishes to save your energy for the whole day.

Chinese Pork Salad

Cooking Time: 10 minutes

Serving Size: 6

Calories: 124

Ingredients:

- ½ cup stir-fry sauce
- ½ red onion
- 3 ounces chow Mein noodles
- 20 ounces pea pods
- 8 ounces mandarin oranges
- 1-pound pork strips (stir-fry)

Method:

1. Marinate pork strips in the sauce for 25 minutes.
2. Stir-fry pork in a large skillet for 6 to 7 minutes.
3. Mix remaining ingredients in a bowl.
4. Mix pork sauce and mixture.
5. Stir and serve.

Chinese-Style Spareribs

Cooking Time: 2 hours

Serving Size: 6

Calories: 77

Ingredients:

- 3 tablespoons dry sherry
- 2 cloves garlic
- 6 pounds pork spareribs
- 2 tablespoons honey
- 2 tablespoons soy sauce
- ¼ cup hoisin sauce
- ¼ cup of water

Method:

1. Take spareribs and cut them into pieces.
2. Mix all ingredients in a bowl.
3. Take a large sealing bag and put ribs into it.
4. Take ¼ cup of mixture and rest aside.
5. Add the remaining mixture in the bag and mix well with ribs.
6. Marinate mixture in the refrigerator for 1 hour.
7. Heat oven at 350°F and take a baking pan.
8. Put ribs in pan and wrap with baking sheet to bake for 90 minutes.
9. Remove the sheet and put the remaining ¼ cup of mixture on the ribs with a brush.
10. Bake for another 30 minutes.
11. Serve hot with sauce.

Crunchy Chinese Pork Salad

Cooking Time: 20 minutes

Serving Size: 4

Calories: 141

Ingredients:

- 3 ounces chow Mein noodles
- 6 cups iceberg lettuce
- 4 slices bacon
- ½ cup green onions
- 3 tablespoons soy sauce
- 8 ounces water chestnuts
- ¾ pound roasted pork loin
- 1 tablespoon ketchup
- 2 tablespoons honey
- 1 teaspoon mustard

Method:

1. Cook bacon until crisp and set it aside.
2. Take a small bowl and stir ketchup, mustard, and soy sauce together.
3. Take a large bowl and mix pork, bacon, lettuce, green onions, and chestnut together.
4. Add noodles in dressing and salad.
5. Mix well and serve.

Chinese Tomato and Egg Sauté

Cooking Time: 30 minutes

Serving Size: 2

Calories: 810

Ingredients:

- 3 pinches shredded coconut
- black pepper
- 1 tablespoon ketchup
- 1 teaspoon sugar
- 1 cup white rice
- ½ teaspoon sesame oil
- 1 teaspoon cornstarch
- 2 scallions
- 1 heirloom tomato
- 1 tablespoon rice wine
- 2 cups of water
- 4 large eggs
- 1 pinch salt

Method:

1. Chop the scallion and slice tomatoes into very little pieces.
2. Put eggs into a bowl and add seasonings.
3. Add rice wine and beat eggs.
4. Heat wok and add 2 tablespoon oil.
5. Add eggs and scramble. Set aside
6. Heat wok and add 1 tablespoon oil.
7. Add tomatoes and scallions.
8. Stir fry and add seasonings.
9. Add 1 cup of water and cooked eggs.

10. Mix and cover for 2-3 minutes until tomatoes make the paste.

11. Heat until sauce thickens as your requirement.

Chinese Meat Filled Buns (Baozi)

Cooking Time: 1 hour 45 minutes

Serving Size: 16

Calories: 105

Ingredients:

- 3 tablespoons sugar
- 1 teaspoon salt
- 50 milliliters cold water
- 300 grams pork (or chicken)
- 1 teaspoon fresh ginger
- 3 cloves garlic
- 2 spring onion
- 1 tablespoon rice wine
- 1 teaspoon sugar
- 3 shiitake mushrooms
- 2 tablespoons soy sauce
- 1 tablespoon oyster sauce
- 400 grams flour
- 1 ½ teaspoons baking powder
- ½ teaspoon sesame oil
- 3 tablespoons pork lard
- 190 milliliters warm water

- 2 teaspoons yeast

Method:

1. Mix flour, baking powder, yeast, sugar, and salt.
2. Add melted lard and warm water to make the dough.
3. Rest it for 30 minutes and knead until smooth.
4. Take other ingredients and mix them in a processor.
5. Take the dough and cut it into small pieces.
6. Prepare pieces into a circle and put fillings.
7. Roll again in a bun shape and set aside for 30 minutes.
8. Steam buns on a greaseproof paper so that they do not stick with sides of the steamer.
9. Steam for 15 to 20 minutes until it looks shiny and feels like buns.
10. Serve with sauce and lettuce.

Shao Bing - Chinese Breakfast Flatbread

Cooking Time: 65 minutes

Serving Size: 4

Calories: 740

Ingredients:

- 2 teaspoons Sichuan peppercorn
- 1 teaspoon spices
- 1 teaspoon chicken
- ¼ teaspoon salt
- 300 grams plain flour
- 1 tablespoon Chinese cooking wine
- ½ teaspoon salt

- 3 tablespoons vegetable oil
- ¼ cup oil
- 1 tablespoon soy sauce
- 250 grams ground beef
- ¼ cup spring onion
- 2 teaspoons ground ginger
- ¼ cup chopped onion
- 2 teaspoons sesame oil
- ¼ cup chopped coriander
- 2 tablespoons spring onion
- 1 ½ tablespoons flour
- 2 teaspoons white pepper
- sesame seeds

Method:

1. Making Dough- mix flour, salt and sugar in a bowl and mix until lumpy. Add yeast, water, and oil. Knead the dough and cover with plastic wrap. Set aside for 30 minutes.

2. Making Oil Paste- take a small pan and heat oil. Add cake flour and mix until smooth. Continue cooking until aromatic. Let it cool.

3. Heat oven at 425°F.

4. Forming Bread- take dough and roll dough. Add oil paste with spatula and roll dough again. Cut into pieces of bread and add sesame seeds on each bread.

5. Bake breads for 12 to 15 minutes until golden brown.

6. Cut the sides and serve with sauce.

Yang Chow Fried Rice

Cooking Time: 25 minutes

Serving Size: 6

Calories: 120

Ingredients:

- 2 large eggs
- 4 cups day-old rice
- 1 teaspoon toasted sesame oil
- ½ teaspoon kosher salt
- ½ teaspoon chicken bouillon
- ½ pound Chinese BBQ pork
- 3 scallions
- ½ teaspoon white pepper
- 3 tablespoons vegetable oil
- ¼ pound shrimp
- 1 tablespoon soy sauce
- 2 tablespoons oyster sauce

Method:

1. Fry shrimps in 1 tablespoon cooking oil. Set aside.
2. Cook chicken bouillon and scallions until softened.
3. Put rice in a wok and make a hole in the center.
4. Add beaten egg and mix with the rice properly.
5. Add other ingredients and chicken mixture in a pan and stir fry to make a paste.
6. Add paste on top of the rice. Serve hot.

Soya Sauce Mushroom Chicken with Braised Eggs

Cooking Time: 105 minutes

Serving Size: 1

Calories: 118

Ingredients:

- 4 cloves garlic
- 1 teaspoon sesame oil
- 4 eggs
- 3 pieces of chicken thighs
- 150 milliliters chicken broth
- 3 pieces of rock sugar
- 1 tablespoon corn flour
- 3 slices ginger
- 1 tablespoon Chinese cooking wine
- potato
- 6 button mushrooms
- 2-star anise
- 3 tablespoons light soy sauce
- 2 tablespoons dark soy sauce
- 1 dash pepper
- 1 cinnamon stick

Method:

1. Rinse chicken and dry with a towel.
2. Clean mushrooms and marinate chicken for 30 minutes.
3. Soak mushrooms for an hour.

4. Heat oil and add ginger, garlic, anise, cinnamon sticks.

5. Add chicken and stir fry for 5 minutes.

6. Add mushrooms and cook with the chicken for 10 minutes.

7. Add all other veggies and stir.

8. Cook on low heat for more than 20 minutes and add other ingredients.

9. Add corn flour to give thickness to the sauce and serve hot.

Chicken Mustard Green Congee – Chinese Breakfast Rice Porridge

Cooking Time: 55 minutes

Serving Size: 6

Calories: 190

Ingredients:

- ¼ cup mustard greens
- 1 tablespoon sesame oil
- 2 garlic cloves
- ¼ cup chives
- 12 ounces chicken tenderloin
- 1 ginger
- ¾ cup sweet rice
- ½ teaspoon dark soy sauce

Method:

1. Boil ginger, garlic on low heat in a pot, and add chicken.

2. Cook for 20 minutes until chicken cooked properly.

3. Shred chicken and discard ginger garlic.

4. Add rice in chicken broth water and cook for 25 minutes.

5. Add other ingredients and cook for more 5 minutes.

6. Rest aside for 10 minutes and serve.

Loaded Breakfast Baked Potatoes

Cooking Time: 80 minutes

Serving Size: 4

Calories: 470

Ingredients:

- 4 russet potatoes
- teaspoons salt
- teaspoons black pepper
- 2 scallions
- 1 tablespoon butter
- 4 large eggs
- 4 strips bacon
- 2 ounces cheddar cheese
- ½ teaspoon salt
- ¼ teaspoon black pepper
- sour cream
- hot sauce

Method:

1. Heat the oven at 400°F and take an aluminum foil.

2. Pierce potatoes with fork and place on aluminum foil sheet.

3. Bake potatoes for 60 to 70 minutes in the oven.

4. Take the potato and cut lengthwise with a knife to add fillings.

5. Heat the skillet and add other ingredients.

6. Stir until cooked.

7. Add mixture into potatoes and bake again for 10 minutes.

8. Serve immediately.

Baked Hash Brown Cups with Eggs

Cooking Time: 27 minutes

Serving Size: 4

Calories: 420

Ingredients:

- ½ cup shredded cheddar cheese
- chives
- ¼ teaspoon black pepper
- canola oil cooking spray
- 8 large eggs
- canola oil cooking spray
- 1 bag hash brown potatoes
- black pepper
- 4 strips bacon

- ½ teaspoon garlic powder
- salt

Method:

1. Heat oven at 400°F.
2. Place shredded potatoes in a bowl and mix with seasonings.
3. Press potatoes until water leaves.
4. Bake potatoes in muffin cups for 20 to 25 minutes.
5. Heat skillet and add beaten eggs.
6. Stir with a rubber spatula. Do not overcook eggs.
7. Add eggs and seasoning on potato and bake again for 3 to 7 minutes until fully melted.
8. Serve with sauce.

Steamed Halibut Fillet with Ginger and Scallions

Cooking Time: 45 minutes

Serving Size: 4

Calories: 500

Ingredients:

- 3 scallions
- 2 tablespoons canola oil
- 4 tablespoons water
- 2 inches fresh ginger
- 1 tablespoon chicken powder
- 2 ½ pounds fillets
- ¼ teaspoon salt
- 2 teaspoons sugar

- 4 baby bok choy
- vegetable oil cooking spray
- 3 tablespoons lite soy sauce
- 4 Chinese black mushrooms
- ¼ teaspoon black pepper

Method:

1. Mix all ingredients in a processor and mix until lightly smooth.
2. Add eggs and blend again.
3. Steam fish fillets and place a lemon slice on each fillet.
4. Bring to boil water and steam for 3 to 4 minutes after the water starts boiling. Do not overcook.
5. Place fillets in a dish and pour the sauce over it. Cool at room temperature. Serve with spinach leaves.

Chapter 4: Chinese Lunch and Snack Recipes

4.1 Chinese Snack Recipes

Seasoned Snack Mix

Cooking Time: 30 minutes

Serving Size: 10

Calories: 450

Ingredients:

- ¼ cup Crisco Butter Flavor
- ¾ teaspoon garlic salt
- ¼ teaspoon cayenne pepper
- 2 cups oyster crackers
- 7 ounces peanuts
- ¾ cup grated Parmesan cheese
- salt

- ¼ teaspoon onion powder
- 3 cups of rice
- 2 teaspoons Worcestershire sauce
- 2 teaspoons Italian seasoning
- 1 square cereal
- 2 cups round toasted oat cereal
- 2 cups pretzel sticks

Method:

1. Preheat oven at 325°F.
2. Melt shortening in the oven and rest it aside.
3. Add Worcestershire sauce, seasoning, garlic, ginger, salt, and pepper in a bowl and stir.
4. Add other ingredients and melted shortenings into the mixture.
5. Mix well and spread evenly on the baking sheet.
6. Bake 16 to 18 minutes in oven and stir after 10 minutes.
7. Cool and store in containers.

Energy Snack Cake

Cooking Time: 85 minutes

Serving Size: 4

Calories: 920

Ingredients:

- 300 grams walnut pieces
- 100 grams flour
- 60 grams of dried cranberries
- 10 dried figs

- ½ teaspoon baking soda
- ¼ teaspoon baking powder
- 3 large eggs
- 15 grams of dried dates
- 80 grams of dried apricots
- ½ teaspoon salt
- 140 grams of sugar
- 1 teaspoon vanilla extract

Method:

1. Mix baking powder, baking soda, flour, and salt in a bowl.
2. Add nuts, dried fruits, and sugar in the mixture.
3. Heat oven to 150°F.
4. Take a small bowl and beat eggs with vanilla extract.
5. Add egg mixture into the flour mixture and mix well.
6. Add other ingredients and pour them into a baking pan.
7. Bake for 60 to 70 minutes.
8. Let it cool and cut into slices.

Taco Snack Mix

Cooking Time: 16 minutes

Serving Size: 4

Calories: 120

Ingredients:

- 2 cups crackers
- 2 cups of corn chips

- 2 cups Rice Chex Cereal
- 1 package McCormick Taco Seasoning Mix
- 2 cups Wheat Chex Cereal
- ½ cup unsalted butter

Method:

1. Microwave butter for 40 seconds until butter melts.
2. Take a bowl and mix cereals, corn chips, cheese crackers.
3. Add seasoning in the mixture and stir well.
4. Microwave mixture uncovered for 6 to 8 minutes until crispy.
5. Cool at room temperature.

One-Bowl Caramel Snack Cake with Caramel Glaze

Cooking Time: 60 minutes

Serving Size: 9

Calories: 610

Ingredients:

- ¾ cup cake flour
- 1 ½ teaspoons baking powder
- ¼ cup confectioners' sugar
- 1 large egg
- 2 large egg yolks
- cooking oil spray
- ¾ cup unsalted butter
- ¾ teaspoon salt

For cake:

- 1 cup dark brown sugar
- 1 cup heavy cream
- 1 tablespoon vanilla extract
- 1 cup all-purpose flour

For caramel:

- ½ cup heavy cream
- 1 teaspoon flaky sea salt
- 1 teaspoon vanilla extract
- 1 cup dark brown sugar

Method:

1. Heat oven at 350°F and Grease the pan with oil. Set aside.
2. Melt butter in the microwave oven and separate ¼ cup.
3. Add brown sugar and cream in remaining butter.
4. Microwave 1 minute and stir. Microwave for more 1 minute until caramel thickens. Set aside to cool down.
5. Use powder ingredients and mix them into the caramel.
6. Stir with a rubber spatula until combine.
7. Bake for 20 minutes on the middle rack.
8. Rotate baking pan and bake for more than 20 minutes until softens.
9. Pour remaining butter and caramel on the cake and set aside.
10. Let it cool down for 10 minutes and cut into pieces.

Snack Dippers with Hillshire Farm Smoked Sausage and Honey Mustard

Cooking Time: 35 minutes

Serving Size: 10

Calories: 170

Ingredients:

- 2 tablespoons yellow mustard
- 1 tablespoon honey
- ¼ cup packed brown sugar
- ¼ cup mayonnaise
- ¼ teaspoon black pepper
- 14 ounces Smoked Sausage

Method:

1. Place sausages in a tray and unwrap. Freeze for 30 minutes.
2. Use a cutting board to cut sausages into ¼ size pieces.
3. Heat oven to 325°F.
4. Transfer sausages in the baking dish and spread brown sugar.
5. Bake sausages for 20 minutes until lightly browned.
6. Mix other ingredients in a bowl and dip sausages to serve.

Afternoon Snack Muffins

Cooking Time: 65 minutes

Serving Size: 4

Calories: 760

Ingredients:

- 4 eggs
- 2 tablespoons chocolate sprinkles
- 1 container yogurt
- 200 grams flour
- 100 grams margarine
- 200 grams of sugar
- 1 teaspoon baking powder
- 1 handful walnuts

Method:

1. Heat oven to 180°C.
2. Grease muffin pan with butter and flour. Set aside.
3. Beat sugar and eggs until the mixture becomes fluffy.
4. Add yogurt and margarine. Beat again.
5. Add baking powder and flour. Beat again until it forms a smooth batter.
6. Add chocolate sprinkles and walnuts. Stir with a spoon.
7. Place dough in muffin cups and bake for 50 minutes.
8. Remove from the oven and let it cool down.

Wheat Bread Snack

Cooking Time: 10 minutes

Serving Size: 4

Calories: 90

Ingredients:

- watercress

- 1 slice whole-wheat bread
- olive oil
- 1 cup skimmed milk

Method:

1. Toast bread to a golden-brown color.
2. Pour watercress and olive oil on toast.
3. Serve with milk.

Apple Peanut Butter Snack

Cooking Time: 10 minutes

Serving Size: 2

Calories: 360

Ingredients:

- 2 tablespoons sunflower kernels
- ¼ cup Smucker's Peanut Butter
- 2 apples
- ¼ teaspoon ground cinnamon
- ¼ cup plain yogurt
- 1 tablespoon apple juice

Method:

1. Cut the apple into small slices.
2. Mix cinnamon, yogurt, peanut butter, apple juice, and kernels in processor and blend well.
3. Apply mixture evenly on sliced apples and let it cool down.

Honey Almond Snack Mix

Cooking Time: 15 minutes

Serving Size: 4

Calories: 320

Ingredients:

- 2 cups of cereal
- 2 cups of rice cereal squares
- 1 cup whole almonds
- ½ teaspoon salt
- ½ teaspoon ground red pepper
- ¼ cup Coconut Oil
- ¼ cup honey

Method:

1. Heat oven to 365°F.
2. Grease pan with baking paper and flour. Set aside.
3. Combine almonds, salt, pepper, and cereals in large bowls.
4. Take a small bowl and mix honey with coconut.
5. Pour in cereal mixture and stir well.
6. Spread into baking pan and bake for 15 to 18 minutes.
7. Let it cool and cut into slices.

Chinese BBQ Pork

Cooking Time: 20 minutes

Serving Size: 4

Calories: 352

Ingredients:

- 1 tablespoon honey
- 2 teaspoons fresh ginger root
- ½ cup dry sherry
- 8 drops red food coloring
- 2 pounds pork loin roast
- 1 teaspoon sesame oil
- 1 whole scallion
- 3 tablespoons soy sauce
- 2 ½ tablespoons hoisin sauce

Method:

1. Cut pork into small pieces.
2. Take a cooking bowl and grease with oil.
3. Place all ingredients in the cooker and mix.
4. Cover and cook for 7 hours on low heat.
5. Serve with fried rice.

Yam Bean, Carrot, and Cucumber Snack

Cooking Time: 45 minutes

Serving Size: 3

Calories: 260

Ingredients:

- Worcestershire sauce
- Peanuts
- 2 carrots
- ½ yam bean

- Unflavored gelatin
- Hot sauce
- Lime juice
- Japanese peanuts
- 1 cucumber
- 6 limes

Method:

1. Grate carrot, yam beans, and cucumber. Drain all thoroughly.
2. Grease baking pan with oil and pour beans.
3. Sprinkle gelatin and lime slices. Press firmly.
4. Add a layer of cucumber and carrots with the same process.
5. Cover and freeze for 30 minutes.
6. Mix other ingredients to make the sauce.
7. Sprinkle peanuts for garnish.

4.2 Chinese Lunch Recipes

These are some Chinese recipes that are common in the Chinese menu and easy to prepare with fewer ingredients.

Stir-Fried Tofu with Rice

Cooking Time: 40 minutes

Serving Size: 2

Calories: 281

Ingredients:

For the Tofu:

- 100 grams of tofu
- 1-inch ginger
- 3 Garlic cloves
- 1-inch red onion
- 1 Lemongrass stick
- 2 Shallots
- A handful of coriander leaves
- 1 teaspoon refined oil
- 2 teaspoon soya sauce

- 2 teaspoon chili paste
- 2 teaspoon honey

For the Fried Rice:

- 2 teaspoon soya sauce
- ½ Lemon
- Carrots
- Coriander leaves
- 1 teaspoon olive oil
- Spring onions
- Salt and pepper
- 1 Fresh red chilly
- 1 Ginger

Method:

1. Add chopped mariner in a preheated pan and stir well.
2. Add seasonings, garlic, shallots, and ginger.
3. Add honey, soy sauce, and chili paste.
4. Add coriander and mix with a rubber spatula. Set aside.
5. Mix carrot, onion, salt, pepper, and ginger in a pan.
6. Drizzle in oil then add chili, lemon juice, and soy sauce.
7. Add coriander in cooked rice and cook for 7 more minutes.
8. Serve rice.

Dim Sums

Cooking Time: 1 hour 20 minutes

Serving Size: 4

Calories: 237

Ingredients:

For Chicken and Prawn Dumplings:

- 5 ml sesame oil
- 2.5 grams white pepper
- 150 grams of chicken
- Wonton skin
- Potato starch
- 150 grams prawn
- 5 grams of sugar
- Salt

For Vegetable Coriander Dumplings:

- 10 grams of water chestnuts
- 10 grams of carrots
- 10 grams button mushrooms
- 5 grams of sugar
- 10 grams garlic
- 10 grams of bamboo shoots
- 5 grams sesame oil
- 10 ml of oil
- 10 grams brown garlic

For Wonton Skin:

- Salt
- 50 grams of wheat starch
- Potato starch

Method:

1. Mix prawns and chicken with salt, potato starch, sesame oil, and sugar.

2. Stuff wanton skin in mixture and steam. Serve with soya sauce.

3. For dumplings, mix all ingredients except wanton skin.

4. Stuff mixture in wanton skin and steam. Serve with sauce.

5. To prepare wanton skin, add potato in wheat starch, salt, and water.

6. Add potato starch and stir till tightens.

7. Cut into pieces and roll balls. Add fillings.

8. For the sauce, fry garlic in oil. Soak chilies and make a paste.

9. Add chili paste when garlic gets brown. Add seasonings.

Hot and Sour Soup

Cooking Time: 1 hour 15 minutes

Serving Size: 4

Calories: 39

Ingredients:

- 1 ½ tablespoon vinegar

- Salt

- 60 grams prawns

- 1 tablespoon soya sauce

- ½ tablespoon chili powder

- 5 grams of carrot

- 5 grams of cabbage
- 1 Egg
- 1 tablespoon coriander
- 1 teaspoon chili oil
- 5 grams of bamboo shoots
- 5 grams black mushrooms
- 5 grams button mushrooms
- 100 grams of chicken
- ½ teaspoon white pepper
- 2 tablespoon corn flour
- 5 grams of bean sprouts
- 5 grams of fresh beans
- 2 cups stock

Method:

1. Cut all vegetables, prawns, and chickens into small pieces.
2. Cook all vegetables with chicken in a wok.
3. Add seasonings and other remaining ingredients into wok.
4. Add corn flour and egg in the end to a thick soup.

Quick Noodles

Cooking Time: 45 minutes

Serving Size: 2

Calories: 188

Ingredients:

- 1 cup carrot, julienne

- 1 tablespoon vegetable oil
- 1 cup onion
- 1 cup spring onions
- 2 packets noodles
- 1 tablespoon ginger and garlic chili paste
- 1 tablespoon coriander
- 1 tablespoon lemon juice
- 1 teaspoon vinegar
- 1 tablespoon soy sauce
- 1 tablespoon Schezuan sauce
- 1 cup pepper
- 1 cup mushrooms
- ½ lettuce
- ½ teaspoon turmeric powder
- 1 teaspoon sugar

Method:

1. Cook noodles using instructions on the pack. Drain and cool in the water.
2. Add oil in noodles and mix to avoid sticking noodles with each other.
3. Heat oil in a wok.
4. Mix vegetables and soya sauce, mushroom, ginger, and garlic paste and fry in wok.
5. Mix remaining ingredients in a small bowl and stir.
6. Add this mixture to vegetable mixture and add noodles. Mix well.

7. Garnish with chopped coriander and serve.

Szechuan Chili Chicken

Cooking Time: 45 minutes

Serving Size: 8

Calories: 179

Ingredients:

- 3 tablespoon brown peppercorn
- Salt
- 2-3 spring onions
- 2 teaspoon white pepper
- 5-6 dry red chilies
- 2-3 tablespoon ginger
- 3 tablespoon green peppercorn
- 10-12 pieces chicken
- 1 tablespoon black vinegar
- 2 teaspoon chili oil
- oil for frying

Method:

1. Fry chicken with ginger until color changes to brown.
2. Drain oil and set it aside.
3. Add onion, garlic, peppercorn, and brown peppercorn.
4. Sauté for 5 minutes and add spices.
5. Stir for more than 10 minutes and add black vinegar.
6. Fry for more than 10 minutes and garnish with peppercorns.

Shitake Fried Rice with Water Chestnuts

Cooking Time: 25 minutes

Serving Size: 2

Calories: 291

Ingredients:

- 1 Cup Shitake mushroom
- 1 tablespoon Ginger
- A pinch of White pepper
- 1 big drop Sesame oil
- 1 cup rice (cooked)
- Green chilies
- 2-3 tablespoon Vegetable oil
- 4 cloves garlic
- 2-3 Water chestnuts
- 1 big tablespoon Celery
- ½ Medium Onion
- 1 big tablespoon Leeks
- Small bunch Parsley
- A dash of Rice wine vinegar
- 1 big drop of Sesame oil
- Salt to season
- 1 stalk Spring onions

Method:

1. Slice mushrooms, chestnuts, and green chilies.
2. Heat wok and add 1 tablespoon vegetable oil.

3. Add celery, onion, and leeks in oil.

4. Add mushrooms, chestnuts, and ginger.

5. Add rice, onion, sauces, and other ingredients.

6. Stir fry and put into the bowl.

Chicken with Chestnuts

Cooking Time: 45 minutes

Serving Size: 4

Calories: 294

Ingredients:

- 5 dried Chinese mushrooms
- 1 tablespoon fish sauce
- 1 tablespoon date puree
- 1 diced green capsicum
- 2 tablespoon sesame oil
- ½ kg chicken mince
- 1 diced red capsicum
- 3 tablespoon white radish
- 50 ml of water
- ½ teaspoon chili flakes
- 12-14 peeled water chestnuts
- 2 tablespoon chopped spring onion
- 1 tablespoon chopped garlic
- 1 tablespoon vinegar
- 1 iceberg lettuce
- 1 tablespoon shredded ginger

- 1 tablespoon soya sauce
- 1 tablespoon chopped coriander

Method:

1. Soak mushrooms in boiling water for 30 minutes and discard stems of mushrooms.
2. Heat oil in wok and fry chicken with ginger until lightly browned.
3. Fry ginger, garlic, and capsicum for 3 minutes.
4. Put the chicken into pan and heat.
5. Add remaining ingredients into chicken except for lettuce and coriander.
6. Add vegetables and mix well.
7. Serve with lettuce and garnish with coriander leaves.

Honey Chili Potato

Cooking Time: 35 minutes

Serving Size: 2

Calories: 586

Ingredients:

For Frying Potatoes:

- 5 tablespoon Corn flour
- 2 Potatoes
- 1 ½ tablespoon Salt
- 2 teaspoon Chili Powder

For Honey Chili Sauce:

- 4 teaspoon Sesame Seeds
- 2 tablespoon Honey

- 1 teaspoon Chili Flakes
- 2 Bulbs Spring Onions
- 1 ½ teaspoon Garlic
- 1 teaspoon Vinegar
- 2 teaspoon Tomato Sauce
- 2 teaspoon Chili Sauce
- 1 teaspoon Ginger
- 2 Whole Red Chilies
- 1 teaspoon salt

Method:

1. Take 2 potatoes and cut them into lengthwise slices.
2. Rinse them with water and soak for 15 minutes.
3. Add slices into a bowl and put some salt, corn flour, chili, and coriander leaves.
4. Mix well until sticky.
5. Take a frying pan and heat 3 tablespoon oil.
6. Fry potatoes into the oil until golden brown and crispy.
7. Do not fry on high flame as it can cause potatoes to burn from the outer side and uncooked from the inner side.
8. When cooked properly, set aside.
9. Take another frying pan and put sesame seeds to heat until golden brown. Set aside.
10. Heat oil in a pan and add chili flakes, tomato sauce, ginger, garlic, and red chilies.
11. Stir well and add vinegar, chili sauce, honey, and salt.
12. Stir and make the sauce.

13. Add fried potatoes in sauce and mix well.

14. Serve potatoes with juice.

Peri-Peri Chicken Satay

Cooking Time: 25 minutes

Serving Size: 2

Calories: 104

Ingredients:

- 50 grams Peri-Peri sauce
- 100 grams of potato fries
- 100 grams of yogurt
- 200 grams of chicken thigh
- salt and pepper
- 5 grams of chili powder
- Oil to fry
- 25 grams ginger garlic paste
- 5 grams coriander leaves

Method:

1. Soak skewers for 60 minutes.
2. Add ginger, garlic, salt, pepper, Peri-Peri sauce, chili, and garlic in a bowl.
3. Mix well and add chicken.
4. Marinate for 2 hours in a sealing bag.
5. Heat grill on medium heat.
6. Place chicken on grill and brush with oil to prevent sticking.
7. Grill for 15 to 20 minutes until brown.

8. Serve chicken with crispy potato fries.

Cantonese Chicken Soup

Cooking Time: 40 minutes

Serving Size: 2

Calories: 132

Ingredients:

- 5 spoons large chicken stock
- 10 Mushrooms
- 1 whole chicken
- 5 Pieces bok choy
- 3-4 spring onions

Method:

1. Cut chicken skin and piece chicken into large slices about 10 to 12.
2. Cut mushrooms into halves.
3. Take a container and layer bok choy, mushrooms, and chicken evenly.
4. Add chicken stock and cook for an hour.
5. Add remaining ingredients and water as your requirement.
6. Cook for more than 20 minutes.
7. Use corn flour to give thickness to the soup.

Vegetable Manchow Soup

Cooking Time: 35 minutes

Serving Size: 2

Calories: 128.8

Ingredients:

- 2 tablespoon French beans
- 2 tablespoon Carrots
- 2 Spring onions
- 1 teaspoon Pepper
- 4 Cups Water
- 2 tablespoon Mushrooms
- 1 teaspoon Ginger
- 1 teaspoon Garlic
- 1 teaspoon Green chilies
- 2 stems Spring onion
- Oil and salt
- 1 tablespoon Coriander leaves
- 2 tablespoon Cabbage
- 1 tablespoon Soya sauce
- 4 tablespoon Corn flour
- 1 cup Water
- 2 tablespoon Capsicum

Method:

1. Stir fry coriander leaves, garlic, green chilies, and ginger for 2 minutes.
2. Cut all vegetables and add them into the ginger-garlic mixture.
3. Add seasonings and sauces. Fry for more than 5 minutes.
4. Add water and wait until it starts boiling.

5. Take a small bowl and mix corn flour in hot water.

6. Add corn flour mixture into boiling water and vegetable mixture.

7. Stir until it starts thickening.

8. Remove from heat and garnish with green onions.

Garlic Soya Chicken

Cooking Time: 35 minutes

Serving Size: 2

Calories: 119.3

Ingredients:

- ¼ teaspoon White Pepper
- 1 teaspoon Ginger Juice
- 450 Gram Chicken Breast
- 1 teaspoon Sesame Oil
- 1 tablespoon ginger, grated
- 1 tablespoon Rice Vinegar
- 2 tablespoon Vegetable oil
- A handful of Snow Peas
- 2 tablespoon Soy Sauce
- 5-6 Garlic cloves
- ½ Cup Red Onion
- 1 teaspoon Red Chili Flakes
- ½ Red Bell Pepper

For the Sauce:

- 2 teaspoon Chinese Rice Wine

- ½ tablespoon Brown Sugar
- 1 teaspoon Corn flour
- 2 teaspoon Dark Soy Sauce

Method:

1. Cut chicken into small pieces.
2. Take a large bowl and mix chicken with sesame oil and white pepper.
3. Marinate chicken for 15 to 20 minutes.
4. Take a small bowl and mix all ingredients of sauces and mix well.
5. Put a frying pan on low heat. Add 2 tablespoon oil and spread it into a frying pan.
6. Gradually add chicken pieces into the frying pan and wait for 5 minutes.
7. The flame should be low. Wait until chicken sides turn into light brown color.
8. Stir chicken until all sides turn brown and remove immediately from the frying pan.
9. Turn the heat up and fry peas and red onion for 1 minute.
10. Stir continuously to prevent burning or overheating.
11. Add bell pepper and cook for one more minute.
12. Mix all ingredients well and when vegetables get crispy, stir in chicken.
13. Make sauce ingredients and cook on low heat until sticky and smooth.
14. Pour sauce on chicken and vegetables.

15. Add 1 tablespoon water and cook for 2 minutes until bubbly and thick.

16. Serve with fried rice and lettuce.

Chapter 5: Chinese Dinner and Dessert Recipes

5.1 Dinner Recipes of Chinese Cuisine

Shrimp Fried Rice

Cooking Time: 20 minutes

Serving Size: 6

Calories: 332

Ingredients:

- 1 package frozen mixed vegetables
- 1-pound medium shrimp
- 4 tablespoons butter
- 4 large eggs
- ¼ teaspoon pepper
- 8 bacon strips

- 3 cups cold cooked rice
- ½ teaspoon salt

Method:

1. Take a large skillet and heat on low flame.
2. Add 1 tablespoon vegetable oil or butter.
3. Beat eggs and pour into skillet.
4. Stir to cook on all sides. Remove from skillet and set aside.
5. Melt butter in the skillet again and add vinegar.
6. Add cooked rice and shrimp into the skillet.
7. Stir and cook for 5 minutes until shrimp color changes to pink.
8. Cut eggs into pieces and add in skillet. Cook on low flame.
9. Remove from flame after 5 minutes and garnish with coriander leaves.

Ginger-Cashew Chicken Salad

Cooking Time: 30 minutes

Serving Size: 8

Calories: 379

Ingredients:

- ¼ teaspoon cayenne pepper
- 4 boneless skinless chicken breast halves
- ½ cup cider vinegar
- 2 teaspoons reduced-sodium soy sauce
- 1 teaspoon salt

- ½ cup molasses
- ½ cup canola oil
- 2 tablespoons minced fresh gingerroot

For Salad:

- 2 tablespoons sesame seeds
- 1 can mandarin oranges
- 1 cup shredded red cabbage
- 3 green onions
- 2 cups Chow Mein noodles
- 8 ounces fresh baby spinach
- ¾ cup salted cashews
- 2 medium carrots

Method:

1. Blend all ingredients in a processor except chicken.
2. Add chicken in a bowl and pour processed ingredients over it.
3. Mix and marinate chicken for 3 hours.
4. Heat the broiler and put the chicken into it.
5. Boil for 20 minutes. Change sides and boil for 15 more minutes.
6. Cut the ingredients of salad and make noodles.
7. Add chicken in a separate dish, add salad and noodles. Serve with sauce.

Beef and Spinach Lo Mein

Cooking Time: 30 minutes

Serving Size: 5

Calories: 363

Ingredients:

- 1 tablespoon water
- 4 teaspoons canola oil
- 1 can sliced water chestnuts
- ¼ cup hoisin sauce
- 2 tablespoons soy sauce
- 1-pound beef top round steak
- 1 package fresh spinach
- 1 red chili pepper
- 6 ounces Spaghetti
- 2 teaspoons sesame oil
- 2 garlic cloves
- ¼ teaspoon crushed red pepper flakes
- 2 green onions

Method:

1. Mix hoisin, soy sauce, garlic, pepper, sesame oil, and water.
2. Separate ¼ cup of mixture in a large bowl.
3. Add beef in this mixture and mix well. Marinate for 10 minutes at room temperature.
4. Prepare spaghetti and follow package directions.
5. Take a skillet and heat it. Add canola oil.
6. Add the beef mixture in parts. Do not load the skillet with the whole mix.

7. Stir-fry beef mixture until pink. Remove and repeat with remaining mixture.

8. Heat a skillet and add remaining ingredients and hoisin mixture.

9. Cook for 15 minutes. Add beef mixture.

10. Add spaghetti and mix well. Cook for 5 minutes and serve hot.

Ginger Pork Lettuce Wraps

Cooking Time: 30 minutes

Serving Size: 2 dozen

Calories: 54

Ingredients:

- 1 tablespoon sesame oil
- 24 Boston lettuce leaves
- 1-pound lean ground pork
- 1 can sliced water chestnuts
- 4 green onions
- 1 medium onion
- ¼ cup hoisin sauce
- 1 tablespoon red wine vinegar
- 1 tablespoon reduced-sodium soy sauce
- 2 teaspoons Thai chili sauce
- 4 garlic cloves
- 1 tablespoon fresh ginger root

Method:

1. Take a large skillet and cook onion with pork for 10 minutes.

2. Remove when the pink color disappears, and onions become tender.

3. Cut into pieces and make crumbles.

4. Blend soy sauce, vinegar, garlic, ginger, and hoisin sauce.

5. Add remaining ingredients and heat for 10 minutes.

6. Place pork on lettuce leaves and mixture over it. Fold and serve.

Mushroom Pepper Steak

Cooking Time: 30 minutes

Serving Size: 4

Calories: 241

Ingredients:

- 1 cup julienned green pepper
- ½ teaspoon minced fresh ginger root
- 1-pound beef top sirloin steak
- 2 medium tomatoes
- 2 cups sliced fresh mushrooms
- 3 teaspoons canola oil
- 1 cup julienned sweet red pepper
- 6 tablespoons reduced-sodium soy sauce
- ¼ teaspoon pepper
- 1 garlic clove

- 6 green onions
- Hot cooked rice
- 1 tablespoon cornstarch
- ½ cup reduced-sodium beef broth

Method:

1. Take a bowl and mix salt, vinegar.
2. Add beef and mix well.
3. Marinate in the refrigerator for 30 to 60 minutes.
4. Take a small bowl and mix corn starch, soy sauce, and remaining broth.
5. Mix until smooth. Set aside.
6. Heat a skillet and add ginger, garlic in vegetable oil.
7. Add beef and discard the remaining marinade.
8. Stir fry beef in oil until no longer pink.
9. Remove from heat and set aside. Keep warm.
10. Stir fry mushrooms, vegetables with remaining ingredients and broth.
11. Add beef and mix well.
12. Cook for 10 minutes and serve with rice.

Asparagus Beef Sauté

Cooking Time: 30 minutes

Serving Size: 4

Calories: 328

Ingredients:

- 1-pound fresh asparagus
- 1 tablespoon canola oil

- 2 garlic cloves
- 1 green onion
- ½ teaspoon salt
- 1 ½ teaspoon lemon juice
- Hot cooked rice
- ½ pound sliced fresh mushrooms
- 1-pound beef tenderloin (¾ -inch cubes)
- ¼ teaspoon pepper
- ¼ cup butter
- 1 tablespoon reduced-sodium soy sauce

Method:

1. Mix salt and pepper with beef.
2. Take a frying pan and add 1 tablespoon cooking oil into it.
3. Add garlic and ginger. Stir fry for 2 minutes.
4. Add beef and fry for 10 minutes until lightly brown.
5. Remove from pan and set aside. Keep warm.
6. Add 1 tablespoon oil in the same skillet and put mushrooms.
7. Add asparagus and cook until tender. Add remaining ingredients and cook for 10 more minutes.
8. Add beef. Heat for 2 minutes and remove. Set aside and serve with rice.

Beef Orange Stir-Fry

Cooking Time: 25 minutes

Serving Size: 2

Calories: 390

Ingredients:

- ¼ cup of orange juice
- 2 teaspoons oil
- 3 cups vegetable (stir-fry)
- 1 tablespoon cornstarch
- 1 tablespoon soy sauce
- 1 garlic clove
- 1 cup hot cooked rice
- ½ pound beef sirloin steak
- ½ teaspoon sesame oil
- red flakes (pepper)
- ¼ cup of cold water

Method:

1. Take a small bowl and combine cornstarch, water, orange juice, soy sauce, pepper flakes, and sesame oil.
2. Stir until smooth. Set aside.
3. Heat wok and add 1 tablespoon vegetable oil. Add beef and heat.
4. Stir fry until golden brown.
5. Stir fry vegetables and cornstarch mixture in a skillet.
6. Add beef and other ingredients. Cook for 2 minutes and serve with rice.

Speedy Salmon Stir-Fry

Cooking Time: 30 minutes

Serving Size: 4

Calories: 498

Ingredients:

- 1 package frozen stir-fry vegetable blend
- 1 tablespoon molasses
- 1 tablespoon reduced-sodium soy sauce
- 1-pound salmon fillets
- 1 teaspoon grated orange zest
- 4 teaspoons canola oil
- 2 cups hot cooked brown rice
- 1 tablespoon sesame seeds
- 1 tablespoon minced fresh ginger root
- ¼ cup reduced-fat honey mustard salad dressing
- 2 tablespoons orange juice

Method:

1. Take a small bowl and mix honey, ginger, mustard, soy sauce, orange zest, and molasses.
2. Heat 2 tablespoon oil in the skillet and add salmon and cook for 5 to 7 minutes until fish becomes soft.
3. In a small frying pan, add oil. Heat and add vegetable mixture, salad dressings, and remaining ingredients.
4. Add salmon and stir gently.
5. Sprinkle sesame seeds and serve with rice.

Asian Glazed Chicken Thighs

Cooking Time: 25 minutes

Serving Size: 4

Calories: 274

Ingredients:

- 4 boneless skinless chicken thighs
- 3 garlic cloves, minced
- ¼ cup of rice vinegar
- ½ teaspoon ground ginger
- Toasted sesame seeds
- 2 teaspoons canola oil
- 3 tablespoons reduced-sodium soy sauce
- 2 tablespoons honey

Method:

1. Take a small bowl and blend honey, soy sauce, and vinegar.
2. In a large skillet, add 1 tablespoon of oil. Add chicken and heat until brown on each side.
3. Add blended mixture and heat for 2 minutes.
4. Add remaining ingredients and cook until it starts boiling.
5. Add in a dish and sprinkle sesame seeds. Serve with rice.

Mandarin Pork Stir-Fry

Cooking Time: 25 minutes

Serving Size: 4

Calories: 473

Ingredients:

- ½ teaspoon garlic powder
- 1 pork tenderloin (cut into 2-inch strips)

- ½ teaspoon ground ginger
- 2 tablespoons soy sauce
- 2 cups uncooked instant rice
- ½ cup of orange juice
- 1 package frozen sugar snap peas
- 1 can mandarin oranges, drained
- ¼ cup of water
- 1 tablespoon cornstarch
- 2 tablespoons canola oil

Method:

1. Follow package direction and cook rice according to these directions.
2. Take a bowl and mix garlic, ginger, and cornstarch.
3. Add orange juice and stir. Add soy sauce and water.
4. Mix until smooth and set aside.
5. Take a large skillet and add 1 tablespoon oil.
6. Add pork and stir fry until lightly brown. Set aside.
7. Add peas in the same skillet and boil until tender.
8. Add orange mixture and pork in skillet.
9. Stir fry for 2 minutes and remove. Serve with rice.

Hoisin-Pineapple Salmon

Cooking Time: 20 minutes

Serving Size: 4

Calories: 349

Ingredients:

- ¼ teaspoon pepper

- ½ cup unsweetened crushed pineapple
- 4 salmon fillets
- ¼ cup orange marmalade
- 2 tablespoons chopped fresh cilantro
- 2 tablespoons hoisin sauce

Method:

1. Heat oven at 400°F.
2. Prepare baking pan and grease with oil. Spread salmon and hoisin sauce.
3. Bake for 15 to 20 minutes or when fish begins to flake.
4. Take a small saucepan and mix pineapple with orange marmalade.
5. Bring to boil and stir continuously.
6. Pour over salmon and sprinkle coriander leaves.

Tropical Sweet and Spicy Pork Tenderloin

Cooking Time: 30 minutes

Serving Size: 4

Calories: 539

Ingredients:

- 2 finely chopped chipotle peppers
- 2 tablespoons olive oil
- 1 medium onion, chopped
- 1 medium green pepper, chopped
- 1 pork tenderloin cut into 1-inches cubes
- 3 garlic cloves, minced
- 1 cup chicken stock

- 1 can pineapple tidbits, drained
- ¼ teaspoon salt
- ¼ teaspoon pepper
- 2 tablespoons reduced-sodium soy sauce
- Hot cooked rice
- ½ cup packed brown sugar
- 1 cup honey barbecue sauce
- 2 teaspoons adobo sauce

Method:

1. Take a large skillet. Heat and add oil.
2. Sprinkle salt and pepper on pork and stir fry for 5 to 7 minutes.
3. Remove when cooked from both sides.
4. Take a pan and add ginger, garlic, chicken stock, onion.
5. Stir for 3 minutes.
6. Add remaining ingredients and cook for 5 minutes.
7. Add pork and cook until tender.
8. Remove and serve with rice.

5.2 Chinese Desserts Recipes

Chinese Almond Cookies

Cooking Time: 40 minutes

Serving Size: 30

Calories: 660

Ingredients:

- ½ teaspoon baking soda

- 2 cups flour
- ½ teaspoon baking powder
- ¼ teaspoon salt
- 2 ½ teaspoons almond extract
- 30 whole almonds
- ½ cup shortening
- ¾ cup white sugar
- 1 egg
- ½ cup butter
- 1 egg beaten

Method:

1. Heat Oven at 325°F.
2. Take a large bowl and add flour.
3. Add salt and mix well.
4. Add baking soda and baking powder. Stir well.
5. In a small bowl, beat butter, shortening, and sugar.
6. Add almond and egg in butter mixture and blend well.
7. Add flour mixture and blend until smooth.
8. Knead the dough and cut into 2 pieces.
9. Refrigerate for 2 hours.
10. Cut the dough into 14 to 15 pieces lengthwise.
11. Grease cookie tray and roll each piece in the round motion.
12. Put round balls into a cookie tray and add almonds in the center of each ball.
13. Grease cookies with beaten egg using a brush.

14. Bake for 15 to 20 minutes until golden brown.

15. Remove and let it cool. Serve when cold and crispy.

Nian Gao

Cooking Time: 60 minutes

Serving Size: 10

Calories: 338

Ingredients:

- 2 ½ cups milk
- One can red azuki beans
- 16 ounces mochiko sweet rice flour
- 1 to 1 ¾ cup sugar
- 1 tablespoon baking soda
- ½ cup unsalted butter
- ¾ cup of vegetable oil
- 3 eggs

Method:

1. Heat oven at 350°F.
2. Grease pan with butter or oil using spray or brush.
3. Mix all ingredients except beans in a processor and blend until smooth.
4. Sprinkle mochiko flour on the baking dish and add half batter.
5. Spread beans on top and add another layer of remaining batter on beans.
6. Bake for 40 to 45 minutes until cooked.
7. Check by using a toothpick if baked well.

8. Serve cold.

Eight Treasure Rice Pudding

Cooking Time: 105 minutes

Serving Size: 8

Calories: 432

Ingredients:

For the Rice:

- 1 cup black raisins
- 1 cup yellow raisins
- ¼ teaspoon salt

For the Fruit:

- Neutral oil for coating bowl
- 2 cups glutinous rice
- 1 tablespoon sunflower oil
- 1 cup sugar-glazed cherries
- 1 dried apricot

For the Filling:

- 1 cup sugar lotus seeds
- 100 grams red bean paste

For the Starch Water:

- 3 tablespoons water
- 2 teaspoon potato starch

For the Sugar Syrup:

- 1 tablespoon honey
- 1 tablespoon sugar

- ½ cup of water

Method:

1. Take a large bowl and put rice in it.

2. Add cold water and cover for 1 hour.

3. Drain and soak rice and steam for 40 minutes in simmering water.

4. Add oil and salt. Combine gently to prevent breaking rice.

5. Cut fruits in small pieces.

6. Take a bowl and grease with oil.

7. Add fruits and a layer of rice. Press gently.

8. Add red bean paste on it and spread with a spoon.

9. Place rice and cherries layer again.

10. Place the bowl in simmering water and steam for 30 minutes.

11. Take a small bowl and mix potato starch water ingredients.

12. Stir until well combined.

13. Place all syrup ingredients and bring to boil. Add starch water and boil for 10 minutes.

14. Remove the bowl from the water and invert it into the dish. Add sugary syrup on top.

Chinese Almond Float Dessert

Cooking Time: 60 minutes

Serving Size: 6

Calories: 312

Ingredients:

- 1 cup of cold water
- 1 can fruit cocktail with syrup
- 1 envelope unflavored gelatin
- 2 teaspoons almond extract
- 1 cup evaporated milk
- 4 tablespoons granulated sugar
- 1 cup boiling water

Method:

1. Take a small bowl and mix sugar with gelatin. Mix well.
2. Add boiling water in the gelatin mixture and stir continuously until dissolved.
3. Add almond extract, milk, and cold water. Mix well.
4. Wait until cool down. Cut into pieces and serve with can fruit.

Candied Banana Fritters

Cooking Time: 30 minutes

Serving Size: 4

Calories: 634

Ingredients:

- 3 to 6 tablespoons white sesame seeds
- ¾ cup of water
- 4 cups oil for deep-frying
- 1 egg, lightly beaten
- 1 cup all-purpose flour

- 5 bananas, firm
- 1 ½ cups granulated sugar
- 2 tablespoons oil

Method:

1. Cut bananas in small pieces about 1 ½ inch.
2. Combine water, egg, and flour. Stir and make the batter.
3. Heat oil in the frying pan. Take a banana slice and dip into the batter.
4. Carefully dip all slices and add them into hot oil for deep frying.
5. Fry until looks golden brown and batter is crispy.
6. Take a bowl and add cold water with ice cubes. Put it into the freezer.
7. Heat oil and add sugar. Stir until golden brown. Avoid high flame. It can cause sugar to burn.
8. Remove the wok and put it into cold water.
9. Use a stick to coat banana slices in syrup and add immediately into cold water until syrup is hardened.
10. Place in a dish and repeat with all slices.

Chinese Bow Tie Dessert with Honey and Brown Sugar

Cooking Time: 35 minutes

Serving Size: 16

Calories: 119

Ingredients:

- 4 to 6 cups oil
- 1 package egg roll wrappers

For the Syrup:

- ½ cup honey
- 1 cup brown sugar
- ½ cup of corn syrup
- ½ cup of water

Method:

1. Cut egg roll wrappers into four equal pieces.
2. Use 2 knives and make a knot like a bow tie on wrappers.
3. Heat wok and then add oil.
4. Fry bow tie for 5 minutes.
5. Boil syrup ingredients for 5 minutes.
6. Dip bow tie in sugar syrup and set aside.

Five-Spice Peanuts

Cooking Time: 40 minutes

Serving Size: 8

Calories: 266

Ingredients:

- 1 tablespoon light corn syrup
- 2 tablespoons butter
- ¼ cup brown sugar
- ½ teaspoon five-spice powder
- 2 cups unsalted peanuts

Method:

1. Take a baking tray and grease with oil.
2. In a large pan, melt butter, syrup, and sugar.

3. Heat on low flame and add five spices powder. Stir well.

4. Boil for 5 minutes and do not stir when it starts boiling.

5. Add on the baking sheet and mix peanuts. Wait to cool down and harden.

6. Cut into pieces and serve cold.

Chinese Sponge Cake

Cooking Time: 40 minutes

Serving Size: 3

Calories: 468

Ingredients:

- ½ tsp. cream of tartar
- ¾ cup sugar
- 1 cupcake flour
- 5 eggs
- 1 tsp. Baking powder
- ¼ tsp. salt
- 1 tsp. almond extract

Method:

1. Prepare pan and wok for steam.

2. Take a large bowl and mix flour, salt, baking powder, and baking soda. Stir well.

3. Take a bowl and separate egg whites from egg yolks. Beat egg whites until fluffy. Add cream and beat.

4. Add ¼ cup of sugar and beat again for 1 minute.

5. Add egg yolk in remaining sugar. Beat for 2 minutes and add almond extract.

6. Gradually add the egg mixture into the flour mixture.

7. Mix with a rubber spatula and set aside.

8. Pour batter into pan and heat wok.

9. Add water in the wok. Wait until it starts boiling.

10. Turn flame to medium and steam cake for 20 to 25 minutes covered.

11. Invert in the plate and cut into pieces.

Dairy-Free Mango Pudding

Cooking Time: 20 minutes

Serving Size: 4

Calories: 259

Ingredients:

- ¼ cup white sugar
- 1 cup good-quality coconut milk
- 1 packet gelatin
- 2 medium to large ripe mangoes
- ½ cup hot water

Method:

1. Take ripe mangoes and peel.

2. Blend mangoes in a processor until smooth. Set aside.

3. Take a pan and add water. Bring to boil.

4. Gradually add gelatin in water. Add milk and sugar.

5. Stir and blend with mango mixture.

6. Pour in a bowl and refrigerate for 2 hours.

Delicious Chinese Raspberry Snowflake Cake

Cooking Time: 25 minutes

Serving Size: 1 cake

Calories: 330

Ingredients:

Raspberry Snowflake Cake

- 450 milliliters water
- 125 grams of potato starch or corn flour
- 3 tablespoons desiccated coconut
- 55 grams raspberries
- 60 milliliters double cream
- 5 leaves gelatin
- 200 grams of sugar
- 200 milliliters whole milk

Coconut Milk Snowflake Cake

- 5 leaves gelatin
- 250 milliliters coconut milk
- 60 milliliters double cream
- 3 tablespoons desiccated coconut
- 125 grams of potato starch or corn flour
- 450 milliliters water
- 200 grams caster sugar

Method:

1. Take a small saucepan and cook water, raspberry, and sugar.

2. Keep whisking until boil and raspberry completely dissolve in sugar.

3. Let it cool down.

4. Add double cream and milk into raspberry jam and bring to boil.

5. Rest aside for 10 minutes and add gelatin. Stir well.

6. Add starch and 100ml additional water.

7. Prepare a baking tray and put mixture.

8. Keep in the refrigerator for 3 hours.

9. Slice and sprinkle coconut. Serve cold.

Fortune Cookies

Cooking Time: 30 minutes

Serving Size: 10

Calories: 133

Ingredients:

- 3 tablespoons vegetable oil
- 8 tablespoons sugar
- ½ teaspoon almond extract
- 3 teaspoons water
- 8 tablespoons all-purpose flour
- 2 large egg whites
- ½ teaspoon vanilla extract
- 1 ½ teaspoons cornstarch
- ¼ teaspoon salt

Method:

1. Heat oven at 300°F.

2. Beat egg, vanilla and almond extract, and vegetable oil in a bowl.

3. Take a large bowl and mix starch, flour, and water. Blend until smooth.

4. Add egg mixture into the flour mixture and blend to make the batter.

5. Grease baking pan with sheet and oil. Add batter with a spoon on sheet.

6. Put that paper in the middle of the cookies and fold edges.

7. Bake for 14 to 16 minutes until brown and crispy.

Chapter 6: Chinese Traditional Wok Recipes and Vegetarian Chinese Meals

6.1 Chinese Famous Wok Recipes

Spicy Oyster Sauce Squid with Green Peppers

Cooking Time: 15 minutes

Serving Size: 2

Calories: 512

Ingredients:

- 1 tablespoon low-sodium light soy sauce
- 1 green pepper (sliced into cubes)
- ½ teaspoon dark soy sauce
- 1 teaspoon oyster sauce
- 1 tablespoon rapeseed oil
- 1 medium white onion (cut into slices)

- 1 tablespoon fresh lemon juice
- A pinch of caster sugar
- 1 red chili (finely chopped)
- 200g whole baby squid (sliced into rings)
- 1 tablespoon rice vinegar

Method:

1. Heat wok and add 1 tablespoon oil.
2. Add sliced onion and rapeseed oil. Heat for 20 minutes until brown and crispy.
3. Add squid and red chili. Heat for 10 seconds. Add rice vinegar.
4. Add green pepper and stir for 1 minute.
5. Add 1 tablespoon water around the edges of the wok to create steam.
6. Cook for 1 minute more and add remaining ingredients.
7. Stir and serve immediately.

Vegetarian Hokkien Mee

Cooking Time: 22 minutes

Serving Size: 2

Calories: 522

Ingredients:

- A knob of fresh ginger (grated)
- 100g Quorn mince
- 1 tablespoon low-sodium light soy sauce
- A drizzle of toasted sesame oil

- 1 tablespoon rapeseed oil
- 2 garlic cloves (chopped)
- 1 teaspoon dark soy sauce
- 2 mini sweet shallots (chopped)
- 1 red chili (chopped)
- 400g cooked egg noodles (200g dried)
- 100g fresh beansprouts
- 3 dried Chinese mushrooms (soaked and finely diced)
- 100ml hot vegetable stock

For Garnish

- Spring onions (sliced)
- Red chili, (sliced into rings)

Method:

1. Heat wok on high flame. Add the rapeseed oil and stir.
2. Add garlic, ginger, chili, and shallots.
3. Heat and stir to explode flavors in the wok for 1 minute.
4. Add dark soy sauce, mushroom, and Quorn. Leave for 2 minutes.
5. Add soy sauce and vegetable stock. Cook for 10 minutes.
6. Add cooked egg noodles and spread sesame oil over it.
7. Stir and serve.
8. You can serve noodles separately in two bowls with the mixture on top of the noodles.

Beijing Egg and Tomato Noodle Soup

Cooking Time: 15 minutes

Serving Size: 2

Calories: 479

Ingredients:

- 1 tablespoon vegetable bouillon powder
- 300g cooked rice noodles (150g uncooked)
- 250g tomatoes (cored and quartered)
- 100g Chinese cabbage (cut into slices)
- 1 tablespoon sesame oil
- 1 tablespoon light soy sauce
- A pinch of white pepper
- 1 egg (beaten)
- 2 spring onions (sliced, to garnish)
- 1 root ginger (peeled and grated)
- 5 fresh shiitake mushrooms (dried and cut into slices)

Method:

1. Heat wok and add ginger, garlic, mushrooms, vegetable powder, and tomatoes.
2. Add 1-liter water in the wok and bring to boil.
3. Cook for 2 minutes until vegetables get softened.
4. Reduce heat to medium and add rice noodles. Add soy sauce and sesame oil.
5. Add remaining ingredients and stir.
6. Add beaten eggs and stir continuously for 2 minutes.
7. Immediately remove from heat and serve.

Radish in Black Rice Vinegar with Crabmeat and Black Sesame Seeds

Cooking Time: 10 minutes

Serving Size: 2

Calories: 333

Ingredients:

- 1 teaspoon rapeseed oil
- 5g black sesame seed (garnish)
- Dried chili flakes (garnish)
- 200g radishes (cut into slices)
- 1 tablespoon black rice vinegar
- 300g radish leaves
- A pinch of caster sugar
- 200g fresh white crab meat

Method:

1. Heat wok on high flame and add the rapeseed oil. Wait for 30 seconds.
2. Add radish sliced and radish leaves in the wok.
3. Stir and add water on the edges of the wok to make steam.
4. Cook for 10 seconds and add remaining ingredients.
5. Remove from heat and serve in a separate dish.
6. Garnish chili flakes and sesame seed on top of the radish.

Lobster Tails, Baby Asparagus and Eggs in Hot Bean Sauce

Cooking Time: 15 minutes

Serving Size: 2

Calories: 230

Ingredients:

- 1 teaspoon corn flour
- 2 spring onions
- 100ml hot vegetable stock
- 1 egg (beaten)
- 1 tablespoon rapeseed oil
- 2 garlic cloves (chopped)
- 200g cooked fresh lobster (sliced into cubes)
- 100g baby asparagus spears
- 1 teaspoon yellow bean paste
- ½ teaspoon dark soy sauce
- 1 tablespoon light soy sauce
- 1 ginger (peeled and grated)
- 1 red chili (chopped)

Method:

1. Heat wok on high flame and add the rapeseed oil. Toss for 5 minutes.
2. Add ginger, garlic, and chili and stir for 2 minutes to release flavor.
3. Add lobsters and stir for 1 minute. Add asparagus and toss for 1 minute more.
4. Add 1 tablespoon water on the edges of the wok to give steam.
5. Add light and dark soy sauce. Stir and add yellow bean paste.
6. Add egg and bring it to boil.

7. Mix the corn flour into 2 tablespoon water and add it into the wok.

8. Stir continuously until thickens.

9. Garnish with onions and serve immediately.

Pineapple Chicken

Cooking Time: 12 minutes

Serving Size: 2

Calories: 240.4

Ingredients:

- A pinch of black pepper
- 1 tablespoon corn flour
- ½ small pineapple (cubes)
- fresh coriander leaves (to garnish)
- 1 tablespoon rapeseed oil
- ½ red pepper (cubes)
- 250g boneless chicken thighs (sliced into cubes)
- sea salt flakes
- 1 spring onion (sliced)
- 2 dried chilies
- roasted cashew nuts

For the Sauce

- 1 teaspoon honey
- ¼ teaspoon Sriracha chili sauce
- 1 tablespoon corn flour
- 100ml pineapple juice

- 1 tablespoon light soy sauce
- 1 lime juice

Method:

1. Take a large bowl and add chicken. Sprinkle pepper and salt. Add corn flour and mix to combine. Set aside.
2. Take all ingredients of the sauce and mix it in a blender. Set aside.
3. Heat a wok on high flame and add the rapeseed oil.
4. Add red chili and stir for flavor.
5. Add chicken pieces and toss for 5 minutes.
6. Add red pepper and pineapple. Cook for 30 seconds.
7. Add sauce and cook until sticky.
8. Add remaining ingredients and cook for 2 minutes more.
9. Remove from flame and garnish with coriander leaves.

Buddha's Stir-Fried Mixed Vegetables

Cooking Time: 15 minutes

Serving Size: 2

Calories: 500

Ingredients:

- 1 tablespoon rapeseed oil
- Ginger root (peeled and grated)
- 4 fresh shiitake mushrooms (dried and sliced)
- 1 cup dried wood ear mushrooms
- 1 cup of fresh beansprouts
- 1 medium carrot

- 1 cup of baby sweetcorn
- ½ teaspoon salted black beans (crushed with rice vinegar 1 tablespoon)
- 1 can of bamboo shoots
- 2 spring onions (garnish)

For the sauce

- 1 tablespoon light soy sauce
- 1 tablespoon vegetarian mushroom sauce
- 100 ml cold vegetable stock
- 1 teaspoon toasted sesame oil
- 1 tablespoon corn flour

Method:

1. Mix all ingredients of sauce in a blender and blend until smooth. Set aside.
2. Heat a wok on high flame and add the rapeseed oil.
3. Add ginger and fry on low heat. Add beans paste and cook for 1 minute.
4. Add vegetables and remaining ingredients except for beansprout. Whisk well.
5. Add sauce and cook for 5 minutes until sticky.
6. Add beansprout and heat for 30 seconds.
7. Transfer to a dish and garnish with onion.

Penang Curry with Chicken

Cooking Time: 35 minutes

Serving Size: 4

Calories: 596

Ingredients:

- 2 peppers fresh red chili peppers
- ¼ cup fresh basil leaves
- 2 tablespoons palm sugar
- 4 cups of coconut milk
- ⅔ pound skinless (boneless and cubed)
- 2 tablespoons fish sauce
- 5 tablespoons Penang curry paste
- cooking oil
- 6 leaf kaffir lime leaves

Method:

1. Heat wok on high flame and add the rapeseed oil.
2. Add curry paste and stir for 2 minutes.
3. Add coconut milk and wait until boiling.
4. Add chicken pieces and cook for 15 minutes.
5. Add remaining ingredients and stir for 2 minutes.
6. Garnish with basil leaves.

Thai Spicy Basil Chicken Fried Rice

Cooking Time: 40 minutes

Serving Size: 6

Calories: 794.1

Ingredients:

- 1 teaspoon white sugar
- ½ cup cilantro sprigs
- 2 peppers serrano peppers (crushed)

- 1 onion (sliced)

- 2 cups sweet basil

- 1-pound boneless chicken breast

- ½ cup sesame oil for frying

- 5 cups jasmine rice (cooked)

- 6 garlic clove (crushed)

- 1 cucumber (sliced)

- 3 tablespoons oyster sauce

- 2 tablespoons fish sauce

- 2 red pepper (sliced)

Method:

1. Take a bowl and mix fish sauce, sugar, and oyster sauce.

2. Heat wok on high flame and add the rapeseed oil.

3. Add serrano pepper and garlic. Stir for 1 minute.

4. Add chicken and sauce mixture. Cook for 5 minutes.

5. Add remaining ingredients except for rice and cook for 10 minutes.

6. Add rice and stir continuously to prevent sticking.

7. Remove from flame and garnish with coriander leaves.

Chinese Buffet Green Beans

Cooking Time: 25 minutes

Serving Size: 6

Calories: 54.5

Ingredients:

- 1-pound fresh green beans (trimmed)
- 2 tablespoons oyster sauce
- 2 teaspoons soy sauce
- 1 tablespoon oil sesame
- 2 cloves garlic (sliced)
- 1 tablespoon white sugar

Method:

1. Heat wok on high flame and add sesame oil.
2. Add garlic and white sugar. Heat until brown.
3. Add green beans and remaining ingredients.
4. Bring to boil and cook for 15 minutes until beans are softened.
5. Garnish with sesame seed and serve.

Summer Special Shrimp and Fruit Fried Rice

Cooking Time: 60 minutes

Serving Size: 2

Calories: 590.8

Ingredients:

- 6 halves walnuts
- 2 cups cold, cooked white rice
- 2 large eggs (beaten)
- 1 tablespoon vegetable oil
- 1 piece of ginger root
- 1 tablespoon soy sauce
- 2 tablespoons cilantro

- ⅔ cup fresh pineapple
- 2 red onions
- 3 green chili peppers
- ½ cup orange segments
- ½ pound shrimp
- salt and pepper

Method:

1. Heat wok on medium flame and add 1 tablespoon oil.
2. Add onion and stir until brown. Set aside.
3. Heat wok on high flame and add shrimp.
4. Stir continuously for 10 minutes until no longer pink in color. Set aside.
5. Wipe wok and heat on high flame. Add ginger, onion, and garlic in 1 tablespoon oil.
6. Stir and heat for 3 minutes until brown on edges.
7. Add pineapple and orange. Stir until pineapple becomes hot.
8. Add remaining ingredients and stir. Add shrimp and onion. Stir for 3 minutes.
9. Garnish with cilantro and serve.

6.2 World Renowned Chinese Recipes

Sichuan Hot Pot

Cooking Time: 1 hour 10 minutes

Serving Size: 1 hot pot

Calories: 259

Ingredients:

For Soup Base:

- 12-14 cups chicken stock
- 10 cloves garlic
- 1 cinnamon stick
- 2 tablespoons oil
- 10 cloves
- 1 tablespoon Sichuan peppercorns
- 10 whole red chilies
- 6 slices ginger
- 3-4 bay leaves
- 1 package spicy hot pot soup base
- 5-star anise

For Dipping Sauce

- Sesame seeds
- Peanuts
- Sesame paste
- Sesame oil
- Cilantro
- Soy sauce
- Chinese black vinegar
- Scallions
- Sacha sauce
- Chili oil
- Garlic

Hot Pot Sides:

- Thinly shaved beef
- Sliced chicken
- Prepared frozen dumplings
- Chinese rice cakes
- Fresh noodles
- Bok choy
- Assorted fish balls
- Thinly sliced fish fillets
- Napa cabbage
- Shiitake mushrooms
- Tofu sheets
- Glass noodles
- Firm tofu
- Soy puffs
- Straw mushrooms
- Green leaf lettuce
- Wood ear mushrooms

Method:

1. To make soup, heat wok and add 1 tablespoon oil and ginger.
2. Stir for 2 minutes. Add garlic, bay leaves, cinnamon stick, cloves, and star anise.
3. Cook for 5 minutes for flavors.
4. Add hot pot soup base, chilies, and peppercorn. Cook for another 2 minutes.

5. Add chicken stock and wait until it starts boiling. Transfer to a broad and deep pot. Set aside

6. Mix all ingredients of dipping sauce and blend until smooth. Set aside.

7. Prepare a hot plate and plugin. Add broth and bring to boil.

8. Pour hot pot side ingredients that you like to add and cook until boil.

9. Place dipping sauce and soup. Serve in the pot.

Braised Pork Ball in Gravy

Cooking Time: 15 minutes

Serving Size: 4

Calories: 684.6

Ingredients:

For meatballs:

- 1 teaspoon salt
- 1 tablespoon dark soy sauce
- 100-gram corn starch
- 1000-gram pork
- 1 leftover steamed bun
- scallion 20 grams
- 2 tablespoon light soy sauce
- 2 tablespoon Shaoxing wine
- 1 cup oil
- 2-gram ginger

For Sauce:

- Sugar ¼ tablespoon
- Corn starch 1 tablespoon
- Dark soy sauce ¼ tablespoon
- 2 slices fresh ginger
- Light soy sauce ½ tablespoon
- Water 1 cup

Method:

1. Add meatball ingredients in a pan and stir continuously in one direction for 5 minutes.
2. Make small round meatballs and set aside.
3. Take all ingredients of the sauce and mix it in a wok or pan.
4. Add oil and stir for 10 minutes.
5. Add meatballs and cook for 30 seconds.
6. Serve hot with rice.

Steamed Garlic Prawns with Vermicelli

Cooking Time: 17 minutes

Serving Size: 2

Calories: 143

Ingredients:

- 10 tiger prawns
- 2 tablespoon light soy sauce
- ¼ teaspoon sugar
- 1 tablespoon cooking oil
- 100 g mung bean vermicelli noodles

- 1 tablespoon water
- 2 tablespoon minced garlic
- 2 tablespoon chopped fresh chili
- 1 tablespoon Shaoxing rice wine
- ¼ teaspoon white pepper
- 1 pinch salt
- scallions for garnishing

Method:

1. Soak noodles and add 1 tablespoon oil to avoid sticking. Set aside.
2. Cut and peel prawns. Put them on noodles.
3. Heat the pan and add oil. Add garlic, water, chili, white pepper, rice wine, soy sauce, and sugar. Heat for 5 minutes until flavored.
4. Add sauce over prawns and noodles.
5. Steam for 5 minutes and serve hot.

Peking Duck

Cooking Time: 1 hour 35 minutes

Serving Size: 4

Calories: 555.7

Ingredients:

- ¼ teaspoon white pepper
- ⅛ teaspoon cloves
- ½ cup plum jam
- 3 tablespoons soy sauce
- 1 tablespoon honey

- 5 green onions
- 1 orange
- 1 tablespoon parsley
- 1 whole duck
- ½ teaspoon cinnamon
- ½ teaspoon ginger
- ¼ teaspoon nutmeg
- 1 ½ teaspoons sugar
- 1 ½ teaspoon white vinegar

Method:

1. Wash duck from inner side and outer side.
2. Mix cinnamon, white pepper, ginger, nutmeg, and cloves.
3. Sprinkle spices mixture on the duck.
4. Add 1 tablespoon vinegar and pour it on the duck.
5. Spread with hands and refrigerate for at least 2 hours.
6. Take a wok and add water. Steam duck from the breast side for 1 hour.
7. Pour lime juice and green onions.
8. Heat oven at 375°F.
9. Remove the skin of the duck and put it in the pan to roast.
10. Roast for 30 minutes. Mix honey with 3 tablespoon soy sauce.
11. Brush it on duck and roast for more than 10 minutes.
12. Mix sugar, chutney, and vinegar to make the sauce.

13. Garnish with parsley and orange slices.

Shrimp Rice Noodle Rolls

Cooking Time: 15 minutes

Serving Size: 8

Calories: 118

Ingredients:

For Shrimp:

- ½ teaspoon sugar
- ¼ teaspoon baking soda
- 2 tablespoons water
- ½ teaspoon cornstarch
- ¼ teaspoon sesame oil
- ¼ teaspoon salt
- 8 ounces shrimp
- ¼ teaspoon white pepper

For Sauce:

- 1 teaspoon oyster sauce
- 1 teaspoon oil
- 2 teaspoons dark soy sauce
- 5 teaspoons sugar
- 1 scallion
- 6 slices ginger
- 2 ½ tablespoons light soy sauce
- ¼ cup of water
- Salt

For the Rice Noodle Rolls:

- 1 cup of water
- Vegetable or canola oil
- 5 tablespoons rice flour
- 1 tablespoon mung bean starch
- 2 tablespoons wheat starch
- 2 tablespoons cornstarch
- ¼ teaspoon salt

Method:

1. Coat shrimps with baking soda, sugar, and water.
2. Refrigerate for 2 hours and wash thoroughly.
3. Coat shrimp with white pepper, sesame oil, cornstarch, and salt.
4. Cover and refrigerate for 1 hour.
5. Mix all ingredients of sauce and heat on low flame.
6. Cook until smooth.
7. Wet a clean cloth and set aside.
8. Steam shrimps for 10 minutes and put in a bowl.
9. Add rice noodles and add shrimps.
10. Cover with wet cloth and roll.
11. Remove the cloth and cut rice noodles lengthwise.
12. Serve with sauce.

Mapo Tofu

Cooking Time: 35 minutes

Serving Size: 6

Calories: 335

Ingredients:

- ¼ teaspoon sugar
- 6-8 dried red chilies
- 1 ½ tablespoon Sichuan peppercorns
- 3 tablespoons ginger
- 3 tablespoons garlic
- ¼ cup low sodium chicken broth
- 1-pound silken tofu
- 1 scallion
- ½ cup oil
- 1-2 fresh chili peppers
- 1 ½ teaspoons cornstarch
- ¼ teaspoon sesame oil
- 8 ounces pork
- 1-2 tablespoons spicy bean sauce

Method:

1. Heat wok and add chilies in oil. Stir for 5 minutes for the fragment. Set aside.
2. Heat wok and add oil. Add peppercorn, garlic, and ginger. Cook for 7 minutes.
3. Add ground pork and cook until pink color disappears.
4. Add bean mixture and chicken broth. Stir well.
5. Add water in cornstarch. Mix and add into bean mixture.
6. Add remaining ingredients and seasonings. Stir for 10 minutes.

7. Serve hot and garnish with onion.

Yang Chow Fried Rice

Cooking Time: 35 minutes

Serving Size: 6

Calories: 301

Ingredients:

- 2 teaspoons salt
- 10 pieces shrimps
- 1 teaspoon garlic
- 3 tablespoons cooking oil
- ¼ cup green onion
- 2 pieces of raw eggs beaten
- 1 teaspoon sugar
- 6 cups cooked white rice
- 1 cup barbecued pork
- 1 ½ tablespoons soy sauce
- ¾ cup green peas
- 1 teaspoon ginger

Method:

1. Take a pan and heat garlic and ginger in oil.
2. Add shrimps and cook for 5 minutes. Set aside.
3. Add eggs and stir for 30 seconds.
4. Add rice in egg and mix thoroughly.
5. Add sauce, sugar, and other spices.
6. Add barbecue pork and cook for 5 minutes.

7. Add shrimp and green peas. Cook for 5 minutes.

8. Add green onions and cook for 1 minute.

9. Transfer to plate and serve.

Wonton Soup

Cooking Time: 40 minutes

Serving Size: 6

Calories: 289.6

Ingredients:

- 2 bok choy
- 2 cloves garlic
- 1 tablespoon ginger
- 4 cups chicken broth
- 3 green onions
- 1 tablespoon sesame oil
- 4 ounces shiitake mushrooms
- 1 tablespoon yellow miso paste

For Wontons

- 1 tablespoon reduced-sodium soy sauce
- 1 tablespoon ginger
- 1 tablespoon oyster sauce
- 1 teaspoon sesame oil
- 8 ounces medium shrimp
- 2 cloves garlic
- 2 green onions
- ½ teaspoon Sriracha

- ¼ teaspoon black pepper
- 36 wonton wrappers

Method:

1. Take a large bowl and combine garlic, ginger, shrimp, Sriracha, soy sauce, sesame oil, and oyster sauce.
2. Put wonton wrappers and pour 1 tablespoon shrimp mixture over it.
3. Fold wrappers and press edges to seal.
4. Take a pan and heat on low flame.
5. Add garlic, ginger, and chicken broth.
6. Add 2 cups water and bring to boil.
7. Add mushrooms and cook for 10 minutes.
8. Add green onions, bok choy, miso paste, and cook for 3 minutes.
9. Add wonton and stir for 2 minutes.
10. Serve hot with sauce.

Chinese Egg Fried Rice

Cooking Time: 20 minutes

Serving Size: 2

Calories: 163

Ingredients:

- 1 big onion diced
- 3 eggs beaten
- 2 spring onion
- 3 tablespoon vegetable oil
- 3 cups cooked rice

Seasonings:

- 2 tablespoon light soy sauce
- 1 teaspoon salt
- ½ teaspoon ground white pepper

Method:

1. Beat eggs and cut vegetables.
2. Heat a wok on high flame and add 1 tablespoon oil.
3. Add eggs and stir continuously.
4. Remove eggs from heat and set aside.
5. Heat wok again and add 1 tablespoon oil.
6. Add eggs and stir immediately. Do not burn the rice.
7. Add vegetables and salt, pepper.
8. Mix again and add soy sauce from the edges of the wok.
9. Cook for 2 minutes and serve hot with parsley and onion garnishing.

French Onion Rice

Cooking Time: 1 hour 30 minutes

Serving Size: 8

Calories: 135

Ingredients:

- 2 cup basmati rice
- 3 cup low-sodium beef broth
- 1 tablespoon thyme leaves
- 1 teaspoon freshly ground black pepper
- ¼ white wine

- 6 cloves garlic, minced
- Lemon wedges
- 6 tablespoon butter
- 1 tablespoon olive oil
- 2 large onions
- 1 ¼ teaspoon kosher salt

Method:

1. Take a large pan and heat. Add butter and onion.
2. Add salt and cook for 30 minutes until caramelized. Set aside.
3. Take a pan and add 1 tablespoon oil.
4. Add rice, garlic thyme, and lemon, wine, and stir well.
5. Add caramelized mixture ¾ and seasoning in rice. Combine and cook for 3 minutes.
6. Add broth and wait to boil.
7. Reduce heat and cook for 15 minutes.
8. Transfer to bowl and add remaining caramelized mixture. Garnish with thyme.

6.3 Recipes of Vegetarian Chinese Meals

15-Minute Garlic Noodles

Cooking Time: 15 minutes

Serving Size: 3

Calories: 426

Ingredients:

- 4 green onions

- 4 tablespoons peanut oil
- 2 teaspoon ginger
- 1 bell pepper
- 4 cloves garlic
- 6 oz. Chow Mein noodles

Sauce:

- 1 tablespoon soy sauce
- ½ teaspoon sesame oil
- ¼ cup chicken broth
- 2 tablespoons Shaoxing wine
- 2 tablespoons oyster sauce

Method:

1. Take a bowl and mix all ingredients of sauce until smooth.
2. Cook noodles by following directions on the package. Rinse with water and add 1 tablespoon oil to prevent sticking.
3. Add oil in a wok or pan and add noodles.
4. Stir noodles to prevent sticking to the wok.
5. Add vegetables and stir for 3 minutes.
6. Add sauce and mix well.
7. Cook for 1 minute and serve immediately.

General Tso Tofu

Cooking Time: 30 minutes

Serving Size: 3

Calories: 345

Ingredients:

- 1 tablespoon maple syrup
- 6 tablespoons cornstarch
- 1 block tofu
- 2 tablespoons soy sauce

Sauce:

- 2 teaspoons cornstarch
- 2 tablespoons Shaoxing wine
- ¼ cup chicken stock
- 2 tablespoons Chinkiang vinegar
- ¼ cup of sugar
- 1 tablespoon light soy sauce
- 1 tablespoon dark soy sauce

Stir fry:

- 2 teaspoons ginger
- 3 to 4 cloves garlic
- 3 tablespoons peanut oil
- 4 green onions
- 2 fresh Thai chili pepper
- 2 bunches broccoli

Method:

1. Marinate tofu with maple syrup and soy sauce in a sealing bag for 10 to 15 minutes.
2. Mix all ingredients of the sauce and stir until combine properly.

3. Gently open the bag of tofu and discard extra liquid. Add cornstarch and mix tofu well.

4. Heat wok and add 1 tablespoon oil.

5. Add broccoli and 3 tablespoon water. Cover immediately to cook broccoli in steam. Heat for 4 minutes and set aside.

6. Clean wok and add 1 tablespoon oil.

7. Add tofu in the wok and cook for 10 minutes until brown. Set aside.

8. Add remaining ingredients in wok and stir well until sauce becomes thick.

9. Transfer tofu on the plate. Pour broccoli and sauce. Serve with rice.

Nepali Momus with Spinach and Ricotta

Cooking Time: 50 minutes

Serving Size: 20

Calories: 75

Ingredients:

- ¼ cup parmesan cheese
- 2 green onions
- 20 round dumplings wrappers
- ¾ cup ricotta cheese
- 5 cups spinach leaves
- 1 clove garlic
- Freshly ground black pepper
- 1 tablespoon butter
- ¾ teaspoon salt

Method:

1. Take a skillet and add spinach and garlic. Add 3 tablespoon water and cook for 5 minutes until spinach wilted. Set aside.

2. Mix all ingredients except dumpling wraps.

3. Add 1 tablespoon mixture in each dumpling and wrap like half-moon shape.

4. Steam dumplings for 10 minutes until cook. Serve with sauce.

Real Deal Sesame Noodles

Cooking Time: 20 minutes

Serving Size: 4

Calories: 166

Ingredients:

- 2 green onions
- 250 grams of noodles

Peanut sauce:

- 2 cloves garlic
- ¼ teaspoon Sichuan peppercorn powder
- 2 tablespoons light soy sauce
- 2 tablespoons Chinkiang vinegar
- 1 tablespoon honey
- ¼ cup natural peanut butter
- 2 teaspoons chili oil
- 1 teaspoon sesame oil
- 1 teaspoon ginger

Topping options:

- tomatoes
- sesame seeds
- 1 cucumber
- 2 carrots

Method:

1. Cook noodles by following package directions. Rinse and add 1 tablespoon oil to prevent sticking.

2. Add peanut butter in warm water and make a smooth paste.

3. Add remaining ingredients and cook for 5 minutes until thick sauce forms.

4. Add noodles in a pan and add the sauce. Mix well. Garnish with sesame seeds and cucumber.

Homemade Vegetarian Oyster Sauce

Cooking Time: 20 minutes

Serving Size: 1

Calories: 40

Ingredients:

- 1 tablespoon dark soy sauce
- 1 teaspoon ginger
- 1 tablespoon light soy sauce
- 1 teaspoon agave syrup
- 2 teaspoons miso paste
- 1.4 oz. shiitake mushrooms
- 2 tablespoons peanut oil

- ¼ teaspoon five-spice powder
- 2 teaspoons sesame oil
- 2 cloves garlic

Method:

1. Wash shiitake mushroom and add hot water in it. Wait for 30 minutes until mushroom tender.
2. Dry mushrooms and cut into small pieces.
3. Take a wok and fry mushrooms in 1 tablespoon oil. Cook for 5 minutes.
4. Add ginger garlic and cook for 1 minute.
5. Add 1 cup of water in the blender and blend the mushroom mixture.
6. Transfer to the frying pan and add remaining ingredients. Add seasonings to taste and cook for 10 minutes.
7. Cooldown and store in a container for 1 week or refrigerator for 1 month.

Carrot Dumplings

Cooking Time: 20

Serving Size: 45 minutes

Calories: 38

Ingredients:

- 45 dumpling wrappers
- 2 teaspoons potato starch

Filling:

- 4 cloves garlic
- 1 tablespoon light soy sauce
- ½ teaspoon salt
- 1-pound carrots
- 3 large eggs
- 1 cup bamboo shoots
- 1 cup shiitake mushrooms
- 2 slices ginger
- 3 tablespoons sesame oil
- ¼ teaspoon white pepper powder

Sauce:

- 2 teaspoons light soy sauce
- 2 tablespoons black vinegar
- 2 teaspoons chili oil

Method:

1. Wash shiitake mushroom and add hot water in it. Wait for 30 minutes until mushroom tender.
2. Dry mushrooms and cut into small pieces.
3. Take a wok and fry mushrooms in 1 tablespoon oil. Cook for 5 minutes.
4. Add ginger, garlic, and carrot and cook for 1 minute.
5. Add 1 cup of water in the blender and blend the mushroom mixture.
6. Transfer to pan and cook until carrots soften. Add eggs and cook for 2 minutes.

7. Add soy sauce, bamboo shoots, salt, and white pepper. Mix and set aside.

8. Combine potato starch with water and brush on dumpling wraps.

9. Add 1 tablespoon mixture overwraps and seal dumplings.

10. Mix all ingredients of the sauce and stir until combine.

11. Steam dumplings for 8 to 10 minutes and serve with sauce.

Di San Xian

Cooking Time: 30 minutes

Serving Size: 2

Calories: 220

Ingredients:

- ½ tablespoon dark soy sauce
- 1 tablespoon Shaoxing wine
- ¼ cup vegetable stock
- ½ tablespoon sugar
- ¼ teaspoon salt
- 1 teaspoon cornstarch
- 1 tablespoon light soy sauce

Stir fry:

- 1 bell pepper
- 2 teaspoons sesame seeds for garnish
- ½ regular eggplant
- 2 green onion

- 2 cloves of garlic
- 2 teaspoons cornstarch
- ¼ cup peanut oil
- 1 small russet potato

Method:

1. Soak eggplants in water for 15 to 20 minutes and sprinkle salt over it.
2. Cut eggplant in small pieces and sprinkle cornstarch.
3. Mix cornstarch, salt, soy sauce, oil, and wine. Set aside.
4. Heat a skillet and add oil. Cook eggplants until golden brown.
5. Remove eggplant and add potato pieces in the skillet.
6. Add garlic and onion and stir fry.
7. Mix sauce until thicken.
8. Add remaining ingredients and eggplants. Mix and serve immediately.

Chinese Broccoli

Cooking Time: 20 minutes

Serving Size: 4

Calories: 90

Ingredients:

- 4 cloves garlic
- 1 bunch Chinese broccoli
- Pinch of salt
- ½ lb. white mushrooms
- 1 tablespoon peanut oil

Sauce:

- 1 tablespoon cornstarch
- 2 tablespoons soy sauce
- 1 cup vegetable stock
- 2 teaspoons sugar
- 1 teaspoon dark soy sauce

Method:

1. Mix all sauce ingredients and set aside.
2. Take a wok and add water. Add broccoli and steam for 5 minutes.
3. Remove excess water and add oil and garlic.
4. Cook for 3 minutes. Add mushroom until golden brown.
5. Add remaining ingredients and sauce. Cook for 2 minutes and serve.

Chinese Banana Fritters

Cooking Time: 25 minutes

Serving Size: 6

Calories: 196

Ingredients:

- Oil for deep frying
- Powdered sugar
- 5 big ripe bananas

Batter

- 1 tablespoon granulated sugar
- ½ cup cornstarch

- 2 tablespoons milk
- ½ cup all-purpose flour
- 1 tablespoon butter
- ½ cup of water

Method:

1. Combine all ingredients of batter and mix until smooth.
2. Heat oil in the pan. Add banana slices in batter and pour in hot oil.
3. Cook for 5 minutes until golden brown.
4. Serve with sugar or maple syrup.

Mango Sago

Cooking Time: 30 minutes

Serving Size: 4

Calories: 340

Ingredients:

- 1 cup full-fat coconut milk
- 2 big mangoes
- ¾ cup evaporated milk
- ½ grapefruit
- ¼ cup tapioca pearls
- ¼ cup of sugar

Method:

1. Boil water and add tapioca pearls until transparent. Add in sieve and merge with tapioca pearls. Set aside
2. Blend half mangoes in milk to make a smooth mixture. Add sugar and blend again.

3. Take a bowl and add tapioca pearls. Add mango paste and coconut oil. Garnish with mango slices.

Conclusion

Chinese foods are very different from all other foods in different countries. Ingredients and taste can vary from region to region in China too, but their preparation method is almost identical. Chinese foods have been prevailing since ancient times and are widely famous for their unique taste and healthy ingredients. There are many benefits of eating Chinese food as it provides nutrients that a body needs and it also uses fewer fat ingredients. Rice is the leading food item in China that is served with every dish and in every meal. Buddhists who cannot consume meat can eat vegetarian dishes. The basic techniques of Chinese food are frying, deep-frying, steaming, boiling, and roasting. Chinese food made at home is very different from the food available at restaurants. There are many health benefits to consuming Chinese food. It helps to regulate your body fluids and enhance your metabolism. Thus, Chinese food is famous in America for its flavors and cooking styles. Vegetarians, lacto-Ovo-vegetarians, Buddhists, Ovo-vegetarians, etc., all can eat Chinese foods due to a wide variety of cooking techniques.

Japanese Home Cooking

Learn How to Prepare Japanese Traditional Food with Over 100 Recipes for Ramen, Sushi, and Vegetarian Dishes

By

Adele Tyler

All trademarks and brands within this book are for clarifying purposes only and are owned by the owners themselves, not affiliated with this document.

Table of contents

We all love to have food conveniently. Everyone loves to order food or get to some restaurant to have their favorite dishes but eating out can be unhealthy to a greater extent. Towards the end of a busy day, eating out or ordering your food might feel like the most convenient and the most straightforward choice. In any case, comfort and restaurant prepared food can negatively affect your health and wellbeing. One of the simplest ways to improve your health is by preparing more home-cooked meals.

Our world comprises of various countries with numerous types of cuisines that are being eaten all around the globe. One such cuisine is called the Japanese cuisine that is, as the name clearly depicts, originated from the Asian country, Japan.

Japanese cooking mainly includes the territorial and conventional nourishments of Japan, which have been developed through hundreds of years of political, monetary, and social changes. The customary cooking of Japan depends on rice with miso soup and different dishes; there is an accentuation on seasonal ingredients.

In this book regarding Japanese home cooking, we will discuss in detail the history as well as the origin of Japanese food and its evolution over the passage of time. You will also get a section in the book where you will learn the reason behind the popularity of Japanese cuisine in the U.S.A. In this book, you will get the knowledge regarding the difference between home cooking and dine in experience while having Japanese food.

There are various different kinds of spices being used in Japanese cooking, out of which many have been discussed in detail in the chapters below. You will learn different recipes, including breakfast, lunch, dinner, dessert, salad, soups, snacks, sushi, alternative, and traditional as well as vegetarian recipes. All the recipes mentioned in this book are extremely easy to make all on your own at home. Now, let us not brag too much and finally start cooking Japanese at home.

Japanese cooking has been around for more than 2,000 years with its strong links from both China and Korea. Although, it has just been a couple of hundreds of years since all the impacts have come to form what is now known as Japanese cuisine. Japanese cooking has overwhelmed the culinary scene. With its one-of-a-kind taste of flavors and fragile mix of sweet and savory, it is no big surprise Japanese meals are so well known. From sushi to ramen, Japanese and Japanese-motivated dishes can be found worldwide, including your own kitchen. You do not need to be a master chef to bring home the exquisite flavors of Japanese cuisine.

Japanese individuals call every supper "Gohan." For instance, breakfast is classified "asa-Gohan." A bowl of steamed rice is included for every single Japanese dinner and is very important for breakfast, lunch, or supper. Side dishes are called okazu and are presented with rice and soup. Rice is a staple of the Japanese eating routine. Rice cakes (mochi) are additionally usually very common. They range from sweet to exquisite and have various preparations from bubbled to barbecued.

1.1 History and Origin of Japanese Food

Japanese cuisine has been influenced by the food customs of other nations but has adopted and refined them to create its own unique cooking style and eating habits. The first foreign influence on Japan was China around 300 B.C. when the Japanese learned to cultivate rice. The use of chopsticks and the consumption of soy sauce and soybean curd (tofu) also came from China.

The Buddhist religion, one of the two major religions in Japan today, was another important influence on the Japanese diet. In the A.D. 700s, the rise of Buddhism led to a ban on eating meat. The popular dish sushi came about as a result of this ban. In the 1800s, cooking styles became simpler. A wide variety of vegetarian foods were served in small portions, using one of five standard cooking techniques.

Starting in the mid-1200s, trade with different nations started bringing Western-style impacts to Japan. The Dutch presented corn, potatoes, and yams. The Portuguese presented tempura. After a boycott of more than 1,000 years, hamburger got back to Japan during the Meiji Period (1868–1912). Western foods, for example, bread, espresso, and frozen yogurt gotten well known during the late 20th century.

Another Western impact has been the presentation of timesaving cooking strategies. These incorporate the electric rice cooker, bundled nourishments, for example, moment noodles, moment miso soup, and moment pickling blends. However, the Japanese are as yet dedicated to their exemplary cooking conventions. All foods were divided into five color groups (green, red, yellow, white, and black-purple) and six tastes (bitter, sour, sweet, hot, salty, and delicate). The Japanese continue to use this cooking system.

1.2 History of Traditional Japanese Dishes

Japan is a small country, but each region or even a city has its own specials. Mainly, there is the Kanto region (eastern area of the main island) food and Kansai region (western area of the main island) food. Generally, Kanto food has intense flavors, and Kansai food is lightly seasoned. Many dishes are cooked differently between the Kansai and Kanto regions.

Milk and other dairy items have neglected to appreciate a similar prominence in Europe as they do in Japan. The main Japanese dairy item known to history was delivered between the eighth and fourteenth hundred years. Cattle were often raised only for drawing carts or ploughing fields. To utilize them for meat or even for milk was, until relatively recently, a long-forgotten practice.

Pepper and cloves were known from the eighth century and were imported either by means of China or legitimately from Southeast Asia, and garlic was additionally developed, taking things down a notch. In any case, these flavors were utilized essentially to make medications and beauty care products.

In the absence of red meat, fish was an effective substitute, and as an island nation, this source of food was abundant and has influenced many of today's most famous dishes. However, before the introduction of modern delivery systems, the difficulty of preserving and transporting fresh marine fish minimized consumption in inland areas where freshwater fish were commonly eaten instead.

Preserving fish additionally got famous, and sushi started as a method for saving fish by placing it in boiled rice. Fish that are salted and set-in rice are saved by lactic corrosive maturation, which forestalls the expansion of the microbes that achieve rot. This more established sort of sushi is still delivered in the zones encompassing Lake Biwa in western Japan, and comparative sorts are likewise known in Korea, southwestern China, and Southeast Asia.

To eat Japanese-style suppers, chopsticks are usually utilized. Also, Japanese people use forks, knives, or spoons, depending on what types of food people are eating. The traditional Japanese table setting is to place a bowl of rice on your left and to place a bowl of miso soup on your right side of the table. Other dishes are set behind these bowls. Chopsticks are placed on a chopstick holder in front of soup and rice bowls.

Today, Japanese cooking is still intensely affected by the four seasons and geology. Fish and vegetables are most ordinarily eaten. While to certain westerners, the food may appear to be practically insipid, freshness, presentation, and balance of flavors to be of paramount importance.

1.3 Evolution of Japanese Food over Time

A significant part of the rice devoured by Japan was imported from other Eastern nations, so once the trade stopped, the rice flexibly dwindled. To additional the issue, returnees from combat areas just as U.S. occupation in Japan raised the populace to numbers higher than those of pre-war levels. Helpless rice harvests in 1944 and 1945 because of climate and war compounded the criticalness of the circumstance, bringing about broad hunger and starvation, especially among youngsters.

This suffering, however, ended up having a silver lining. During the U.S. occupation of Japan following World War II, the United States government supplied Japan with large quantities of wheat flour to rehabilitate the Japanese economy as a strategic move during the cold war. This wheat flour served as a substitute for rice, and was used mainly to make wheat noodles for Chinese noodle soup at the time referred to as shina soba or chuka soba. This noodle soup is often sold in Japanese black markets from yatai or small food carts, which later became known as ramen.

The daily diet of the Japanese people has changed drastically over the past years, with corresponding changes in agricultural production. In the early post-war years of food shortage, people ate sweet potatoes, barley, and millet more than white rice, which was scarce and expensive. Vegetables and fish in small quantities served as side dishes.

Although rice regained its traditional place at the center of the preferred Japanese diet by the early 1950s, western staples of meat, bread, and dairy products soon made inroads. Many people credit the national school lunch program with changing the diet preferences of the younger generation because it served milk and a roll along with a hot dish.

Japanese now eat much more meat, bread, and dairy products, while consumption of rice has declined. By the 1970s, western style restaurants and fast foods further changed the eating habits of urban Japanese. Instead of the traditional diet of rice for breakfast and dinner and noodles for lunch, most urban Japanese now eat a western breakfast and lunch, with rice remaining the staple food only for most dinners.

1.4 Popularity of Japanese Dishes in the U.S.A

Japanese food is getting more mainstream, alongside a developing movement towards sound reasoning. The quantity of Japanese cafés is developing, even in America. While the taste is a reason for the popularity, the colorful plating of items that allow for dishes to also be enjoyed visually is another.

After Italian, Chinese, and Mexican, Japanese food is presumably the most mainstream ethnic cooking in the United

States. Before 1970 only a few big cities, and a few Japanese-American communities in Hawaii and California, had Japanese restaurants; the foods, and the manners and customs, attracted few mainstream American diners. The popularity of sushi would change all that. While Americanised sushi variations like the ever-popular California roll made the form popular, once introduced to sushi, Americans began to crave it, even if it meant eating raw fish.

However, real Japanese food is available and popular at restaurants all over the United States of America. Restaurants will, naturally, avoid many Japanese foods that will never appeal to American taste: the pungent, sticky fermented soy paste called natto is a perfect example, although even this is available in Japanese groceries.

A real Japanese restaurant has a staff of Japanese chefs. Good Japanese cooking is subtle and takes a long time to master. Sushi chefs are particularly highly trained and are skilled at avoiding health issues when dealing with raw seafood. A number of pan-Asian restaurants offer Japanese food in combination with Chinese or Korean food. The Japanese dishes at these restaurants should be reliable if prepared by a genuine Japanese chef.

Thirty years ago, the typical Japanese restaurant served a little of everything. Now Japanese food is so popular that the market supports numerous specialties eating concepts such as the famous sushi, tempura, shabu yautia, udon and soba, ramen, teriyaki, bento box, nabe, yakiniku, sukiyaki, and donburi.

Japanese cooking incorporates the local and conventional nourishments of Japan, which have created through hundreds of years of political, financial, and social changes. The customary cooking of Japan depends on rice with miso soup and different dishes; there is an emphasis on seasonal ingredients. Side dishes often consist of fish, pickled vegetables, and vegetables cooked in broth.

Seafood is common, often grilled, but also served raw as sashimi or in sushi. Seafood and vegetables are also deep-fried in a light batter, as tempura. Apart from rice, staples include noodles, such as soba and udon. Japan also has many simmered dishes such as fish products in broth called oden, or beef in sukiyaki and nikujaga.

2.1 Difference between Home Cooking Vs. Dine-in Experience

While many restaurants and fast-food outlets offer us convincing marketing statements that they offer healthy and nutritional food, studies frequently find that this is not the case. The sugar and sodium substance of most handled foods cause them to be not kidding dangers to our wellbeing. These are likewise similar characteristics which permit these foods to get addictive. The eatery business supports overconsumption and extravagance in foods that we know to be undesirable for our bodies.

Neither is restaurant food as healthy for us as what we would make at home. At the same time, the cost of eating out puts a large strain on many of our food budgets. Cooking at home is the best choice for having a consistently healthy, budget-friendly diet.

Individuals all around the globe are occupied with work, school and other additional exercises. Nobody actually has the opportunity to cook, so families are continually going out to eat at an eatery. At the point when a family eats at home, they, will pay not as much as cafés in light of the fact that when they purchase food from the market they purchase for better quality and a superior cost. It is very simple. There is most likely even a not insignificant rundown of advantages that a considerable lot of you previously experienced eating at home yourselves. Following are the differences between home cooking and dine-in experience:

1. **You can save money.**

In the long run, preparing meals at home may save you money. A group of fundamental ingredients frequently comes in at a lower sticker price than a single restaurant dish.

You can likewise wind up getting more suppers out of a formula you make at home than if you request takeout, or have extras to take to work the following day. After only a couple weeks, you could see perceptible reserve funds begin to accumulate.

2. Keep up calorie count.

The average fast food order ranges between 1,100 to 1,200 calories total that is almost all of a woman's recommended daily calorie intake (1,600 to 2,400 calories) and almost two thirds of a man's daily intake (2,000 to 3,000 calories). Furthermore, if you think independent cafés, and modest chains do any better, reconsider. Making a meal yourself means you can make sure the portion sizes and calorie counts are where you want them to be. Recipes often come with nutritional information and serving size suggestions, which makes that even easier.

3. It is fun to cook.

At the point when you are making a meal without any preparation, you will find and explore different avenues regarding various ingredients, flavours, and foods. And as with any activity, the more time you spend in the kitchen, the better you become at creating fantastic meals. You would be missing out this fun if you would keep on ordering your food or going for dine-in to any restaurant.

4. Save plenty of time.

Part of ordering take-out means waiting for the food to arrive or driving to get it. Depending on where you live, what time you order, and whether or not the delivery person is good with directions, this could actually take more time than if you would simply make a meal at home.

Cooking at home does not have to take a lot of time if you do not want it to.

By using different services, you eliminate the need to look for recipes or grocery shop. Everything you need comes right to your door; in the exact pre-portioned amounts you will be using.

5. You will feel healthy

Some research specialists recommend that individuals that more frequently prepare food themselves, instead of getting a take-out meal, have a generally more beneficial eating regimen. These examinations additionally give us the idea that café suppers ordinarily contain higher measures of sodium, immersed fat, absolute fat, and large number of calories than home-prepared meals. While cooking without anyone else at home you have full scale authority over what is going in your food. That can improve things fundamentally to your overall prosperity.

6. More family times.

Cooking together can offer you an event to reconnect with your assistant just as loved ones. Cooking has various favourable circumstances as well. The American Psychological Association communicates that trying new things together like learning another formula together can help keep a couple related and busy with their relationship.

The most important fact is that food simply tastes better when it is been prepared in home rather than any restaurant. Thus, it is smarter to cook home and eat well instead of taking off to an eatery only because of your apathetic daily schedule.

2.2 Health Benefits of Japanese Food

The Japanese eating regimen depends on the rule of wellbeing and life span. Japanese food is not just elegant and mouth-watering yet additionally offers different medical advantages.

Japanese food generally comprises of natural ingredients, refined sugar or other food sources, and high measures of grains and vegetables. Following are a portion of the numerous medical advantages of appreciating Japanese food:

1. Large variety of fruits and vegetables.

The Japanese eating regimen comprises of a wide scope of vegetables, which contains fundamental minerals to help generally sustenance. For instance, kelp is profoundly nutritious, including a lot of iodine that can enable your body to save a sound thyroid. Likewise, high measures of organic product are burned-through for breakfast and treat, which has high measures of fibre and water content.

2. Healthy drinks.

Japanese eateries generally incorporate green tea with their suppers, which have various medical advantages. Green tea is known to help direct pulse, lower glucose, support the safe framework, lower cholesterol, and hinder the maturing cycle. It likewise contains a large portion of the measure of caffeine that espresso does, and assists breaks with bringing down oils in your stomach related framework. Green tea additionally makes a loose and centred mental perspective because of it being wealthy in cancer prevention agents.

3. Reduced risk of various cancers.

Japan has had an extremely low risk for hormone-dependent cancers such as breast and prostate cancers. This is attributed to the high consumption of vegetables, fruits, healthy fats, high-fibre foods, and overall lower calorie intake.

4. Lower chances of cardiac diseases.

Japan has one of the lowest rates for the development of heart disease in the world and even more compared to developed countries. The reasoning behind these low instances of heart diseases is that the Japanese diet is filled with foods that help improve heart health.

Furthermore, Japanese food lacks ingredients in their diet which promotes poor cardiac health like high levels of saturated fats, modified carbohydrates from processed foods, and lower levels of sugar consumption. Soy is commonly in many Japanese dishes, and it is known to decrease the risk of heart attacks, as well as, regulate blood pressure. The Japanese use soy as an alternative to red meat, which can be very high in saturated fats.

5. High amount of protein.

The Japanese culture comprehends that eating excellent wellsprings of protein advances a more advantageous way of life. A significant number of the dishes in Japanese food are brimming with protein, which is staggeringly helpful to your body. Fish, chicken, and even tofu are probably the most widely recognized staples in Japanese food. When you eat a lot of protein, you create stronger building blocks for your bones, your muscles, your cartilage, your skin, and even your blood.

Protein also provides large amounts of iron, which keeps your blood oxygenated, so it continues to flow through your body as efficiently as possible. Likewise, the Japanese eating regimen utilizes a ton of fish rather than red meats since it brings down the dangers of coronary episodes. By consuming more fish, you are also gaining a great source of omega 3 fatty acids and brain-boosting nutrients.

The traditional Japanese diet combines simple soups, steamed rice or noodles, fish, seafood, tofu or natto, and a variety of minimally processed sides. The traditional Japanese diet focuses on whole, minimally processed, nutrient-rich, seasonal foods. It is particularly rich in seafood, vegetables, and fruit, and limits meat, dairy, and snacks. It may improve digestion, aid weight management, help you live longer, and protect against various diseases.

2.3 Different Properties of Spices used in Japanese Food

Spices are utilized for flavor and for stylish allure in Japanese cooking. Probably the most widely recognized are: shiso, akajiso, mistuba, kaiware, sancho, and chrysanthemum leaves. Shichimi Togarashi is the most famous flavoring other than soy sauce.

1. Mitsuba.

Mitsuba is a tasty kind of parsley with a fresh surface and an invigorating fragrance. Added as an exquisite embellishment to flavorful custard dishes, soups, and sashimi, it is likewise southern style entire in tempura or added to plates of mixed greens. Mitsuba can be utilized at whatever point more grounded tasting parsley is required.

2. Akajiso

Akajiso or red shiso is also used to dye pickled plums red. These umeboshi are used throughout Japanese cuisine as a garnish or as a flavoring in sauces, dressings, rice balls and other dishes. A specialty gin made in Kyoto is made from red shiso and flavoured with yusu, sansho pepper, and juniper berries. This gin which is lighter than its western counterpart has a smooth but complex flavor.

3. Sansho

Sansho is a pretty herb with a dainty balanced design that is a good seasoning for soups and fish dishes, in particular eel specialties or chicken. With its refreshing mint like flavor, sansho is a popular herb enhancer in Japan. Apart from its leaf, the seed pods of the sansho plant give a tingling dimension to eel or chicken dishes; its flavor is lemony and peppery and can deliver a flavorful punch.

4. Yuzu Koshu

Japan's local specialty spice, yuzu kosho, is made of the peel of the Asian citrus yuzu, salt, and chili pepper. You can commonly find it as a tube or jar of yellow paste in Japanese supermarkets. Traditionally used in nabe, or Japanese hotpot, yuzu kosho also pairs wonderfully with miso, tonkatsu (fried pork cutlet), yakitori (grilled meat skewers), sashimi, and all manner of Japanese noodle dishes.

5. Ponzu

Ponzu is the citrus sauce that even those who hate citrus will love. Made from the juice of any citrus fruit, soy sauce, mirin (rice wine), and dashi (Japanese soup stock), this tangy vinaigrette like sauce can brighten the flavor of your gyoza, stir-fry, marinated meats, and tofu dishes.

6. Chrysanthemum

Although somewhat bitter in taste, chrysanthemum leaves are often added to hot pot dishes and stir fries. The buds and flowers are infused to make a celebratory herbal tea served on special occasions like weddings.

7. Wasabi

In case you are acquainted with any topping on this rundown, it is most likely wasabi. Wasabi is notable for being the threateningly hot green glue that goes with sushi, verifiably thought to have restorative properties when eaten with crude fish. Yet, you can likewise utilize it to decorate soba noodles, or even make a wasabi dressing for sushi bowls and cooked fish.

8. Shichimi Togarashi

Shichimi togarashi is a flavorful mixture of sansho, hemp seeds, ground nori, black and white sesame seeds, white poppy seeds, ground chilies, shiso, and ginger and dried tangerine peel. These ingredients vary according to the region, but basically it is a zesty chili powder used to flavor Udon. This popular seven spice seasoning originated in the 1600s when chilies were first introduced to Japan and has been enjoyed ever since as a seasoning for udon, ramen, hot pot, and chicken dishes.

9. Rayu

Commonly found in Japanese-style Chinese food, rayu is chili oil made with sesame oil, garlic, ginger, onion, spices, and sometimes sesame seeds. You may have seen this signature red oil available at the tables of most ramen shops. It also serves as a great dipping sauce for meals and can spice up any regular bowl of rice, noodles, or tofu.

10. Kaiware

Kaiware is a type of radish sprout with a hot, peppery flavor like watercress. Useful as a spicy garnish, it is excellent in sandwiches, stir fries, salads and sushi. Often it is sprinkled on top of tuna or beef tataki to give a peppery accent to the other ingredients.

11. Shiso

Shiso consists of large aromatic leaves, either purple or green, with a refreshing scent and flavor. When served raw with sushi or sashimi, shiso is said to prevent food poisoning because of its antiseptic or antibacterial qualities. Other medicinal characteristics include anti-inflammatory powers with illnesses such as allergies, colds, and arthritis.

Otherwise, shiso leaves are used as a garnish for sashimi, wrapped around onigiri, used to flavor pickled plums, deep fried in tempura batter, or added to rice dishes.

Shiso is also a refreshing herb to add to salads, egg sandwiches, or in sauces such as pesto or gremolata. Very easy to grow in pots on your patio, shiso will grow waist high and propagate easily if the conditions are right.

12. Furikake

Furikake is a broad term that applies to any dry Japanese spices made to be sprinkled over cooked rice. Common varieties might include salmon flakes, bits of dried omelet, sesame seeds, wasabi, seaweed flakes, bonito flakes, and nearly any other Japanese seasoning you can think of! You can try out special prefectural varieties, or simply stick with safe old seaweed flavor to spice up your rice, noodles, fried chicken, or salads.

13. Aonori

Aonori, or dried seaweed flakes, are a ubiquitous Japanese seasoning that lends its familiar earthy flavor to much of Japanese cuisine. Traditionally, it goes atop takoyaki, okonomiyaki, and yakisoba.

You will discover a great deal of these fixings in standard Japanese cooking, so unquestionably adventure outside your customary range of familiarity with some conventional and extraordinary Japanese dishes. In any case, the beautiful universe of Japanese flavors and sauces additionally has a lot of space for experimentation.

Rather than the sweet oats or additionally filling bacon and egg dishes that fill in as the cornerstone of numerous American breakfast menus, Japanese morning meals centre on pungent, appetizing flavours that fulfil and empower you for the afternoon. The components of this hearty-yet-not-too-filling breakfast might seem more like lunch or dinner to Americans, and that is by design. Following are some amazing Japanese breakfast recipes:

3.1 Japanese Omelette

Cooking Time: 5 minutes

Serving Size: 1

Ingredients:

- Soy sauce, one tbsp.
- Eggs, four
- Sugar, one tbsp.
- Mirin, one tbsp.

- Salt, as required
- Cooking oil, as required

Method:

1. First, beat your eggs well in a bowl using either a fork, or chopsticks if you are an expert chopstick user.

2. Add one tablespoon each of soy sauce, mirin and sugar and a little salt to your mix.

3. Put a small amount of cooking oil in your pan and bring it up to medium heat. Keep some kitchen roll handy to help keep the pan oiled during cooking.

4. Add a small amount of your egg mix into the heated pan. Once the egg is cooked slightly so that the top is still slightly uncooked, push it over to the side of your pan.

5. Add a little more oil to the pan using the kitchen roll and add another small amount of the egg mix to your pan.

6. You can then begin to roll the first bit of egg over the mix you just put in the pan until you have a small roll of egg.

7. Continue adding a small amount of egg while oiling the pan each time in between.

8. Your omelette is now done so remove from the pan and wait to cool before slicing it up into thin pieces with a sharp knife.

9. Your dish is ready to be served.

3.2 Breakfast Ramen

Cooking Time: 25 minutes

Serving Size: 6

Ingredients:

- Sage leaves, a bunch
- Unsalted butter, a quarter cup
- Bacon, eight strips
- Enki mushrooms, a bunch
- Miso soup, two cups
- Broth, twelve cups
- Poached eggs, six
- Ramen noodles, six cups
- Tomato, one
- Salt, as required
- Cooking oil, as required
- Avocado, one

Method:

1. Preheat oven to 400 degrees. Lay a piece of parchment paper on a baking sheet.

2. Spread the bacon strips on the sheet and bake for about twenty minutes. Watch carefully as time will vary with ovens. They will crisp up with no need to turn the pieces over. Save your bacon grease in a jar because you can use it to make the ramen soup bases. Remove from the oven and set on a paper towel.

3. Heat the butter in a small skillet over high heat until the butter starts to brown. Immediately scatter the sage leaves in the pan and cook for about 10 seconds.

4. Boil a pot of water for your noodles. In a separate saucepan, bring two cups miso base, and twelve cups

(2.8 L) of broth to a boil, then lower the heat and let it simmer until it is ready to be served.

5. Boil the noodles. If fresh, boil for about one minute, if packaged, boil for about two minutes. As soon as they are done, drain well and separate into serving bowls.

6. Pour two cups of soup over each bowl of noodles.

7. Top each bowl with mushrooms, avocado slices, tomatoes, poached egg, a crumbled up half strip of bacon, and crispy sage; lay another whole piece of bacon on the side.

8. Drizzle the browned butter over the top for added flavour.

9. You dish is ready to be served.

3.3 Japanese Style Pancakes

Cooking Time: 40 minutes

Serving Size: 4

Ingredients:

- Milk, one and a half cup
- Baking powder, two tsp.
- Sugar, three tbsp.
- Kosher salt, half tsp.
- Unsalted butter, four tbsp.
- Eggs, four
- Vanilla extract, one tsp.
- Cream of tartar, a quarter tsp.
- Maple syrup, as required

- All-purpose flour, one and a half cup

Method:

1. Whisk together the flour, sugar, baking powder and salt in a large bowl.
2. Whisk together the milk, melted butter, vanilla and egg yolk in a medium bowl until combined.
3. Beat the egg whites and cream of tartar in another large bowl with an electric mixer on medium-high speed until stiff peaks form, about two minutes.
4. Stir the milk mixture into the flour mixture until just combined. Then gently fold in the remaining egg whites until just combined.
5. Coat a large non-stick skillet with non-stick cooking spray and heat over medium-low heat.
6. Put the prepared ring moulds in the middle of the skillet and fill each with half cup of batter.
7. Cover the skillet with the lid and cook until the batter rises to the tops of the ring moulds and is golden on the bottom for about five minutes.
8. Release the bottom of the pancakes with a spatula. Grasp the sides of the ring moulds with tongs to stabilize them and then carefully flip.
9. Cover and cook until golden on the other side, about five minutes more. Transfer to a plate and remove the mould.
10. Serve with butter and maple syrup.

3.4 Japanese Breakfast Rice Bowl

Cooking Time: 3 minutes

Serving Size: 1

Ingredients:

- Egg, one
- Thinly sliced nori, as required
- Hondashi, a pinch
- Mirin, half tsp.
- Soy sauce, half tsp.
- MSG, a pinch
- Furikake, as required
- Cooked white rice, one cup

Method:

1. Place rice in a bowl and make a shallow scoop in the centre.
2. Break the whole egg into the centre.
3. Season with half teaspoon soy sauce, a pinch of salt, a pinch of MSG, half teaspoon mirin, and a pinch of Hondashi.
4. Stir vigorously with chopsticks to incorporate egg; it should become pale yellow, frothy, and fluffy in texture.
5. Taste and adjust seasonings as necessary.
6. Sprinkle with furikake and nori, make a small scoop in the top, and add the other egg yolk.
7. Your dish is ready to be served.

3.5 Tamagoyaki

Cooking Time: 10 minutes

Serving Size: 2

Ingredients:

- Eggs, three
- Olive oil, one tsp.
- Shirodashi, two tsp.
- Salt, pinch
- Water, two tbsp.

Method:

1. Crack the eggs into a medium size mixing bowl.
2. Add seasoning and mix them all together gently to avoid too much bubble forming.
3. Strain the egg mixture through a sieve a few times.
4. Pour about two tbsp. oil in a small bowl and soak kitchen paper and set aside.
5. Heat two tsp. olive oil in the frying pan over medium heat till you can feel the heat when you hover your hand over the pan.
6. Pour a quarter of egg mixture into the pan.
7. Break any bubbles that have been formed with the edge of the chopsticks and scramble gently and slightly.
8. When the surface is solidified a little, fold and push the egg to one end of the pan with chopsticks.
9. Repeat the procedure and make an egg roll.
10. Your dish is ready to be served.

3.6 Tonkatsu

Cooking Time: 10 minutes

Serving Size: 4

Ingredients:

- Eggs, two
- Flour, as required
- Tonkatsu sauce, for serving
- Shredded Napa cabbage, as required
- Bread crumbs, as required
- Pork loins, four pieces
- Oil, for frying
- Salt, pinch
- Pepper, as required

Method:

1. Pound to flatten the loin cutlet to about a quarter inch. Salt and pepper both sides of each cutlet.

2. Dredge each in flour, then dip into beaten eggs and press into bread crumbs to coat both sides.

3. Heat a large skillet with about half inch of oil until hot.

4. Lay the cutlets in the hot oil. Deep-fry until golden brown, about five minutes, turning them once or twice.

5. Drain the cutlets on paper towels and cut the pork into bite-size strips that can be eaten with chopsticks.

6. Arrange the pork on a platter lined with the shredded cabbage, and garnish with lemon wedges.

7. Serve the sauce on the side for dipping, or pour it over the pork and cabbage.

3.7 Japanese Egg Omelette Sandwich

Cooking Time: 5 minutes

Serving Size: 2

Ingredients:

- Eggs, two
- Japanese soup stock, half tsp.
- Hot water, one tsp.
- Soy sauce, one tsp.
- Mayonnaise, as required
- Bread slices, four
- Oil, for frying
- Salt, pinch
- Pepper, as required

Method:

1. Melt the Japanese soup stock in hot water, and keep it cool.
2. Mix all ingredients using a whisk.
3. Put oil thinly to a 12 cm × 12 cm heat-resistant container.
4. Wrap the container and warm one minute thirty seconds with microwave.
5. Take it out and keep it cool. Wipe off extra moisture with kitchen paper.

6. Spread the mayonnaise over one side of breads. Put on omelette and cut it into four pieces.

7. Your dish is ready to be served.

3.8 Japanese Rolled Omelette

Cooking Time: 10 minutes

Serving Size: 4

Ingredients:

- Eggs, six
- Daikon, for serving
- Soy sauce, one tsp.
- Salt, one tsp.
- Mirin, one tbsp.
- Caster sugar, one tbsp.
- Shiso leaves, as required
- Oil, for frying

Method:

1. Mix the dashi stock with mirin, sugar, soy sauce, and salt.

2. Add to the beaten eggs and stir well. Heat the omelette pan over medium heat.

3. Pour in some egg mixture and tilt the pan to coat evenly.

4. When the omelette starts to set, roll it up towards you, using a pair of chopsticks or a spatula.

5. Keep the rolled omelette in the pan and push it back to the farthest side from you.

6. Again, pour in some egg mixture into the empty side, lift up the first roll with chopsticks and let the egg mixture runs underneath.

7. When it looks half set, roll the omelette around the first roll to make a single roll with many layers.

8. Repeat the process until all egg mixture is used up.

9. Move the roll gently onto a sushi rolling mat covered with a clear sheet of plastic wrap.

10. Roll the omelette firmly into the mat and leave to sushi rolled for five minutes.

11. Grate the daikon with a daikon grater or with a very fine grater.

12. Cut the rolled omelette into one-inch slices crossways. Lay the shiso leaves on a plate and place a few pieces of omelette on top.

13. Put a small heap of grated daikon to one side and add and serve.

3.9 Hiroshima Okonomiyaki

Cooking Time: 30 minutes

Serving Size: 2

Ingredients:

- Water, two tbsps.
- Eggs, three
- Bacon, six strips
- Cabbage, 150g
- Okonomiyaki flour, half cup
- Okonomiyaki sauce, two tbsp.

- Spring onions, as required
- Bonito flakes, as required
- Yakisoba noodles, two cups
- Pickled ginger, one tsp.
- Oil, for frying
- Aonori seaweed, as required

Method:

1. Begin by chopping your green onion and cabbage. Try to chop your cabbage as finely as possible.

2. Grab a bowl and mix the okonomiyaki flour with the water, and one egg until you have a smooth batter with no lumps.

3. Now the fun part, take a frying pan or hot plate, and grease with a splash of vegetable oil and place on a medium heat.

4. Make sure the pan is evenly heated before the next step or the okonomiyaki will be difficult to be shaped.

5. Add just under half the batter to the pan in a nice even circle, remember not to make the circle too wide otherwise it will not be able to keep its shape.

6. Next, add half of the cabbage and half of the bean sprouts on top of the batter, before adding a layer of bacon.

7. Pour one tbsp. of the batter on the top of the mix to hold everything together and let the okonomiyaki cook for about ten minutes before flipping it over with a spatula to cook on the other side.

8. Grab another pan and cook one serving of yakisoba with a bit of vegetable oil and the sauce provided in the packet.

9. Once the yakisoba is cooked, with a spatula move the okonomiyaki on top of the noodles.

10. Crack an egg in a bowl and break the yolk before pouring in the first pan to the side of the okonomiyaki.

11. Place the okonomiyaki over the egg and leave to cook for two minutes.

12. Once done, flip the completed okonomiyaki over onto a plate and smother in a criss-cross pattern with okonomiyaki sauce and mayonnaise.

13. The final touch is to sprinkle the spring onion, aonori seaweed, katsuobushi and pickled ginger on the top.

3.10 Japanese Hibachi Style Fried Rice

Cooking Time: 20 minutes

Serving Size: 4

Ingredients:

- Toasted sesame oil, one tbsp.

- Salt, as required

- Ground black pepper, as required

- Eggs, two

- Cooked rice, four cups

- Soy sauce, two tbsp.

- Chopped onion, one

- Butter, four tbsp.

Method:

1. Heat a wok or large skillet over medium-high heat.

2. In a small bowl, lightly whisk together the eggs, salt, and ground black pepper.

3. Add one tablespoon of butter into the heated wok or skillet. Once the butter melts, add in the eggs and scramble until they are no longer thin but still a soft scramble.

4. Carefully remove the cooked eggs from the skillet or wok back into the small bowl. Set aside.

5. Add in another one tablespoon of butter into the heated wok or skillet. Once the butter melts, add in the chopped onion and move around in the pan until the onion is lightly coated with the butter. Allow the onion to continue to cook until it becomes translucent.

6. Add in the remaining two tablespoons of butter into the wok or skillet along with the cooked onion. Once it melts add in the cooked rice.

7. Add in the soy sauce and toasted sesame oil with the rice. Stir the rice frequently, breaking it up as needed. Once the fried rice has been heated thoroughly and has also lightly browned, add in the egg and stir to evenly distribute.

8. Serve warm with some yum sauce.

3.11 Japanese Breakfast Skillet

Cooking Time: 20 minutes

Serving Size: 2

Ingredients:

- Japanese sweet potato, half cup

- Sliced carrots, half cup

- Fresh ginger, half tsp.

- Mirin, a quarter cup

- Sliced mushrooms, one cup

- Tamari, two tbsp.

- White onions, half cup

- Sesame oil, two tbsp.

- Organic tempeh, one block

- Vegetable broth, two cups

Method:

1. In a medium pot that will fit the block of tempeh, combine the tempeh and the vegetable broth and bring to a boil.

2. Immediately reduce to heat and simmer gently for fifteen minutes. When done, dice into small cubes and set aside.

3. In a large skillet, warm the oil and then add the diced potatoes and sliced carrots. Adjust heat to medium high and cook for fifteen minutes until the vegetables have a nice, golden color to them.

4. Add in the onions and tempeh and continue sautéing for about three minutes.

5. Add the cabbage, garlic, ginger and mushrooms, then give it a quick stir. The pan should be very dry.

6. Now deglaze with the mirin and tamari.

7. Stir for a few minutes to coat everything in the glaze.

8. Your dish is ready to be served.

All the recipes mentioned above are very easy to make at home.

If you are an accomplished home cook or new to cooking, Japanese food is a delectable food to prepare at home. This rundown of essential Japanese plans is an extraordinary beginning stage for learning to cook all by yourself. It is useful to know the Japanese food technique. When you ace these, you can go for more complicated plans and procedures.

4.1 Onigiri

Cooking Time: 20 minutes

Serving Size: 3

Ingredients:

- Nori sheet, as required
- Umeboshi, one
- Soy sauce, half tsp.
- Mirin, half tsp.

- Tuna, one cup
- Japanese mayonnaise, two tbsp.
- Salted salmon, one piece
- Cooked rice, two cups

Method:

1. Cook the rice according to your rice cooker or if you do not have a rice cooker, follow the instructions here.
2. Transfer the cooked rice to a separate bowl to cool it down.
3. Prepare all the fillings that you are going to use and set aside.
4. Prepare seaweed sheet.
5. Place cling wrap over a rice bowl.
6. Place some of the cooked rice over the centre of the cling wrap.
7. Put about 1tsp of umeboshi on the centre of the rice then cover with the rice around.
8. Wrap the cling wrap over the rice and squeeze and mould the rice into a triangle shape with your hands.
9. Remove the cling wrap and cover the bottom of the rice triangle with a nori sheet.
10. Your dish is ready to be served.

4.2 Natto

Cooking Time: 20 minutes

Serving Size: 1

Ingredients:

- Scallions, for garnish
- Natto, one tbsp.
- Soy sauce, half tsp.
- Saikkyo, one and a half tsp.
- Tofu, half block
- Miso, two tbsp.
- Wakame seeds, a handful
- Dashi, two cups

Method:

1. Bring the dashi to a simmer in a soup pot and place the spoonful of natto into the liquid. Simmer for two minutes.

2. Place the miso pastes into the pot and use the back of a spoon to dissolve the pastes into the dashi.

3. Add the wakame and the tofu and simmer for 30 seconds longer.

4. Garnish with scallions.

5. Serve immediately.

4.3 Agedashi Tofu

Cooking Time: 20 minutes

Serving Size: 3

Ingredients:

- Flavoured oil, three cups
- Corn starch, four tbsp.
- Soy sauce, two tbsp.

- Katsuobishi, as required
- Tofu, one block
- Mirin, two tbsp.
- Daikon radish, as required
- Scallions, as required
- Shichimi Togarashi, a handful
- Dashi, one cup

Method:

1. Gather all the ingredients.

2. Wrap the tofu with three layers of paper towels and place another plate on top. Drain the water out of tofu for fifteen minutes.

3. Peel and grate the daikon and gently squeeze water out. Cut the green onion into thin slices.

4. Put dashi, soy sauce, and mirin in a small saucepan and bring to boil.

5. Remove the tofu from paper towels and cut it into eight pieces.

6. Coat the tofu with potato starch, leaving excess flour, and immediately deep fry until they turn light brown and crispy.

7. Remove the tofu and drain excess oil on a plate lined with paper towels or wire rack.

8. To serve, place the tofu in a serving bowl and gently pour the sauce without wetting the tofu.

9. Garnish with grated daikon, green onion, katsuobushi, and shichimi togarashi.

4.4 Nasu Dengaku

Cooking Time: 30 minutes

Serving Size: 4

Ingredients:

- Japanese eggplant, three
- Flavoured oil, one tbsp.
- Sake, two tbsp.
- Sugar, two tbsp.
- Miso, four tbsp.
- Sesame seeds, as required
- Tofu, one block
- Mirin, two tbsp.
- Daikon radish, three
- Konnyaku, a handful

Method:

1. Combine sake, mirin, sugar, and miso in a saucepan.

2. Mix well to combine and then bring to a gentle simmer over the lowest heat. Stir constantly and cook for few minutes.

3. When the miso is thickened, it is ready to use.

4. Use the miso glaze to slather on the foods you prepare below.

5. Wrap the tofu with two sheets of paper towel and press the tofu between two plates for 30 minutes.

6. Once the tofu is dried, cut it into small bite-sized pieces.

7. Cut the eggplant in half lengthwise and cut it in a crisscross pattern. This will help the eggplant absorb more flavors.

8. Immediately soak in water to prevent the eggplants from changing colors, and to remove the bitter taste. Drain and dry with a paper towel.

9. Place the tofu and eggplants on a rimmed baking sheet lined with parchment paper or silicone baking sheet. With a brush, apply vegetable oil on top and bottom of tofu and eggplants.

10. Bake at 400 degrees for twenty minutes, or until the eggplant is tender. Transfer the baking sheet to the working surface.

11. Meanwhile, carefully spoon some of the miso glaze onto your tofu and eggplants and spread evenly. Broil for five minutes, or until the top has nice char and caramelization.

12. Transfer to a serving platter, sprinkle with sesame seeds and serve immediately.

4.5 Omurice

Cooking Time: 20 minutes

Serving Size: 2

Ingredients:

- Boneless chicken, one pound
- Olive oil, one tbsp.
- Mixed vegetables, half cup
- Salt and pepper, as required
- Cooked Japanese rice, one and a half cup

- Soy sauce, one tsp.
- Ketchup, one tbsp.
- Milk, two tbsp.
- Eggs, two
- Cheese, a handful

Method:

1. Gather all the ingredients.
2. Chop the onion finely.
3. Cut the chicken.
4. Heat the oil in a non-stick pan and sauté the onion until softened.
5. Add the chicken and cook until no longer pink.
6. Add the mixed vegetables and season with salt and pepper.
7. Add the rice and break into small pieces.
8. Add ketchup and soy sauce and combine everything evenly with a spatula. Transfer the fried rice to a plate and wash the pan.
9. We will make the omelette one at a time. Whisk the egg and milk in a small bowl.
10. Heat the olive oil in the pan over medium high heat.
11. When the pan is hot, pour the egg mixture into the pan and tilt to cover the bottom of the pan. Lower the heat when the bottom of the egg is set.
12. Put the cheese and the divided fried rice on top of the omelette.

13. Use the spatula to fold both sides of omelette toward the middle to cover the fried rice. Slowly move the omurice to the edge of the pan.

14. Hold a plate in one hand and the pan in the other hand flip the pan and move the omurice to the plate.

15. While it is still hot, cover the omurice with a paper towel and shape it. Drizzle the ketchup on top for decoration.

4.6 Okonomiyaki

Cooking Time: 30 minutes

Serving Size: 4

Ingredients:

- Dashi, one cup
- Oyster sauce, one tbsp.
- Nagaimo, as required
- Salt, as required
- Flour one and a half cup
- Sugar, half tsp.
- Baking powder, half tsp.
- Sliced pork belly, half pound
- Milk, two tbsp.
- Eggs, four
- Cabbage, one

Method:

1. Mix all the batter ingredients.
2. Peel and grate nagaimo in a small bowl.

3. Add the grated nagaimo and dashi in the bowl.

4. Mix all together till combined. Cover the bowl with plastic wrap and let it rest in the refrigerator for at least an hour.

5. Cut the pork belly slices in half and set aside.

6. Take out the batter from the refrigerator and add eggs, tempura scraps, and pickled red ginger in the bowl. Mix well until well-combined.

7. Add chopped cabbage to the batter. Mix well before adding the rest.

8. In a large pan, heat vegetable oil on medium heat. Spread the batter evenly. If you are new to making okonomiyaki, make a smaller and thinner size so it is easier to flip.

9. Place the sliced pork belly on top of Okonomiyaki and cook covered for five minutes.

10. Gently press the okonomiyaki to fix the shape and keep it together. Cover and cook for another five minutes.

11. Flip over one last time and cook uncovered for two minutes. If you are going to cook next batch, transfer to a plate.

12. Serve with your preferred toppings.

4.7 Cheesy Ramen Carbonara

Cooking Time: 30 minutes

Serving Size: 4

Ingredients:

- Dashi, one cup
- Olive oil, one tbsp.

- Bacon slices, six
- Salt, as required
- Minced garlic, two
- Parsley, as required
- Parmesan cheese, half cup
- Milk, two tbsp.
- Eggs, two
- Ramen pack, three

Method:

1. Combine all the ingredients.
2. Boil noodles according to package instructions.
3. Save a quarter cup of cooking water to loosen sauce later, if needed. Drain noodles and toss with olive oil so that they do not stick.
4. Heat medium skillet over medium heat. Cook bacon pieces until brown and crisp. Add the noodles to the skillet and toss with the bacon until the noodles are coated in the bacon fat.
5. Beat eggs with fork and mix in parmesan cheese. Pour egg-cheese mixture to skillet and toss with bacon and noodles.
6. Divide between bowls. Garnish with parsley and freshly ground pepper.

4.8 Yakisoba

Cooking Time: 30 minutes

Serving Size: 4

Ingredients:

- Fish sauce, two tbsp.
- Egg, one
- Soy sauce, half cup
- Cooked Japanese rice, three cups
- Tomatoes, two
- Cilantro, half cup
- Salt and pepper, to taste
- Vegetable oil, two tbsp.
- Japanese chili peppers, three
- Toasted walnuts, half cup
- Chicken breast, eight ounces
- Onion, one
- Scallions, half cup
- Minced garlic, one tsp.

Instructions:

1. Heat a large nonstick pan over high heat.
2. Meanwhile, season chicken lightly with salt and pepper.
3. When the wok is very hot, add two tsp of the oil.
4. When the oil is hot, add the chicken and cook on high until it is browned all over and cooked through.
5. Remove chicken and set aside, add the eggs, pinch of salt and cook a minute or two until done.
6. Add the remaining oil to the wok and add the onion, scallions and garlic.

7. Sauté for a minute, add the chili pepper if using, tomatoes and stir in all the rice.

8. Add the soy sauce and fish sauce stir to mix all the ingredients.

9. Keep stirring a few minutes, and then add egg and chicken back to the wok.

10. Adjust soy sauce if needed and stir well for another 30 seconds.

11. Your dish is ready to be served.

4.9 Baked chicken Katsu

Cooking Time: 25 minutes

Serving Size: 4

Ingredients:

- Boneless chicken breast pieces, one pound
- Panko, one cup
- All-purpose flour, half cup
- Water, one tbsp.
- Egg, one
- Salt and pepper, to taste
- Tonkatsu sauce, as required

Instructions:

1. Gather all the ingredients. Adjust an oven rack to the middle position and preheat the oven to 400 degrees. Line a rimmed baking sheet with parchment paper.

2. Combine the panko and oil in a frying pan and toast over medium heat until golden brown. Transfer panko into a shallow dish and allow to cool down.

3. Butterfly the chicken breast and cut in half. Using a mallet or rolling pin, pound the chicken to equal thickness if necessary. Season salt and pepper on both sides of the chicken.

4. In a shallow dish, add flour and in another shallow dish, whisk together the egg and water.

5. Coat each chicken piece in the flour and shake off any excess flour. Dip into the egg mixture and then coat with the toasted panko, pressing firmly to adhere to the chicken.

6. Place the chicken pieces on the prepared baking sheet for about twenty minutes. Serve immediately or transfer to a wire rack so the bottom of the katsu does not get soggy from the moisture.

7. Serve with salad and tonkatsu sauce on the side.

4.10 Hayashi Ground Beef Curry

Cooking Time: 15 minutes

Serving Size: 2

Ingredients:

- Onion, one
- Carrots, half cup
- Ground beef, half pound
- Canola oil, one tbsp.
- Ketchup, two tbsp.
- Salt and pepper, to taste
- Corn starch, one tsp.
- Beef broth, one cup

- Sake, one tbsp.
- Boiled egg, one
- Worcestershire sauce, one tbsp.

Instructions:

1. Slice onion half. One half will be for frying; the other will go in with the dry curry.
2. Slice one half into thin half-moons. Finely chop the other one.
3. Boil egg and cut into small pieces or mash with a fork. Season well with salt and pepper.
4. Heat oil and add onions and carrots.
5. Sprinkle corn starch on top of ground beef and add to the vegetables. Add a quarter cup beef broth and break the ground beef while stirring.
6. Add beef broth, ketchup, sake, and Worcestershire sauce.
7. Mix well and cook for ten minutes or until all the liquid has evaporated. Season with salt and pepper.
8. Fry onions in a separate pan until crispy.
9. Put rice on a plate, top with curry, eggs and fried onions.

4.11 Ramen Noodle Skillet with Steak

Cooking Time: 15 minutes

Serving Size: 2

Ingredients:

- Onion, one
- Carrots, half cup

- Ground beef, half pound
- Canola oil, one tbsp.
- Ketchup, two tbsp.
- Salt and pepper, to taste
- Corn starch, one tsp.
- Beef broth, one cup
- Sake, one tbsp.
- Boiled egg, one
- Worcestershire sauce, one tbsp.

Instructions:

1. In a large skillet over medium-high heat, heat oil.

2. Add steak and sear until your desired completion, about five minutes per side for medium, then transfer to a cutting board and let it rest for five minutes, and then slice it.

3. In a small bowl, whisk together soy sauce, garlic, lime juice, honey, and cayenne until combined and set aside.

4. Add onion, peppers, and broccoli to skillet and cook until tender, then add soy sauce mixture and stir until fully coated.

5. Add cooked ramen noodles and steak and toss until combined.

6. Your dish is ready to be served.

4.12 Chicken Teriyaki

Cooking Time: 15 minutes

Serving Size: 2

Ingredients:

- Sesame oil, one tsp.
- Broccoli, for serving
- Honey, one tbsp.
- Ketchup, two tbsp.
- Salt and pepper, to taste
- Corn starch, one tsp.
- Cooked white rice, one cup
- Garlic and ginger, one tbsp.
- Boiled egg, one
- Soy sauce, one tbsp.

Instructions:

1. In a medium bowl, whisk together soy sauce, rice vinegar, oil, honey, garlic, ginger, and corn starch.

2. In a large skillet over medium heat, heat oil. Add chicken to skillet and season with salt and pepper. Cook until golden and almost cooked through.

3. Cover chicken and simmer until sauce is thickened slightly and chicken is cooked through.

4. Garnish with sesame seeds and green onions.

5. Serve over rice with steamed broccoli.

4.13 Japanese Salmon Bowl

Cooking Time: 30 minutes

Serving Size: 4

Ingredients:

- Chili sauce, one tsp.

- Soy sauce, one tsp.
- Rice, two cups
- Sesame oil, one tbsp.
- Ginger, two tbsp.
- Salt and pepper, to taste
- Sesame seeds, one tsp.
- Vinegar, one tsp.
- Shredded nori, as required
- Salmon, half pound
- Shredded cabbage, one cup

Instructions:

1. Place the rice, three cups of water and half teaspoon of salt in a large pot and bring to the boil.

2. Reduce the heat to low, place the lid on top and cook for fifteen minutes or until water is absorbed.

3. Remove from heat and let stand covered for five minutes.

4. Place the vinegar, soy sauce, chilli sauce, sesame oil, sesame seeds and ginger in a bowl and mix well.

5. Add the salmon and gently stir until completely coated.

6. Place the shredded cabbage and sesame oil in a bowl and mix until well combined.

7. Place a large spoonful of rice in each bowl, add the cabbage and squeeze over the mayonnaise.

8. Garnish with toasted shredded nori and toasted sesame seeds.

4.14 Scattered Sushi Rice/Chirashi-zushi

Cooking Time: 30 minutes

Serving Size: 4

Ingredients:

- Japanese rice, two cups
- Rice vinegar, a quarter cup
- Salt, one tsp.
- Sugar, two tbsp.
- Shitake mushrooms, eight
- Sashimi, half pound
- Eggs, three
- Mirin, one tsp.
- Sesame seeds, as required
- Tuna, half pound

Instructions:

1. Combine the ingredients.

2. Put rice in a large bowl and wash it with cold water. Repeat washing until the water becomes almost clear. Drain the rice in a colander and set aside for thirty minutes.

3. Place the rice in a rice cooker and add about two cups of water. Let the rice soak in the water for at least thirty minutes. Start the cooker.

4. In a small saucepan, mix rice vinegar, sugar, and salt. Put the pan on low heat and heat until the sugar dissolves. Cool the vinegar mixture.

5. Spread the hot steamed rice into a large plate or a large bowl. Sprinkle the vinegar mixture over the rice and quickly mix into the rice using a shamoji.

6. Meanwhile, remove stems from shiitake and slice thinly. Heat half cup of the reserved water used for rehydrating shiitake in a medium pan.

7. Add shiitake, soy sauce, sugar, and mirin. Simmer shiitake on low heat until the liquid is almost gone.

8. Make the omelettes by beating eggs in a bowl with sugar.

9. Oil a medium skillet and pour a scoop of egg mixture and make a thin omelette.

10. Serve sushi rice on a large plate or individual bowls.

11. Spread simmered shiitake, cucumber, imitation crab meat, and omelette strips over rice. Place tuna sashimi on top. Garnish with sesame seeds.

4.15 Broiled Shrimp and Vegetables/ Kushiyaki

Cooking Time: 10 minutes

Serving Size: 4

Ingredients:

- Lime juice, three tbsp.
- Shrimp, two pounds
- Salt and pepper, to taste
- Chili, one tbsp.
- Mix vegetables, one cup
- Sashimi, half pound
- Eggs, three

- Mirin, one tsp.
- Sesame seeds, as required

Instructions:

1. Marinate the shrimp with the spices, lime juice and olive oil.
2. Meanwhile, chop and slice the veggies.
3. Add one tablespoon of olive oil in a skillet and bring to medium heat.
4. Sauté the veggies until they obtain a golden colour and are tender. Remove and set aside in a bowl.
5. In the same skillet, sauté the shrimp until they are fully cooked. Then return the cookies veggies to the skillet, and sauté with the shrimps for two minutes.
6. Remove and serve.

4.16 Chicken in a Pot/Mizutaki

Cooking Time: 10 minutes

Serving Size: 4

Ingredients:

- Negi, one
- Mizuna, four
- Napa cabbage, eight
- Carrot, half cup
- Chicken thighs, one pound
- Kombu, half pound
- Sake, one tsp.
- Ginger, one tsp.

- Sesame seeds, as required

Instructions:

1. Mix all the ingredients.

2. In a large bowl, add five cups of water, and kombu to make cold brew kombu dashi. Set aside while you prepare the chicken.

3. Fill a medium pot with water and add the bone-in, skin-on chicken thigh pieces. Turn the heat on medium-low.

4. Bring the water to a boil and cook for one minute and discard the water.

5. Rinse the chicken, especially around the bone area, under lukewarm water.

6. In the cold brew kombu dashi, add the chicken thigh pieces you just rinsed.

7. Also add the chicken pieces sake, and ginger.

8. Bring it to a boil over medium heat.

9. Reduce the heat to medium-low and cook covered for thirty minutes. During this time, start preparing other ingredients. After thirty minutes, remove and discard the ginger slices.

10. Your dish is ready to be served.

Regardless of the season, most Japanese meals are served with a salad to keep things in balance. A well-composed salad refreshes your palate, provides a pop of colour, and its crisp flavours enhance everything else on the table.

5.1 Japanese cucumber Salad (Sunomo)

Cooking Time: 10 minutes

Serving Size: 8

Ingredients:

- Peanuts, half cup
- Soy sauce, three tbsp.
- Sesame oil, one tsp.
- Sugar, one tbsp.
- Wine vinegar, three tbsp.
- Small cucumber, twelve ounces

- Garlic, one

- Fresh cilantro, as required

Instructions:

1. Whisk the dressing together and be sure to taste it to adjust anything you like.

2. Finely grind the peanuts in a food processor using the pulsing button. You want them to be very fine but be careful not to go too far and turn them into peanut butter.

3. Thinly slice the cucumbers in the diagonal shape.

4. If you would like to remove part of the peel first, you can run a zesting tool down the sides, or simply run the tines of a fork down the sides to create a decorative edge.

5. Put the cucumbers in a bowl and toss with enough dressing to coat thoroughly, you may not need all of it.

6. Toss with the crushed peanuts, sprinkle with chili flakes, and top with cilantro leaves.

7. Serve immediately or chill until ready to serve.

5.2 Japanese Watercess Salad

Cooking Time: 10 minutes

Serving Size: 2

Ingredients:

- Peanut butter, three tbsp.

- Rice vinegar, one tbsp.

- Honey, one tsp.

- Sugar, one tbsp.

- Wine vinegar, three tbsp.
- Watercress, six cups
- Mirin, two tbsp.

Instructions:

1. In a medium size pot, bring water, salted with one tablespoon kosher salt, to boil.
2. Put the peanut butter, honey, rice vinegar, soy sauce, and mirin in a medium bowl.
3. Rinse the watercress, drain and separate the leaves from the stems.
4. Roughly chop the stems and add to the boiling water along with the leaves.
5. Cook until the stems are tender but yielding a soft crunch.
6. Drain, rinse under cold water and softly squeeze out excess water.
7. Gently pat the watercress, dry with a paper towel and add to a mixing bowl.
8. Pour the dressing over the watercress and toss until the watercress is evenly coated.

5.3 Kani Salad

Cooking Time: 10 minutes

Serving Size: 4

Ingredients:

- Carrot, one medium
- Cucumber, two medium sized
- Ripe mango, one cup

- Japanese mayonnaise, one tbsp.
- Half lemon
- Salt and pepper to taste
- Kani, 150 g

Instructions:

1. Peel the carrots and trim off the ends.

2. Do the same with the cucumber but do not include the core with seeds.

3. Shred the crab sticks by hand by gently pressing a piece from end to end to loosen the strips and then separate each strip from one another.

4. Peel the ripe mango.

5. In a large bowl, add the cucumber, carrots, Kani, mango and Japanese mayo. Squeeze the juices of half a lemon on top and toss.

6. Season with salt and pepper as needed, and give it another toss until all ingredients are well blended.

7. Serve immediately or refrigerate until ready.

8. Serve on top of a layer of iceberg or romaine lettuce.

5.4 Oshitashi

Cooking Time: 5 minutes

Serving Size: 1

Ingredients:

- Spinach, one pound
- Sesame seeds, one tbsp.
- Soy sauce, one tbsp.

- Mirin, one tbsp.

Instructions:

1. Toast the sesame seeds in a skillet until lightly coloured.

2. Add the spinach to a large saucepan of boiling water and cook two to three minutes until wilted.

3. Have an ice bath ready.

4. Drain the spinach in a colander.

5. Squeeze dry and place in a bowl.

6. Mix the cooked spinach with the soy sauce, mirin and sesame seeds.

7. Serve at room temperature.

5.5 Japanese Cabbage Salad

Cooking Time: 5 minutes

Serving Size: 1

Ingredients:

- Coleslaw mix, one cup

- Sesame seeds, one tbsp.

- Soy sauce, one tbsp.

- Mirin, one tbsp.

- Bonito flakes, as required

Instructions:

1. Mix all the ingredients for the dressing together in a bowl and pour it over the shredded coleslaw mix.

2. Toss well and top with sesame seeds and bonito flakes.

5.6 Ramen Noodle Salad

Cooking Time: 15 minutes

Serving Size: 1

Ingredients:

- Cabbage and onion, one cup
- Sesame seeds, one tbsp.
- Soy sauce, one tbsp.
- Sugar, one tbsp.
- Vinegar, one tbsp.
- Butter, as required
- Ramen noodles, one pack
- Almonds, as required

Instructions:

1. Combine the oil, vinegar, sugar, and soy sauce in a jar and shake until the sugar is dissolved.

2. Melt the butter in a large skillet over medium heat. While the butter is melting, crush the ramen noodles while still inside the package.

3. Remove the seasoning packet and throw away.

4. Add the noodles, almonds, and sesame seeds to the melted butter in the skillet.

5. Sauté while stirring frequently, until the noodle mixture is golden brown.

6. Shred the cabbage and combine the cabbage and onions in a large mixing bowl. Add the noodle mixture.

7. Pour the dressing over the salad and toss well to combine.

8. Serve immediately.

5.7 Pork Chimichurri Salad

Cooking Time: 15 minutes

Serving Size: 2

Ingredients:

- Pork chops, one pound
- Greens, six ounces
- Cherry tomatoes, two cups
- Olive oil, one tbsp.
- Vinegar, one tbsp.
- Parsley, as required
- Chipotle, half
- Oregano leaves, as required
- Salt and pepper, as required
- Chimichurri dressing, per taste

Instructions:

1. In a food processor, combine olive oil, vinegar, parsley, oregano leaves, and chipotle. Season with salt and pepper and set aside.

2. Preheat a broiler. Line a rimmed baking sheet with foil and spray with cooking oil.

3. Place pork on the baking sheet and sprinkle both sides with salt and pepper. Broil until internal temperature reaches 145 degrees, five minutes per side. Remove pork from broiler and let it rest for five minutes.

4. Meanwhile, in a large bowl, combine greens, cherry tomatoes, cheese, and chimichurri dressing to taste. Arrange salad on plates or a platter.

5. Arrange on top of salad, drizzle with additional dressing, and serve.

5.8 Spring Green Salad

Cooking Time: 30 minutes

Serving Size: 4

Ingredients:

- Salad potatoes, half pound
- Petits pois, half cup
- Asparagus, half cup
- Olive oil, four tbsp.
- Pumpkin seeds, one tbsp.
- Spring onions, four
- Baby courgettes, one cup
- Whole grain mustard, as required
- Salt and pepper, as required
- Honey, per taste
- Lemon juice, as required

Instructions:

1. To make the dressing, put all the ingredients in a small food processor or blender and process until smooth and emulsified. Season well.

2. Cook the potatoes in lightly salted boiling water for ten minutes, or until just tender, adding the petits pois for the last two minutes.

3. Drain and place in a wide, shallow serving bowl.

4. Heat a large griddle pan or heavy-based frying pan until hot. Add a tablespoon of olive oil and add the asparagus in a single layer.

5. Cook for five minutes, or until lightly charred. Remove from the pan and add to the potato mixture.

6. Wipe out the pan and add the remaining olive oil. When hot, add the courgettes, sliced side down, and cook for five minutes, or until lightly charred. Add to the potato mixture with the lettuce and spring onions.

7. Stir the dressing then pour over the salad and mix well. Scatter over the pumpkin seeds and serve.

5.9 Japanese Corn Salad

Cooking Time: 30 minutes

Serving Size: 4

Ingredients:

- Mayonnaise, one tbsp.

- Cabbage, one

- Corn, half cup

- Sugar, one tbsp.

- Salt and pepper, as per taste

- Ground sesame seeds, two tbsp.

Instructions:

1. Shred the cabbage and drain the excess water. To allow a nice texture, do not shred it too thinly.

2. To prepare the dressing, mix the ingredients together.

3. In another bowl, mix the cabbage and corn. Add the dressing and you are done.

4. Add the dressing right before serving as the cabbage tends to get watery.

5. Your dish is ready to be served.

The Japanese cuisine contains a variety of healthy and nutritious soups that are loved by many people all over the world. Following are the yummy and easy to make soup recipes that you can try on your own.

6.1 Miso soup

Cooking Time: 15 minutes

Serving Size: 4

Ingredients:

- Water, four cups
- Miso paste, three tbsp.
- Green onions, two
- Dashi granules, two tbsp.
- Tofu, one block

Instructions:

1. In a medium saucepan over medium-high heat, combine dashi granules and water; bring to a boil.

2. Reduce heat to medium, and whisk in the miso paste, and then stir in tofu.

3. Separate the layers of the green onions, and add them to the soup.

4. Simmer gently for a few minutes before serving.

5. Your soup is ready to be served.

6.2 Ochazuke

Cooking Time: 5 minutes

Serving Size: 1

Ingredients:

- Dashi, one tbsp.
- Soy sauce, one tsp.
- Japanese green tea leaves, one
- Water, one cup
- Salt and pepper to taste
- Mirin, one tsp.

Instructions:

1. Combine all the ingredients in a small saucepan and bring it to a boil.

2. Pour the soup into a small teapot.

3. Put tea leaves in the pot.

4. Bring the water to the appropriate temperature for your tea and pour it into the pot.

5. Set aside for two minutes.

6. Your soup is ready to be served.

6.3 Ozoni

Cooking Time: 20 minutes

Serving Size: 4

Ingredients:

- Dashi, one cup
- Soy sauce, one tbsp.
- Sake, one tbsp.
- Chicken strips, one pound
- Water, two cups
- Salt and pepper to taste

Instructions:

1. Mix all the ingredients together and let it simmer.

2. Your soup is ready to be served.

6.4 Japanese Clear Onions Soup

Cooking Time: one hour

Serving Size: 5

Ingredients:

- Vegetable oil, two tbsp.
- Onion, one
- Carrot, one cup
- Garlic and ginger paste, one tbsp.
- Chicken broth, one cup

- Beef broth, one cup
- Salt and pepper as required

Instructions:

1. Place a large stock pot over medium-high heat.

2. Add the oil and place the onion, garlic, carrots, and ginger in the pot.

3. Sear the veggies on all sides to caramelize, making sure not to burn the garlic.

4. Pour in the chicken broth, beef broth, and water.

5. Bring to a boil.

6. Lower the heat to a low boil and simmer for at least one hour.

7. Use a skimmer to remove the vegetables from the broth.

8. Taste, then adjust salt as needed.

9. Your dish is ready to be served.

6.5 Wonton Dumplings Soup

Preparation time: 12 minutes

Cooking Time: 30 minutes

Serving: 6

Ingredients:

- Wonton wrappers, twenty-four
- Finely chopped scallion, one tsp.
- Finely chopped ginger, one tsp.
- Soy sauce, one tbsp.
- Brown sugar, one tsp.

- Chicken breast, shredded, two
- Fresh spinach, one cup
- Shrimp, one pound
- Water chestnuts, eight ounces
- Mushroom, sliced, one cup
- Rice wine, one tbsp.
- Ground pork, eight ounces

Instructions:

1. Bring chicken stock to a rolling boil, and then add all the ingredients.
2. Cook until chicken and shrimps are cooked through, for about 10 minutes.
3. In a bowl, mix the pork, ground shrimp, brown sugar, rice wine or sherry, soy sauce, scallions and chopped ginger.
4. Blend well and set aside for 25-30 minutes for flavors to blend.
5. Add one tsp. of the filling in the center of each wonton wrapper.
6. Wet the edges of each wonton with a little water and press them together with your fingers to seal.
7. To cook, add wontons to the boiling chicken stock and cook for 4-5 minutes.
8. Transfer to individual soup bowls and serve.

6.6 Kimchi and Tofu Soup

Cooking Time: 20 minutes

Serving Size: 2

Ingredients:

- Vegetable oil, one tbsp.
- Scallions, six
- Kimchi, half cup
- Chicken broth, one cup
- Soy sauce, three tbsp.
- Salt and pepper, as per taste
- Garlic and ginger paste, one tbsp.
- Tofu, one block
- Daikon, one

Instructions:

1. Heat oil in a large saucepan over high.
2. Cook white and pale-green parts of scallions, garlic, and ginger, stirring often, until softened and fragrant, about three minutes.
3. Add broth, then whisk in the soy sauce.
4. Add daikon and gently simmer until daikon is tender, fifteen minutes.
5. Add kimchi and tofu.
6. Simmer until tofu is heated through.
7. Carefully divide among bowls.
8. Your soup is ready to be served.

6.7 Shio Koji Mushroom Soup

Cooking Time: 20 minutes

Serving Size: 2

Ingredients:

- Soup stock, two cups
- Different mushrooms, two cups
- Salt and pepper to taste
- Shio koji, two tbsp.

Instructions:

1. Slice the mushrooms into thin slices or pieces and boil in plenty of water for about two mins.
2. Drain and add the shio koji seasoning to the hot mushrooms.
3. Wait about fifteen minutes for the flavours to develop.
4. In another saucepan, bring soup stock to the boil.
5. Add the mushrooms and salt and allow everything to heat through.
6. Spoon into bowls and serve with some nice crusty bread.

6.8 Yudofu

Cooking Time: 15 minutes

Serving Size: 2

Ingredients:

- Tofu, one block
- Mitsuba, as required
- Sake, one tbsp.
- Mirin, one tsp.
- Vegetable stock, three cups
- Water, one cup

Instructions:

1. Mix all the ingredients well and let it simmer for fifteen minutes.

2. Your soup is ready to be served.

6.9 Ojiya Rice Soup

Cooking Time: 20 minutes

Serving Size: 2

Ingredients:

- Japanese rice, one cup
- Vegetable stock, two cups
- Mixed vegetable, one cup
- Soy sauce, one tsp.
- Mirin, half tsp.
- Salt and pepper, to taste
- Water, two cups

Instructions:

1. Mix all the ingredients well and let it simmer for fifteen minutes.

2. Your soup is ready to be served.

6.10 Oshiruko Sweet Red Bean Soup

Cooking Time: 20 minutes

Serving Size: 3

Ingredients:

- Azuki sweet red beans, one cup

- Mochi rice cakes, four
- Vegetable stock, four cups

Instructions:

1. Start by adding the azuki and one cup for water to a large pan and bring it to the boil. You can adjust the amount of water depending if you prefer a thick or thin soup.

2. You can cook the mochi in a variety of ways, but grilling them gives great results so place the mochi under a hot grill for five to ten minutes.

3. Once the mochi begin expanding in the grill, they are ready and can be put into serving bowls.

4. After the azuki and water mix is boiled, take it off the heat and pour over the mochi in the serving bowls and enjoy.

6.11 Bean Paste Soup

Cooking Time: 15 minutes

Serving Size: 2

Ingredients:

- Bean paste, five tbsp.
- Vegetable soup, two cups
- Soy sauce, one tsp.
- Mirin, one tsp.
- Salt and pepper to taste

Instructions:

1. Mix all the ingredients well and let it simmer for fifteen minutes.

2. Your soup is ready to be served.

6.12 Egg Drop Soup

Cooking Time: 30 minutes

Serving: 6

Ingredients:

- Cornstarch, two tbsp.
- Eggs, two
- Green Onions, chopped, three
- Ginger, grated, half tsp.
- Water, two tbsp.
- Chicken broth, four cups
- Soy Sauce, one tbsp.

Instructions:

1. Mix all the ingredients together, and boil it for about thirty minutes.

2. Add the cornstarch in the end, and mix properly.

3. Your soup is ready to be served.

Japanese snacks are appreciated worldwide for the variety of snacks. The tastes are unique and also healthy. Following are some amazing snack recipes that you can try at home.

7.1 Japanese Summer Sandwiches

Cooking Time: 5 minutes

Serving: 2

Ingredients:

- Bread slices, six

- Strawberry, one cup

- Whipped cream, one cup

Instructions:

1. First you should prepare your bread.

2. Either whip half cup of whipping cream in a bowl until stiff and spread evenly on the bread.

3. Next, wash, cut off the stems and chop each strawberry in half down the middle.

4. Your sandwich is ready to be served.

7.2 Fresh Spring Rolls with Japanese Style Sauce

Cooking Time: 20 minutes

Serving: 4

Ingredients:

- Prawns, half pound
- Green beans, one cup
- Mint or coriander leaves, as required
- Rice paper wrapper, twelve
- Spring onion, half cup
- Mayonnaise, two tbsp.
- Bean chili paste, one tsp.
- Miso paste, one tsp.

Instructions:

1. Fill a small saucepan with some water and add a little salt.

2. Add the prawns and boil until they are bright pink for about five mins.

3. In a separate saucepan, boil the green beans for five mins.

4. Lay the rice paper on clean cloth.

5. Arrange the mint or coriander leaves on the bottom of the rice paper and add the prawn halves in the middle.

6. Top with the green beans and one whole chives or spring onion.

7. Sprinkle a little salt on top to taste.

8. Fold the sides in and tightly roll to ensure all ingredients are inside.

9. Make the dipping sauce by mixing all the ingredients together.

10. Serve spring rolls with the dipping sauce as a snack or side.

7.3 Karaage Japanese Fried Chicken

Cooking Time: 30 minutes

Serving: 6

Ingredients:

- Soy sauce, three tbsp.

- Boneless Chicken thighs, one pound

- Sake, one tbsp.

- Gaelic and ginger paste, one tsp.

- Katakuriko potato starch, a quarter cup

- Japanese mayonnaise, as required

- Cooking oil, as required

Instructions:

1. Cut chicken into bite-size pieces.

2. Add the ginger, garlic, soy sauce and cooking sake to a bowl and mix until combined.

3. Add the chicken, coat well, and allow marinating for twenty minutes.

4. Drain any excess liquid from the chicken and add your katakuriko potato starch. Mix until the pieces are fully coated.

5. Heat some cooking oil in a pan to around 180 degrees and test the temperature by dropping in some flour.

6. Fry a few pieces at a time for a few minutes until they are deep golden-brown colour, then remove and allow to drain on a wire rack or kitchen roll.

7. Serve hot or cold with some lemon wedges and a squeeze of Japanese mayonnaise.

7.4 Tazukuri Candied Sardines

Cooking Time: 15 minutes

Serving: 4

Ingredients:

- Toasted sesame seeds, one tbsp.
- Honey, one tbsp.
- Soy sauce, one tbsp.
- Sugar, one tbsp.
- Honey, one tbsp.
- Flavored oi, one tbsp.
- Sake, one tsp.
- Baby sardines, one cup

Instructions:

1. Gather all the ingredients. You will also need a baking sheet lined with parchment paper.

2. Put dried baby sardines in a frying pan, and toast them on medium-low heat for a few minutes or until crispy.

3. Add the sesame seeds in the frying pan and toast for two minutes.

4. Make sure to shake the pan constantly so the sesame seeds do not burn.

5. In the same frying pan, add sake, soy sauce, and sugar.

6. Add honey and oil.

7. Bring to a simmer on medium-low heat and reduce the sauce until the sauce gets thicken and you can draw a line on the surface of the pan with a silicone spatula.

8. Add the sardines back to the pan and coat with the sauce.

9. Once the sardines are coated with the sauce nicely, transfer back to the parchment paper.

10. Your dish is ready to be served.

7.5 Kuromame Sweetened Black Soybean

Cooking Time: 4 hours

Serving: 8

Ingredients:

- Water, five cups

- Sugar, two tbsp.

- Soy sauce, one tbsp.

- Edible gold leaf flakes, as required

- Black soybeans, one cup

- Kosher salt, as required

Instructions:

1. Gather all the ingredients.

2. Rinse black soybeans under running water and discard bad ones.

3. Put black soybeans and water in a large pot and let it soak overnight.

4. After being soaked, add sugar and salt and gently mix.

5. Start cooking over medium heat. Once boiling, you start to see white bubbles. When it is done, put an Otoshibuta and a regular pot lid.

6. The otoshibuta is to keep the soybeans under the cooking liquid.

7. Reduce heat to low and simmer for four hours or until the beans are tender.

8. Check inside the pot a few times to make sure there is enough cooking liquid.

9. Check if the beans are tender by mashing a bean with two fingers.

10. When the means are tender, add soy sauce and mix well.

11. Remove from the heat and place the parchment paper on top of the surface to prevent the beans from getting wrinkles.

12. Once cooled, keep in the refrigerator overnight so the soybeans will turn darker and absorb more flavour.

13. Your dish is ready to be served.

7.6 Takoyaki Octopus Balls

Cooking Time: 30 minutes

Serving: 6

Ingredients:

- Dashi stock powder, one tbsp.
- Eggs, two
- Flour, half cup
- Chopped boiled octopus, half cup
- Chopped spring onion, half cup
- Water, as required
- Tempura flakes, half tsp.
- Red picked ginger, half tsp.

Instructions:

1. Grab a large bowl and mix together eggs, flour, water and a little dashi stock.

2. Place your takoyaki plate on the gas stove on medium heat and heat up a small amount of oil in each hole.

3. Cut up your octopus into small pieces.

4. Place a piece of octopus in each of the semi-circular holes, and then fill up each hole to the top with the batter mix.

5. Now you can add the chopped spring onion, red pickled ginger and tempura flakes to each hole.

6. Once the takoyaki are about half cooked, you will need to flip them over.

7. Usually, you can only flip each takoyaki about three quarters of the way round so allow it to cook a little more before flipping it again.

8. Place a few takoyaki on a plate and smother them with loads of takoyaki sauce and Japanese mayonnaise.

9. Your dish is ready to be served.

7.7 Yakitori Grilled Skewers

Cooking Time: 10 minutes

Serving: 12

Ingredients:

- Teriyaki sauce, half cup

- Green shallots, two

- Chicken thigh, two pounds

Instructions:

1. Heat teriyaki sauce in a small saucepan medium-high heat. Bring to simmer and reduce to thicken the sauce.

2. Cut the white end part of the shallots into long pieces.

3. Prepare the skewers.

4. Preheat the BBQ grill and coat with olive oil.

5. Place the yakitori chicken skewers on the grill side to cook the chicken till browned.

6. Turn the skewers over and cook till other side browned or chicken meat change whitish colour.

7. Brush the Teriyaki sauce over the chicken skewers. When one side is coated, turn the skewers over and Brush Yakitori sauce over the side.

8. Repeat the above process one more time then turn the heat off.

9. Serve the yakitori skewers on rice or serve with green salad.

7.8 Sweet Ginger Meatballs

Cooking Time: 30 minutes

Serving: 4

Ingredients:

- Ginger and garlic paste, one tbsp.
- Eggs, one
- Ground turkey, one pound
- Sesame oil, half tsp.
- Soy sauce, four tbsp.
- Bread crumbs, half cup
- Hoisin, two tbsp.
- Diced scallions, as required
- Sesame seeds, as required

Instructions:

1. Pre-heat oven to 400 degrees and lightly grease a large baking sheet.

2. In a large bowl, add turkey, garlic, ginger, and mix well.

3. Then add egg, panko, sesame oil, and soy sauce, and mix well.

4. Roll out the meatballs and place on baking sheet.

5. Bake for ten mins and then rotate pan and bake for another ten minutes.

6. Heat a large sauté pan to medium.

7. Transfer meatballs to a large sauté pan that will fit them all.

8. In a small bowl mix the remaining soy sauce and hoisin.

9. Coat and turn meatballs in sauce as it bubbles and thickens and let cook for a couple of minutes.

10. Remove meatballs, add to a bowl and pour remaining sauce on meatballs.

11. Serve as an appetizer or over a layer of rice.

7.9 Satsuma Age Fried Fish Cake with Vegetables

Cooking Time: 30 minutes

Serving: 4

Ingredients:

- Sugar, two tbsp.
- Eggs, one
- Fish fillet, one pound
- Salt, as required
- Ginger juice, half tsp.

- Water, two tbsp.
- Mix vegetables, two cups
- Soy Sauce, one tbsp.

Instructions:

1. Cut fish fillet into small pieces so that it is easier to make paste in a food processor.
2. Add fish pieces, sake, ginger juice, salt and sugar to a food processor and whizz until the mixture becomes paste.
3. Add egg to the fish paste and blend well.
4. Add all the vegetable mixture in a large bowl and mix well ensuring that vegetable pieces are evenly coated with corn flour.
5. This will allow the vegetables to stick to the paste better.
6. Add the fish paste to the bowl and mix well.
7. Heat oil in a deep-frying pan or a skillet to 170 degrees.
8. Take the fish cake mixture and make a ball.
9. Fry until bottom side of the fish cake is golden brown.
10. Turn it over to cook until golden brown.
11. Remove the fish cake and drain oil on a rack or kitchen paper.
12. Serve while hot or at room temperature with lemon wedges, or grated ginger.

7.10 Sweet and Salty Nori Seaweed Popcorn

Cooking Time: 30 minutes

Serving: 6

Ingredients:

- Black sesame seeds, one tbsp.

- Brown sugar, one tbsp.

- Salt, half tsp.

- Coconut oil, half tsp.

- Popcorn kernel, half cup

- Butter, two tbsp.

- Nori seaweed flakes, one tbsp.

Instructions:

1. In a pestle and mortar, grind the nori seaweed flakes, sesame seeds, sugar and salt to a fine powder.

2. Melt the coconut oil in a large, heavy-bottomed saucepan.

3. Add popcorn kernels, cover with a lid and cook over a medium heat until they pop.

4. Immediately add the rest of the corn after the corn is popped, replace the lid and cook, shaking the pan occasionally until all the kernels are popped.

5. Transfer the popped corn to a large bowl and pour over the melted butter, if using.

6. Sprinkle over your sweet and salty nori mixture and use your hands to mix well until every piece is coated.

7. Top with the remaining sesame seeds.

Japanese cuisine is famous for its amazing dessert ranges. Here in this section where we will discuss the yummiest dessert recipes of Japan.

8.1 Kinako Dango

Cooking Time: 5 minutes

Serving: 4

Ingredients:

- Kinako, half cup
- Granulated sugar, two tbsp.
- Cold water, half cup
- Dango powder, one cup
- Kosher salt, half tsp.

Instructions:

1. In a mixing bowl add Dango powder and water. Mix well until well combined.
2. Grab a little dough and shape into a ball.
3. Lay it on a plate and repeat until all the dough is used.
4. Set aside a bowl of cold water.
5. Add dango balls to boiling water and boil until they rise to the top.
6. Drain and add to cold water. Leave for a few minutes until they cool down and drain.
7. In another mixing bowl, add kinako, sugar and salt, and mix well.
8. Put a half of the kinako mixture in a serving bowl, add dango balls, and top with leftover kinako.
9. Your meal is ready to be served.

8.2 Japanese Style Pumpkin Pudding

Cooking Time: 25 minutes

Serving: 2

Ingredients:

- Pumpkin puree, one cup
- Sugar, three tbsp.
- Vanilla extract, one tsp.
- Eggs, two
- Gelatin powder, two tbsp.
- Maple syrup, as required

Instructions:

1. Dissolve the gelatin powder with the milk.

2. Meanwhile, put the pumpkin puree and sugar in a bowl, stir, and microwave on high for thirty seconds.

3. Stir in the milk and gelatin mix and add it to the pumpkin and sugar. Stir in the eggs and vanilla extract and combine well.

4. Get rid of the unblended bits left in the strainer.

5. Place a deep pan or pot over a burner and put the ramekins inside.

6. Turn the heat on and bring the water to a boil.

7. Turn the heat off and check the firmness of the puddings. The texture should be a little firm but still creamy like pudding.

8. Cool the puddings in the fridge until they are completely chilled.

9. Pour two tablespoons of pure maple syrup on top of each pudding before serving.

8.3 Dorayaki

Cooking Time: 15 minutes

Serving: 6

Ingredients:

- Honey, two tbsp.
- Eggs, two
- Sugar, one cup
- Flour, one cup
- Baking powder, one tsp.

- Red bean paste, half cup

Instructions:

1. Gather all the ingredients.

2. In a large bowl, combine eggs, sugar, and honey and whisk well until the mixture becomes fluffy.

3. Sift flour and baking powder into the bowl and mix all together.

4. The batter should be slightly smoother now.

5. Heat a large non-stick frying pan over medium-low heat. It is best to take your time and heat slowly.

6. When you see the surface of the batter starting to bubble, flip over and cook the other side.

7. Put the red bean paste in the centre.

8. Wrap dorayaki with plastic wrap until ready to be served.

8.4 Fluffy Japanese Cheesecake

Cooking Time: 50 minutes

Serving: 4-5

Ingredients:

- Vanilla ice cream
- Brownie mix, one box
- Hot fudge sauce

Instructions:

1. Preheat oven to 350 degrees.

2. Cut strips of foil to line jumbo muffin tin cups.

3. Layer strips in crisscross manner to use as lifting handles when brownies are done.

4. Spray foil in a pan with cooking spray.

5. Prepare brownie batter as described on the back of the box or according to your favorite recipe.

6. Divide batter evenly among muffin tin cups. Muffin cups will be about 3/4 full.

7. Place muffin tin on the rimmed baking sheet and bake in preheated oven for 40-50 minutes.

8. Remove from oven and cool in the pan for 5 minutes, then transfer to a cooling rack for ten additional minutes.

9. You may need to use a butter knife or icing spatula to loosen the sides of each brownie and then lift out of the muffin pan using the foil handles.

10. Serve warm brownie on a plate topped with a scoop of vanilla ice cream and hot fudge sauce.

8.5 Matcha Ice cream

Cooking Time: 5 minutes

Serving: 2

Ingredients:

- Matcha powder, three tbsp.
- Half and half, two cups
- Kosher salt, a pinch
- Sugar, half cup

Instructions:

1. In a medium saucepan, whisk together the half and half, sugar, and salt.

2. Start cooking the mixture over medium heat, and add green tea powder.

3. Remove from the heat and transfer the mixture to a bowl sitting in an ice bath. When the mixture is cool, cover with plastic wrap and chill in the refrigerator.

4. Your dish is ready to be served.

8.6 Taiyaki

Cooking Time: 15 minutes

Serving: 5

Ingredients:

- Cake flour, two cups
- Baking powder, one tsp.
- Baking soda, half tsp.
- Sugar, one cup
- Egg, two
- Milk, half cup

Instructions:

1. Sift the cake flour, baking powder and baking soda into a large bowl.

2. Add the sugar and whisk well to combine.

3. In a medium bowl, whisk the egg and then add the milk.

4. Combine the dry ingredients with wet ingredients and whisk well.

5. Pour the batter into a measuring cup or jug.

6. Heat the Taiyaki pan and grease the pan with vegetable oil using a brush.

7. Fill the Taiyaki pan mould about 60% full over medium-low heat.

8. Close the lid and immediately turn.

9. Then flip and cook. Open and check to see if Taiyaki is golden coloured.

10. Let Taiyaki cool on a wire rack.

11. Your dish is ready to be served.

8.7 Zenzai

Cooking Time: 15 minutes

Serving: 4

Ingredients:

- Mochi, one cup
- Red beans, one cup
- Sugar, three tbsp.

Instructions:

1. Place red beans, and five cups of water in a pot.

2. Bring to a boil and cook for five minutes, and then, strain the beans and discard the water they were cooked in.

3. Now, drain the beans, reserving the water they were cooked in.

4. Put drained beans into the pot, add sugar, and cook over medium heat for ten minutes, stirring constantly.

5. Then, pour in the water from cooking the beans, season with sugar, and stir over low heat.

6. Bake mochi over a grill or in a toaster oven until they expand and brown slightly.

7. Put mochi into a serving bowl and cover with a scoop of bean soup.

8. Your dish is ready to be served.

8.8 Okoshi

Cooking Time: 10 minutes

Serving: 3

Ingredients:

- Cooked rice, one cup
- Tempura oil, one tbsp.
- Sugar, one cup
- Puffed rice, one cup
- Peanuts, half cup

Instructions:

1. Spread the cooked rice on a baking sheet in a thin layer and place it on a flat sieve or a serving tray.

2. When the rice becomes translucent and crispy, it is ready for further preparation. First, break down any lumps using your fingers.

3. Line a mould for okoshi with baking paper.

4. Heat tempura oil to 180 degrees and deep fry the rice.

5. Mix sugar with water and cook over medium heat until the syrup starts simmering, then lower the heat and, if you wish, add peanuts.

6. Combine fried, puffed rice and sugar syrup quickly, and transfer to a container. Cover the top with a baking sheet, and press with a heavy and flat object.

7. Cut into small pieces and serve.

8.9 Dango

Cooking Time: 10 minutes

Serving: 6

Ingredients:

- Joshinko rice flour, one cup
- Shiratamako rice flour, one cup
- Sugar, half cup
- Hot water, as required

Instructions:

1. Mix together the joshinko non-glutinous rice flour, shiratamako glutinous rice flour and sugar.

2. Add the hot water little by little, mixing well.

3. Cover the bowl you mixed your dango mixture in and microwave for a few minutes. Dampen your hands again and roll the dough into evenly sized balls.

4. Your dish is ready to be served.

8.10 Kasutera

Cooking Time: 50 minutes

Serving: 24

Ingredients:

- Milk, one cup

- Honey, two tbsp.
- Flour, two cups
- Sugar, one cup

Instructions:

1. Set the oven to preheat to 170 degrees.
2. First, coat the bottom and the sides of a baking pan with butter or shortening, and then line it with baking paper, so that a portion of the paper is hanging over the sides of the pan.
3. Sprinkle the bottom of the pan with sugar.
4. Bring a pot of water to a boil, and then remove from the heat.
5. Whisk milk and honey together and double sift the flour.
6. Add the eggs and the sugar to the bowl.
7. Next, whisk in the milk and honey mixture, and then add flour tablespoon by tablespoon, whisking all the time until incorporated.
8. When the cake is cool enough to handle, put the cake into a plastic bag and seal. Refrigerate for a few hours.
9. Your dish is ready to be served.

8.11 Daifuku

Cooking Time: 10 minutes

Serving: 6

Ingredients:

- Swedish dried peas, two tbsp.

- Caster sugar, two tbsp.
- Rice flour, two cups
- Potato starch, one cup
- Anko red bean paste, two tbsp.

Instructions:

1. Place the Swedish red peas in a small saucepan and pour enough water to cover the red peas.
2. Bring it to simmer over low heat and cook for ten minutes.
3. Divide the anko sweet red bean paste into six balls.
4. Place the Shiratamako in a mixing bowl and add sugar and water.
5. Cover your hand with katakuriko potato starch and spread the mochi dough out with your hand.
6. Place the Swedish red peas over the mochi dough and fold the mochi dough in half.
7. Take one piece of dough on your palm and flat it.
8. Close the mochi ends at the top with your well dusted finger and shape it into a nice round shaped daifuku mochi.

Japanese ramen and sushi are famous worldwide. They are appreciated by many individuals all around the globe. Following are some recipes you can make at home:

9.1 Shoyu Ramen

Cooking Time: 30 minutes

Serving: 4

Ingredients:

- Chashu, one cup
- Nitamago, as required
- Shiitake, as required
- La-yu, as required
- Nori, half cup
- Ramen, four packs

- Dashi, half cup

Instructions:

1. In a pot of salted boiling water, cook ramen, stirring with tongs or chopsticks until cooked, about one minute.

2. In a small saucepan over medium heat, warm dashi and shiitake until barely simmering.

3. Cook for one minute and remove from heat.

4. Set shiitake aside.

5. Add dashi and noodles to serving bowl.

6. Top with chashu, nitamago, shiitake, green onion, a drizzle of la-yu, and nori, if desired.

9.2 Miso Ramen

Cooking Time: 10 minutes

Serving: 2

Ingredients:

- Miso paste, two tbsp.
- Mix vegetables, one cup
- Ramen, two packs
- Soy sauce, one tbsp.

Instructions:

1. Cook the ramen, and boil the vegetables.

2. Now mix all the remaining ingredients, and serve hot.

9.3 Simple Homemade Chicken Ramen

Cooking Time: 10 minutes

Serving: 2

Ingredients:

- Chicken, one cup
- Ramen noodles, two packs
- Oil, one tsp.
- Salt and pepper to taste

Instructions:

1. Cook the ramen, and chicken.
2. Now mix all the other ingredients, and serve hot.

9.4 Vegetarian Ramen

Cooking Time: 10 minutes

Serving: 2

Ingredients:

- Mix vegetables, one cup
- Ramen noodles, two packs
- Oil, one tsp.
- Salt and pepper to taste

Instructions:

1. Cook the ramen, and vegetables.
2. Now mix all the other ingredients, and serve hot.

9.5 Ramen Noodles

Cooking Time: 10 minutes

Serving: 2

Ingredients:

- Ramen noodles, two packs
- Miso paste, two tbsp.
- Soy Sauce, one tbsp.

Instructions:

1. Mix all the ingredients together, and cook well for ten minutes.
2. Your dish is ready to be served

9.6 Pork Ramen

Cooking Time: 10 minutes

Serving: 2

Ingredients:

- Pork meat, one cup
- Ramen noodles, two packs
- Oil, one tsp.
- Salt and pepper to taste

Instructions:

1. Cook the ramen, and pork meat.
2. Now mix all the ingredients, and serve hot.

9.7 Instant Ramen

Cooking Time: 10 minutes

Serving: 2

Ingredients:

- Instant ramen noodles, two packs
- Instant spice mix, two tbsp.
- Water, three cups

Instructions:

1. Mix all the ingredients together and cook for ten minutes.
2. Your dish is ready to be served.

9.8 Sushi

Cooking Time: 5 minutes

Serving: 4

Ingredients:

- Sesame oil, half tsp.
- Green onions/scallions, two
- Toasted white sesame seeds, two tbsp.
- Spicy Mayo, two tbsp.
- Sushi rice (cooked and seasoned), one and a half cup
- Sashimi-grade tuna, four ounces
- Sriracha sauce, three tsp.

Instructions:

1. In a medium bowl, combine the tuna, Sriracha sauce, sesame oil, and some of the green onion.

2. Lay a sheet of nori, shiny side down, on the bamboo mat. Wet your fingers in water and spread ¾ cup of the rice evenly onto nori sheet.

3. Sprinkle the rice with sesame seeds.

4. Turn the sheet of nori over so that the rice side is facing down.

5. Line the edge of nori sheet at the bottom end of the bamboo mat.

6. Place half of the tuna mixture at the bottom end of the nori sheet.

7. Grab the bottom edge of the bamboo mat while keeping the fillings in place with your fingers, roll into a tight cylinder form.

8. With a very sharp knife, cut the roll in half and then cut each half into three pieces.

9. Put a dollop of spicy mayo on top of each sushi and garnish with the remaining green onion.

10. Your dish is ready to be served.

9.9 Japanese Sushi Rolls

Cooking Time: 60 minutes

Serving: 4

Ingredients:

- Lemon, half

- Nori sheets, two

- Sushi rice, two cups

- Shrimp tempura, eight pieces
- Tobiko, two tbsp.
- Unagi (eel)
- Persian/Japanese cucumbers, one
- Avocados, one

Instructions:

1. Gather all the ingredients.
2. Cut cucumber lengthwise into quarters.
3. Remove the seeds, and then cut in half lengthwise.
4. Cut the avocado in half lengthwise around the seed, and twist the two halves until they are separate.
5. Hack the knife edge into the pit. Hold the skin of the avocado with the other hand, and twist in counter directions.
6. Remove the skin, and slice the avocado widthwise.
7. Gently press the avocado slices with your fingers, and then keep pressing gently, and evenly with the side of the knife until the length of avocado is about the length of sushi roll.
8. Wrap the bamboo mat with plastic wrap, and place half of the nori sheet, shiny side down.
9. Turn it over and put the shrimp tempura, cucumber strips, and tobiko at the bottom end of the nori sheet.
10. If you like to put unagi, place it inside here as well.
11. From the bottom end, start rolling nori sheet over the filling tightly, and firmly with bamboo mat until the bottom end reaches the nori sheet.

12. Place the bamboo mat over the roll and tightly squeeze the roll.

13. Using the side of the knife, place the avocado on top of the roll.

14. Place plastic wrap over the roll and then put the bamboo mat over.

15. Cut the roll into 8 pieces with the knife.

16. Put tobiko on each piece of sushi, and drizzle spicy mayo, and sprinkle black sesame seeds on top.

17. Your dish is ready to be served.

Japanese cuisine remains rooted in its traditions, while embracing a certain amount of fusion from other cultures. Following are some traditional and alternative recipes:

10.1 Sashimi

Cooking Time: 20-30 seconds

Serving: 3

Ingredients:

- Tuna, one pound
- Salmon, one pound, sesame oil, two tbsp.
- Coriander leaves, as required

Instructions:

1. Drizzle the tuna and salmon with sesame seed oil, turning it over to ensure even coverage on all sides.

2. Sprinkle a generous helping of dried and chopped coriander leaves over the tuna, and salmon filet.

3. Cook the fish for only fifteen to twenty seconds.

4. Your dish is ready to be served with your preferred sauce.

10.2 Unadon

Cooking Time: 20-30 seconds

Serving: 3

Ingredients:

- Sesame oil, two tbsp.
- Unagi eel, two pounds
- Japanese pepper one tbsp.
- Coriander leaves, one tbsp.

Instructions:

1. Drizzle the unagi with sesame seed oil, turning it over to ensure even coverage on all sides.
2. Sprinkle a generous amount of Japanese pepper, and chopped coriander leaves over the unagi.
3. Cook the fish for only fifteen to twenty seconds.
4. Your dish is ready to be served.

10.3 Tempura

Cooking Time: 10 minutes

Serving: 2

Ingredients:

- Plain flour, four tbsp.
- Prawns, one pound
- Mix vegetables, one cup

- Mayonnaise, half tsp.
- Water, two tbsp.

Instructions:

1. Prepare the prawn and vegetables and set aside.
2. Place the flour, and add icy cold water and mayonnaise.
3. Set aside in fridge until all ingredients and oil are ready.
4. Fill a deep pan or deep-fryer with vegetable oil and heat until 180 degrees.
5. Add each ingredient to the batter individually to coat them and put them into the oil.
6. Fry each ingredient.
7. Your dish is ready to be served with your preferred sauce

10.4 Soba

Cooking Time: 10 minutes

Serving: 2

Ingredients:

- Japanese noodles, one pack
- Sesame seeds, as required
- Sesame oil, one tbsp.
- Green Onions, chopped, three
- Ginger, grated, half tsp.
- Soy Sauce, one tbsp.

Instructions:

1. Boil the noodles properly and then mix all the ingredients together while on heat.

2. Your dish is ready to be served.

10.5 Udon

Cooking Time: 15 minutes

Serving: 2

Ingredients:

- Cornstarch, two tbsp.

- Japanese noodles, one pack

- Green Onions, chopped, three

- Ginger, grated, half tsp.

- Water, two tbsp.

- Chicken broth, four cups

- Soy Sauce, one tbsp.

Instructions:

1. Mix all the ingredients together and let it cook for fifteen minutes.

2. Now add the corn flour mixed in water.

3. Cook for five minutes.

4. Your dish is ready to be served.

10.6 Sukiyaki

Cooking Time: 30 minutes

Serving: 6

Ingredients:

- Dried vermicelli, two cups
- Tofu slices, six
- Shiitake mushrooms, half cup
- Enoki mushrooms, half cup
- Napa cabbage, one cup
- Tong ho, half cup
- Scallions, one cup
- Vegetable oil, two tbsp.
- Beef slices, six slices

Instructions:

1. Prepare all your sukiyaki ingredients, the tofu slices, rehydrated shiitake mushrooms, enoki mushrooms, napa cabbage, tong ho, and scallions.

2. Soak the dried vermicelli noodles in water for ten minutes.

3. Heat a tablespoon vegetable oil in the pan.

4. Fry the white parts of the scallions in the oil for two minutes.

5. In the pan with the scallions, add the sliced beef.

6. Sear the beef for a few seconds, and add a drizzle of your sukiyaki sauce.

7. Add the rest of your sukiyaki sauce and two cups stock.

8. Bring to a boil, and add the tofu, mushrooms, napa cabbage, and tong ho to the pot in sections.

9. Also drain the vermicelli noodles you soaked and add them to the pot.

10. Remove the cover, and add the beef back to the pot.

11. Sprinkle with the chopped scallions, and enjoy with rice and egg yolk.

10.7 Oden

Cooking Time: 30 minutes

Serving: 6

Ingredients:
- Dashi, three cups
- Fish cakes, six
- Fish balls, six
- Eggs, six
- Konnyaku, two
- Kombu, two
- Japanese mustard, two tbsp.
- Soy sauce, two tsp.
- Mirin, two tsp.
- Sake, two tsp.
- Togarashi, as required

Instructions:
1. Rinse the fish cakes and fish balls with running water, remove the excess oil from the fish cakes and fish balls.

2. In a soup pot, bring the dashi, water, kombu strips to boil.

3. Add the daikon and stew on low heat until they are cooked through.

4. Add the hard-boiled eggs, konnyaku, and fish cakes.

5. Add the soy sauce, mirin and sake. Turn the heat to low and simmer for fifteen minutes.

6. Serve the Oden warm with Japanese mustard and Togarashi.

10.8 Gohan - Steamed Rice

Cooking Time: 10 minutes

Serving: 2

Ingredients:

- Japanese rice, one cup
- Water, one and a half cup
- Salt for taste

Instructions:

1. Wash the rice and then cook it properly.
2. Pour water into a pan and boil it and add rice as well as salt.
3. Cover for ten minutes.
4. Your dish is ready to be served.

10.9 Tonkatsu

Cooking Time: 15 minutes

Serving: 4

Ingredients:

- Pork loin, one pound
- Eggs, two
- Bread crumbs, half cup
- Cabbage, one

Instructions:

1. Slash the fat rimming one side of the loin cutlet to keep the meat from curling when deep fried.

2. Sprinkle salt and pepper both sides of each cutlet.

3. Dredge each in flour, then dip into beaten eggs and press into bread crumbs to coat both sides.

4. Heat a large skillet with about half inch of oil until hot.

5. Deep-fry until golden brown, about five minutes, turning them once or twice. Drain the cutlets on paper towels and cut the pork into bite-size strips that can be eaten with chopsticks.

6. Arrange the pork on a platter lined with the shredded cabbage, and garnish with lemon wedges.

7. Serve your preferred sauce on the side for dipping, or pour it over the pork and cabbage.

10.10 Wagashi

Cooking Time: 30 minutes

Serving: 3

Ingredients:

- Shiro-an, one cup
- Water, half cup
- Sugar, half cup
- Rice flour, one cup

Instructions:

1. Combine the water, sugar, and rice flour.

2. Stir this in with 600 grams of the shiroan and heat over medium heat.

3. You should end up with a tacky dough that can be shaped with your fingers.

4. Let it cool down.

5. Make into various shapes.

6. Your dish is ready to be served.

10.11 Japanese Matcha Green Tea

Cooking Time: 5 minutes

Serving: 1

Ingredients:

- Matcha tea leaves, one tsp.

- Water, one cup

Instructions:

1. Mix all the ingredients together and then let it boil for five minutes.

2. Drain the tea. Your tea is ready.

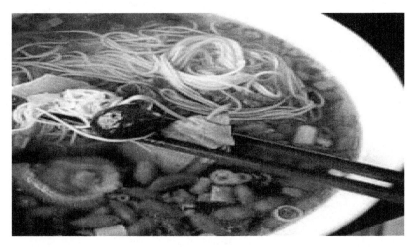

Japan is known for its variety of vegetarian cuisine, Japanese love vegetables, and tend to make more vegetarian meals. Following are some amazing vegetarian recipes:

11.1 Kenchin Vegetable Soup

Cooking Time: 30 minutes

Serving: 3

Ingredients:

- Dashi, one cup

- Mix vegetables, one cup

- Taro, half cup

- Abura age, one cup

- Mirin, two tbsp.

- Soy Sauce, one tbsp.

- Salt, as required

- Sesame oil, two tbsp.

Instructions:

1. Begin by peeling your daikon, burdock and carrot, and then cut them into bite sized chunks.

2. Scrub the taro well with a vegetable brush, making sure any dirt is removed.

3. In a bowl, soak the abura age in hot water to remove any excess oil, and then slice into bite sized pieces.

4. Add the dashi, vegetables and abura age fried tofu to a pan and bring to boil. Add the soy sauce, mirin, salt and sesame oil, and simmer until the vegetables are tender and soft.

5. Serve and garnish with the spring onion.

11.2 Vegan Japanese Omelette

Cooking Time: 10 minutes

Serving: 2

Ingredients:

- Vegan mayo, as required
- Wheat flour, one cup
- Nori, one
- Soy sauce, one tsp.
- Water, one cup
- Salt and pepper to taste
- Oil, two tbsp.

Instructions:

1. In a large mixing bowl, combine all ingredients and stir together so you have a thick dough.

2. Heat a drop of oil in a frying pan and heat on high.

3. Add a scoop of dough and flatten.

4. Reduce flame to medium heat and gently sear each side of the omelette for five minutes.

5. Serve your dish with vegan mayo.

11.3 Japanese Vegetable Pancake

Cooking Time: 25 minutes

Serving: 2

Ingredients:

- Dashi, half cup
- Eggs, two
- Bacon slices, three
- Okonomiyaki sauce, as required
- Mayyonaise, two tbsp.
- Cabbage, half cup
- Green onion, as required
- Flour, one tbsp.

Instructions:

1. Mix the flour, dashi, egg and cabbage in a large bowl.

2. Heat oil in large pan over medium heat, pour in mixture, flatten, top with the bacon slices and cook until golden brown on both sides, about ten minutes per side.

3. Top with okonomiyaki sauce, mayonnaise, and green onion slices.

4. Your dish is ready to be served.

11.4 Vegetarian Japanese Curry

Cooking Time: 30 minutes

Serving: 4

Ingredients:

- Mixed vegetables, two cups
- Green Onions, chopped, three
- Ginger, grated, half tsp.
- Tomato puree, one cup
- Vegetable broth, two cups
- Salt and pepper as required
- Soy Sauce, one tbsp.

Instructions:

1. Mix all the ingredients together, and let it simmer for thirty minutes.
2. Your meal is ready to be served.

11.5 Vegetable Tempura

Cooking Time: 10 minutes

Serving: 2

Ingredients:

- Plain flour, four tbsp.
- Mix vegetables, one cup
- Mayonnaise, half tsp.
- Water, two tbsp.

Instructions:

1. Place the flour, and add icy cold water and mayonnaise.
2. Set aside in fridge until all ingredients and oil are ready.
3. Fill a deep pan or deep-fryer with vegetable oil and heat until 180 degrees.
4. Add each ingredient to the batter individually to coat them and put them into the oil.
5. Fry each ingredient.
6. Your dish is ready to be served with your preferred sauce.

11.6 Japanese Edamame

Cooking Time: 10 minutes

Serving: 2

Ingredients:

- Edamame, one cup
- Soy Sauce, one tbsp.
- Sesame oil, one tsp.
- Salt and pepper to taste

Instructions:

1. Boil edamame for a few minutes.
2. In a pan over high heat, add sesame oil.
3. When the oil is hot, almost smoking, add edamame pods and fry for two minutes.
4. Add soy sauce and stir until the sauce is evaporated.

5. Season with salt and lots of black pepper.

6. Your dish is ready to be served.

11.7 Japanese Eggplant Curry

Cooking Time: 30 minutes

Serving: 4

Ingredients:

- Eggplant, two
- Green Onions, chopped, three
- Ginger, grated, half tsp.
- Tomato puree, one cup
- Vegetable broth, two cups
- Salt and pepper as required
- Soy Sauce, one tbsp.

Instructions:

1. Mix all the ingredients together, and let it simmer for thirty minutes.

2. Your meal is ready to be served.

11.8 Mushroom and Tofu Potstickers

Cooking Time: 15 minutes

Serving: 5

Ingredients:

- Sesame oil, two tbsp.
- Mushrooms, one cup
- Red pepper, half tsp.

- Cabbage, half cup
- Wonton wrappers, ten
- Scallions, half cup
- Ginger and garlic paste, half tsp.
- Olive oil, two tbsp.
- Tofu, one block
- Soy Sauce, one tbsp.

Instructions:

1. Heat a frying pan and add the olive oil.
2. Sauté the crumbled tofu, mushrooms, cabbage, ginger, and garlic for a few minutes.
3. When the tofu and mushrooms are almost cooked, add the scallions, soy sauce, sesame oil, and optional red pepper flakes, stirring well to combine.
4. Add the mixture to wonton wrappers and then steam them for five minutes.
5. Your dish is ready to be served with your preferred sauce.

11.9 Vegetable Teppanyaki

Cooking Time: 10 minutes

Serving: 2

Ingredients:

- Mixed vegetables, two cups
- Sesame oil, two tbsp.
- Salt and pepper to taste
- Cooking wine, two tbsp.

- Soy Sauce, one tbsp.

Instructions:

1. In a skillet over high heat, add two tablespoon oil.
2. Add carrots and cook until almost tender.
3. Add the rest of the vegetables and stir fry.
4. Pour in soy sauce and cooking wine.
5. Season with salt and pepper.
6. Your meal is ready to be served.

11.10 Naturally Sweet Red Bean Daifuku

Cooking Time: 10 minutes

Serving: 6

Ingredients:

- Sweet red beans, two tbsp.
- Caster sugar, two tbsp.
- Rice flour, two cups
- Potato starch, one cup

Instructions:

1. Place the sweet red beans in a small saucepan and pour enough water to cover the red peas.
2. Bring it to simmer over low heat and cook for ten minutes.
3. Place the red beans in a mixing bowl and add sugar and water.
4. Cover your hand with katakuriko potato starch and spread the mochi dough out with your hand.

5. Place the Swedish red peas over the mochi dough and fold the mochi dough in half.

6. Close the mochi ends at the top with your well dusted finger and shape it into a nice round shaped daifuku mochi.

7. Your dish is ready to be served.

11.11 Japanese Carrot Pickles

Cooking Time: 5 hours

Serving: 3-4

Ingredients:

- Rice vinegar, half cup

- Sugar, two tbsp.

- Sesame seeds, as required

- Carrots, two cups

Instructions:

1. In a large cup, whisk together the rice vinegar and sugar until it dissolves completely.

2. Pour the vinegar mixture over all of the carrots, and leave it for five hours.

3. Sprinkle sesame seeds on top and serve.

11.12 Mango Mochi

Cooking Time: 20 minutes

Serving: 5-6

Ingredients:

- Potato starch, two tbsp.

- Water, as required
- Rice flour, one cup
- Green Onions, chopped, three
- Mongo bites, one cup
- Whipped cream, one cup
- Sugar, two cups
- Cream stabilizer one tbsp.

Instructions:

1. In a small cup, add sugar and cream stabilizer.
2. In another bowl, add whipping cream and blend with an electric hand mixer for a few seconds. Then add the sugar mix.
3. Add the whipped cream in the moulds.
4. Place the mango bits on the cream. Then cover with the remaining whipped cream.
5. In a bowl, add glutinous rice flour, sugar and water.
6. Heat over medium heat, stir constantly, until smooth and silky.
7. Spread the potato starch onto your working surface or chopping board.
8. Pull out one filling from the freezer.
9. Pull the edges of the mochi disc over the filling so as to cover it.
10. Your dish is ready to be served.

11.13 Japanese Green Avocado Salad

Cooking Time: 10 minutes

Serving: 2

Ingredients:

- Cucumber, one
- Snowpeas, half cup
- Avocado, one
- Cabbage, half
- Green salad dressing, half cup
- Salt and pepper, per taste

Instructions:

1. Bring a small saucepan of water to a boil and blanch the snowpeas.
2. Peel the cucumber and slice into very thin rounds.
3. For the dressing, whisk all the ingredients together in a small bowl.
4. Combine all the green ingredients in a large bowl, pour the dressing over the top and gently toss with your hands to coat them.
5. Your dish is ready to be served.

11.14 Sweet Potatoes and Avocado Green Salad

Cooking Time: 10 minutes

Serving: 2

Ingredients:

- Sweet potato, one
- Avocado, one
- Green salad dressing, half cup
- Salt and pepper to taste
- Cucumber, one

Instructions:

1. Boil the sweet potato for ten minutes.
2. Cut into pieces and mix the rest of the ingredients.
3. Your dish is ready to be served.

11.15 Japanese Baked Sweet Potato

Cooking Time: 30 minutes

Serving: 3

Ingredients:

- Sweet potatoes, three
- Soy Sauce, one tbsp.
- Sesame oil, two tbsp.
- Salt and pepper, to taste

Instructions:

1. Cut the sweet potatoes into half and add the rest of the ingredients on it.
2. Bake it at 180 degrees for ten minutes.
3. Your dish is ready to be served.

11.16 Japanese Fried Rice

Cooking Time: 30 minutes

Serving Size: 4

Ingredients:

- Fish sauce, two tbsp.
- Egg, one
- Soy sauce, half cup
- Cooked Japanese rice, three cups
- Tomatoes, two
- Cilantro, half cup
- Salt and pepper, to taste
- Vegetable oil, two tbsp.
- Toasted walnuts, half cup
- Chicken breast, eight ounces
- Onion, one
- Scallions, half cup
- Minced garlic, one tsp.

Instructions:

1. Heat a large nonstick pan over high heat.
2. Meanwhile, season chicken lightly with salt and pepper.
3. When the pan is very hot, add two tsp of the oil.
4. When the oil is hot, add the chicken and cook on high until it is browned all over and cooked through.

5. Remove chicken from pan and set aside, add the eggs, pinch of salt and cook a minute or two until done.

6. Add the remaining oil to the pan and add the onion, scallions and garlic.

7. Sauté for a minute, add the chili pepper if using, tomatoes and stir in all the rice.

8. Add the soy sauce and fish sauce stir to mix all the ingredients.

9. Keep stirring a few minutes, and then add egg and chicken back to the wok.

10. Adjust soy sauce if needed and stir well another 30 seconds.

11. Your dish is ready to be served.

11.17 Kenchinjiru

Cooking Time: 30 minutes

Serving: 3

Ingredients:

- Dashi, one cup
- Mix vegetables, one cup
- Taro, half cup
- Abura age, one cup
- Mirin, two tbsp.
- Soy Sauce, one tbsp.
- Salt, as required
- Sesame oil, two tbsp.
- Japanese seven spice, two tbsp.

- Sesame oil, two tbsp.
- Sake, one tsp.
- Tofu, one block.

Instructions:

1. Mix all the ingredients together and let it simmer for thirty minutes straight.
2. Serve and garnish with the spring onion.

The recipes mentioned in this chapter are very easy to make and will fill your craving needs for delicious Japanese cuisine.

Conclusion

Japanese Cuisine is known for its variety of dishes and its vast combination of rare spices that are usually grown only in Japan. This cuisine has been out there from the 18th century but has entered the United States of America from the times when trade began between the two countries, and Japanese people started to move in to America for various purposes.

Today, Japanese cuisine is not only liked by Japanese people residing all over the world but also by other people that live in America. There are various restaurant chains and eateries that make delicious Japanese food but what is better than cooking your favorite meals all by yourself at home.

This book contains all the details that you need to know regarding Japanese cuisine. You can get to know about its history, the different spices that are used in Japanese meals and their various health benefits. So, now you have all the knowledge you need to start cooking Japanese food on your own. This book also contains more than 100 different recipes that include breakfast, lunch, dinner, soups, salads, sweets, traditional as well as vegetarian meals. So, do not wait more, start cooking from today and eat your favorite Japanese healthy and yummy meals at home.

Thai Cookbook

Learn How to Prepare Traditional and Modern Thai Comfort Food at Home, Cooking Over 100 Dishes Plus Vegetarian and Spicy Slow Cooker Recipes

By

Adele Tyler

Table of contents

Introduction

Food is an integral part of our daily routine. Without the intake of healthy, nutritious, and tasty food, life can really turn into a challenge. Often, cooking is considered a tough job due to lack of our knowledge and skills regarding it. But it is the other way round, once you start getting familiar with the skill of cooking. Cooking is an art, and you can also be an artist if you start cooking food at your home.

This book is majorly about Thai cuisine. Thai food is the public cooking of Thailand. Thai cooking places accentuation on light meals with amazing aromatic segments and a spicy or zesty edge. Thai cooking is about the shuffling of different components to make an amicable completion. Like an unpredictable melodic harmony, it must have a smooth surface, yet it does not make a difference what is going on underneath. Simplicity is not the proclamation here, by any means.

In this cookbook, you will learn the history and origin of Thai food as well as the history of traditional Thai dishes. You are going to get all the information regarding the evolution of Thai cuisine over the years. You will get to know the reasons behind the popularity of Thai food across the U.S.A.

You will always be finding yourself at ease while cooking Thai food at home, and find exactly why cooking Thai food at home is way better than any Dine-in experience.

There are various health benefits of having Thai food at home, and you will learn all of these benefits when you go through the different properties of spices used in Thai foods. You will get over 100 different breakfast, lunch, dinner, and dessert, famous, alternative, vegetarian, and slow cooker recipes that you can easily start cooking at home with the detailed instructions present below each recipe.

Preparing your Thai food at home without the need to order food from some restaurant can become very easy once you start reading this book. So, why wait for more? Let us dive deep into the world of Thai cuisine.

Chapter 1: Introduction to Thai Food

Thailand is the most acclaimed nation in the whole world for its cooking. Traversing from the southern landmass toward the northern regions, the nation offers a various mix of madly flavorful food.

The south of Thailand is acclaimed for its fiery curries, weighty utilization of coconut milk, and amazing fish recipes. The northeastern part is notable for its veggie filled plates of mixed greens and spices, barbecued meat, hotdogs, and clingy rice. Bangkok, the biggest city, draws in Thais from all around the nation to make an endless blend of enticing flavors to taste.

From streak cooked sautés to hand beaten servings of mixed greens, if you appreciate eating, you will be in heaven with the assortment and amount of food in this cuisine.

1.1 History and Origin of Thai Food

Thai food began with the individuals who emigrated from the southern Chinese territories to cutting edge Thailand, hundreds of years back. Truly there were multiple Szechwan impacts in Thai cooking; however, throughout the long term, numerous different impacts have influenced Thai food.

In the past, Buddhist priests brought an Indian touch to the food, and southern Muslim states affected the cooking in the south of Thailand. A lot later, Thai food was impacted by European cuisine after contact with Portuguese ministers and Dutch brokers. During these occasions, there was some impact from the Japanese.

Thailand is a major nation with an assorted topography, and throughout the long term, this has prompted the improvement of local divergences in its style of foods.

1.2 History of Traditional Thai Dishes

Thai food was customarily eaten while sitting on mats or covers on the floor; these customs actually are still found in the more traditional family units. Currently, there are four distinct styles of cooking in Traditional Thai cuisine:

- Southern Thai cooking is the most mainstream outside of Thailand since that is the primary traveler area of the nation. In southern cooking, there is considerably more utilization of coconut milk in numerous dishes. Coconut replaces Ghee for fricasseeing, and there is a substantial utilization of fish in the dishes.

- The food in the north east is impacted by Laos; when in doubt, the food is exceptionally spiced, and clingy glutinous rice is the favored staple for north-eastern dishes. Despite the fact that there are a lot of meat dishes, generally, meat was scant in the towns, and the principle wellspring of protein were shrimp and freshwater fish.

- The central area offers food that is halfway between the north and south; however, fragrant Jasmine rice is preferred by many to the clingy assortment. What makes the focal area food unique is that it is home to illustrious cooking.

- The cooking in northern Thailand is commonly milder than in the remainder of the nation; clingy rice is preferred, customarily it is massaged into little balls with the fingers.

1.3 Evolution of Thai Food over Time

Traditionally, Thai cooking sets aside a great deal of effort to plan. Consequently, planning food requires loads of participation and cooperation, including the relatives to cook it all together as a feast. The food clarifies the Thai life and its conventions, customs, and culture. Thai families are huge and well-weave. In cooking, Thai relatives help each other as a group. In cooking curries, youngsters help with light work like nipping off basil leaves, and grown-ups press coconut meat and pound chilies and flavors.

In the present day, making Thai food is a lot simpler as all the things are promptly accessible in general stores, yet there is an analysis that it does not have the customary standards of the past.

1.4 Popularity of Thai Dishes in the U.S.A

Thai food is not the only cuisine to have been changed in the excursion across seas. Various eateries in the USA serve dishes that regard the intricacy of Thai food and its equalization of sweet, sharp, salt, and zest. They are important for an ocean change that, as of late, has delivered amazing and acclaimed Thai cafés around the entire nation.

Eateries serving great Thai food, as they do now, did not exist twenty years before because there was no network to help it grow.

Utilizing a strategy currently known as gastro diplomacy or culinary discretion, the legislature of Thailand has purposefully supported the presence of Thai cooking outside of Thailand to build its fare and the travel industry incomes, just as its noticeable quality on the social and conciliatory stages.

The techniques for accomplishing this expansion were complex, run in equal by different divisions of the legislature. The Ministry of Commerce's Department of Export Promotion, in all probability run by officials as opposed to restaurateurs, drew up models for three diverse "Ace Eateries," which financial specialists could pick as such a pre-assembled eatery plan, from stylish to menu contributions.

Since huge business sectors like the United States have been immovably settled as admirers of coconut milk and nut sauce, the Thai government has been making a push to expand the presence of Thai cooking in new areas, particularly the Middle East.

Chapter 2: Thai Food: Home Cooking Vs. Dine- in Experience

Individuals all around the globe are occupied. Everyone is either occupied with work, school or other additional daily activities. Nobody actually has the opportunity to cook, so families are continually going out to eat at any preferred eatery. In this chapter we will discuss the difference between eating at home and eating at an eatery as far as the value, tidiness, taste and administration are concerned.

2.1 Difference between Home Cooking Vs. Dine-in Experience

With applications that permit you to arrange with simply a couple of taps, it tends to be incredibly enticing to swear off preparing supper at home. Yet, there are frequently compromises for comfort. Café suppers can contain loads of unhealthy substances.

There is additionally a great deal past what is in the supper that you pass up when you are eating from a take-away meal box. Following are the differences between home cooking and dine-in experience:

1. Healthy Food

Some research studies propose that individuals more frequently, instead of getting a take-out meal, have a generally more beneficial eating regimen. These examinations additionally show that café suppers ordinarily contain higher measures of sodium, immersed fat, absolute fat, and large number of calories than home-prepared dinners. While by cooking yourself at home, you have all the authority over what is going in your food. That can improve things significantly to your general wellbeing.

2. More Family Time

Cooking together can offer you an occasion to reconnect with your accomplice as well as friends and family. Cooking has different advantages too. The American Psychological Association expresses that trying new things together like learning another recipe together can help keep a couple associated and occupied with their relationship.

3. Save Plenty of Time

Part of ordering take-out means waiting for the food to arrive or driving to get it. Depending on where you live, what time you order, and whether or not the delivery person is good with directions, this could actually take more time than if you would simply make a meal at home.

Cooking at home does not have to take a lot of time if you do not want it to.

By using different services, you eliminate the need to look for recipes or grocery shop. Everything you need comes right to your door; in the exact pre-portioned amounts you will be using.

4. Save Money

In the long run, preparing meals at home may save you money. A group of basic ingredients often comes in at a lower price tag than a single restaurant dish. You can also end up getting more meals out of a recipe you make at home than if you order takeout, or have leftovers to take to work the next day. After just a few weeks, you could see noticeable savings start to pile up.

5. It is Fun

When you are making a meal from scratch, you get to discover and experiment with different ingredients, seasonings, and cuisines. And as with any activity, the more time you spend in the kitchen, the better you become at creating fantastic meals. You would be missing out this fun if you would keep on ordering your food or going for dine-in to any restaurant.

6. Personalization

Cooking at home gives you the opportunity to eat the foods you love exactly how you enjoy eating them. While, going for dine-in you would have to consume the food however it is prepared.

7. Maintain Calorie Count

The average fast-food order ranges between 1,100 to 1,200 calories total that is almost all of a woman's recommended daily calorie intake (1,600 to 2,400 calories) and almost two thirds of a man's daily intake (2,000 to 3,000 calories). And if you think independent restaurants and smaller chains do any better, think again.

Those eateries pump in even more calories, with an average of 1,327 calories per meal. Making a meal yourself means you can make sure the portion sizes and calorie counts are where you want them to be. Recipes often come with nutritional information and serving size suggestions, which makes that even easier.

So, it is better to cook home and eat healthy rather than heading off to a restaurant just due to your lazy routine.

2.2 Health Benefits of Thai Food

Thai food is ordinarily loved in the United States; however, you may puzzle over whether this cooking is healthy or not. The conventional eating routine of Thailand highlights vivid vegetables, fish, and meats that are presented with rice or noodles and prepared with spices and flavors like turmeric, galangal, Thai basil, and lemongrass. Food served at Western Thai eateries shares numerous parts of valid Thai cooking, despite the fact that it has some striking contrasts.

Thai menus in America may have bigger segments, more seared nourishments, and recipes that are higher in salt and sugar. Following are the health benefits of Thai food:

- Several of the most common Thai ingredients are nutritious on their own, but there are other healthy aspects of Thai food in general. For one, Thai meals often feature a good balance of macronutrients such as protein, fats, and carbs.

- Curries, stir-fries, and soups are made with a variety of vegetables, include a protein source like tofu, lean meat, or seafood, and contain coconut milk, peanut sauces, or other fat.

- The most commonly used veggies in Thai meals are non-starchy, such as peppers, tomato, cabbage, broccoli, carrots, and onions. These veggies are loaded with fiber, vitamins, minerals, and a variety of compounds that contribute to good digestion and overall health.

- Eating meals that largely comprise on non-starchy veggies and also contain protein and fat can help you maintain stable blood sugar levels throughout the day. This, in turn, leads to sustained energy and may aid weight loss.

Thai cuisine is known for incorporating regional herbs and spices, fresh vegetables, and lean proteins that add both flavor and nutrition to meals. However, some Westernized Thai dishes are deep fried, served in large portions, or contain excessive amounts of added sugar and salt. To choose a healthy Thai meal, opt for the dishes that are loaded with plant foods, contain a protein source, and feature a variety of herbs and spices.

2.3 Different Properties of Spices used in Thai Food

A large portion of the ingredients found in Thai food are a clear reflection of the environment that is warm with fertile land and abundant water. Recipes depend on fish, peculiar products of the soil, a few sorts of noodles and sauces.

Rice is the pillar of most dinners, giving an ideal similarity to the wide assortment of tastes and colors that encompass it. Hot flavoring mixes are utilized to season everything from the day's catch to the easy to make servings of rice or noodles.

Following are some of the main seasonings used in Thai cooking:

- **Cinnamon:** Thai cooks favor Chinese cinnamon, or Cinnamomum cassia, which is better, somewhat spicier, and more exceptional in color and flavor than Cinnamomum zeylanicum. Cinnamon's fragrance and flavor add to both sweet and exquisite Thai dishes, just as zest mixes.

- **Cumin:** Thai cooks roast aromatic, earthy cumin seed in a dry pan to bring out its flavor, and then grind it for use in curry pastes and other spice blends. Cumin is also a primary ingredient in many spice blends, soups, stews, and meat, bean and rice dishes.

- **Cilantro:** Also known as Chinese parsley, Thais use this soft, leafy plant for its distinctive flavor and earthy or musty aroma.

- **Basil:** Basil is used both as a flavoring and a garnish in Thai cooking, and handfuls are sometimes tossed into soups, curries and stir fries just before serving.

- **Cardamom:** The fragrant cardamom seedpod is used in the whole form in a few Thai dishes of Indian origin, like Mussamun Curry. A bit lemony, cardamom also has a slightly peppery and sweet taste and scent. Thai cooks often combine cardamom with other aromatic spices, like cinnamon, nutmeg, and mace.

- **Garlic:** Thai cooks value garlic for its health properties, aroma, and the fact that its flavor blends well with a variety of other spices. Garlic is a main ingredient in the traditional Big Four Seasonings Blend, along with salt, cilantro root, and white peppercorns.

- **Curry Powders and Pastes:** Thais commonly blend their own curry powders and pastes by grinding various herbs and spices in a mortar and pestle. Curries are used to flavor coconut milk, salad dressings, noodle sauces, seafood and meat dishes, vegetable dishes and soups.

- **Lemongrass:** The fresh, light, lemony flavor and scent of lemongrass is a staple in Thai cuisine. Thai cooks use the bulb and base leaves of lemongrass to season sauces, soups, stir-fries and curries. It enhances meats, poultry, seafood, and vegetables, and it's especially delicious with garlic, chilies and cilantro.

- **Nutmeg:** Thai cooks appreciate the intense aroma and sweet, spicy flavor of nutmeg in recipes for sweet and savory dishes. They use a grater to finely powder the whole spice.

- **Turmeric:** The robes of Buddhist monks in Thailand are colored with an ancient yellow dye made from turmeric. Its flavor is sweet, warm, and a little peppery, but it is used primarily for color in many Thai dishes, including curries, condiments, and seafood and grain dishes.

- **Cloves:** This dark brown, aromatic spice is used whole in the Thai kitchen. Its taste is distinct, sharp, and warm or sweet, and you will find it in both sweet and savory recipes.

- **Chili peppers:** Thai food is hot, thanks to its liberal use of fresh and dried chili peppers. Although chili peppers are not native, they are now essential to Thai cuisine.

- **Coriander:** The intensely aromatic and slightly piquant flavor of coriander seeds is prized in Thai cooking. Thai cooks often roast and then pound the seeds to release the flavor; they also use the root and the leaf (cilantro) of the plant.

- **Galangal:** A relative of ginger, this pale-yellow spice has a sharp, lemony, peppery hot taste. It is also known as galingale, Java root, or Siamese ginger. Large, thin pieces of galangal are used to flavor Thai soups, stews and curries; for pastes it is finely chopped and pounded. Ginger may be substituted for galangal in most of the Thai recipes.

- **Mace:** The sweet scent of "closed blossom," as the Thai cooks refer to mace, is enjoyed in dishes that have been influenced by Indian and Indonesian cookery. It is mildly nutty, warm taste is found in soups, stuffing, sauces and baked goods. It complements seafood, meats, and cheese, as well as some beverages.

Thai cuisine will appeal to any cook who loves the art of seasoning. And while many dishes are very hot, those prepared at home can be adjusted to just the right degree for your own tastes.

Chapter 3: The World of Thai Breakfast Recipes

Food is enormously significant in Thai culture, with Thais utilizing food as a typical friendly exchange. There are numerous well-known dishes in Thailand and a lot of territorial specialties. Following are some amazing breakfast recipes that you can easily make at home:

3.1 Thai Breakfast Omelette Recipe

Cooking Time: 15 minutes

Serving Size: 2

Ingredients:

- Vegetable oil, one and a half tbsp.

- Sliced mushrooms, one cup

- Eggs, eight

- Sliced red capsicum, one large

- Chopped tomatoes, two media sized
- Bean sprouts, one cup
- Fresh coriander leaves, half cup
- Fish sauce, one tbsp.
- Lime juice, two tbsp.
- Sliced red chili, one long
- Green beans, one cup

Instructions:

1. Whisk eggs, lime juice, fish sauce, quarter cup water and half of the chili in a large jug.
2. Heat two teaspoons of oil in a medium non-stick frying pan over medium-high heat. Cook mushrooms and capsicum, stir, for five minutes or until golden and tender.
3. Add tomato. Cook, stirring, for two minutes or until slightly softened. Meanwhile, place green beans in a heatproof bowl.
4. Cover with boiling water.
5. Wait for few minutes and then drain.
6. Rinse under cold water.
7. Combine mushroom mixture, beans and sprouts in a bowl.
8. Wipe the pan clean. Heat one teaspoon of remaining oil in pan over medium-high heat. Pour quarter of the egg mixture into pan.
9. Swirl to coat.
10. Cook for 30 seconds or until just set.
11. Slide omelet onto a plate.

12. Cover to keep warm.

13. Repeat with remaining oil and egg mixture to make 4 omelets.

14. Place quarter of the mushroom mixture over one half of each omelet.

15. Fold over to enclose filling.

16. Serve by sprinkling with coriander and remaining chili.

3.2 Yam Kai (Thai Eggs) with Leftover Grains Recipe

Cooking Time: 10 minutes

Serving Size: 2

Ingredients:

- Vegetable oil, one and a half tbsp.
- Cooked pork chops, one cup
- Eggs, four
- Sliced scallions, four
- Sliced shallots, two medium sized
- Cooked barley, one cup
- Fresh coriander leaves, half cup
- Fish sauce, one tbsp.
- Lime juice, two tbsp.
- Sliced red chili, one long

Instructions:

1. In a medium bowl, stir together the lime juice, fish sauce, one teaspoon of the chili, and the cooked grain of your choice.

2. Put the eggs and the remaining half teaspoon of chili paste in a small bowl and beat with a fork to combine.

3. In a large heavy sauté pan, heat half tablespoon of the oil over medium-high heat.

4. Add the shallots, the white sections of the scallions, and the pork, if using, and cook, stirring occasionally, until the shallots are very dark brown and shriveled for about four minutes.

5. Add the scallion greens and the remaining half tablespoon of oil and cook for one minute.

6. Pour in the egg mixture and cook without disturbing for thirty seconds, then turn and stir, breaking it up a little but keeping good-size pieces together, cooking until just set for about one minute.

7. Pour in the grain mixture and cook, turning with a spatula, until heated through for about one minute.

8. Your dish is ready to be served.

3.3 Thai Breakfast Rice Soup with Shrimp Recipe

Cooking Time: 10 minutes

Serving Size: 4

Ingredients:

- Soy sauce, one and a half tbsp.
- Pork stock, three cups
- Jasmine rice, four cups
- Garlic cloves, four
- White peppercorns, one tsp.
- Cilantro, one cup

- Shrimps, 150 grams
- Fish sauce, one tbsp.

Instructions:

1. Pound white peppercorns until fine, then add garlic and cilantro and pound until fine.

2. Add half of this paste to your small pieces of shrimps and mix well.

3. Sauté the small pieces of shrimp in a pan with a little bit of oil just until it is cooked through.

4. Deglaze the pan with some stock as needed and scrape any bits of herb stuck to the bottom.

5. Remove from pan and set aside.

6. If using whole garnish shrimp, sear the whole shrimp over medium high heat until browned and cooked through.

7. Bring the stock to a boil in a pot, add the other half of the herb paste and simmer for one minute.

8. Season with fish sauce and soy sauce, then taste and adjust seasoning.

9. When ready to serve, bring the broth to a boil then add the rice and the shrimp.

10. Bring the soup back to a simmer, and immediately turn off the heat.

11. Serve immediately, if you let this sit, the rice will continue to absorb liquid.

12. Ladle into a bowl, and top with all the condiments as desired.

3.4 Noodles Stuffed Thai Omelette Recipe

Cooking Time: 15 minutes

Serving Size: 4

Ingredients:

- Soy sauce, two tbsp.
- Eggs, eight
- Dried chilies, half tsp.
- Sesame oil, one tbsp.
- Cornstarch, one tsp.
- Button mushrooms, one cup
- Rice noodles, 150 grams
- Sesame seeds, one tbsp.
- White wine vinegar one tbsp.
- Green pepper, one
- Carrots, two
- Canola oil, six tbsp.
- White cabbage, one cup
- Fresh ginger, one tsp.
- Salt and pepper to taste

Instructions:

1. Mix the cornstarch with cold water in a bowl.
2. Add the eggs and whisk together until mixed.
3. Stir in the chilies and season with pepper.
4. Heat one teaspoon of the canola oil in a 20 cm nonstick frying pan over medium heat.

5. Pour in one-quarter of the egg mixture, tipping the pan to spread out the egg in a thin, even layer.

6. Cook for two minutes or until set and golden-brown.

7. Slide the omelet out of the pan onto a plate.

8. Make three more omelets in the same way, stacking them up interleaved with parchment paper.

9. Set aside and keep warm.

10. While making the omelets, soak the rice noodles in boiling water to cover for four minutes, or according to the package instructions, then drain.

11. Heat the remaining two teaspoons canola oil with the sesame oil in a wok or large frying pan.

12. Add the mushrooms, carrots, pepper and cabbage and stir-fry for few minutes or until just tender.

13. Add the soy sauce, vinegar, ginger and rice noodles.

14. Gently toss together until hot.

15. Divide the vegetable and noodle mixture among the Thai omelets and fold them over in half.

16. Sprinkle with the sesame seeds, if using, and serve immediately.

3.5 Thai Breakfast Rice Soup Recipe (Jok)

Cooking Time: 50 minutes

Serving Size: 2

Ingredients:

- Soy sauce, one and a half tbsp.

- Vegetable oil, half cup

- White vinegar, a quarter cup

- Long red chili, one
- Garlic cloves, ten
- Pork mince, 150 grams
- Long grain rice, one cup
- Scallions, to serve
- Garlic cloves, four
- Eggs, four
- White peppercorns, one tsp.
- Cilantro, one cup
- Fresh ginger, one tsp.
- Fish sauce, one tbsp.

Instructions:

1. Place eggs in a heat-proof bowl.
2. Pour over boiling water and allow to stay for ten minutes.
3. Remove eggs and set aside for later.
4. Rinse the rice briefly under running water.
5. Place the rice in a large saucepan with five cups of water.
6. Bring to boil over high heat, then reduce the heat to low and gently simmer for fifteen minutes.
7. Frequently use a wooden spoon to stir and break up the rice grains and to make sure that the rice is not sticking to the bottom of the pan.
8. The rice should be of a thick porridge consistency.
9. Meanwhile, make the pork balls.

10. Use a mortar and pestle to pound the garlic cloves to a paste.

11. Mix the garlic with the pork mince, pepper and fish sauce.

12. Heat four cups of water in a large pot over high heat.

13. When simmering, add teaspoonful of the pork mixture.

14. Simmer for three to four minutes or until the pork balls are cooked through. Remove from heat.

15. Season the stock with fish sauce and white pepper to taste.

16. For the garlic oil, heat the vegetable oil in a small saucepan over medium heat.

17. Add the garlic and gently fry for about two minutes or until just starting to turn golden.

18. Pour into a heat-proof jar or bowl and set aside until ready to serve.

19. For the chili vinegar, combine the chili and vinegar in a small bowl and set aside.

20. To serve, place the pork soup back onto high heat and bring to a simmer.

21. Add half of the rice porridge mixture and stir through.

22. Heat over medium-high heat until just simmering.

23. The soup should have a thick soupy consistency.

24. You can add more or less of the rice porridge mixture according to your taste. Crack one egg into each bowl and ladle the hot rice soup over the top.

25. Top the soup with coriander and spring onion.

26. Serve with fish sauce, ginger, garlic oil, chili vinegar, and pepper.

3.6 Spicy Thai Breakfast Noodles Recipe

Cooking Time: 25 minutes

Serving Size: 4

Ingredients:

- Chili garlic sauce, two tbsp.
- Fresh cilantro leaves, half cup
- Thai basil leaves, a quarter cup
- Beef broth, one can
- Minced lemon grass, one tsp.
- Egg, one large
- Rice stick noodles
- Thai chilies, two
- Jalapeno, one large
- Sliced green onions, half cup
- White peppercorns, one tsp.
- Cilantro, one cup
- Fresh ginger, one tsp.
- Fish sauce, one tbsp.
- Soy sauce, one tbsp.
- Chinese 5 spice, half tsp.

Instructions:

1. Slice vegetables.
2. Mix everything together in a large microwavable bowl.
3. Microwave for five minutes.
4. Make sure your broth is bubbling.

5. Add rice stick noodles to broth mixture.

6. Stir well.

7. The rice stick noodles are cooked in ten seconds in heated broth or water.

8. Quickly add an egg and mix well.

9. It will cook in the broth.

10. Garnish soup with additional fresh Cilantro and sesame seeds.

11. Serve with sides of Garlic Chili Sauce, Fish Sauce and Soy Sauce.

3.7 Pad Thai Omelette Recipe

Cooking Time: 10 minutes

Serving Size: 2

Ingredients:

- Tamarind paste, one and a half tbsp.
- Shrimps, two ounces
- Chili sauce, one tsp.
- Palm sugar, two tsp.
- Shitake mushrooms, two
- Bean sprouts, one cup
- Finely chopped shallot, one
- Eggs, four
- Oil, one tbsp.
- Sliced scallions, four
- Green onion, one

- Chopped roasted peanuts, one tbsp.
- Eggs, two
- Birds eye chili, one
- Fish sauce, two tbsp.
- Cilantro, to taste
- Butter, one tsp.

Instructions:

1. Heat the water, tamarind, fish sauce, sugar and chili until the sugar is dissolved and set aside.
2. Heat oil in a pan over medium-high heat.
3. Add the shrimp, shiitake, shallot and garlic and sauté for two minutes.
4. Add the sauce, bean sprouts, green onion and peanuts and cook for one minute.
5. Add the chili and cilantro and remove from heat and set aside.
6. Wipe out the pan and melt the butter over medium heat.
7. Mix the eggs and the fish sauce, pour them into the pan and cook until almost set, about two minutes.
8. Spoon the shrimp mixture onto half of the omelet and fold the other half over.
9. Your dish is ready to be served.

3.8 Boiled Eggs with Thai Dipping Sauce Recipe

Cooking Time: 10 minutes

Serving Size: 2- 4

Ingredients:

- Green onions, a quarter cup
- Eggs, five
- Red cayenne chili, two tbsp.
- Fish sauce, two tsp.
- Fresh lime juice, two tbsp.
- Erythritol sweetener, one tsp.

Instructions:

1. Place a medium sized pot quarter filled with water onto the stove.
2. Bring to boil.
3. Once water is being boiled, gently place the eggs into the hot water, and cook for five minutes.
4. While the eggs are being cooked, slice the green onions and chili, set aside.
5. Into a small bowl, mix together the lime juice, fish sauce and erythritol.
6. Remove the eggs from the hot water, run under cold water for one minute and peal shells.
7. Slice in half and place into a wide bowl.
8. Place the lime dipping sauce into the middle, and cover with green onions and chili.
9. Dip the eggs into the dipping sauce, and enjoy.

3.9 Thai Vegetable Omelette Recipe

Cooking Time: 10 minutes

Serving Size: 2

Ingredients:

- Water, two tbsp.
- Turmeric powder, one pinch
- Salt to taste
- Garlic cloves, four
- Eggs, two
- Mix veggies, one cup
- Olive oil

For Thai Dressing:

- Fish sauce, half tbsp.
- Brown sugar, half tbsp.
- Chopped small chili, one
- Water, one tbsp.
- Peanut oil, one tsp.
- Rice vinegar, half tbsp.
- Sweet chili sauce, half tbsp.

Instructions:

1. Heat up a cast iron skillet with some oil and quickly stir-fry garlic, bok choy, broccoli, asparagus, snow peas, mushrooms, and bean sprouts or any other vegetable of your choice.

2. Season with salt and pepper and cook until veggies are tender but still crisp. Set aside.

3. In a medium bowl, beat together the eggs, water, salt and turmeric.

4. Wipe the cast iron skillet clean with paper towel, and add a bit more oil.

5. Heat the skillet up again, and pour in the beaten eggs.

6. Cook over low heat until the eggs start to set.

7. Remove the skillet from the heat, while the hot skillet continues to cook the omelet further, top it with the cooked assorted vegetables, and then fold the omelet over them.

8. Drizzle with Thai dressing and serve with remaining dressing on the side.

3.10 Khai Yat Sai Recipe

Cooking Time: 10 minutes

Serving Size: 2

Ingredients:

- Scallions, four
- Mixed mushrooms, 250g
- Salt to taste
- Garlic cloves, one
- Eggs, four
- Cilantro, half cup
- Thai chili, half tsp.
- Thai basil, two springs
- Fish sauce, two tbsp.
- Oyster sauce, two tbsp.

- Black sesame seeds, two tbsp.

- Pepper to taste

- Vegetable oil, as required

Instructions:

1. Thinly slice scallions, separating the greens from the whites.

2. Mince the garlic. Roughly chop mushrooms and cilantro.

3. Mince the Thai chili.

4. In a frying pan, sauté chopped mushrooms with some vegetable oil until soft.

5. Add chopped garlic and scallion whites.

6. Add tomato paste over high heat and let fry shortly.

7. Season it with salt.

8. Add most of the chopped cilantro when it is almost done and mix together well.

9. Remove from heat and set aside.

10. In a bowl, whisk the eggs together with fish sauce, half of black sesame seeds, and chopped Thai chili.

11. Season with salt and pepper if necessary.

12. Pour half of the mixture into a big frying pan with hot oil to make a crepe.

13. Add half of the prepared mushroom mixture on one side of the crepe, and then fold it in half to form an omelet.

14. Repeat the process and make another omelet with the remaining egg and mushroom mixture.

15. Garnish with oyster sauce, scallion greens, Thai basil, remaining black sesame seeds and cilantro and serve.

3.11 Thai Scrambled Eggs Recipe

Cooking Time: 10 minutes

Serving Size: 4

Ingredients:

- Salt to taste
- Baby plum tomatoes, four
- Eggs, four
- Cilantro, half cup
- Spring onions, four
- Tortilla, as required
- Pepper to taste
- Butter, as required

Instructions:

1. Put the butter, spring onions and chili in a small pan.
2. Cook for a couple of minutes until softened.
3. Beat together the eggs and milk.
4. Add to the pan and cook them until scrambled.
5. Stir in the tomatoes and coriander leaves, if using.
6. Serve with griddled tortillas.

3.12 Kai Jeow Recipe

Cooking Time: 10 minutes

Serving Size: 1

Ingredients:

- Soy sauce, one tsp.
- Chopped scallions, one
- Eggs, two
- Cilantro, for garnish
- Salt to taste
- Sirarcha, as per taste
- Pepper to taste
- Olive oil, one tsp.

Instructions:

1. Heat the oil in a frying pan or wok until very hot.
2. Beat the eggs, chopped spring onion, soy sauce, salt and pepper.
3. Pour into the hot pan.
4. Cook for few minutes until lightly browned, flip and cook for further two minutes on the other side.
5. Serve immediately, drizzled with sriracha sauce to taste.

3.13 Thai Breakfast Baskets Recipe

Cooking Time: 20 minutes

Serving Size: 4

Ingredients:

- Minced green onion, one
- Minced jalapeno, a quarter cup

- Egg roll wrappers, eight

- Mango, one small

- Queso fresco, a quarter cup

- Avocado, one small

- Salsa Verde, a quarter cup

- Sesame oil, one tsp.

- Pumpkin seeds, to garnish

- Lime juice, one tsp.

Instructions:

1. Press wraps into nonstick muffin cups.

2. Bake at 375 degrees for seven minutes or till lightly browned and crisp.

3. Remove baskets from cups to wire rack to cool.

4. Combine remaining ingredients in medium sized bowl; fill each basket, dividing equally.

5. Garnish with pumpkin seeds and serve.

3.14 Thai Breakfast Bake Recipe

Cooking Time: 35 minutes

Serving Size: 4

Ingredients:

- Minced garlic, one tsp.

- Minced onion, one

- Diced tomatoes, one medium

- Grated potatoes, four cups

- Ground cumin, half tsp.

- Salt, half tsp.
- Ground coriander, half tsp.
- Red bell pepper, one small
- Coconut aminos, half tsp.
- Coconut milk, a quarter cup
- Ghee, one tsp.
- Eggs, four
- Lime juice, one tsp.

Instructions:

1. Preheat the oven to 350 degrees.
2. In a cast iron pan, melt the ghee over medium heat.
3. Add the onion, garlic, ginger, and red pepper and sauté until the onion starts to get translucent.
4. Add the coconut milk, coconut aminos, lime juice, spices, sand salt and mix.
5. Cook for another five minutes.
6. Add the tomato and sweet potato and mix well to combine.
7. Turn the stovetop off and transfer the pan to the oven and bake for twenty-five minutes.
8. Remove from the oven, and turn the oven to broil.
9. Make four little wells in the sweet potatoes and crack an egg in each.
10. Place the pan back in the oven on the top rack for five minutes depending on how you like your eggs to be cooked.
11. Your dish is ready to be served.

3.15 Thai Breakfast Bowl Recipe

Cooking Time: 1 minutes

Serving Size: 6

Ingredients:

- Chopped bell peppers, one
- Minced garlic, one
- Shredded carrots, five
- Toasted cashews, one cup
- Coconut milk, fourteen ounces
- Salt, half tsp.
- Shredded kale leave, two and a half cups
- Blackberries, one and a half cup
- Shredded Napa cabbage, two and a half cups
- Yellow curry powder, one tbsp.
- Ghee, one tsp.
- Garlic chili paste, one tsp.
- Lime juice, one tsp.

Instructions:

1. Place the dressing ingredients into a high-speed blender.
2. Blend on high speed for about 30 seconds, until smooth and creamy throughout.
3. Add salad ingredients to a large bowl and toss with as much dressing as you would like.
4. Add a little bit it at a time.

5. Serve right away.

3.16 Thai Breakfast Quesadilla Recipe

Cooking Time: 10 minutes

Serving Size: 2

Ingredients:

- Red bell peppers, a quarter cup
- Flour tortillas, two (12-inch size)
- Small green onion
- Thai peanut satay sauce, two tablespoons
- Grilled chicken (spicy seasoning optional), four ounces
- Reduced fat monetary jack cheese, half cup

Instructions:

1. Heat a skillet over medium-low heat.
2. Place two tortillas on a clean workspace.
3. Top one tortilla with Monterey Jack cheese, sliced chicken, peanut satay sauce, sliced red peppers, and green onions.
4. Place the second tortilla on top of the ingredients.
5. Spray top of the tortilla lightly with nonstick olive oil cooking spray.
6. Transfer quesadilla into preheated skillet.
7. Cook for five minutes, or until golden brown.
8. Spray top tortilla, and then flip in skillet.
9. Cook until golden brown.
10. Serve right away.

3.17 Thai French Toast Recipe

Cooking Time: 5 minutes

Serving Size: 6

Ingredients:

- Sweetened condensed milk, for garnish
- Eggs, two
- White bread, six slices
- Granulated sugar, two tablespoons
- Whole milk, half cup
- Vegetable oil, half cup
- Kosher salt, a pinch

Instructions:

1. In a medium bowl, whisk together the milk, eggs, sugar, and salt until combined.

2. Pour the mixture into a shallow dish, and then dip each slice of bread into the batter, stacking the slices and letting them sit in the dish while you heat the oil.

3. In a wok, heat the vegetable oil to 325 degrees and line a sheet pan with a wire rack.

4. Working with two slices at a time, shake off any excess batter, and fry, flipping once until golden brown, two minutes per side.

5. Transfer each slice to the prepared sheet pan to drain.

6. Divide the French toast between plates and top each piece with a heavy drizzle of sweetened condensed milk, and then serve.

3.18 Thai Breakfast Porridge Recipe

Cooking Time: 5 minutes

Serving Size: 4

Ingredients:

- Vegetable stock, six cups
- Sesame seeds, one tbsp.
- White rice, one cup
- Poached eggs, four
- Sautéed red cabbage, one cup
- Kimchi, half cup
- Chives, for garnish

Instructions:

1. Bring water to a boil and add the rice. Bring all ingredients to a simmer, and cover the pan.

2. Continue to simmer for thirty minutes until the rice porridge is very creamy.

3. While the rice is simmering, you can prepare the optional garnishes.

4. Remove from heat, add your desired garnishes, and serve warm.

Chapter 4: Thai Lunch and Dinner Recipes

Thai lunch and dinner recipes consist of amazing dishes that are healthy, nutritious and flavorful at the same time. Following are some amazing Thai lunch and dinner recipes that you can easily make at home:

4.1 Pad Thai Recipe

Cooking Time: 15 minutes

Serving Size: 4

Ingredients:

- Chopped green onions, three
- Eggs, two
- Fresh bean sprouts, half cup
- Garlic cloves, three
- Oil, three tbsp.

- Shrimp or chicken, eight ounces
- Limes, two
- Red bell pepper, one
- Flat rice noodles, eight ounces
- Dry roasted peanuts, two cups
- Soy sauce, one tbsp.
- Light brown sugar, five tbsp.
- Fish sauce, three tbsp.
- Creamy peanut butter, two tbsp.
- Rice vinegar, two tbsp.
- Sirarcha hot sauce, one tbsp.

Instructions:

1. Cook noodles according to package instructions, just until tender.
2. Rinse under cold water.
3. Mix the sauce ingredients together. Set aside.
4. Heat one and a half tablespoons of oil in a large saucepan or wok over medium-high heat.
5. Add the shrimp, chicken or tofu, garlic and bell pepper.
6. The shrimp will cook quickly, about two minutes on each side, or until pink.
7. If using chicken, cook until just cooked through, about five minutes, flipping only once.
8. Push everything to the side of the pan.
9. Add a little more oil and add the beaten eggs.
10. Scramble the eggs, breaking them into small pieces with a spatula as they cook.

11. Add noodles, sauce, bean sprouts and peanuts to the pan.

12. Toss everything to combine.

13. Top with green onions, extra peanuts, cilantro and lime wedges.

14. Your dish is ready to be served.

4.2 Easy Thai Noodles Recipe

Cooking Time: 25 minutes

Serving Size: 3

Ingredients:

- Coleslaw mix, one bag
- Green onions, a quarter cup
- Shredded carrots, half cup
- Honey roasted peanuts, half cup
- Oil, three tbsp.
- Rotisserie chicken, two cups
- Linguini noodles, five ounces
- Cilantro, a quarter cup
- Soy sauce, one tbsp.
- Honey, five tbsp.
- Sesame oil, three tbsp.
- Red chili flakes, two tbsp.
- Minced garlic, four

Instructions:

1. Cook linguini noodles according to the package instructions.

2. Drain when fully cooked.

3. While noodles are being cooked, whisk together in a small bowl, the soy sauce, honey, sesame oil, garlic and red pepper flakes.

4. Pour sauce onto drained noodles, and toss together.

5. Add shredded cabbage, shredded carrots and shredded cilantro to noodle mixture and mix.

6. Then gently stir in half of the chopped cilantro, green onions and peanuts, reserving the other half for garnish.

7. Serve warm or cold and garnish with remaining cilantro, green onions and chopped peanuts.

8. Your dish is ready to be served.

4.3 Thai Red Curry Recipe

Cooking Time: 20 minutes

Serving Size: 4

Ingredients:

- Coleslaw mix, one bag
- Green onions, a quarter cup
- Thai basil, half cup
- Kefir lime leaves, half cup
- Oil, one tbsp.
- Boneless chicken thigh, eight pieces

- Coriander, for garnish
- Soy sauce, one tbsp.
- Honey, five tbsp.
- Brown sugar, half tbsp.
- Red curry paste, five tbsp.
- Minced garlic and ginger, one tsp.
- Cooked jasmine rice

Instructions:

1. Heat one tablespoon of vegetable oil in a large saucepan over a medium heat and fry one tablespoon of ginger and one tablespoon of garlic paste for 2 minutes. Add the red curry paste, sizzle for a few seconds, and then pour in the coconut milk.

2. Bring to the boil, reduce to a simmer, stir a little and wait for the oil to rise to the surface.

3. Add the skinless, boneless chicken thighs, cut into chunks, and kaffir lime leaves, and simmer for twelve minutes or until the chicken is cooked through.

4. Add Soy sauce and a pinch of brown sugar, then taste if you like it a little saltier, add more Soy sauce; if you like it sweeter, add a little more sugar.

5. Bring to the boil, take off the heat and add Thai basil.

6. Spoon the curry into four bowls and top with the red chili, a thumb-sized piece of ginger and a few extra basil leaves.

7. Serve with jasmine rice.

4.4 Thai Green Chicken Curry Recipe

Cooking Time: 20 minutes

Serving Size: 2

Ingredients:

- Shredded carrots, two
- Green curry paste, a quarter cup
- Lime, half
- Cherry tomatoes, half cup
- Oil, one tbsp.
- Boneless chicken, eight pieces
- Coriander, for garnish
- Soy sauce, one tbsp.
- Coconut cream, five tbsp.
- Brown sugar, half tbsp.
- Uncooked jasmine rice, one pack

Instructions:

1. In a medium saucepan, bring the water to the boil.
2. Add the jasmine rice, stir, cover with a lid and reduce the heat to low.
3. Slice the carrot (unpeeled) into half-moons.
4. Roughly chop the coriander.
5. Slice the lime into wedges.
6. Cut the chicken breast into thin strips.
7. In a small bowl, combine the Thai green curry paste, coconut cream, the soy sauce, sugar, a good squeeze of lime juice and a drizzle of olive oil.

8. In a large frying pan, heat a drizzle of olive oil over a high heat.

9. When the oil is hot, add the chicken with a pinch of salt and pepper and cook, tossing, until browned and cooked through.

10. Transfer to a plate and repeat with the remaining chicken.

11. Add the Asian greens, carrot and Thai green curry paste and cook until fragrant.

12. Simmer the Vegetables.

13. Season to taste with salt and pepper.

14. Divide the jasmine rice between bowls and top with the Thai green chicken curry.

15. Sprinkle with some of the coriander and squeeze over lime juice to serve.

4.5 Thai Peanut Chicken and Noodles Recipe

Cooking Time: 30 minutes

Serving Size: 4

Ingredients:

- Rice vinegar, two tbsp.
- Sesame oil, one tbsp.
- Water, half cup
- Soy sauce, half cup
- Sirarcha hot sauce, one tbsp.
- Cucumber slices and roasted peanuts
- Coriander, for garnish

- Peanut oil, one tbsp.

- Chicken tenders, one pound

- Peanut butter, two tbsp.

- Minced garlic, half tbsp.

- Rice noodles, one pack

- Onion, one

Instructions:

1. For sauce, whisk together the wet ingredients.

2. Bring a large saucepan of water to a boil; remove from heat.

3. Add noodles; let stand until noodles are tender but firm, five minutes.

4. Drain; rinse with cold water and drain well.

5. In a large skillet, heat one tablespoon peanut oil over medium-high heat; sauté chicken until no longer pink, five minutes.

6. In the same pan, sauté onion in remaining oil over medium-high heat until tender.

7. Stir in sauce; cook and stir over medium heat until slightly thickened.

8. Add noodles and chicken; heat through, tossing to combine. If desired, top with cucumber and chopped peanuts.

9. Serve immediately.

4.6 Thai Salad with Walnut Butter Recipe

Cooking Time: 5 minutes

Serving Size: 6

Ingredients:

- Rice vinegar, two tbsp.
- Sesame oil, one tbsp.
- Soy sauce, half cup
- Sirarcha hot sauce, one tbsp.
- Red cabbage, three cups
- Cilantro, half cup
- Red pepper, one
- Walnut butter, two tbsp.
- Toasted walnuts, half cup
- Dry noodles, one pack
- Carrot, one

Instructions:

1. Cook noodles according to package, rinse and set aside.
2. Prepare sauce by whisking all of the ingredients together in a bowl.
3. Add noodles, sliced veggies, cilantro, and toasted walnuts to another large bowl.
4. Pour sauce on top of noodle and veggie bowl and toss till fully coated.
5. Add sesame seeds on top.
6. Serve cold.

4.7 Thai Chicken Fried Rice Recipe

Cooking Time: 30 minutes

Serving Size: 4

Ingredients:

- Fish sauce, two tbsp.
- Egg, one
- Soy sauce, half cup
- Cooked brown jasmine rice, three cups
- Tomatoes, two
- Cilantro, half cup
- Salt and pepper, to taste
- Vegetable oil, two tbsp.
- Thai chili peppers, three
- Toasted walnuts, half cup
- Chicken breast, eight ounces
- Onion, one
- Scallions, half cup
- Minced garlic, one tsp.

Instructions:

12. Heat a large nonstick wok over high heat.
13. Meanwhile, season chicken lightly with salt and pepper.
14. When the wok is very hot, add two teaspoons of the oil.
15. When the oil is hot, add the chicken and cook on high until it is browned all over and cooked through.
16. Remove chicken from wok and set aside, add the eggs, pinch of salt and cook a minute or two until done.

17. Add the remaining oil to the wok and add the onion, scallions and garlic.

18. Sauté for a minute, add the chili pepper if using, tomatoes and stir in all the rice.

19. Add the soy sauce and fish sauce stir to mix all the ingredients.

20. Keep stirring a few minutes, and then add egg and chicken back to the wok.

21. Adjust soy sauce if needed and stir well for another 30 seconds.

22. Your dish is ready to be served.

4.8 Thai Rice Noodles with Chicken and Asparagus Recipe

Cooking Time: 40 minutes

Serving Size: 4

Ingredients:

- Asparagus, half pound
- Brown sugar, one tbsp.
- Soy sauce, a quarter cup
- Fish sauce, one tbsp.
- Chili garlic sauce, one tbsp.
- Oil, two tbsp.
- Chicken breast, eight ounces
- Rice noodles, half pound
- Minced garlic, one tsp.

Instructions:

1. Pour noodles into bowl and cover with hot tap water.
2. Soak for twenty minutes.
3. Heat oil in large skillet over medium-high heat.
4. Add garlic and stir fry until golden.
5. Add fish sauce or salt and chicken.
6. Stir fry until done.
7. Add soy sauce, chili pepper sauce, and brown sugar.
8. Mix until sugar is dissolved.
9. Drain noodles and add to skillet along with asparagus.
10. Stir fry noodles until firm but tender.
11. Your dish is ready to be served.

4.9 Thai Green Curry Soup Recipe

Cooking Time: 20 minutes

Serving Size: 4

Ingredients:

- Sliced mushrooms, one cup
- Vegetable stock, four cups
- Broccoli florets, three cups
- Coconut milk, a quarter cup
- Brown sugar, one tbsp.
- Soy sauce, one tsp.
- Thai green curry paste, two tbsp.
- Sesame oil, two tbsp.
- Salt to taste

- Crushed peanuts, one tbsp.

- Spring onion greens, one tbsp.

- Rice noodles, half pound

- Fresh basil, half cup

- Lime, two

- Minced garlic, one tsp.

Instructions:

1. Heat oil in a saucepan.

2. Add the vegetables (broccoli, mushroom) and stir fry them over high heat for five minutes.

3. Transfer to a plate and set aside.

4. In the same saucepan, add the garlic, ginger, and green curry paste.

5. Sauté the curry paste for few minutes to combine it evenly with the oil.

6. Add the coconut milk, brown sugar, and soy sauce.

7. Stir until the curry paste is nicely dissolved.

8. Next, add the vegetable stock, salt, and stir to combine.

9. Taste and add more coconut milk for a milder taste or green chilies to make it spicy.

10. Add the vermicelli noodles.

11. Simmer the soup till noodles are cooked.

12. This takes five minutes over medium heat.

13. Once noodles are cooked, add stir fry vegetables and give the soup a good stir. At this stage, if the soup seems too thick add more vegetable stock to get the desired consistency, simmer, and turn off the heat.

14. Just before serving, garnish the soup with fresh herbs, crushed peanuts, and juice of lemon.

15. Serve the soup warm.

4.10 Thai Chicken Coconut Curry Recipe

Cooking Time: 25 minutes

Serving Size: 6

Ingredients:

- Yellow onion, one
- Ground coriander, one tbsp.
- Soy sauce, a quarter cup
- Fish sauce, one tbsp.
- Coconut milk, one cup
- Shredded carrots, one cup
- Garlic and ginger paste, one tbsp.
- Oil, two tbsp.
- Fresh spinach leaves, three cups
- Cilantro, a quarter cup
- Brown sugar, two tbsp.
- Salt and pepper to taste
- Thai red curry paste, three tbsp.
- Chicken breast, one pound
- Rice to serve
- Lime juice, two tbsp.

Instructions:

1. To a large skillet, add the oil, onion, and sauté over medium-high heat until the onions begin to soften for about five minutes; stir intermittently.

2. Add chicken and cook for about five minutes, or until chicken is done; flip and stir often to ensure even cooking.

3. Add the garlic, ginger, coriander, and cook for about one minute, or until fragrant; stir frequently.

4. Add the coconut milk, carrots, Thai curry paste, salt, pepper, and stir to combine.

5. Reduce the heat to medium, and allow mixture to gently boil for about five minutes, or until liquid volume has reduced as much as desired and thickens slightly.

6. Add the spinach, lime juice, and stir to combine.

7. Cook until spinach is wilted and tender.

8. Taste and optionally add brown sugar, additional curry paste, salt, and pepper to taste.

9. Evenly sprinkle with the cilantro and serve immediately.

4.11 Thai Crunch Salad with Peanut Butter Dressing Recipe

Cooking Time: 5 minutes

Serving Size: 4-6

Ingredients:

- Shredded green cabbage, two cups
- Shredded red cabbage, two cups

- Sliced red bell pepper, one cup
- Shredded carrots, one cup
- Sliced yellow bell pepper, one cup
- Shredded carrots, one cup
- Green onions, a quarter cup
- Toasted Almonds, half cup
- Honey, two tbsp.
- Cilantro, a quarter cup
- Brown sugar, two tbsp.
- Salt and pepper to taste
- Sesame oil, one tsp.
- Peanut butter, half cup
- Fish sauce, two tsp.
- Lime juice, two tbsp.

Instructions:

1. Combine all of the dressing ingredients in a high-powered blender and blend until smooth and creamy.
2. Add all of the salad ingredients to a large bowl.
3. Drizzle your desired amount of the peanut dressing over the salad.
4. Toss the salad until well combined and coated in the dressing.
5. Your dish is ready to be served.

4.12 Thai Basil Chicken Recipe

Cooking Time: 20 minutes

Serving Size: 6

Ingredients:

- Fresh Thai basil leaves, two cups
- Oyster sauce, two tsp.
- Honey, two tbsp.
- Boneless chicken, two pounds
- Brown sugar, two tbsp.
- Salt and pepper to taste
- Canola oil, one tsp.
- Lime juice, two tbsp.
- Lime wedges, 4
- Crushed red chili flakes, two tsp.
- Fish sauce, two tsp.
- Minced garlic, two tbsp.

Instructions:

1. In a large bowl, stir together sliced chicken, oyster sauce, soy sauce, fish sauce, lime juice and brown sugar until evenly coated.
2. Allow chicken to marinate while preparing the rest of the meal.
3. Heat canola oil in a large skillet or wok over medium-high heat.
4. Add garlic and red pepper flakes and sauté until fragrant for about thirty seconds.
5. Add chicken and sauce and increase heat to high.

6. Cook, stirring frequently, until chicken is cooked through and no longer pink for about five minutes.

7. Add basil leaves and continue to cook, stirring occasionally, until basil leaves have wilted for about four minutes.

8. Your dish is ready to be served.

4.13 Thai Fish Curry Recipe

Cooking Time: 30 minutes

Serving Size: 4

Ingredients:

- Coconut cream, two cups
- Coconut milk, one cup
- Barracuda fish, 800 g
- Salt, to taste
- Kaffir lime leaves, twenty
- Lemongrass, two stalks
- Turmeric, one tsp.
- Thai dry chilies, two
- Black pepper, one tsp.
- Shrimp paste, two tbsp.
- Lime wedges, 4
- Crushed red chili flakes, two tsp.
- Bean sprouts
- Lemon basil
- Chinese long beans

- Fresh rice noodles, two pounds

- Minced garlic, two tbsp.

- Deep fried chilies

Instructions:

1. Gut and clean the fish, then cut into medium sized pieces.

2. Bring a pot of water to boil, and then boil the fish for about ten minutes until fully cooked.

3. Remove the fish from the water, drain fully, and leave to cool.

4. Once the fish is cool, carefully take off the skin and debone all the meat from the fish, and flake the fish in your fingers so it is almost like deboned minced fish.

5. Discard the bones and skin.

6. Set aside the fish for later.

7. Cut off the ends of the lemongrass and tear off the outer few layers, then shave the lemongrass into small pieces.

8. Cut the turmeric into small pieces as well.

9. Then add the lemongrass, turmeric, garlic, and peppercorns, and pound for about thirty minutes until a relatively smooth paste.

10. Once the paste is pretty smooth, the final step is to add the shrimp paste, and pound and mix for another five minutes.

11. Set aside.

12. In a large pot or sauce pan, add all the coconut milk and curry paste, then turn on medium heat.

13. Stir gently, and only in one direction, making sure all the curry paste dissolves into the coconut milk.

14. Add the minced fish, season with salt, and tear the kaffir lime leaves in half and add them to the curry.

15. Keep stirring in one direction, and once it comes to a boil, turn down the heat.

16. Keep stirring gently for about five minutes once it comes to a boil.

17. Your dish is ready to be served.

4.14 Pork Pad Thai Recipe

Cooking Time: 15 minutes

Serving Size: 4

Ingredients:

- Chopped green onions, three
- Eggs, two
- Fresh bean sprouts, half cup
- Garlic cloves, three
- Oil, three tbsp.
- Limes, two
- Red bell pepper, one
- Flat rice noodles, eight ounces
- Dry roasted peanuts, two cups
- Soy sauce, one tbsp.
- Light brown sugar, five tbsp.
- Fish sauce, three tbsp.

- Creamy peanut butter, two tbsp.
- Rice vinegar, two tbsp.
- Sirarcha hot sauce, one tbsp.
- Pork strips, half pound

Instructions:

1. Place all sauce ingredients in a jar and shake until well combined.
2. Bring 4 quarts of water to a boil.
3. Remove from heat and drop noodles in.
4. Stir to separate and cover with a lid.
5. Let them soak for six minutes.
6. Heat two tablespoon oil in a large skillet over medium-high heat.
7. Add the garlic and pork strips and cook until evenly browned on all sides and fully cooked.
8. Add the sprouts, carrots, pepper, and noodles in with the pork and stir fry for one to two minutes.
9. Take the pan off the heat and mix in the sauce, green onions, and peanuts.
10. Top with cilantro and sesame seeds and serve.

4.15 Beef Pad Thai Recipe

Cooking Time: 15 minutes

Serving Size: 4

Ingredients:

- Chopped green onions, three
- Eggs, two

- Fresh bean sprouts, half cup
- Garlic cloves, three
- Oil, three tbsp.
- Limes, two
- Red bell pepper, one
- Flat rice noodles, eight ounces
- Dry roasted peanuts, two cups
- Soy sauce, one tbsp.
- Light brown sugar, five tbsp.
- Fish sauce, three tbsp.
- Creamy peanut butter, two tbsp.
- Rice vinegar, two tbsp.
- Sirarcha hot sauce, one tbsp.
- Beef strips, half pound

Instructions:

1. Place all sauce ingredients in a jar and shake until well combined.
2. Bring 4 quarts of water to a boil.
3. Remove from heat and drop noodles in.
4. Stir to separate and cover with a lid.
5. Let them soak for six minutes.
6. Heat two tablespoon oil in a large skillet over medium-high heat.
7. Add the garlic and beef strips and cook until evenly browned on all sides and fully cooked.

8. Add the sprouts, carrots, pepper, and noodles in with the beef and stir fry for one to two minutes.

9. Take the pan off the heat and mix in the sauce, green onions, and peanuts.

10. Top with cilantro and sesame seeds and serve.

4.16 Thai Chopped Salad with Sesame Garlic Dressing Recipe

Cooking Time: 5 minutes

Serving Size: 4-6

Ingredients:

- Shredded green cabbage, two cups
- Shredded red cabbage, two cups
- Sliced red bell pepper, one cup
- Shredded carrots, one cup
- Sliced yellow bell pepper, one cup
- Shredded carrots, one cup
- Green onions, a quarter cup
- Toasted Almonds, half cup
- Honey, two tbsp.
- Cilantro, a quarter cup
- Brown sugar, two tbsp.
- Salt and pepper to taste
- Sesame oil, one tsp.
- Sesame, half cup
- Fish sauce, two tsp.

- Garlic paste, two tbsp.

Instructions:

1. Combine all of the dressing ingredients in a high-powered blender and blend until smooth and creamy.

2. Add all of the salad ingredients to a large bowl.

3. Drizzle your desired amount of the sesame garlic dressing over the salad.

4. Toss the salad until well combined and coated in the dressing.

5. Your salad is ready to be served.

4.17 Quick Thai Salad Recipe

Cooking Time: 5 minutes

Serving Size: 4-6

Ingredients:

- Cucumber cubes, two cups
- Bean sprouts, two cups
- Spring onion, one cup
- Shredded carrots, one cup
- Fresh mint leaves
- Fresh basil leaves
- Brown sugar, two tbsp.
- Peanuts
- Lime juice, two tsp.
- Fish sauce, two tsp.

Instructions:

1. In a bowl, mix together the veg and herbs.

2. Make the dressing by mixing together the fish sauce, lime juice and sugar.

3. When ready to serve, pour the dressing over the salad, toss to coat and scatter over the peanuts.

4.18 Thai Chicken Salad Recipe

Cooking Time: 5 minutes

Serving Size: 8

Ingredients:

- Carrots, one cup
- Cucumber, one cup
- Bok choy, two cups
- Cucumber, one cup
- Fresh mint leaves
- Green cabbage, three cups
- Chicken breast, two pounds
- Peanuts, half cup
- Olive oil, two tsp.
- Fish sauce, two tsp.
- Chili garlic sauce, two tsp.
- Honey, one tbsp.
- Peanut butter, two tbsp.
- Soy sauce, two tsp.

Instructions:

1. Whisk all the ingredients for the dressing together in a bowl or give them a shake in a mason jar.

2. You can microwave the peanut butter for fifteen seconds to soften it for easier mixing, if needed.

3. Add all the salad ingredients to a large bowl along with the dressing.

4. Toss everything well and serve right away.

Chapter 5: Thai Dessert Recipes

This chapter contains amazing Thai dessert recipes that you can easily make in your kitchen without any stress.

5.1 Thai Coconut Pudding Cake Recipe

Cooking Time: 30 minutes

Serving Size: 8

Ingredients:

- Eggs, two
- Coconut milk, one cup
- Rice flour, half cup
- Vanilla extract, one tsp.
- Coconut extract, one tsp.
- Sugar, a quarter cup
- Dry shredded coconut

- Coconut cream

Instructions:

1. Place one cup coconut milk in a mixing bowl.
2. Crack in the eggs, and add a pinch of salt.
3. Beat well with a fork or whisk until smooth.
4. Sprinkle the rice flour over and beat until smooth.
5. Add the coconut extracts and sugar.
6. Taste-test the batter for sweetness, adding a little more sugar if desired. Grease 4 ramekins with a few drops of cooking oil.
7. Ladle the batter into these ramekins, filling to 3/4.
8. Place ramekins inside a long baking dish.
9. Pour some water into this dish so that it reaches the sides of the ramekins. Place carefully in the oven.
10. Bake at 375 degrees minutes, or until the cakes are set.
11. Add a dollop of the coconut cream and a sprinkling of toasted coconut, if desired.
12. Your cake is ready to be served.

5.2 Mango Sticky Rice Recipe

Cooking Time: 25 minutes

Serving Size: 4

Ingredients:

- Water, one and a half cup
- Ripe mangoes, two
- Thai sweet rice, one cup
- Coconut milk, one can

- Salt, a quarter tsp.
- Brown sugar, five tbsp.

Instructions:

1. Soak rice in one cup water for twenty minutes.
2. Do not drain the rice.
3. Add half cup more water, plus half can of the coconut milk, the salt, and one tablespoon of the brown sugar.
4. Stir well.
5. Add coconut milk, salt, and some of the brown sugar to the saucepan.
6. Bring to a gentle boil, and then partially cover with a lid.
7. Reduce heat to medium-low, or just until you get a gentle simmer.
8. Simmer thirty minutes, or until the coconut water is absorbed by the rice.
9. Turn off the heat but leave the pot on the burner with the lid on tight.
10. Allow it to stay for five minutes.
11. To make the sauce, warm the remaining coconut milk over medium-low heat.
12. Add three tablespoons of brown sugar, stirring to dissolve.
13. Taste-test sauce for sweetness, adding more sugar if desired.
14. Prepare the mangoes by cutting them open and slicing each into bite-sized pieces.
15. Scoop some warm rice into each serving bowl, and then drizzle lots of the sweet coconut sauce over the top.

16. It should look like an English pudding with custard sauce, with the rice whirling in sauce.

17. Arrange mango slices on the rice and finish with a drizzle of more sauce.

5.3 Kanom Tuy Recipe

Cooking Time: 25 minutes

Serving Size: 4

Ingredients:

- Coconut milk, one can
- Salt, a pinch
- Sugar, a quarter cup
- Rice flour, a quarter cup

Instructions:

1. Place coconut milk in non-stick skillet to medium heat.
2. Add rice flour to milk while milk is cold or warm but not hot and mix well.
3. Add sugar and pinch of salt.
4. Stir until mixture starts to get thick.
5. Add warm water and mix well then take it off the heat, pour into small Thai style ceramic dish.
6. Let it set in the fridge.
7. Your dish is ready to be served.

5.4 Khanom Krok Recipe

Cooking Time: 25 minutes

Serving Size: 4

Ingredients:

- Coconut milk, one can
- Salt, a pinch
- Sugar, a quarter cup
- Rice flour, a quarter cup
- Cooked jasmine rice, 50 g
- Water, one cup
- Shredded coconut, half cup

Instructions:

1. Whisk the rice flour, sugar and salt together until there are no more clumps of flour.
2. Add coconut milk and whisk until sugar is dissolved.
3. Heat pan at 325.
4. To test pan for readiness, sprinkle a bit of water onto the pan, and if it sizzles away immediately, it is hot enough.
5. Brush half of the holes with coconut oil.
6. Then add some of the filling by dunking the teaspoon right into the middle of the shell and wiggle it slightly.
7. After a minute or two of cooking, the cakes should be partially set, go ahead and add your toppings.
8. Your dish is ready to be served.

5.5 Bua Loy Recipe

Cooking Time: 25 minutes

Serving Size: 4

Ingredients:

- Coconut milk, one can
- Pandan water, half cup
- Sugar, a quarter cup
- Pandan leaf, one
- Salt, a quarter tsp.
- Rice flour, a quarter cup
- Sticky rice flour, 50 g
- Water, one cup
- Sweet potato, 50 g

Instructions:

1. To make the sweet potato dumplings, mash the steamed sweet potato and add sticky rice flour.
2. Knead until combined into sandy textured dough.
3. Add water, one teaspoon at a time, until the dough comes together with sheen.
4. This is typically five to six teaspoons.
5. Roll into small marble sized balls.
6. Prepare the pandan bua loy as above by mixing the pandan water with the sticky rice flour.
7. Add more flour if the dough is too thin, or more pandan water if too thick.
8. Roll the dough into marble sized balls.
9. Make the coconut milk soup by adding the coconut milk, both kinds of sugar, salt, and knotted pandan leaf to a small saucepan and simmer for a few minutes.
10. Do not boil.

11. Discard the pandan leaf.

12. Bring a pot of water to the boil and tip in all of the dumplings.

13. Boil for a minute, or until all of the balls are floating.

14. Strain with a spider or mesh strainer and divide up amongst some bowls.

15. Pour the warm sweetened coconut milk over and serve.

5.6 Tub Tim Grob Recipe (Red Rubies Dessert)

Cooking Time: 25 minutes

Serving Size: 4

Ingredients:

- Crushed ice
- Ripe jackfruit
- Coconut milk, one cup
- Pandan leaf, one
- Salt, a quarter tsp.
- Sugar, half cup
- Red food color, few drops
- Water, one cup
- Chestnuts, 50 g
- Tapioca starch, half cup

Instructions:

1. Cut water chestnuts into about one cm. cubes.

2. Add just enough water to cover chestnuts, and then add red food coloring until the water is bright red.

3. Boil pandan leaves in water for ten minutes.

4. Then add sugar and stir to dissolve.

5. Chill completely.

6. Boil coconut milk, salt, water and pandan leaves for five minutes.

7. Bring a big pot of water to a boil.

8. Meanwhile, drain the chestnuts and place in a mixing bowl.

9. Sprinkle about the tapioca starch and toss to coat.

10. Keep adding until all pieces are completely coated in starch and are not sticking together.

11. For a thin coating, you will need about a quarter cup total.

12. For thicker coating you may need up to half cup.

13. Once done, put them in a strainer and shake off excess starch.

14. Prepare an ice water bowl for chilling the rubies after cooking.

15. To cook the rubies, sprinkle half of the rubies into rapidly boiling water, then stir briefly.

16. Boil them for about few minutes.

17. Scoop out a small amount with a slotted skimmer then dunk them into the cold-water bowl, keeping them in the skimmer for a few seconds just until the coating settles into a clear gel.

18. To serve, put a scoop of the rubies into a serving bowl, add jackfruit or young coconut meat if using.

19. Spoon the syrup over, just until it almost covers the rubies.

20. Top with a couple of tablespoons of coconut milk.

21. Your dish is ready to be served.

5.7 Thai Custard Recipe

Cooking Time: 50 minutes

Serving Size: 4

Ingredients:

- Coconut cream, one cup
- Eggs, four
- Vanilla extract, one tsp.
- Palm sugar, half cup

Instructions:

1. Whisk the eggs.
2. Add the coconut cream and the palm sugar.
3. Add in the vanilla extract.
4. Put the custard in steam safe bowls.
5. Add the bowls into layered steamer.
6. Steam for fifty minutes or until the custard reaches 170 degrees
7. As the custard becomes firm, it will expand.
8. You can check to see if the custard is done by poking a toothpick into the custard.
9. Your dish is ready to be served.

5.8 Thai Banana in Coconut Milk Recipe

Cooking Time: 10 minutes

Serving Size: 2

Ingredients:

- Coconut milk, one cup
- Banana, four
- Salt, one tsp.
- Palm sugar, half cup

Instructions:

1. In a medium saucepan, bring the coconut milk to a gentle boil.
2. Add the sliced bananas and reduce the heat to a simmer.
3. Cook until the banana pieces are tender but not falling apart, stirring occasionally, about five minutes.
4. Add sugar and stir until it is fully dissolved.
5. Sprinkle with salt.
6. Serve warm.

5.9 Thai Pumpkin in Coconut Milk Recipe

Cooking Time: 10 minutes

Serving Size: 2

Ingredients:

- Coconut milk, one cup
- Pumpkin pieces, four
- Salt, one tsp.

- Palm sugar, half cup

Instructions:

1. In a medium saucepan, bring the coconut milk to a gentle boil.

2. Add the sliced pumpkins and reduce the heat to a simmer.

3. Cook until the pumpkin pieces are tender but not falling apart, stirring occasionally, about five minutes.

4. Add sugar and stir until it is fully dissolved.

5. Sprinkle with salt.

6. Serve warm.

5.10 Khanum Tako Recipe

Cooking Time: 10 minutes

Serving Size: 2

Ingredients:

- Screwpine leaves, thirty
- Water, three cups
- Chestnuts, twelve
- Palm sugar, half cup
- Coconut cream, two cups
- Corn flour, one tbsp.
- Rice flour, two tsp.
- Salt, half tsp.

Instructions:

1. Wash the screwpine leaves and wipe dry.
2. Prepare the screwpine leaf juice.
3. Cut the screwpine leaves into short lengths.
4. Place into a blender with the water and process until fine.
5. Strain the juice through a muslin cloth and discard the pulp.
6. Place the arrowroot flour, screwpine leaf juice, water and sugar in a saucepan. Mix well.
7. Cook, stirring over medium heat until the mixture is thick, shiny and translucent.
8. Add the chestnuts and mix well.
9. Remove from the heat.
10. Pour the arrowroot mixture evenly into the screwpine leaf cases until they are half-full.
11. Refrigerate for about thirty minutes until the arrowroot layer is set.
12. In the meantime, prepare the coconut cream topping.
13. Place the coconut cream into a clean saucepan and sift in the rice flour and corn flour.
14. Add the salt.
15. Mix well and cook over medium heat until the coconut cream is thickened.
16. Pour the coconut cream topping over the set arrowroot layer.
17. Set aside to cool and set.
18. Serve chilled or at room temperature.

5.11 Red Sticky Rice Recipe

Cooking Time: 10 minutes

Serving Size: 2

Ingredients:

- Palm sugar, one cup
- Glutinous rice, one cup
- Coconut cream, two cups
- Sesame seeds

Instructions:

1. Wash and soak the glutinous rice for at least three hours.
2. Drain and steam the rice for ten mins.
3. In a brass wok or a heavy-base pan add palm sugar and stir until the sugar is dissolved then add coconut cream followed by salt.
4. When the sugar and coconut cream has merged and thickened add cooked rice and stir for around ten minutes.
5. Wait for the rice to cool down and transfer it to a tray. Add sesame seeds on top.
6. Now your caramel rice is ready to eat.

5.12 Thai Pumpkin Pudding Recipe

Cooking Time: 40 minutes

Serving Size: 4-6

Ingredients:

- Tapioca flour, one cup

- Rice flour, half cup
- Pumpkin, three cups
- Coconut cream, half cup
- Arrowroot starch, half tbsp.
- Salt, half tsp.
- Sugar, half cup

Instructions:

1. Mix tapioca flour, rice flour and arrowroot starch together.
2. Gradually add coconut cream, stir constantly until all the coconut cream is used up.
3. It will take about fifteen minutes.
4. Add sugar, pumpkin, salt and coconut milk; continue stirring until sugar and salt are all dissolved.
5. Pour the mixture into a baking pan, spread out evenly, steam over boiling water for twenty minutes or until done.
6. Remove from the heat and allow to cool.
7. Your dish is ready to be served.

5.13 Thai Black Rice Pudding Recipe

Cooking Time: 120 minutes

Serving Size: 4-6

Ingredients:

- Cold water, one cup
- Black rice, one cup
- Salt, half tsp.

- Sugar, half cup
- Coconut milk, one cup

Instructions:

1. Place rice in a bowl and rinse with water by stirring in a counter clockwise motion.

2. Do this repeatedly until the water is clear and clean, indicating the rice is clean.

3. Pick out any odd grains.

4. In a medium saucepan, stir rice, salt, sugar and water and bring to a boil.

5. Stir well and reduce heat to low.

6. Cover and simmer gently for two hours until all of the water has been absorbed and the rice is tender.

7. Stir in the coconut milk and serve immediately as a hot dish.

5.14 Thai Coconut Sticky Rice Recipe

Cooking Time: 25 minutes

Serving Size: 4

Ingredients:

- Water, one and a half cup
- Thai sweet rice, one cup
- Coconut milk, one can
- Salt, a quarter tsp.
- Brown sugar, five tbsp.

Instructions:

1. Soak rice in one cup water for twenty minutes.

2. Do not drain the rice.

3. Add half cup more water, plus half can of the coconut milk, the salt, and one tablespoon of the brown sugar.

4. Stir well.

5. Coconut milk, salt, and some of the brown sugar are added to the saucepan.

6. Bring to a gentle boil, and then partially cover with a lid.

7. Reduce heat to medium-low, or just until you get a gentle simmer.

8. Simmer for thirty minutes, or until the coconut water has been absorbed by the rice.

9. Turn off the heat but leave the pot on the burner with the lid on tight.

10. Allow it to stay for five minutes.

11. Let simmered sticky rice remain in the saucepan.

12. To make the sauce, warm the remaining coconut milk over medium-low heat.

13. Add three tablespoons of brown sugar, stirring to dissolve.

14. Taste-test sauce for sweetness, adding more sugar if desired.

15. Your dish is ready to be served.

5.15 Thai Tea Pudding Recipe

Cooking Time: 25 minutes

Serving Size: 4

Ingredients:

- Condensed milk, one and a half cup
- Thai tea leaves, three tbsp.
- Coconut milk, one can
- Vanilla extract, a quarter tsp.
- Cornstarch, five tbsp.

Instructions:

1. Heat one cup milk to a simmer.
2. Add the Thai tea and let steep for three minutes, no longer or it could become bitter.
3. Drain through a fine sieve.
4. In a sauce pan, whisk together the cornstarch, tea infused milk and remaining milk, condensed milk and vanilla.
5. Place over medium-low heat and bring to a low boil, stirring constantly.
6. Set heat for a constant low boil.
7. Stir constantly for one and a half minutes, scraping the sides and bottom of the pan.
8. Remove from the heat and pour into four pudding cups.
9. Let cool, then refrigerate.
10. Serve cold.

5.16 Thai Sweet Corn Pudding Recipe

Cooking Time: 50 minutes

Serving Size: 4

Ingredients:

- Water, two cups
- Corn ears, three
- Coconut milk, one can
- Vanilla extract, a quarter tsp.
- Sugar, five tbsp.
- Salt, half tsp.
- Tapioca peals, half cup
- Tapioca starch, half tsp.

Instructions:

1. Combine corn cobs and two cups of water in a pot.
2. Bring to a boil.
3. Cover and reduce heat to low and simmer for thirty minutes.
4. Meanwhile, cover tapioca pearls with a half inch of cold water and let stand.
5. Remove corn cobs from hot water and discard.
6. Add corn kernels, coconut milk, sugar, and salt to the pot.
7. Stir to combine. Return to a boil and then simmer for ten minutes.
8. Drain tapioca pearls and add them to pot.
9. Simmer for one minute.

10. Dissolve cornstarch in one tablespoon of water.

11. Remove from heat to cool down.

12. Serve at room temperature or chilled.

5.17 Thai Peanut Ice-cream Recipe

Cooking Time: 45 minutes

Serving Size: 8

Ingredients:

- Cream cheese, two cups
- Corn syrup, two tbsp.
- Coconut milk, four tbsp.
- Vanilla extract, a quarter tsp.
- Sugar, five tbsp.
- Salt, half tsp.
- Peanut butter, half cup
- Salt, half tsp.

Instructions:

1. Mix the coconut milk with the cornstarch in a small bowl to make smooth slurry. Using a hand mixer or a stand mixer with the whisk attachment, mix the cream cheese, peanut butter, and salt in a medium metal bowl until smooth.

2. Combine the remaining coconut milk, sugar, corn syrup, and honey in a 4-quart saucepan, bring to a rolling boil over medium-high heat, and boil for four minutes.

3. Remove from the heat and gradually whisk in the coconut milk cornstarch slurry. Bring this mixture back

to a boil over medium-high heat and cook, stirring once in a while with a spatula, until slightly thickened, about one minute.

4. Remove the pot from the heat.

5. Whisking, gradually pour the hot milk mixture into the peanut butter mixture.

6. Refrigerate for an hour and serve cold.

5.18 Thai Black Beans in Coconut Milk Recipe

Cooking Time: 10 minutes

Serving Size: 2

Ingredients:

- Coconut milk, one cup
- Black beans, one cup
- Salt, one tsp.
- Palm sugar, half cup

Instructions:

1. In a medium saucepan, bring the coconut milk to a gentle boil.

2. Add the black beans and reduce the heat to a simmer.

3. Cook until the black beans are tender but not falling apart, stirring occasionally, about five minutes.

4. Add sugar and stir until it is fully dissolved.

5. Sprinkle with salt.

6. Serve warm.

Chapter 6: Thai Famous and Alternative Recipes

This Chapter contains those famous and alternative Thai recipes that are known worldwide and eaten only by real Thai People and you have been longing to make them in your kitchen.

6.1 Thai Chicken Risotto Recipe

Cooking Time: 40 minutes

Serving Size: 6

Ingredients:

- Lime wedges
- Shallots, for garnish
- Green beans, 200g
- Fish sauce, two tbsp.
- Coconut cream, two tbsp.
- Minced garlic, one tsp.

- Arborio rice, one and a half cup
- Thai red curry paste, half cup
- Skinless chicken thigh filets, 500g
- Peanut oil, one tbsp.
- Red chili, one
- Onion, one
- Kaffir lime leaves, four

Instructions:

1. Preheat the oven to 180 degrees.
2. Heat the oil in a flameproof casserole over medium-high heat.
3. In batches, add the chicken and cook, turning, for few minutes until browned. Remove the chicken from the casserole and set aside.
4. Reduce heat to medium and add the onion, chili, garlic and half the kaffir lime leaves.
5. Cook, stirring constantly, for few minutes until the onion is soft, then add the rice and curry paste and cook, stirring to coat the grains, for a further one minute.
6. Return the chicken to the casserole with the stock and half cup water.
7. Bring to a simmer, then cover with a lid and cook in the oven for twenty-five minutes or until most of the liquid has been absorbed.
8. Remove from the oven and stir in the coconut cream, fish sauce and beans, then cover and let it stay for ten minutes.

9. Top risotto with coriander, fried Asian shallots and remaining kaffir lime leaves and serve with lime halves.

6.2 Thai Chicken Meatballs Recipe

Cooking Time: 20 minutes

Serving Size: 4

Ingredients:

- Lime wedges
- Fish sauce, two tbsp.
- Fresh mint leaves, two tbsp.
- Minced garlic and ginger, one tsp.
- Thai red curry paste, half cup
- Chicken mince, 500g
- Brown sugar, one tbsp.
- Red chili, one
- Kaffir lime leaves, four

Instructions:

1. Combine mince, garlic, ginger, kaffir lime leaves, mint and coriander in a bowl.
2. Using clean hands, roll the leveled tablespoons of mixture into balls.
3. Place on a large plate.
4. Refrigerate for thirty minutes.
5. Meanwhile, place fish sauce, lime juice, sugar and chili in a small bowl.
6. Stir until sugar dissolves.

7. Heat oil in a large, non-stick frying pan over medium heat.

8. Cook meatballs, in two batches, turning, for ten minutes or until light golden and cooked through.

9. Serve with dipping sauce and lime wedges, sprinkled with extra mint springs.

6.3 Hot and Sour Noodle Soup with Prawns Recipe

Cooking Time: 15 minutes

Serving Size: 4

Ingredients:

- Lime wedges
- Fish sauce, two tbsp.
- Tamarind paste, two tbsp.
- Minced garlic and ginger, one tsp.
- Glass noodles, 500g
- Water, four cups
- Tomatoes, two
- Red chili, one
- Prawns, 500g
- Snake beans, one cup
- Kaffir lime leaves, four

Instructions:

1. Place the stock, kaffir lime leaves, chili, ginger, fish sauce, tamarind paste, and water in a large heavy-based saucepan, and bring to the boil over high heat.

2. Reduce heat to medium-low and simmer for five minutes.

3. Meanwhile, place the glass noodles or vermicelli in a large heatproof bowl and pour over enough boiling water to cover.

4. Set aside for three minutes to soften, then rinse and drain well and divide among serving bowls.

5. Add the green or snake beans to the soup and simmer for a further two minutes.

6. Add the tomatoes and prawns, and then remove from the heat.

7. Wait for one minute until prawns are just cooked, then ladle soup over the noodles and garnish with coriander.

8. Serve immediately, with lime cheeks if desired.

6.4 Thai Coconut Soup with Prawns and Mushrooms Recipe

Cooking Time: 15 minutes

Serving Size: 2

Ingredients:

- Lime wedges
- Lemon grass, two sticks
- Fish sauce, two tbsp.
- Mushrooms, one cup
- Coconut milk, one cup
- Prawns, 500g
- Galangal, one can

- Chicken stock, two cups
- Minced garlic, one tsp.
- Palm sugar, two tbsp.
- Shallot, one
- Kaffir lime leaves, four

Instructions:

1. Bruise the chilies and repeatedly hit the lemongrass with the back of a knife, trimming the top and bottom ends and removing the outer layer if dirty or tough.

2. Add them and the coconut milk to a pan on low-medium heat and then tear the kaffir lime leaves and drop them in as well.

3. Reduce the coconut milk all the way down until it splits.

4. Remove the aromatics just before that occurs.

5. As the coconut milk reduces, peel and slice the shallot and three cloves of garlic. Slice the mushroom, as well, into suitable size of pieces.

6. Fry off the shallot, garlic and mushrooms in the coconut oil that has formed in the pan, increasing the heat to medium high.

7. Cook until the onions are soft and translucent.

8. Add the prawns and stir, flash cooking to get some color on the outside.

9. Add the stock and stir everything together, cooking for further five minutes.

10. Stir in some palm sugar and season with fish sauce and lime juice, to taste.

11. Garnish with basil and a wedge of lime.

6.5 Thai Som Tum without Papaya Recipe

Cooking Time: 15 minutes

Serving Size: 2

Ingredients:

- Lime wedges
- Unsalted cashews, two cups
- Fish sauce, two tbsp.
- Thai chili paste, one tbsp.
- Shredded carrot, one cup
- White cabbage, one cup
- Green snake beans, two cups
- Minced garlic, one tsp.
- Palm sugar, two tbsp.
- Bird's eye chili, one

Instructions:

1. In a small pan, dry roast cashews over medium high heat, tossing frequently. Roast until nuts are nearly blackened in small spots for about four minutes.

2. Combine the lime juice, chili paste, fish sauce and sugar in a small bowl.

3. Whisk to combine evenly.

4. Using a mortar and pestle, gently pound the garlic and bird's eye chili until both are crushed and broken into small pieces.

5. Add carrot and beans to the mortar and pound until carrots are moist and beans are crushed.

6. Pour contents of mortar into a small bowl.

7. Add cabbage and cashews.

8. Add liquid into the bowl bits at a time until vegetables are heavily dressed, stirring to combine.

9. Serve immediately or refrigerate and serve within a couple of hours, garnished with lime wedges.

6.6 Thai Green Curry Coconut Sauce Recipe

Cooking Time: 15 minutes

Serving Size: 2

Ingredients:

- Thai green curry paste, two tbsp.
- Unsweetened coconut milk, one cup
- Fish sauce, two tbsp.
- Lime juice, one tbsp.
- Fresh basil, one cup
- Chicken stock, one cup
- Minced ginger, one tsp.
- Brown sugar, two tbsp.
- Cilantro, a quarter cup

Instructions:

1. In a medium saucepan, whisk a quarter cup of the coconut milk with the curry paste.

2. Stir in the remaining coconut milk, the stock, lemon zest, ginger, lime zest, two tablespoons of the fish sauce and the brown sugar and bring to a simmer.

3. Cook the sauce over moderately high heat until reduced by one-quarter for about fifteen minutes.

4. Using a slotted spoon, remove the lemon zest, ginger and lime zest and discard. Stir in the lime juice, cilantro, basil and the remaining one tablespoon of fish sauce; transfer to a bowl.

5. Your curry paste is ready to serve.

6.7 Thai Pandan Chicken Recipe

Cooking Time: 20 minutes

Serving Size: 4

Ingredients:

- Pandan leaves, sixteen
- Skinless chicken thighs, 350 grams
- Fish sauce, two tbsp.
- Coriander roots, four
- Soy sauce, two tbsp.
- White peppercorns, half tsp.
- Oyster sauce, two tbsp.
- Minced garlic, one tsp.
- Coconut milk, two tbsp.
- Tamarind juice, one tbsp.
- Sesame seeds, one tbsp.
- Sirarcha hot sauce, one tbsp.

Instructions:

1. With a pestle and mortar, pound and grind coriander roots, garlic, white peppercorns, one teaspoon of light soy sauce, two tablespoons of oyster sauce and two tablespoon of coconut cream until well combined.

2. In a bowl, mix chicken pieces with marinade until evenly coated.

3. Let it marinate for thirty minutes.

4. In a small pot, on high heat, mix palm sugar, one tablespoon of sweet soy sauce, one tablespoon of light soy sauce, one tablespoon of sriracha hot sauce and one tablespoon of tamarind juice until sugar dissolves and sauce thickens.

5. Set aside to cool and transfer to the sauce dish.

6. Twist the middle part of the pandan leaf to prepare a pocket where you can put a piece of marinated chicken.

7. Wrap the pandan leaf around the chicken by looping the ends of the leaves into the pocket. Cut off any excess leaf.

8. In a pan or pot on medium-high heat, heat up enough oil for deep frying. When the oil is hot enough, about 180 degrees Celsius, deep-fry wrapped chicken for four minutes until the chicken is golden brown.

9. Remove deep-fried pandan-wrapped chicken from hot oil and place on a plate lined with a paper towel to drain excess oil.

10. Place Thai pandan chicken on a serving plate.

11. Sprinkle sesame seeds on the dipping sauce.

12. Serve hot with dipping sauce on the side.

6.8 Thai Beef Salad Recipe

Cooking Time: 5 minutes

Serving Size: 2

Ingredients:

- Tomatoes, two
- Cucumber, two
- Onion, one
- Mint leaves, a handful
- Basil leaves, a handful
- Lime leaves, a handful
- Oyster sauce, two tbsp.
- Barbequed beef strips, half pound
- Thai dressing, as required

Instructions:

1. Place the tomato, cucumber, onion, chili, mint, coriander, basil, peanuts and lime leaves in a large bowl.
2. Place beef strips in the salad.
3. Drizzle the dressing and gently toss to combine.
4. Divide salad among bowls and serve immediately.

6.9 Thai Mango Salad Recipe

Cooking Time: 5 minutes

Serving Size: 2

Ingredients:

- Tomatoes, two
- Cucumber, two
- Onion, one
- Mint leaves, a handful
- Basil leaves, a handful
- Lime leaves, a handful
- Oyster sauce, two tbsp.
- Mango chunks, one cup
- Thai dressing, as required

Instructions:

1. Place the tomato, cucumber, onion, chili, mint, coriander, basil, peanuts and lime leaves in a large bowl.
2. Put mango chunks in the salad.
3. Drizzle the dressing and gently toss to combine.
4. Divide salad among bowls and serve immediately.

6.10 Thai Spicy Lemongrass Soup Recipe

Cooking Time: 25 minutes

Serving Size: 2

Ingredients:

- Tomatoes, two
- Mushrooms, half cup
- Chicken strips, one cup
- Galangal, one cup

- Lemon grass, three
- Cilantro, half cup
- Makrut lime leaves, a handful
- Oyster sauce, two tbsp.
- Fish sauce, two tbsp.
- Thai dressing, as required

Instructions:

1. Whisk together the fish sauce, lime or lemon juice and chili paste in a small bowl.

2. Combine the lemongrass, galangal, makrut lime leaves and water or broth in a medium saucepan over high heat.

3. Bring to a boil; cook for few minutes, then use a slotted spoon to discard the solids.

4. Add the chicken to the pan, making sure the pieces do not stick together.

5. Once the liquid returns to a boil, add the mushrooms and tomatoes.

6. Cook for few minutes, until the chicken is cooked through and the tomatoes get softened, reducing the heat as needed to keep the soup from boiling over.

7. Remove from the heat; stir in the fish sauce mixture, scallion and cilantro. Serve hot.

6.11 Thai Grilled Salmon Recipe

Cooking Time: 25 minutes

Serving Size: 2

Ingredients:

- Salmon fillet, two pounds
- Lemon, two, cut in halves
- Butter, half cup
- Thai seasoning, two tbsp.
- Steamed rice, two cups
- Parsley, half cup
- Minced garlic, one tsp.
- Salt and pepper to taste

Instructions:

1. Season the salmon with salt, pepper, and Thai seasoning, rubbing them well on both sides.

2. Allow the salmon to briefly marinade on a slotted tray, at least for fifteen minutes.

3. Place the salmon on the grill skin side down and brush with oil on both sides. You may also use cooking spray.

4. Cook the salmon, flipping it regularly until it is cooked through.

5. Bring your butter out from the chiller and slice a half cm. thick ring.

6. Return any excess back to the chiller, and discard any paper wrapping of the cut portion.

7. Once the salmon is cooked, serve it with rice, lemon wedges, garlic butter on top, and your choice of vegetables.

6.12 Thai Cucumber Salad Recipe

Cooking Time: 5 minutes

Serving Size: 4-6

Ingredients:

- Cucumber, eight
- Toasted Almonds, half cup
- Honey, two tbsp.
- Cilantro, a quarter cup
- Brown sugar, two tbsp.
- Salt and pepper to taste
- Sesame oil, one tsp.
- Peanut butter, half cup
- Fish sauce, two tsp.
- Lime juice, two tbsp.

Instructions:

1. Combine all of the dressing ingredients in a high-powered blender and blend until smooth and creamy.
2. Add all of the salad ingredients to a large bowl.
3. Drizzle your desired amount of the dressing over the salad.
4. Toss the salad until well combined and coated in the dressing.
5. Your dish is ready to be served.

6.13 Thai Turkey Meatballs Recipe

Cooking Time: 20 minutes

Serving Size: 4-6

Ingredients:

- Lime zest, two
- Turkey leg piece, 500g
- Spring onions, three
- Cilantro, a quarter cup
- Chopped coriander, a handful
- Lime wedges
- Micro leaves
- Garlic cloves, two

Instructions:

1. Simply mix all the ingredients together.
2. Form into eight patties and leave in the fridge for twenty mins to rest and for the flavors to blend.
3. For cooking, either use the barbecue or gently fry in a little oil.
4. Scatter over the herbs and serve with lime wedges.

6.14 Thai Red Curry Paste Recipe

Cooking Time: 10 minutes

Serving Size: 6

Ingredients:

- Cumin seeds, two teaspoons

- Medium red chilies, four
- Garlic cloves, four
- Coriander seeds, two teaspoons
- Chopped coriander, a handful
- Hot paprika, two tsp.
- Grated lemon zest, two
- Lemon grass, four stems

Instructions:

1. Begin by splitting the chilies in half and removing and discarding the seeds.

2. Now take a small frying pan and pre-heat it over a medium heat, then add the coriander and cumin seeds and toss them around in the dry pan to roast them and draw out their flavors.

3. After about five minutes tip them into a mortar and crush them finely to a powder.

4. Now simply place the chilies, spices and all the other ingredients in a food processor and whiz them to a coarse paste.

5. Then freeze in the portions of two tablespoons.

6.15 Thai Seafood Soup Recipe

Cooking Time: 120 minutes

Serving Size: 2

Ingredients:

- Fish sauce, two tbsp.
- Mix seafood, three cups

- Garlic cloves, four

- Coriander seeds, two teaspoons

- Chopped coriander, a handful

- Hot paprika, two tsp.

- Grated lemon zest, two

- Kaffir lime leaves, four

Instructions:

1. Mix all the ingredients together and cover them to simmer in 2 liters of water for two hours.

2. Your soup is ready to be served.

6.16 Thai Peanut Sauce Recipe

Cooking Time: 10 minutes

Serving Size: 6

Ingredients:

- Peanut butter, half cup

- Garlic and ginger paste, half tsp.

- Water, as required

- Unseasoned rice vinegar, one tbsp.

- Maple syrup, one tbsp

Instructions:

1. Mix all the ingredients together.

2. Pour the mixture in a jar and store.

3. Use your sauce on anything you prefer.

6.17 Thai Chicken Soup Recipe

Cooking Time: 50 minutes

Serving Size: 2

Ingredients:

- Soy sauce, one and a half tbsp.
- Vegetable oil, half cup
- White vinegar, a quarter cup
- Long red chili, one
- Garlic cloves, ten
- Chicken mince, 150 grams
- Scallions, to serve
- Garlic cloves, four
- White peppercorns, one tsp.
- Cilantro, one cup
- Fresh ginger, one tsp.
- Fish sauce, one tbsp.

Instructions:

1. Mix all the ingredients together and cover them to simmer in 1.5 liters of water for fifty minutes.
2. Your soup is ready to be served.

6.18 Thai Turkey Soup Recipe

Cooking Time: 50 minutes

Serving Size: 2

Ingredients:

- Soy sauce, one and a half tbsp.
- Vegetable oil, half cup
- White vinegar, a quarter cup
- Long red chili, one
- Garlic cloves, ten
- Turkey mince, 150 grams
- Scallions, to serve
- Garlic cloves, four
- White peppercorns, one tsp.
- Cilantro, one cup
- Fresh ginger, one tsp.
- Fish sauce, one tbsp.

Instructions:

1. Mix all the ingredients together and cover it to simmer in 1.5 liters of water for fifty minutes.
2. Your soup is ready to be served.

Chapter 7: Thai Vegetarian and Slow Cooker Recipes

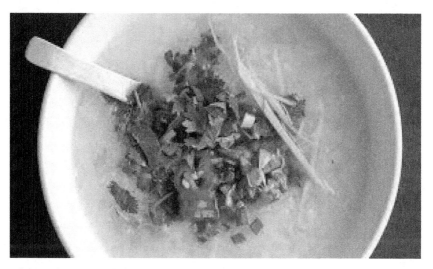

This chapter focuses on Thai vegetarian and slow cooker recipes that you will find very easy to make on your own.

7.1 Rainbow Vegetarian Pad Thai with Peanuts and Basil Recipe

Cooking Time: 5 minutes

Serving Size: 4

Ingredients:

- Fresh Thai herbs, half cup

- Zucchini, one

- Red bell pepper, one

- Eggs, one

- Carrots, two

- Brown rice noodles, four ounces

- Peanuts, half cup
- Vegetable oil, two tbsp.
- Basil sauce, as required

Instructions:

1. Place the uncooked noodles in a bowl of cold water to soak.
2. Cut the zucchini, red pepper, and onion into noodle-like shapes.
3. Shake up the sauce ingredients in a jar.
4. Heat a tablespoon of oil over medium high heat.
5. Add the veggies and stir fry with tongs.
6. Add another tablespoon of oil to the pan.
7. Add the noodles to the hot pan and stir fry for a minute, using tongs to toss. Add the basil sauce and stir fry for another minute or two, until the sauce starts to thicken and stick to the noodles.
8. Add eggs into the mixture and cook.
9. Add in the vegetables, toss together, and remove from heat.
10. Stir in the peanuts and herbs and serve immediately.

7.2 Thai Vegetarian Green Curry Recipe

Cooking Time: 40 minutes

Serving Size: 4

Ingredients:

- Salt, a pinch
- Red bell pepper, one

- Coconut milk, one cup
- Red bell pepper, one
- Thai green curry paste, four tbsp.
- Butternut squash, one
- Vegetable oil, two tbsp.
- Chili, one tsp.
- Water, 200ml
- Shallots, half cup
- Brown rice, four

Instructions:

1. Add the shallots with a pinch of salt and fry for ten mins over a medium heat until softened and beginning to caramelize.

2. Add the curry paste and chili to the dish and fry for two mins.

3. Tip in the squash and pepper, and then stir through the coconut milk along with 200ml water.

4. Season and stir through half of the coriander. Spoon the curry into deep bowls, scatter with the remaining coriander and serve with rice and lime wedges for squeezing over.

7.3 Vegetarian Coconut Curry Recipe

Cooking Time: 40 minutes

Serving Size: 4

Ingredients:

- Corn, half cup

- Salt, a pinch
- Coconut milk, one cup
- Vegetable oil, two tbsp.
- Chili, one tsp.
- Water, 200ml
- Shallots, half cup
- Carrots, one cup
- Cooked brown rice, four cups

Instructions:

1. Add the shallots and carrots with a pinch of salt and fry for ten minutes over a medium heat until softened and begin to caramelize.
2. Add coconut milk into the mixture.
3. Season and stir through half of the coriander and corn.
4. Spoon the curry into deep bowls, scatter with the remaining coriander and serve with rice and lime wedges for squeezing over.

7.4 Vegetarian Pad Thai Recipe

Cooking Time: 15 minutes

Serving Size: 4

Ingredients:

- Chopped green onions, three
- Fresh bean sprouts, half cup
- Garlic cloves, three
- Oil, three tbsp.

- Limes, two
- Red bell pepper, one
- Flat rice noodles, eight ounces
- Dry roasted peanuts, two cups
- Soy sauce, one tbsp.
- Light brown sugar, five tbsp.
- Fish sauce, three tbsp.
- Creamy peanut butter, two tbsp.
- Rice vinegar, two tbsp.
- Sirarcha hot sauce, one tbsp.

Instructions:

1. Cook noodles according to package instructions, just until tender.
2. Rinse under cold water.
3. Mix the sauce ingredients together. Add garlic and bell pepper in a wok.
4. Push everything to the side of the pan.
5. Add noodles, sauce, bean sprouts and peanuts to the pan.
6. Toss everything to combine.
7. Top with green onions, extra peanuts, cilantro and lime wedges.
8. Your dish is ready to be served.

7.5 Thai Vegetarian Red Curry Recipe

Cooking Time: 40 minutes

Serving Size: 4

Ingredients:

- Salt, a pinch
- Red bell pepper, one
- Coconut milk, one cup
- Red bell pepper, one
- Thai red curry paste, four tbsp.
- Butternut squash, one
- Vegetable oil, two tbsp.
- Chili, one tsp.
- Water, 200ml
- Shallots, half cup
- Brown rice cooked, four cups

Instructions:

1. Add the shallots with a pinch of salt and fry for ten minutes over a medium heat until softened and begin to caramelize.

2. Add the red curry paste and chili to the dish and fry for two minutes.

3. Tip in the squash and pepper, and then stir through the coconut milk along with 200ml water.

4. Season and stir through half the coriander. Spoon the curry into deep bowls, scatter with the remaining coriander and serve with rice and lime wedges for squeezing over.

7.6 Thai Vegetarian Fried Rice with Cashews Recipe

Cooking Time: 30 minutes

Serving Size: 4

Ingredients:

- Fish sauce, two tbsp.
- Soy sauce, half cup
- Cooked brown jasmine rice, three cups
- Tomatoes, two
- Cilantro, half cup
- Salt and pepper, to taste
- Vegetable oil, two tbsp.
- Thai chili peppers, three
- Toasted walnuts, half cup
- Onion, one
- Scallions, half cup
- Roasted cashews, half cup
- Minced garlic, one tsp.

Instructions:

1. Heat a large nonstick wok over high heat.
2. When the wok is very hot, add two tsp. of oil.
3. Add the remaining oil to the wok and add the onion, scallions and garlic.
4. Sauté for a minute, add the chili pepper if using, tomatoes and stir in all the rice.

5. Add the soy sauce and fish sauce. Stir to mix all the ingredients.

6. Keep stirring a few minutes and then add cashews on top.

7. Your dish is ready to be served.

7.7 Thai Vegetarian Noodles Recipe

Cooking Time: 25 minutes

Serving Size: 3

Ingredients:

- Coleslaw mix, one bag
- Green onions, a quarter cup
- Shredded carrots, half cup
- Honey roasted peanuts, half cup
- Oil, three tbsp.
- Linguini noodles, five ounces
- Cilantro, a quarter cup
- Soy sauce, one tbsp.
- Honey, five tbsp.
- Sesame oil, three tbsp.
- Red chili flakes, two tbsp.
- Minced garlic, four

Instructions:

1. Cook noodles. While noodles are being cooked, whisk together in a small bowl the soy sauce, honey, sesame oil, garlic and red pepper flakes.

2. Pour sauce onto drained noodles, and toss together.

3. Add shredded cabbage, shredded carrots and shredded cilantro to noodle mixture and mix.

4. Then gently stir in half of chopped cilantro, green onions and peanuts, reserving the other half for garnish.

5. Your dish is ready to be served.

7.8 Thai Vegetarian Kebabs Recipe

Cooking Time: 10 minutes

Serving Size: 4

Ingredients:

- Eggplant, one
- Pineapple, one can
- Tofu, two ounces
- Wooden skewers
- Maple syrup, one tbsp.
- Peanut butter, half cup
- Thai red curry paste, two tbsp.
- Rice vinegar, one tsp.
- Soy sauce, two tbsp.
- Garlic and ginger paste, one tsp.

Instructions:

1. Whisk together all of the marinade ingredients.

2. Cut the squash, pineapple and eggplant, and divide the pieces into eight equal piles. Cut the tofu and add the pieces to the piles.

3. Place the squash, pineapple and eggplant and tofu on the skewers, alternating as you go.

4. Lay the assembled kebabs on a cutting board or baking sheet, and brush with some of the marinade.

5. Grill on medium-high, or broil on high on a baking sheet or broiler pan, for about five minutes per side, or until the squash is tender.

6. Your kebabs are ready to be served.

7.9 Thai Vegetarian Soup Recipe

Cooking Time: 20 minutes

Serving Size: 4

Ingredients:

- Sliced mushrooms, one cup
- Vegetable stock, four cups
- Broccoli florets, three cups
- Coconut milk, a quarter cup
- Brown sugar, one tbsp.
- Soy sauce, one tsp.
- Thai green curry paste, two tbsp.
- Sesame oil, two tbsp.
- Salt to taste
- Crushed peanuts, one tbsp.
- Spring onion greens, one tbsp.
- Rice noodles, half pound
- Fresh basil, half cup

- Lime, two
- Minced garlic, one tsp.

Instructions:

1. Mix all the ingredients together and let it simmer for one hour.

2. Your soup is ready to be served.

7.10 Thai Yellow Curry Recipe

Cooking Time: 40 minutes

Serving Size: 4

Ingredients:

- Salt, a pinch
- Red bell pepper, one
- Coconut milk, one cup
- Red bell pepper, one
- Butternut squash, one
- Vegetable oil, two tbsp.
- Water, 200ml
- Shallots, half cup
- Brown rice, four

Instructions:

1. Add the shallots with a pinch of salt and fry for ten minutes over a medium heat until softened.

2. Tip in the squash and pepper, and then stir through the coconut milk along with 200ml water.

3. Season and stir through half of the coriander. Spoon the curry into deep bowls, scatter with the remaining

coriander and serve with rice and lime wedges for squeezing over.

7.11 Thai Tofu Green Curry Recipe

Cooking Time: 40 minutes

Serving Size: 4

Ingredients:

- Corn, half cup
- Salt, a pinch
- Coconut milk, one cup
- Thai green curry paste, four tbsp.
- Vegetable oil, two tbsp.
- Chili, one tsp.
- Tofu, two cups
- Water, 200ml
- Shallots, half cup
- Brown rice, four

Instructions:

1. Add the shallots with a pinch of salt and fry for ten mins over a medium heat until softened and begin to caramelize.

2. Add the curry paste and chili to the dish and fry for two minutes.

3. Tip in the tofu, and then stir through the coconut milk along with 200ml water.

4. Season and stir through half of the coriander and corn. Spoon the curry into deep bowls, scatter with the

remaining coriander and serve with rice and lime wedges for squeezing over.

7.12 Thai Tofu Green Curry with Quinoa Recipe

Cooking Time: 40 minutes

Serving Size: 4

Ingredients:

- Quinoa, four cups
- Salt, a pinch
- Coconut milk, one cup
- Thai green curry paste, four tbsp.
- Vegetable oil, two tbsp.
- Chili, one tsp.
- Tofu, two cups
- Water, 200ml
- Shallots, half cup

Instructions:

1. Add the shallots with a pinch of salt and fry for ten minutes over a medium heat until softened and begin to caramelize.

2. Add the curry paste and chili to the dish and fry for two mins.

3. Tip in the tofu, and then stir through the coconut milk along with 200ml water.

4. Season and stir through half of the coriander and corn. Spoon the curry into deep bowls, scatter with the remaining coriander and serve with cooked quinoa and lime wedges for squeezing over.

7.13 Thai Vegan Drunken Noodles Recipe

Cooking Time: 15 minutes

Serving Size: 2

Ingredients:

- Green onion, one
- Bell pepper, one
- Thai basil, a handful
- Garlic and ginger paste, one tsp.
- Sesame oil, two tbsp.
- Soy sauce, one tsp.
- Oyster sauce, one tsp.
- Fish sauce, one tsp.
- Salt and black pepper, to taste
- Red Thai chili, one
- Shallots, half cup

Instructions:

1. Cook the vegetables in the sesame oil.
2. Add spices and sauces into the mixture and then add the noodles and mix thoroughly.
3. Your dish is ready to be served.

7.14 Thai Pumpkin and Veggie Curry Recipe

Cooking Time: 40 minutes

Serving Size: 4

Ingredients:

- Corn, half cup
- Red bell pepper, two
- Pumpkin, two
- Salt, a pinch
- Coconut milk, one cup
- Thai red curry paste, four tbsp.
- Vegetable oil, two tbsp.
- Chili, one tsp.
- Butternut squash, two cups
- Water, 200ml
- Shallots, half cup
- Brown rice, four cups

Instructions:

1. Add the shallots with a pinch of salt and fry for ten minutes over a medium heat until softened.

2. Add the curry paste and chili to the dish and fry for two mins.

3. Tip in the pumpkin, vegetables, and then stir through the coconut milk along with 200ml water.

4. Season and stir through half of the coriander and corn. Spoon the curry into deep bowls, scatter with the

remaining coriander and serve with rice and lime wedges for squeezing over.

7.15 Thai Veggie Burger Recipe

Cooking Time: 10 minutes

Serving Size: 4

Ingredients:

- Thai red curry paste, two tbsp.
- Salt, a pinch
- Mix vegetables, two cups
- Thai red curry paste, four tbsp.
- Vegetable oil, two tbsp.
- Green onions, half cup
- Cilantro, half cup
- Garlic and ginger paste, one tsp.
- Thai pickles, as required
- Bread buns, four

Instructions:

1. Mix all the stuff for the burger mixture together and make patty.
2. Fry the patties and then assemble the patty burger by adding pickles into it.
3. Your burger is ready to be served.

7.16 Thai Vegetarian Quinoa Chili Recipe

Cooking Time: 120 minutes

Serving Size: 6-8

Ingredients:

- Quinoa, two cups
- Coconut milk, half cup
- Vegetable broth, half cup
- Thai red curry paste, four tbsp.
- Olive oil, two tbsp.
- Green onions, half cup
- Chili powder, one tsp.
- Curry paste, one tbsp.
- Green bell pepper, one
- Sweet potato, one cup
- Tomatoes, one cup
- Salt and pepper, to taste
- Garlic and ginger paste, one tsp.
- Thai pickles, as required
- Greek yoghurt, as required

Instructions:

1. In a large Dutch oven or soup pot, whisk together the chili powder; curry paste, cumin and a few tablespoons of broth over medium-low heat until smooth.

2. Add in onion, green pepper, garlic, sweet potato and olive oil and sauté for five minutes or until veggies are tender.

3. Add in remaining broth, beans, quinoa, coconut milk, tomatoes, salt and pepper and bring to a boil.

4. Reduce to simmer and cook for about an hour, or until flavors are mixed and quinoa is cooked.

5. Serve topped with sliced green onions and plain Greek yogurt.

7.17 Thai Slow Cooker Vegetable Massaman Curry Recipe

Cooking Time: 3 hours

Serving Size: 6

Ingredients:

- Quinoa, two cups
- Coconut milk, half cup
- Vegetable broth, half cup
- Tomatoes, half cup
- Brown sugar, one tsp.
- Tamari sauce, one tbsp.
- Cauliflower, one
- Potato, one cup
- Green beans, one cup
- Salt and pepper, to taste
- Sirarcha hot sauce, one tsp.
- Peanut butter, half cup
- Peanuts, half cup

Instructions:

1. Stir in the broth, tomatoes, fish sauce, tamari and brown sugar.

2. Add the cauliflower and potatoes, and toss to coat. Cover and cook until the vegetables are tender.

3. Combine the coconut milk and peanut butter in a heatproof bowl and microwave until warm.

4. Pour the coconut milk mixture into the slow cooker, and add the green beans and peanuts. Cover and cook until warmed through.

5. Add the sriracha, and season with salt and pepper.

6. Serve the curry over rice or quinoa, and sprinkle with chopped peanuts and cilantro.

7.18 Thai Slow Cooker Yellow Curry Recipe

Cooking Time: 2 hours

Serving Size: 4

Ingredients:

- Salt, a pinch
- Chickpeas, two cups
- Coconut milk, one cup
- Butternut squash, one
- Vegetable oil, two tbsp.
- Water, 500ml
- Carrots, two cups
- Brown rice, four cups

Instructions:

1. Tip in the chickpeas, butternut squash and carrots. Then stir through the coconut milk along with 500ml water.

2. Season and stir through half of the coriander.

3. Spoon the curry into deep bowls, scatter with the remaining coriander and serve with rice and lime wedges for squeezing over.

7.19 Thai Slow Cooker Pineapple Vegetarian Curry Recipe

Cooking Time: 2 hours

Serving Size: 4

Ingredients:

- Salt, a pinch
- Pineapple, two cups
- Coconut milk, one cup
- Mix vegetables, one cup
- Vegetable oil, two tbsp.
- Water, 200ml
- Curry powder, two tsp.
- Crushed red pepper, one tbsp.
- Minced garlic, half tsp.
- Brown rice, four cups

Instructions:

1. Whisk together the coconut milk, curry powder, salt, crushed red pepper and garlic in a slow cooker.

2. Add the remaining ingredients and cook for two hours.

3. Your dish is ready to be served with brown rice or jasmine rice.

7.20 Thai Slow Cooker Vegetable and Tofu Stew Recipe

Cooking Time: 3 hours

Serving Size: 4

Ingredients:

- Salt, a pinch
- Tofu, two cups
- Coconut milk, one cup
- Mix vegetables, one cup
- Vegetable oil, two tbsp.
- Water, 200ml
- Crushed red pepper, one tbsp.
- Minced garlic, half tsp.
- Curry powder, two tsp.

Instructions:

Whisk together the coconut milk, curry powder, salt, crushed red pepper and garlic in a slow cooker.

1. Add the remaining ingredients and cook for three hours.

2. Your dish is ready to be served with brown rice or jasmine rice.

7.21 Thai Slow Cooker Potato Soup Recipe

Cooking Time: 120 minutes

Serving Size: 2

Ingredients:

- Potato, three cups
- Garlic cloves, four
- Water, four cups
- Coriander seeds, two teaspoons
- Chopped coriander, a handful
- Hot paprika, two tsp.
- Grated lemon zest, two
- Kaffir lime leaves, four
- Coconut milk, one cup

Instructions:

1. Mix all the ingredients together and cover it to simmer for two hours.
2. Your soup is ready to be served.

7.22 Thai Slow Cooker Green Tofu Soup Recipe

Cooking Time: 120 minutes

Serving Size: 3

Ingredients:

- Tofu, three cups
- Garlic cloves, four
- Water, four cups

- Thai green curry paste, two tbsp.
- Coriander seeds, two teaspoons
- Chopped coriander, a handful
- Hot paprika, two tsp.
- Grated lemon zest, two
- Kaffir lime leaves, four
- Coconut milk, one cup

Instructions:

1. Mix all the ingredients together and cover it to simmer for two hours.
2. Your soup is ready to be served.

7.23 Thai Slow Cooker Eggplant Curry Recipe

Cooking Time: 3 hours

Serving Size: 4

Ingredients:

- Salt, a pinch
- Eggplant, two cups
- Coconut milk, one cup
- Cilantro, one cup
- Vegetable oil, two tbsp.
- Water, 500ml
- Crushed red pepper, one tbsp.
- Minced garlic, half tsp.
- Curry powder, two tsp.

- Brown or jasmine rice, two cups

Instructions:

1. Whisk together the coconut milk, curry powder, salt, crushed red pepper and garlic in a slow cooker.

2. Add the remaining ingredients and cook for three hours.

3. Your dish is ready to be served with brown rice or jasmine rice.

7.24 Thai Slow Cooker Chicken Curry Recipe

Cooking Time: 3 hours

Serving Size: 4

Ingredients:

- Salt, a pinch
- Chicken breast pieces, two pounds
- Coconut milk, one cup
- Cilantro, one cup
- Vegetable oil, two tbsp.
- Water, 500ml
- Crushed red pepper, one tbsp.
- Minced garlic, half tsp.
- Curry powder, two tsp.
- Brown or jasmine rice, two cups

Instructions:

1. Whisk together the coconut milk, curry powder, salt, crushed red pepper and garlic in a slow cooker.

2. Add the remaining ingredients and cook for three hours.

3. Your dish is ready to be served with brown rice or jasmine rice.

7.25 Thai Slow Cooker Pumpkin Soup Recipe

Cooking Time: 2 hours

Serving Size: 4

Ingredients:

- Corn, half cup
- Pumpkin, two cups
- Salt, a pinch
- Coconut milk, one cup
- Thai red curry paste, four tbsp.
- Vegetable oil, two tbsp.
- Chili, one tsp.
- Water, 500ml

Instructions:

1. Add the curry paste and chili to the dish and fry for two mins.

2. Tip in the pumpkin, and then stir through the coconut milk along with 500ml water.

3. Season and stir through half of the coriander and corn.

4. Your soup is ready to be served.

7.26 Thai Slow Cooker Peanut Chicken Curry Recipe

Cooking Time: 3 hours

Serving Size: 4

Ingredients:

- Salt, a pinch
- Chicken breast pieces, two pounds
- Coconut milk, one cup
- Cilantro, one cup
- Vegetable oil, two tbsp.
- Water, 200ml
- Peanuts, half cup
- Crushed red pepper, one tbsp.
- Minced garlic, half tsp.
- Curry powder, two tsp.
- Brown or jasmine rice, two cups

Instructions:

1. Whisk together the coconut milk, curry powder, salt, crushed red pepper and garlic in a slow cooker.

2. Add the remaining ingredients and cook for three hours.

3. Your dish is ready to be served with brown rice or jasmine rice.

7.27 Thai Slow Cooker Beef Curry Recipe

Cooking Time: 4 hours

Serving Size: 4

Ingredients:

- Salt, a pinch
- Beef pieces, two pounds
- Coconut milk, one cup
- Cilantro, one cup
- Vegetable oil, two tbsp.
- Water, 500ml
- Crushed red pepper, one tbsp.
- Minced garlic, half tsp.
- Curry powder, two tsp.
- Brown or jasmine rice, two cups

Instructions:

1. Whisk together the coconut milk, curry powder, salt, crushed red pepper and garlic in a slow cooker.
2. Add the remaining ingredients and cook for four hours.
3. Your dish is ready to be served with brown rice or jasmine rice.

7.28 Thai Slow Cooker Coconut Curry Lentils Recipe

Cooking Time: 4 hours

Serving Size: 4

Ingredients:

- Salt, a pinch
- Brown lentils, two cups
- Coconut milk, one cup
- Carrots, one cup
- Tomatoes, two cups
- Cilantro, one cup
- Vegetable oil, two tbsp.
- Water, 500ml
- Crushed red pepper, one tbsp.
- Minced garlic, half tsp.
- Curry powder, two tsp.
- Brown or jasmine rice, two cups

Instructions:

1. Whisk together the coconut milk, curry powder, salt, crushed red pepper and garlic in a slow cooker.

2. Add the remaining ingredients and cook for four hours.

3. Your dish is ready to be served with brown rice or jasmine rice.

7.29 Thai Slow Cooker Chicken Carrot Potato Soup Recipe

Cooking Time: 3 hours

Serving Size: 4

Ingredients:

- Potato, three cups

- Garlic cloves, four
- Water, four cups
- Carrots, three cups
- Chicken, two pounds
- Coriander seeds, two teaspoons
- Chopped coriander, a handful
- Hot paprika, two tsp.
- Grated lemon zest, two
- Kaffir lime leaves, four
- Coconut milk, one cup

Instructions:

1. Mix all the ingredients together and cover it to simmer for three hours.
2. Your soup is ready to be served.

7.30 Thai Slow Cooker Butternut Squash Soup Recipe

Cooking Time: 3 hours

Serving Size: 4

Ingredients:

- Butternut Squash, three cups
- Garlic cloves, four
- Water, four cups
- Coriander seeds, two teaspoons
- Chopped coriander, a handful
- Hot paprika, two tsp.

- Grated lemon zest, two
- Kaffir lime leaves, four
- Coconut milk, one cup

Instructions:

1. Mix all the ingredients together and cover it to simmer for three hours.
2. Your soup is ready to be served.

7.31 Thai Slow Cooker Coconut Quinoa Curry Recipe

Cooking Time: 3 hours

Serving Size: 4

Ingredients:

- Salt, a pinch
- Coconut milk, one cup
- Cilantro, one cup
- Vegetable oil, two tbsp.
- Water, 500ml
- Crushed red pepper, one tbsp.
- Minced garlic, half tsp.
- Curry powder, two tsp.
- Quinoa, two cups

Instructions:

1. Whisk together the coconut milk, curry powder, salt, crushed red pepper and garlic in a slow cooker.

2. Add the remaining ingredients and cook for three hours.

3. Your dish is ready to be served.

7.32 Thai Slow Cooker Whole Cauliflower Curry Recipe

Cooking Time: 3 hours

Serving Size: 4

Ingredients:

- Salt, a pinch
- Coconut milk, one cup
- Cilantro, one cup
- Cauliflower, one whole
- Vegetable oil, two tbsp.
- Water, 500ml
- Crushed red pepper, one tbsp.
- Minced garlic, half tsp.
- Curry powder, two tsp.
- Quinoa, two cups

Instructions:

1. Whisk together the coconut milk, curry powder, salt, crushed red pepper and garlic in a slow cooker.

2. Add the remaining ingredients and cook for three hours.

3. Your dish is ready to be served with any rice of your choice.

7.33 Thai Slow Cooker Salmon Curry Recipe

Cooking Time: 2 hours

Serving Size: 4

Ingredients:

- Salt, a pinch
- Salmon filet pieces, two pounds
- Coconut milk, one cup
- Cilantro, one cup
- Vegetable oil, two tbsp.
- Water, 500ml
- Crushed red pepper, one tbsp.
- Minced garlic, half tsp.
- Curry powder, two tsp.
- Brown or jasmine rice, two cups

Instructions:

1. Whisk together the coconut milk, curry powder, salt, crushed red pepper and garlic in a slow cooker.
2. Add the remaining ingredients and cook for two hours.
3. Your dish is ready to be served with brown rice or jasmine rice.

7.34 Thai Slow Cooker Chicken Pumpkin Curry Recipe

Cooking Time: 3 hours

Serving Size: 4

Ingredients:

- Salt, a pinch
- Chicken breast pieces, two pounds
- Coconut milk, one cup
- Cilantro, one cup
- Vegetable oil, two tbsp.
- Water, 500ml
- Pumpkin, two cups
- Crushed red pepper, one tbsp.
- Minced garlic, half tsp.
- Curry powder, two tsp.
- Brown or jasmine rice, two cups

Instructions:

1. Whisk together the coconut milk, curry powder, salt, crushed red pepper and garlic in a slow cooker.
2. Add the remaining ingredients and cook for three hours.
3. Your dish is ready to be served with brown rice or jasmine rice.

7.35 Thai Slow Cooker Noodles Soup Recipe

Cooking Time: 2 hours

Serving Size: 4

Ingredients:

- Rice noodles, three cups
- Garlic cloves, four

- Chicken broth, four cups
- Coriander seeds, two teaspoons
- Chopped coriander, a handful
- Hot paprika, two tsp.
- Grated lemon zest, two
- Kaffir lime leaves, four
- Coconut milk, one cup

Instructions:

1. Mix all the ingredients together and cover it to simmer for two hours.
2. Your soup is ready to be served.

All the recipes in this chapter are easy to make on your own.

Conclusion

While living a busy life food becomes the only source of happiness for individuals in the 21st century. Different cuisines are available in the world, each of them being totally different from the other. Thai cuisine covers dishes from Thailand and Thai foods are extremely popular in the U.S.A.

In this book, we have discussed different aspects of Thai cuisine along with the Thai recipes. We have discussed in detail the history and origin of Thai foods. Light was thrown upon the evolution of Thai foods over time and the reason behind the popularity of this cuisine in the U.S.A. We have also discussed the advantages of cooking Thai food at home rather than going out for meals or having it delivered to your door stop.

The various spices used in Thai cooking have enormous amount of amazing properties that can have a positive and healthy impact on our overall health. This cookbook includes 100+ recipes that contain breakfast, lunch, dinner, dessert, famous, alternative, as well as slow cooker and vegetarian recipes that you can easily make at home without supervision of any kind. So, why to order or go out for Thai food when you can be the chef at your home? Now make your family and loved ones crave for this delicious food.

Mexican Food

How to Prepare Traditional Mexican Food at Home with Over 100 Recipes Cookbook

By

Adele Tyler

Table Of Content

Introduction

Mexican food is considered as one of the most famous cuisines in the world. Whether we talk about enchiladas, tacos, or tortillas, it is loved by people from different countries in the world. Mexican delights have satisfied the taste buds of many food-lovers. Popular Mexican recipes are available in many restaurants worldwide, as Mexican dishes are much more than just spicy salsa and guacamole. They have the culinary influence of many cultures that have led to today's Mexican colorful and vibrant cuisine. Traditional Mexican food has a wide variety of colorful and healthy ingredients used in it. Mexican recipes are prepared with fresh produce, fiber-packed tortillas, protein-filled beans, and nutritious spices like garlic, chilies, cloves, cumin, and cinnamon.

The best way to celebrate Mexican food's rich history is to try and make these delicious and tasty recipes at home. They are super easy to make. This cookbook has over 100 Mexican recipes for you, from breakfast, lunch, dinner, soups, and desserts, to vegetarian as well as non-vegetarian. This cookbook will help you become pro at making this cuisine at home. There is no other way to have full control over what you eat than to cook at home. You can always customize your recipes, making it healthier without compromising its taste and pure essence.

Knowing about the food history of a particular culture has always been fun. It connects us more to that culture and its cuisines. A small part of this book has been dedicated to the history of Mexican food, the traditional Mexican food ingredients, and the evolution of Mexican food in the United States. In chapter two, the health benefits of Mexican food, and the preference of its homemade cooking has been addressed, which is crucial to maintain a balance in your recipes.

You will find different varieties of Mexican breakfast recipes in this cookbook, from Mexican Baked Eggs, Breakfast Tostada, and Sunrise Sausage Enchiladas to Breakfast Tacos and Eggs & Chorizo Wraps.

In this cookbook, there is a long list of delicious Mexican lunch and dinner recipes. From trying Prawn & Chorizo Quesadilla, Grilled Cumin Lime Chicken, and Mexican Lasagna to Chicken Fajitas and Refried Beans, you will never be short of the choices. For a healthy eating lifestyle, the addition of soup in your daily meal plan can do a lot of good. Find a variety of Mexican soups recipes in this cookbook that are super easy to make at home. A separate portion has been reserved for healthy Mexican vegetarian recipes for veggie-lovers to make the most out of the fresh vegetables.

No menu is complete without salads and desserts. Make the best out of this cookbook, and try some mouth-watering salad and dessert dishes. You will also find the most famous Mexican tacos, burritos, and quesadillas recipes in this cookbook. Each dish is filled with tasty, healthy, and colorful ingredients. Whether you are cooking just for yourself or preparing for a family gathering, this cookbook has a much more satisfying list of incredible recipes to get ready for Mexican Feast.

Chapter 1: History of Mexican Food

Mexican food has a diverse and long history. Some people believe that traditional Mexican food has a significant influence of Mayan Indians, who were gatherers and nomadic hunters. Corn tortillas having bean paste in it was a very common food for them apart from fish, wild and tropical fruits. On the other hand, salsa was derived from the Aztec market. In Spanish, it is used for the sauce. In modern salsa, you can find tomatillo, red tomatoes, chipotle, and avocado. These core ingredients are the same as the past recipe of salsa. In 1885, enchilada was first used in the U.S., but Aztecs had the direct link with the concept and recipe of tortillas as they used it as a wrap.

Aztecs domesticated the tomatillo, which is a fruit. Tomatillo means plump and round. Today, a fruit very similar to tomatillo is very common in the U.S. It provides a tart flavor green sauces. Let's look at the influence of different cultures on Mexican food and Mexican food evolution in the U.S.

1.1 Influence of Different Cultures on Mexican Food

Mexican food has significant influences of different cultures due to the past colonization eras. That increased later on due to the trade between various colonies and countries when globalization started to grow. Mexican food is thus a result of many diverse cultural influences. It has also adopted ingredients and different cooking styles from various cultures.

Mayan Influence

Mayan Indians brought significant culinary influence on Mexican food. They used to live in the Yucatan in Southeast Mexico.

As mentioned earlier, Mayan Indians were gatherers and hunters, so most of their food included many animals like deer, raccoons, armadillos, rabbits, rattlesnakes, spider monkeys, iguanas, pigeons, frogs, turtles, and turkeys. Apart from that, their food also included beans, tropical fruits, and corn. These influences still have been retained in Mexican cooking. This type of food is now well known as Comida prehispánica, or pre-Hispanic cuisine. It is looked at as an exotic cuisine in Mexico's food today.

Aztec Influence

Aztec tribes conquered Mexico and rules over it in the mid-1300s. They added salt, chili peppers, chocolate, and honey into the culinary mix of Mayan Indians. Avocados, tomatoes, and squash became popular. Salt and chili peppers became as crucial for them as they are today in our cuisines. It had a significant influence on their food. Modern Azteca Mexican cuisines still use those traditional Mayan ingredients while adding new flavors as well.

Spanish Influence

Like many countries in the world, Mexico was also under colonization. Spanish invaded colonized Mexico in 1521. They introduced their dishes and recipes to Mexican culture like olive oil, rice, garlic, cinnamon, coriander, and other spices. They brought domesticated animals like sheep, pigs, cows, goats, and chickens. The goats, sheep, and cows were sources of dairy, and cheese became the main ingredient in most of the dishes. They also brought changes to cooking methods.

After the invasion, the Spanish soldiers found out that the cuisine consisted of corn-based recipes with herbs and chilies, tomatoes, and beans.

Then they combined imported addition of rice, pork, beef, chicken garlic, onions, and wine with the local foods of Mexico that mostly included beans, tomatoes, chocolate, corn, avocado, vanilla, papaya, chili peppers, pineapple, squash, peanuts, sweet potato, turkey, and fish.

The Spanish influence led to many dishes such as Chile Rellenos, lomo en adobo, and quesadillas.

French Influence

When the French invaded Mexico, they brought a variety of fantastic baked foods with them. Mexican bolillo and sweetbreads are some examples of French influence. They also introduced various cooking techniques. The combination of their techniques with the Mexican ingredients proved to be fantastic. Mexican ingredients like avocados and squash blossoms were perfect for the French style crepes, mousse, and soups.

1.2 Traditional Mexican Food Ingredients

The three ingredients that have always been in Mexican food before the arrival of Spanish influence are beans, corn, and chilies. Corn was being used in all forms, but mostly consumed as a tortilla. In making quesadillas and tacos today, tortilla is used. Apart from that, tomatoes, avocado, and rice are also used in Mexican dishes today.

Before the arrival of Spaniards, meat was not abundant, so Mexicans used to include beans and corn as the main nutritional ingredients. Heavy spices and chiles were used for a complex flavor in their dishes.

Chile Peppers

The use of chiles is the specialty of Mexican food, and it makes perfect sense as chiles have their deep roots in Mexico. They have always been part of Mexican cuisine.

Even if you go back to thousands of years, the use of chiles was common. Different types of chiles are used in Mexican food like aromatic ancho, spicy jalapeno, and fiery serrano. They are the main ingredients in most of the Mexican food, even the classic cuisines as well. Chiles are not just used as a spice, but they also add a special flavor to recipes. Many recipes almost use some kind of chile. They are used as whole, fresh, smoked, powdered, or dried.

Beans

Another ingredient that is most widely used is frijoles or beans. You hardly find any kitchen in Mexico that is without a wide variety of beans. They have different types. Most known are the black beans, pinto beans, brownish, and the black beans flor de junio and golden Peruvian. Beans are used in dishes like refried beans, soups, bean salads, and the traditional recipe of frijoles de olla.

Corn

Corn is the key source of grain in Mexico. Mostly it is dried. It is widely used in making tamales, beverages, soups, and tortillas. The corn tortilla is included in almost every recipe in Mexico. Apart from that, huitlacoche grown on corn ears is found in various dishes in Mexican food like omelets, succotash, as a filling in tamales or tacos.

Avocado

The Hass avocado is cultivated in Mexico. It is the main and key ingredient in "guac". It is also found in salsas, salads, and tacos topping.

Tomatoes

Vegetables are widely used in Mexican food, especially tomatoes. The raw and fresh tomatoes are the key ingredient found in salsas.

They have also used as fillings toppings for burritos and tacos. They are not commonly employed in making a red sauce in Mexico with red chiles as their main ingredient. The freshly cooked as well as canned tomatoes add flavor to salads, rice, and soups.

Herbs

Mexican oregano and cilantro are the most commonly found herbs in Mexican cuisines. Cilantro is mostly used fresh that brings brightness and also the citrus essence to recipes. The vibrant green color is snipped and adds a sense of esthetics to salsas, guacamole, and other dishes. The Mexican oregano is locally used in Mexico. It can be utilized as dried or fresh.

1.3 Evolution of Popular Mexican Foods in U.S.

Mexican food has influenced many American cuisines for years. In the 20th century, many Mexican-inspired recipes have been there in almost every corner of the U.S., making their way to the mainstream dishes. Apart from the traditional recipes like tacos, tortillas, tamales, salsas, enchiladas, many new recipes emerged in the U.S. that was a perfect blend of regional American, Mexican, and Latino culture.

Enchiladas

Enchiladas are mostly topped with onion rings, fresh cheese, and fresh cream in Mexico. But in the U.S., enchilada is usually topped with the melted cheese, and then served with pico de gallo, Mexican rice, refried beans, shredded lettuce, and guacamole. Enchilada is a straightforward dish, though it does not look like that, nut it surely is.

Tacos

In Mexico, you can enjoy tacos with pork, beef, or chicken. Tacos have their roots back to mid-19th century.

Mexico was developing in its industrialization during this period. Early tacos were used to be filled with organ meats (inexpensive) and some other ingredients. Tacos were brought to the U.S. in the early 1900s. They had the same appearance as we see them in Mexican-American style taco today; the U-shaped tortilla shells filled with iceberg lettuce, ground beef, and the cheddar cheese.

Salsa

Salsa is a sauce in Mexican recipes. Some people think salsa is a spicy tomato-based red sauce. But, in Mexico, it is a term used for the sauce. Salsa has a long history back to the era of Aztecs in Mexico. It is found in different forms like salsa verde, which is made of tomatillos, cilantro, jalapenos, pico de gallo, that uses chopped tomatoes, garlic, and seasoned with lime juice and oil. Pace Foods introduced to salsa in the U.S. in 1947. Today, you can easily find salsa at any grocery store to enjoy it with the tortilla chips.

Tex-Mex

Refried Beans

The taste of Mexican food and the popularity of Mexican Cuisine led to the several variations in its recipes across many countries and regions. Tex-Mex dish evolved in Southwest America in Texas-Mexico. It is a variation of the traditional recipe with an American touch. The best example of Tex-Mex recipes is refried beans. Tex-Mex is, however, different from the original Mexican recipe. It includes, to a certain extent, some of the same ingredients, but it is not exactly like that.

New Mexican Cuisine

New Mexican Cuisine is a kind of the regional cuisine that originates from New Mexico in the U.S., and also in southern Colorado. It is known as a subset of the Mexican-American cuisine. The American consumers' liking Mexican food has certainly evolved since a long time.

Mexican food is a perfect blend of all the cultures mentioned above. However, you can still find diversity in the recipes as per the Mexican regional differences. Mexican food has variations according to the region, local climate, ethnic differences, and geography. Northern Mexico is best known for beef and meat recipes. Southeastern Mexico is famous for spicy vegetables and chicken-based recipes. Seafood is also commonly used in Mexican states that border the Gulf of Mexico or the Pacific Ocean.

Chapter 2: Health Benefits of Homemade Mexican Food

There are some valid reasons to dine in restaurants, including saving time and convenience. There is also another reason not to cook at home: there are a lot of people who think they cannot cook or lack proper cooking skills. So, they consider it more expensive and time-consuming. But if we can spend most of our day time on our phones and the internet, then why not spend time on cooking, which is a meditation in itself. This attitude has led to many diseases like diabetes and obesity in many countries. Restaurant food has some unhealthy portions of our diet, which we can control at home.

Let's look at some general benefits of cooking and eating at home:

- When we dine at a restaurant, there is no way we can find out what goes into our dishes. While cooking at home, they are unlimited healthy options. We can limit the use of certain ingredients to shape it in healthy cuisine.
- Restaurants have a fixed menu to choose from, while at home, we have plenty of options to select and follow some healthy diet plans. We can make whatever we want.
- Developing a healthy eating habit to adopt a healthy lifestyle, and doing that on our terms is only possible at home, not at restaurants. Homemade food offers us a great amount of flexibility.
- Cooking at home bring the family together and strengthens the bond by spending more time together and try new things in the kitchen.
- Cost is cut by a considerable fraction when we choose to cook at home. We have a lot of freedom at all stages of cooking to make it budget-friendly.

Health Benefits of Mexican Food

Mexican food incorporates different pungent flavors in its cuisines. From vegetables to beans, there is a wide variety to choose the ingredients and make healthy Mexican food options without compromising the taste.

Let's look at some fantastic presence of nutrition that we can find in Mexican food:

Fiber

A variety of beans is used in Mexican food. All of these varieties include fiber as a healthy source, a balanced diet. Many people do not take enough fiber that can cause many digestive problems. Tacos or burritos that are made with beans prove to be the healthiest choice. Whole beans have more fiber than refried beans, which are a little bit less nutritious.

Protein

In Mexican food, we can find meat like pork, beef, shrimp, or chicken. When we include lean meat in our diet, it helps in increasing the protein intake. Protein improves the health of muscles and boosts energy levels. Fried meat is delicious, but it adds saturated fats that are not healthy.

Capsaicin

It helps in marinating cholesterol and blood pressure levels, and improve circulation. We can find this in jalapenos, which is used in making Mexican sauces.

Minerals and Vitamins

A variety of vegetables are used in Mexican dishes. These vegetables are the source of some essential nutrients. Onions and tomatoes, for example, are rich in vitamin C.

on the other hand, avocado, which is the key ingredient in making guacamole, provides some healthy unsaturated fats, fiber, and potassium.

Restaurant vs. Homemade Mexican Food

When we think about Mexican food at restaurants, many think of heavy cheeses, fried tortillas, and sour cream in recipes. But, the fact is that traditional Mexican food is much not about that. It is the effect of different cultures that have made the Mexican food what it is today.

Let's see what differentiates homemade Mexican dishes from restaurant dining:

- American restaurants have introduced the heavy use of ingredients like cheese and sour cream. However, at home, there are many endless alternatives to creating a healthy and delicious Mexican recipe. It is not about avoiding those ingredients altogether, it is about limiting the amount that makes it unhealthy.
- Many American households use Mexican food ingredients a lot. People following a healthy eating lifestyle know that keeping balance is the only key to stay healthy. Choose beans and right meats, avoid too much use of cheeses. We can do that at home.
- Authentic and traditional Mexican food always has fresh ingredients in it. Many restaurant chains use the slogan of fresh Mexican food, but never know what is being used back in the kitchen because fresh and healthy go hand-in-hand. We can enjoy both only at home. If eating a healthy bowl is the choice, go for brown rice, lean meat, and beans. Toppings of fresh lettuce and homemade salsa make it even more robust.
- Tacos are a healthy Mexican food option. But if we cook at home, we can choose what we put in a taco shell, and control their portions.
- Use of lean steak, grilled chick, and grilled fish in tacos make an excellent protein-filled diet. There are many healthy options for topping too. Avoid sour cream if

you want to make it healthier. We can choose to control these things at home.

- Choosing to make Mexican food healthy is much easier than we think. We can always use the right substitutes. Doing so will not compromise on its essence but makes it even tastier. Add the healthy flavors avocados, onions, and peppers as Mexican ingredients to make the best out of a day's meals.

Chapter 3: Mexican Breakfast Recipes

Cook and enjoy some delicious and healthy Mexican breakfast recipes given in this chapter.

3.1 Eggs and Chorizo Wraps

Ingredients

- 12 ounces chorizo
- 2 tbsp. milk
- 6 eggs, large
- 1 cup cheddar cheese, shredded
- 6 tortillas (6 inches)
- Green onions, thinly sliced
- Fresh cilantro
- Salsa (optional)

Instructions

1. Take a large skillet and cook the chorizo. Keep the heat medium until it is cooked. Drain and put it back to the pan.
2. Take a bowl, and whisk milk and eggs until blended.
3. Pour egg mixture into chorizo. Stir continuously until eggs are thoroughly cooked.
4. Pour cheese in it.
5. Place 1/2 cup mixture in each tortilla.
6. Then add onion, cilantro, and salsa. Fold the tortilla and roll-up.
7. Serve and Enjoy!

3.2 Breakfast Tacos

Ingredients

- 1/2 cup black beans
- 1/2 cup pico de gallo
- 1/2 cup avocado, cubed
- 1 tbsp. lime juice
- 1/2 pound pork sausage
- 1 cup O'Brien potatoes, frozen
- 7 large eggs
- 1/2 cup Monterey Jack shredded cheese
- 2 tbsp. milk
- 6 flour tortillas (8 inches), warmed
- Fresh cilantro, optional
- Sour cream

Instructions

1. Mix avocado, black beans, lime juice, and pico de gallo. Set the mixture aside.
2. Take a large skillet, and cook crumble sausage and potatoes. Keep the heat medium for 5-6 minutes until potatoes are cooked.
3. Mix eggs and milk together. Cook the mixture, and stir continuously and keep the heat medium until eggs are cooked.
4. Pour in the cheese.
5. Put egg mixture into each tortilla.
6. Put a mixture of black bean over top of it.
7. Garnish with cilantro and sour cream.
8. Serve and Enjoy!

3.3 Sunrise Sausage Enchiladas

Ingredients

- 1 pound pork sausage
- 20 ounces hash brown shredded potatoes
- 2 tbsp. canola oil
- 1/2 tsp. salt
- 1/4 tsp. cayenne pepper
- 1/2 tsp. chili powder
- 1/4 tsp. pepper
- 2 cups cheddar cheese, shredded
- 1 can green chiles, chopped
- 8 flour tortillas (8 inches)
- 2 cans enchilada sauce

For Topping:

- Red onion, chopped
- Red pepper, sweet and chopped
- Fresh cilantro, chopped

Instructions

1. Take a skillet and cook sausage on medium heat. Make sure it is not pink anymore. Remove drippings from it while taking it out of the skillet.
2. Heat oil in a pan over medium heat. Cook potatoes until its color is brown. Then turn off the heat.
3. Mix in chiles, seasonings, sausage, and cheese.
4. Put 1/2 cup of filling on a tortilla; fold it and place it in a baking dish.
5. Top it with sauce, then cover and refrigerate it overnight.
6. Preheat the oven to 375°. Take out enchiladas from the refrigerator.
7. Bake it for 30 minutes while being covered.
8. Put the remaining cheese. Then bake while being uncovered till the point it is lightly brown.

9. Put toppings and serve.

3.4 Sausage Tortilla Breakfast Bake

Ingredients

- 1/2 cup tomatoes
- 1/2 green chiles
- 8 ounces turkey breakfast sausage
- 4 corn tortillas (8 inches)
- 1/4 cup pepper jack cheese, shredded
- 1/2 cup Monterey Jack cheese, shredded
- 2 green onions
- 3/4 cup milk, fat-free
- 6 eggs
- 3/4 tsp. paprika
- Sour cream
- 1/4 tsp. ground cumin
- Salsa, optional
- Green onions chopped, optional

Instructions

1. Preheat the oven to 350°. Take a skillet and cook sausage over the medium heat. Make sure its color is not pink anymore. Put tomatoes in it.
2. In a dish plate, place half of the tortillas. Put half of the mixture, green onions, and cheeses. Repeat this process while making layers.
3. Whisk eggs, paprika, milk, and cumin in a bowl. Then pour it over the layers.
4. Bake while keeping it uncovered for about half an hour.
5. Serve with green onions, sour cream, and salsa.

3.5 Egg Burritos

Ingredients

- 12 eggs
- 12 chopped bacon strips
- 1/2 tsp. salt
- 12 flour tortillas (6 inches)
- 1/4 tsp. pepper
- 1 1/3 cups cheddar cheese
- 4 thinly sliced green onions

Instructions

1. Take a skillet, and cook in it the bacon until it is crisp.
2. Whisk together salt, eggs, and pepper.
3. Over the medium heat, cook egg mixture in a skillet. Stir continuously till the eggs are cooked, and then remove the skillet from heat.
4. Pour 1/4 cup of egg mixture on each tortilla, and sprinkle with bacon, cheese, and green onions.
5. Make burritos, and serve.

3.6 Ramona's Chilaquiles

Ingredients

- 1/2 pound chorizo or pork sausage
- 1/2 pound ground beef
- 1 onion, chopped
- 1 can tomatoes
- 1 minced garlic clove
- 1 cup Monterey Jack cheese, shredded
- 6 ounces tortilla chips
- Chopped cilantro

For Topping:

- Diced avocado
- Sour cream
- Red onion, sliced

Instructions

1. Preheat the oven to 350°.
2. Take a skillet, and cook chorizo and beef with garlic and onion over the medium heat.
3. Stir in tomatoes and bring it to boil.
4. Take a greased baking dish and layer half of the beef mixture, 2 cups of chips, and 1/2 cup of cheese. Repeat this in layers.
5. In the end, bake it while being uncovered till the point cheese is melted.
6. Serve with toppings on it.

3.7 Huevos Rancheros with Tomatillo Sauce

Ingredients

- 2 tbsp. chopped onion
- 5 tomatillos, cut in half
- 1 serrano pepper
- 1 tsp. chicken bouillon granules
- 3 garlic cloves
- 1 can Southwestern black beans
- 1 cup Manchego cheese, shredded
- 8 eggs
- 8 tostada shells
- 1/2 cup sour cream

For Topping:

- Sliced avocado
- Chopped tomato
- Minced cilantro

Instructions

1. Finely chopped onion, the tomatillos, garlic, pepper, and bouillon, and set aside.
2. Take a saucepan, and cook the beans on low heat.
3. Break eggs into a skillet. Cover it and cook the eggs on low heat
4. Add cheese.
5. While serving, put beans over the tostada shells.
6. Put toppings of sour cream, tomatillo sauce, and eggs.
7. Garnish with avocado, tomato, and cilantro.

3.8 Avocado Quesadillas

Ingredients

- 1 mashed avocado
- 2 flour tortilla
- 50g cheddar cheese, grated

Instructions

1. Sprinkle half cheese on one tortilla wrap.
2. Spread the avocado on it.
3. Put the remaining cheese.
4.
5. Heat a pan over the medium heat. Put the quesadilla in it, and cook till the point it is golden brown.
6. Cook the other side of quesadilla by gently flipping it.
7. Serve hot!

3.9 Breakfast Tortas

Ingredients

- 3/4 cup black beans, refried
- 3 ciabatta rolls
- 1/4 cup sour cream
- 2 tsp. lime juice
- 1/4 cup fresh cilantro
- 4 drops chipotle pepper sauce

- 4 eggs
- 1/8 tsp. salt
- 1/2 cup Monterey Jack cheese, shredded
- 4 bacon strips, cooked and halved
- 1 tsp. olive oil
- 1/2 avocado, sliced
- 2 chopped green onions
- 1/3 cup salsa

Instructions

1. Cut one third from the top of each roll, and empty the bottom part.
2. Put roll bottoms on a baking sheet.
3. Take a bowl, mix sour cream, beans, lime juice, cilantro, salt, and chipotle pepper sauce.
4. Place 1/4 cup of this mixture inside each roll. Place an egg on it.
5. Bake it at 400° for almost 10 minutes.
6. Spread cheese over the eggs. Brush roll with olive oil and put it on the baking sheet.
7. Put toppings of avocado, bacon, salsa, and onions on each roll.
8. Replace the roll tops, and serve.

3.10 Mexican Baked Eggs

Ingredients

- 1 onion, chopped
- 1 1/2 tbsp. olive oil
- 1/3 tsp. chili flakes
- 2 tsp. cumin
- 1 tsp. paprika
- 450g kidney beans
- 1 large red capsicum, chopped
- 450g tomatoes, diced
- 4 eggs

- 1/2 cup water
- 1/3 cup coriander
- 1 avocado, sliced
- Salt, to season
- Pepper, to season
- Lime wedges, Sour cream, and tortillas, to serve

Instructions

1. Preheat the oven to 180°C. Take a pan and heat oil over the medium heat.
2. Put chili, onion, paprika, salt, cumin, and pepper, and cook for 5 minutes.
3. Add kidney beans, capsicum, water, and tomatoes in it.
4. After bringing it to boil, put the heat down, and cook for almost 10 minutes.
5. Put the mixture into four dishes. Fill them with each bean mixture, and put the egg.
6. Bake for 15-16 minutes.
7. Serve with sour cream, coriander, lime, avocado, and tortillas.

3.11 Breakfast Burrito Casserole

Ingredients

- 1/3 cup milk
- 8 eggs
- 1/2 tsp. salt
- 1 pound pork sausage
- 1/2 teaspoon pepper
- 1 cup sour cream
- 1 can chicken soup
- 6 flour tortillas (8 inches)
- 1 1/2 cups salsa
- 2/3 cup cheddar cheese, shredded
- 2/3 cup mozzarella cheese, shredded

Instructions

1. Preheat the oven to 350°. Mix milk, eggs, pepper, and salt.
2. Take a skillet, cook the egg mixture and stir it continuously over the medium heat till the point it is thickened.
3. Cook sausage in the same skillet, and keep the heat medium, then drain it.
4. Mix soup and sour cream together. Spread half mixture on a baking dish. Make a layer with half of the tortilla slices, scrambled eggs, half of the salsa, sausage. Then put the remaining sour cream mixture and tortillas.
5. Pour remaining salsa and cheeses.
6. Bake for almost 30-35 minutes while keeping it uncovered.
7. Serve with green onions and enchilada sauce.

3.12 Breakfast Tostada

Ingredients

- 1 tbsp. vegetable oil
- 4 slices bacon
- 15-ounces canned black beans
- Kosher salt and black pepper, to taste
- 4 tostada shells
- 1 egg
- 1/4 cup Cheddar cheese
- 1/4 avocado, diced
- 1 tbsp. sour cream
- 1 tbsp. salsa
- 1 tbsp. cilantro leaves

Instructions

1. Preheat oven to 400^0 F.
2. Take a skillet, and cook the bacon over the medium heat till the point it is crisp.

3. Take a saucepan and keep the medium heat. Put vegetable oil, salt, black beans, and pepper. Mash the black beans.
4. Take a baking sheet and layer one tostada shell, one tbsp. Cheese and two tbsp. Beans. Repeat this with all layers of tostada shells. Bake till the point cheese is melted, and edges of tostadas start to turn into golden color.
5. Take a pan and heat oil over the medium heat.
6. Cook egg in it for about 5 minutes.
7. Put tostada on a plate, and top it with diced avocado, the fried egg, salsa, a remaining cheese, sour cream, and cilantro. Serve with bacon, and enjoy.

3.13 Mexican Sweet Potato Hash

Ingredients

- 1 1/2 tbsp. olive oil
- 2 pounds sweet potatoes
- 1 cup onion
- 1/2 cup bell pepper, green
- 1/2 cup bell pepper, red
- 3 cloves garlic
- 4 eggs
- 12 ounces soy chorizo

Instructions

1. Boil water in a pot, and add sweet potatoes to it. Boil till the point potatoes are tender. Then drain them and set aside.
2. Take a skillet and heat the oil over the medium heat. Add onion, red and green bell pepper in it. Saute it for almost 5 minutes
3. Add sweet potatoes and garlic. Saute for almost 4 minutes.
4. Add chorizo, and cook for almost 5 minutes.
5. Put the flame low and add eggs on the top of potato hash.
6. Cover it, and cook for 5 minutes
7. Serve and Enjoy!

3.14 Spicy Jalapeno Eggs and Sweet Pepper

Ingredients

- 4 slices sourdough
- 4 eggs
- 10 vine tomatoes
- 1 jalapeno
- 1 small sweet bell pepper, yellow, orange, or red
- 4 garlic cloves
- 2 tbsp. butter
- 1 tbsp. olive oil
- Salt, to taste
- Pepper, to taste
- Basil, for garnishing

Instructions

1. Preheat oven to the high broil.
2. Put tomatoes slices in an oven pan. Add salt, pepper, and olive oil. Then broil for almost 8 minutes.
3. Chop garlic. And add butter in it.

4. Spread mixture onto sourdough slices.
5. Cut jalapeno and sweet pepper.
6. When tomatoes are cooked, take the pan out of the oven and push tomatoes to the oven pan's edges.
7. Break eggs in the middle, and put the sliced jalapeno and pepper around eggs.
8. Add pepper and salt, and put it back for almost 6-8 minutes.
9. Put garlic slices of sourdough to toast.
10. Take a sourdough slice and top it with tomatoes, and egg.
11. Garnish it with basil, and serve.

3.15 Best-Ever Migas

Ingredients

- 6 corn tortillas
- 3 tbsp. of vegetable oil
- 1 jalapeño, chopped
- 1/2 onion, diced
- 3 cloves garlic, chopped
- 5 eggs
- 1/2 cups mild salsa
- Kosher salt, to taste
- 1/4 cups cilantro leaves
- 2 radishes, sliced
- 1 avocado, sliced
- 1/4 cups crumbled cotija cheese
- Hot sauce

Instructions

1. Take a pan and heat oil over the medium heat. Add corn tortillas in it, and cook for 5 minutes.
2. Put onion, garlic, and jalapeño in it, and cook for 4 minutes. Put the heat down to low.
3. Add eggs and salt.

4. Stir continuously till the point everything is mixed well.
5. Add salsa.
6. Top with radishes, cilantro, cheese, avocado, and hot sauce.
7. Serve and Enjoy!

Chapter 4: Mexican Lunch Recipes

Here are given some delicious and easy Mexican lunch recipes in this chapter. These recipes are fun to cook at home and perfect to enjoy with your family.

4.1 Prawn and Chorizo Quesadilla

Ingredients

- 1/2 red onion
- 1 tbsp. of olive oil
- 1 red pepper
- 1 garlic clove
- 70g chorizo, chopped
- 1 tbsp. of chipotle paste
- 1/2 tsp. coriander
- 1/2 tsp. cumin
- 2 flour tortillas
- 1 lime
- 100g prawns, chopped
- Guacamole, optional

Instructions

1. Take oil in a pan, and fry pepper and onion for almost 10 minutes.
2. Put the chorizo in it, and cook for another 5 minutes. Add the chipotle paste, garlic, cumin, prawns, and ground coriander, then cook for another 2 minutes.
3. Season with lime juice.
4. Put the mixture on a tortilla and place the second tortilla on it.
5. In a frying pan over high heat, add quesadilla and cook each side for almost 2 minutes.
6. Cut into pieces and serve.

4.2 Mexican-Style Stuffed Peppers

Ingredients

- 1 pound lean beef
- 4 red or green bell peppers
- 1 onion, diced
- 2 tsp. of chili powder
- 3 minced cloves garlic
- 1/2 tsp. cumin
- 1 can divided enchilada sauce
- 1 can tomatoes diced with peppers
- 2 cups of cheddar cheese
- 2 cups rice, cooked

Instructions

1. Preheat the oven to 375^0. Cut bell peppers into half. Put it in a baking dish.
2. Fry garlic, beef, and onion in a skillet. Pour in cumin, chili powder, diced tomatoes, and 2/3 cup enchilada sauce. Then let it simmer for 2-3 minutes.
3. Turn down the heat and add cooked rice in it.
4. Put beef mixture into the pepper. Add remaining cheese and enchilada sauce.
5. Bake while keeping uncovered till the point peppers and cheese is cooked. It might take around 30 minutes.
6. Put some taco toppings on it and serve.

4.3 Mexican Corn Salsa

Ingredients

- 1/4 cup minced red onion minced
- 2 cups fresh corn kernels
- 1/3 cups minced bell pepper, green or red
- 1/3 tsp. sea salt
- 2 1/2 lime juice

- 1 1/2 tbsp. fresh Jalapeño
- 3 tbsp. finely chopped cilantro
- Ground pepper

Instructions

1. Take a large bowl, and mix corn kernels, bell pepper, red onion, jalapeño, lime juice, cilantro, and salt.
2. Refrigerate it for about 24 hours to get the best taste.

4.4 Turkey Taco Lettuce Wraps

Ingredients

- 3/4 cup yellow onion, chopped
- 1 tbsp. of olive oil
- 1 pound ground turkey
- Salt, to taste
- Black pepper, to taste
- 3 cloves garlic
- 1/2 cup chicken broth
- 1/2 cup of tomato sauce
- 1 tsp. cumin
- 1 tbsp. of chili powder
- 1/2 tsp. of paprika

For Serving

- Iceberg or lettuce leaves
- Mexican cheese
- Roma tomatoes
- Red onion
- Avocado
- Cilantro
- Sour cream

Instructions

1. Heat the olive oil in a skillet.
2. Saute onion for 2 minutes. Then add garlic and turkey, pepper, and salt. Cook for 5 minutes.
3. Then add cumin, chili powder, paprika, chicken broth, and tomato sauce. Reduce the heat to simmer. Cook for 5 minutes.
4. Put the mixture on top of lettuce leaves, and serve with toppings of your choice.

4.5 Shrimp Enchiladas

Ingredients

- 1 bell pepper, red
- 1 1/2 tbsp. of olive oil
- 1/2 diced sweet onion
- 1 minced jalapeno
- Corn kernels
- 1 clove minced garlic
- 1 package seasoning mix
- 1 pound shrimp
- 1 can green chilies
- 1 package of Colby Jack cheese
- 1/2 cup of sour cream
- 10 corn tortillas
- 1 cup Monterey Jack cheese
- 2 cans enchilada sauce
- Fresh cilantro

Instructions

1. Preheat the oven to 350^0 and take a baking dish.
2. Take a skillet and heat oil over the medium heat. Add onion, red pepper, jalapeno, and corn. Cook until tender.

3. Add shrimp and garlic. Cook for almost 2 minutes. Then put taco seasoning mix in it, and cook.
4. Turn down the heat.
5. Add green chilies, Colby Jack cheese, and sour cream.
6. Put tortillas in the microwave for 30-35 seconds, till the point they are warm.
7. Place the mixture in the center of a tortilla, then roll it up. Put it in the baking dish.
8. Put enchilada sauce on the tortilla.
9. Add Monterey Jack cheese on top of it.
10. Bake for almost 30 minutes.
11. Take out and serve.

4.6 Mexican Quiche

Ingredients

- 6 ounces shredded cheddar cheese
- 1 pie crust, refrigerated
- 1 can tomatoes with green chilies
- 2 ounces black olives
- 1 can green chilies
- 3 eggs
- 1/2 tsp. of chili powder
- 1 cup of sour cream
- 1/2 tsp. paprika
- 1/8 tsp. cayenne pepper
- 1/4 tsp. cumin
- 1/8 tsp. garlic powder

Instructions

1. Place the pie crust on the pie plate.
2. Put cheddar over the bottom of the crust.
3. Then put tomatoes with green chilis and olives on it.
4. Mix eggs, chili powder, sour cream, paprika, cayenne, cumin, and garlic powder. Pour this mixture over the pie crust.

5. Bake at 350^0 for an hour.
6. Wait for 5 minutes to let it settle and then serve.

4.7 Grilled Cumin Lime Chicken

Ingredients

- 3-4 limes
- 3 chicken breasts
- 3 tbsp. olive oil
- 2 tsp. cumin
- 1 tbsp. kosher salt
- 2 tsp. black pepper
- 7 tbsp. vegetable oil
- 2-3 tbsp. salt

Instructions

1. Cut the chicken breast horizontally.
2. Put all chicken breast slices in a bowl. Add salt and put some water over chicken. Refrigerate it overnight for better taste.
3. Take it out and then pat dry it. Add lime juice and olive oil to it. Marinate the chicken and refrigerate it for another 3-7 hours.
4. Mix the ground pepper, cumin, and kosher salt in a bowl. Rub this mixture on the chicken.
5. Grill the chicken from each side.
6. Serve with chimichurri sauce and salsa.

4.8 Spicy Black Beans and Yellow Rice

Ingredients

For Beans

- 4 finely minced garlic cloves
- 3 tbsp. olive oil
- 1 small white onion
- 3 cups black beans, cooked
- 1 jalapeno, minced
- 1 tsp. of chili powder
- 2 1/2 cups vegetable stock
- 1/2 tsp. cumin powder
- 1/2 bell pepper, red

For Rice

- 1/2 tsp. turmeric
- 1 cup of rice
- 1/2 tsp. grated ginger
- Salt, to taste
- 1/4 tsp. coriander

Instructions

1. In a pot, heat olive oil, garlic cloves, and jalapeño pepper on low heat.
2. Then add chili powder, beans, 1/2 cup of stock, cumin, and cook for 25-35 minutes. In the end, add bell pepper and salt.
3. Add garlic cloves in the remaining olive oil
4. and heat them. Pour the remaining stock, bring it to boil. Add rice, reduce the heat, and cook for almost 15-20 minutes.
5. When rice is cooked, add spices.
6. Arrange black beans and rice on a serving platter.

4.9 Chicken Tostadas

Ingredients

- 3 tomatoes, diced
- 8 tostada shells or corn tortillas
- 4 avocados, diced
- 1/4 cup finely chopped cilantro
- 3 tbsp. finely chopped red onion
- 1 tsp. cumin
- 3/4 tsp. salt
- 1 tsp. of chili powder
- Lime juice
- 3 cups chicken, shredded
- 15 ounces can drained and rinsed black beans
- 1/2 cup Cotija or feta cheese

Instructions

1. For making tostada shells, arrange tortillas in a baking sheet, ad make a single layer. Bake each side at 400⁰ for around 6 minutes.
2. Meanwhile, make guacamole salsa by mixing avocado, tomato, red onion, cumin, cilantro, chili powder, lime juice, and salt.
3. For assembly, put guacamole salsa, chicken, beans, and cheese on each shell.

4.10 Chicken, Cheese, and Chili Quesadillas

Ingredients

For Quesadillas:

- 6 ounces Colby, Monterey, Cheddar, or Jack cheese
- 12 corn tortillas
- 1 tbsp. jalapenos
- 4 tbsp. butter
- 1 cup chicken, cooked

For Salsa and Topping:

- 1/4 red onion
- 2 tomatoes
- 2-3 tbsp. cilantro
- Kosher salt
- Hot sauce, to taste
- 1 avocado, sliced

Instructions

1. Put tortillas on a surface, and equally divide the jalapenos, cheese, and the chicken.
2. Put remaining tortillas on the top and seal them gently.
3. Melt butter in a skillet. Fry both sides of quesadilla carefully. Make sure it does not burn. Add more butter if required.
4. In the meantime, prepare the salsa.
5. Take tomatoes, and cut them into halves. Peel off their skin. Then add onion, cilantro, salt, and hot sauce to taste.
6. Then, cut the quesadillas into 4 pieces.
7. Serve with avocado and salsa.

4.11 Refried Beans

Ingredients

- 1/2 cup onion
- 1 tbsp. olive oil
- 1/4 tsp. sea salt
- 1/2 tsp. of chili powder
- 2 cloves minced garlic
- 1/4 tsp. cumin
- 1/2 cup water
- 2 cans pinto beans
- 1 tbsp. lime juice, to taste
- 2 tbsp. chopped cilantro

Instructions

1. Heat the olive oil in a saucepan. Add salt and onions. Cook for 5-8 minutes.
2. Then add cumin, chili powder, and garlic. Stir constantly.
3. Add water and beans. Stir, and cook for about 5 minutes.
4. Lower the heat a little bit and use a masher to mash up beans.
5. Continue cooking, and often stir for some more minutes.
6. Add lime juice and cilantro.
7. Serve and Enjoy!

4.12 Mexican Lunch Loaf

Ingredients

- 2 tsp. baking powder
- 1 cup plain flour
- 1 tsp. Mexican chilli powder
- 2 tbsp. caster sugar
- 1 cup polenta
- 1 tsp. sea salt
- 125g can of corn kernels
- 1 red capsicum, diced
- 1/2 cup grated cheese
- 1 tbsp. finely chopped coriander leaves
- 3 onions, sliced
- 1 1/4 cups buttermilk
- 2 tbsp. olive oil
- 1 egg
- 1 red chilli, sliced
- Cherry tomatoes and Sliced avocado for serving

Instructions

1. Preheat the oven to 180^0 C, and grease a loaf pan.
2. Mix baking powder, chilli powder, and flour in a bowl.
3. Add sugar, polenta, salt, corn, capsicum, onion, cheese, and coriander.
4. Add pepper. Make space at the center.
5. Put buttermilk, oil, and egg in it. Transfer this mixture to the pan, and top it with sliced chilli.
6. Bake for almost 1 hour.
7. Make slices and serve with cherry tomatoes and avocado.

Chapter 5: Mexican Dinner Recipes

In this chapter, you will have some amazing, tasty, and fresh Mexican dinner recipes. Enjoy cooking, and have fun with an exciting mix of flavors.

5.1 Chicken and Bean Enchiladas

Ingredients

- 2 sliced red onion
- 1 tbsp. rapeseed oil
- 2 sliced red peppers
- 2 tsp. chipotle paste
- 2 crushed garlic cloves
- 2 chicken breasts
- Chopped coriander, a small bunch
- 500ml passata
- 400g can kidney beans or black beans
- 1 tsp. sugar or ketchup
- 50g cheddar, grated
- 6 tortillas
- Green salad, for serving

Instructions

1. Heat the oven to 200⁰C.
2. Heat oil in a pan. Add peppers, onions, and garlic.
3. Then, cook for around 15 minutes.
4. Add the chipotle paste, and fry for 2 minutes.
5. Add chicken, and cook.
6. Add coriander, beans, and 140 ml of passata, then turn down the heat.
7. Pour remaining passata, ketchup, and the crushed garlic.
8. Put the mixture over the tortillas, and fold its sides, and roll it up.

9. Put the passata in a baking dish, and put enchiladas on the top.
10. Pour the remaining sauce, then add grated cheese.
11. Bake it for around 25-30 minutes.
12. Serve and Enjoy!

5.2 Cheesy Mexican Cauliflower Rice

Ingredients

- 1 chopped onion
- 1 tbsp. olive oil
- 2 cloves crushed garlic
- 1/2 tsp. cumin
- 1 tsp. oregano, dried
- 65 g cauliflower, grated
- Black pepper, to taste
- Salt, to taste
- 1 tbsp. tomato pureé
- 1 can black beans
- 250 g rotisserie chicken, shredded
- 175 g sweetcorn
- 2 thinly sliced jalapeños
- 200 g tomatoes
- 5 g coriander, freshly chopped
- 100 g Monterey jack cheese, grated
- 100 g cheddar cheese, grated
- Lime wedges, to serve

Instructions

1. Heat oil in a skillet over the medium heat.
2. Put the onion in it and cook for around 5 minutes.
3. Then add oregano, garlic, and cumin. Cook for 1 minute.
4. Add cauliflower in a dishtowel and drain any excess liquid.

5. Add more oil if required, and add grated cauliflower, pepper, and salt. Stir occasionally while cooking.
6. Add the tomato paste, black beans, chicken, tomatoes, corn, coriander, and jalapenos.
7. Add cheeses over it, then cover and cook until it melts.
8. Serve and Enjoy!

5.3 Chicken Fajitas

Ingredients

For Chicken:

- Salt, to taste
- 1 1/4 pounds chicken breasts
- 2 tbsp. olive oil
- 3 bell peppers, different colors
- 1 onion

For Marinade:

- 3 tbsp. olive oil
- 2 tbsp. lime juice
- 1 minced garlic clove
- 1/2 tsp. ground cumin
- 1/2 tsp. salt
- 1/2 tsp. chili powder
- 1/4 cup cilantro, chopped
- 1/2 minced jalapeño

For Serving:

- Salsa
- 10 flour tortillas
- Sliced avocado
- Iceberg lettuce
- Sour cream

Instructions

1. Cut chicken breasts into slices horizontally.
2. Mix together all the ingredients. Then put the chicken in it to marinate and mix well. Marinate for up to 9-10 hours in the refrigerator.
3. Take the chicken out, and sprinkle salt on the chicken slices.
4. Heat oil in a frying pan, and heat chicken for around 2-3 minutes on high heat. Turnover and cook the other side until it is well seared.
5. Cover seared breasts with foil then set aside.
6. Cook the onions and peppers on high heat. Spread the peppers and onions in the pan for around 2 minutes.
7. Put vegetables and cook for 2-3 minutes.
8. Cut chicken pieces, and serve with warm tortillas, onions and peppers, shredded cheese, guacamole, salsa, and iceberg lettuce, whatever you like.

5.4 Mexican Lasagna

Ingredients

- 1 can refried beans
- 2 pounds beef
- 1 can green chilies, chopped
- 2 tbsp. hot salsa
- 1 envelope of taco seasoning
- 12 ounces lasagna noodles, uncooked
- 1 jar mild salsa
- 4 cups Monterey Jack cheese, shredded
- 2 cups of water
- 1 can ripe olives, sliced
- 2 cups of sour cream
- 1 chopped tomato
- 3 chopped green onions

Instructions

1. Preheat the oven to 350°.
2. Take a skillet, and cook beef over the medium heat.
3. Add beans, chilies, hot salsa, and taco seasoning.
4. In a baking dish, put meat mixture and 1/3 of noodles. Add one cup of cheese. Then, repeat these layers twice.
5. Add water and salsa. Cover it and bake for around one hour.
6. Add sour cream, onions, olives, tomatoes, and the remaining cheese. Bake it while keeping it uncovered for 5 minutes.
7. Cut and server.

5.5 Slow-Cooker Enchiladas

Ingredients

- 1 can black beans
- 1 pound beef
- 1 cup frozen, roasted, or canned corn kernels,
- 1 can chopped green chiles
- 1 cup salsa,
- 2 tsp. taco seasoning mix
- 4 flour tortillas
- 1 can enchilada sauce
- 2 cups Mexican blend cheese, shredded

For Serving

- 1 diced tomato
- 1 diced avocado
- 2 tbsp. chopped cilantro leaves

Instructions

1. Take a skillet and heat oil over the medium heat. Then, add beef and cook for 3-5 minutes. Crumble the beef, and drain any excess fat, then turn down the heat.
2. Add corn, black beans, green chiles, salsa, enchilada sauce, and taco seasoning.

3. Coat the slow cooker from inside with a nonstick spray. Then put one tortilla in a slow cooker.
4. Place one-third of beef mixture on top of it, and sprinkle with a half cup of cheese. Repeat this with two more layers.
5. Put tortilla, cheese, and enchilada sauce.
6. Cook it on the low heat for around 3-4 hours.
7. Garnish with tomato, avocado, and cilantro.
8. Serve and Enjoy!

5.6 Garlic Beef Enchiladas

Ingredients

- 1 onion, chopped
- 1 pound beef
- 2 tbsp. all-purpose flour
- 1 tsp. salt
- 1 tsp. chili powder
- 1 tsp. garlic powder
- 1/4 tsp. rubbed sage
- 1/2 tsp. ground cumin
- 1 can stewed tomatoes

For Sauce:

- 5 minced garlic cloves
- 1/3 cup butter
- 1/2 cup of all-purpose flour
- 1 can tomato sauce
- 1 can beef broth
- 1 1/2 tbsp. chili powder
- 1 1/2 tsp. rubbed sage
- 1 1/2 tsp. ground cumin
- 1/2 tsp. salt
- 2 cups Monterey Jack cheese, shredded
- 10 flour tortillas

Optional Toppings:

- Fresh cilantro
- Grape tomatoes
- Chopped red onion
- Jalapeno peppers, sliced.

Instructions

1. Preheat the oven to 350°.
2. Take a skillet, and cook onion and beef over the medium heat.
3. Add seasonings and flour.
4. Stir in tomatoes and bring it to boil. Lower the heat, then simmer for 15 minutes.
5. Heat butter in a pan over the medium heat.
6. Cook garlic in it for around 1 minute. Mix flour, and blend it gradually.
7. Add broth, and bring it to boil. Cook for almost 2 minutes.
8. Add seasonings and tomato sauce.
9. Pour sauce into a baking dish. Place beef mixture on each tortilla.
10. Add cheese on top of it.
11. Top with some more sauce.
12. Bake it covered for around 30-35 minutes.
13. Then add the remaining cheese.
14. Bake it while keeping it uncovered till the point cheese is melted, 10-15.
15. Serve with your favorite toppings.

5.7 Roast Vegie Quesadillas

Ingredients

- 500g peeled sweet potato
- 1 red onion
- 1 tbsp. olive oil
- 150g broccoli
- 8 flour tortillas
- 240g mozzarella or cheddar, grated
- 85g sour cream
- 1-2 tbsp. pesto

Instructions

1. Preheat the oven to 200ºC. Put the onions and the sweet potato in a roasting pan, and drizzle it with season and oil.
2. Then roast it for 20 minutes.
3. Put broccoli to a pan. Mix the veggies, and roast them for another 10 minutes.
4. Take a frying pan and heat the oil over the medium heat.
5. Put one tortilla in the pan. Add 1/8 of the cheese. Then add 1/4 of the veggie mixture.
6. Add another 1/8 of the cheese. Put another tortilla on it, and seal it.
7. Cook it for around 1-2 minutes
8. Turn it and cook for another 1-2 minutes. Repeat this with all remaining tortillas, veggies, and cheese.
9. Mix pesto and sour cream in a bowl. Make pieces of quesadillas, and serve with pesto cream.

5.8 Corn, Black Bean, and Spinach Enchiladas

Ingredients

For Sauce:

- 1/4 cup of tomato paste
- 3 cups of vegetable broth
- 1/4 cup of all-purpose flour
- 2 tsp. cumin
- 2 tbsp. of olive oil
- 1/4 tsp. garlic powder
- 1/4 tsp. chili powder
- 1/4 tsp. onion powder
- Salt, to taste
- Pepper, to taste

For Enchiladas:

- 1 1/2 cups corn
- 15 ounces can black beans
- 6 ounces fresh spinach
- 1/3 cup cilantro
- 6 green onions
- 2 tsp. cumin
- 8 flour tortillas
- 1 cup vegan cheese, shredded

Instructions

1. Heat the oil in a skillet over the medium heat.
2. Put in tomato paste, cumin, flour, onion powder, garlic powder, and chili powder, and cook for one minute.
3. Add broth, and bring it to boil. Cook for 8-10 minutes until it gets slightly thickened.
4. Add pepper and salt to taste and put it aside.
5. Put spinach in a pan and heat for 2 minutes over the medium heat.

6. Take a bowl, and mix black beans, vegan cheese, wilted spinach, green onions, corn, cilantro, and cumin.
7. Preheat the oven to 375⁰C. Spray a baking dish, and add some sauce to the bottom.
8. Fill tortillas with the mixture, and roll-up.
9. Pour the remaining sauce on top of enchiladas.
10. Add 1/4 cup of cheese on the top.
11. Bake it for 20 minutes, garnish with green onions and cilantro.
12. Serve and Enjoy!

5.9 Zucchini and Cheese Quesadillas

Ingredients

- 4 flour tortillas
- 2 cups zucchini
- 3/4 cup Cotija cheese, Monterey Jack, or shredded cheddar
- 1 jalapeño chile, sliced
- 2/3 cup scallions
- 1 1/3 tbsp. olive oil
- 3/4 cup tomato salsa
- 1 diced avocado
- Lime wedges, to serve

Instructions

1. Put half of the zucchini in between two tortillas. Top it with half of the cheese.
2. Then add the remaining cheese and zucchini.
3. Sprinkle half of the scallions and chile.
4. Put the remaining two tortillas on top of it, and seal it gently.
5. Take a nonstick skillet and heat oil over the medium heat. Then brush the pan with one teaspoon of oil.
6. Put one quesadilla in the pan and cook until it is golden brown.

7. Brush the top with one teaspoon of more oil and flip the quesadilla.
8. Repeat this with the second quesadilla.
9. Cut out quesadillas into pieces.
10. Add remaining scallions, avocado and chile. Then serve with lime and salsa.

5.10 Mushroom Quesadillas

Ingredients

- 1 pound mushrooms, thickly sliced
- 2 tbsp. olive oil
- 1 finely chopped clove garlic
- 1/4 tsp. salt
- 1/2 thinly sliced bunch scallions
- 1/8 tsp. black pepper
- Cilantro leaves
- 1 1/2 cups grated cheddar and Monterey Jack
- 10 corn tortillas

For Serving:

- Salsa

Instructions

1. Heat the oil in a skillet over the medium heat the oil.
2. Put mushrooms in the pan. Cook for 5 minutes.
3. Put scallions and garlic to the pan. Cook for 2-4 minutes, then add pepper and salt.
4. Place one tortilla in a pan and add 2 tablespoons mushrooms and cheese. Add 2 tablespoons more cheese and cilantro leaves.
5. Put one more tortilla on the top and seal it lightly.
6. Cook both sides and repeat this with all tortillas, filling, and cheese.
7. Cut all quesadilla into pieces.
8. Serve hot with salsa and jalapeño peppers.

Chapter 6: Mexican Soup Recipes

Cook and enjoy some of the most satisfying Mexican soup recipes given in this chapter to satisfy your cravings.

6.1 Chicken Tortilla Soup

Ingredients

- 1 onion, diced
- 2 tbsp. vegetable oil
- 2 tbsp. minced garlic
- 6 cups chicken broth
- 2 finely diced jalapenos
- 14.5 ounces can diced tomatoes
- 3 chicken breasts
- 14.5 ounces can black beans
- Salt, to taste
- Black pepper, to taste
- 2 limes
- 1 cup Monterrey cheese, shredded
- 8-inch tortilla
- 1 cup cilantro leaves, roughly chopped
- 1 sliced avocado

Instructions

1. Take a saucepan and heat the oil.
2. Add onions. Cook for around 2 minutes.
3. Add jalapenos and garlic.
4. Add tomatoes, chicken broth, and beans to the pot. Bring it to boil.
5. Lower the heat and add chicken breasts, and cook for 20-25 minutes.
6. When it is cook, take it out and let it cool so you could easily shred it.
7. Add fresh cilantro and lime juice.

8. Take a bowl and add shredded chicken in it. Pour soup over it.
9. Put a grilled tortilla, lime wedge, cheese, and avocado slices on top, and serve.

6.2 Chicken Enchilada Soup

Ingredients

- 1/2 cup chopped onion
- 2 tsp. of olive oil
- 3 cloves minced garlic
- 8 ounces can tomato sauce
- 3 cups chicken broth
- Chipotle chili, to taste
- 15 ounces can black beans
- 1/4 cup cilantro, chopped
- 14.5 ounces can diced tomatoes
- 1 tsp. cumin
- 2 chicken breasts
- 2 cups of frozen corn
- 1/2 tsp. oregano

For Topping:

- 1/4 cup scallions, chopped
- 3/4 cup cheddar cheese, shredded
- 1/4 cup cilantro, chopped
- 6 tbsp. sour cream
- 1 small avocado, diced

Instructions

1. Take a saucepan and heat oil over the medium heat.
2. Put garlic and onion and cook for 3-4 minutes.
3. Add chipotle adobo sauce, tomato sauce, and chicken broth, and bring it to boil.
4. Put cilantro in it and turn down the heat.

5. Add diced tomatoes, oregano, drained beans, cumin, corn, and stir.
6. Put chicken breasts, and cook for 5-6 hours on the low heat.
7. Shred the chicken and put it back to the soup.
8. Add cumin and salt to taste.
9. Pour in bowls and put avocado, cheese, cilantro, sour cream, tortilla chips, and scallions. Enjoy!

6.3 Burrito Bowl Soup

Ingredients

- 1 large onion, diced
- 2 tbsp. of canola oil
- 2 garlic cloves, minced
- 15 ounces canned tomatoes
- 1 tbsp. of cumin
- 15 ounces canned black beans
- 6 cups of chicken broth
- 2 cups of frozen corn
- 15 ounces green chile sauce
- 2 cups of mozzarella
- 1 cups of white rice
- Kosher salt to taste
- Chopped avocado

For Serving:

- Hot sauce
- Crushed tortilla chips
- Sour cream

Instructions

1. Take a large pot and heat oil over the medium heat.
2. Put garlic cloves and onion in it and cook for 6-8 minutes.
3. Put cumin.

4. Add black beans, frozen corn, and tomatoes. Stir constantly.
5. Add green chile sauce, chicken broth, and white rice in it and bring it to boil.
6. Lower the heat and cook while keeping it covered.
7. Stir constantly. When rice is tender, add mozzarella in it. Cook until it is melted.
8. Add salt and put avocado, hot sauce, tortilla chips, and sour cream on the top.

6.4 Hominy Beef Chili

Ingredients

- 1 beef chuck
- 2 tbsp. of canola oil
- 1 can hominy
- 1 can diced tomatoes
- 1 can beef broth
- 1 finely chopped sweet red pepper
- 1 can green chiles, chopped
- 1/2 cup onion, chopped
- 2 minced garlic cloves
- 1 tbsp. chili powder
- 1 tbsp. paprika
- 2 tsp. ground cumin
- 1/2 tsp. pepper
- 1/2 tsp. salt
- 1 1/2 cups of frozen corn

Instructions

1. Take a skillet and heat the oil in a pan over the medium heat.
2. Add beef in it.
3. Stir in broth, hominy, red pepper, tomatoes, onion, garlic, chiles, and seasonings.
4. Cover it and cook for almost 6-7 hours on low heat.

5. Mix corn and cook.
6. Serve with sour cream and cheese, and Enjoy!

6.5 Mexican White Chili

Ingredients

- 3 tbsp. olive oil
- 3 pounds of chicken breast
- 2 1/2 tbsp. chile powder
- Salt, to taste
- 3 tbsp. cumin
- Cayenne pepper, to taste
- 3 tbsp. minced garlic
- 3 cups of chopped onion
- 1 can of white beans
- 2 tsp. oregano
- 6 cups cheese, shredded
- 1 can green chiles, chopped
- 4–6 cups of chicken broth
- 2 cups of sour cream

For Garnishing:

- Sour cream
- Cilantro leaves, chopped
- Scallions, chopped
- Hot sauce
- Monterey Jack or Shredded cheddar cheese

Instructions

1. Preheat oven to 350°F.
2. Put the chicken in a pan. Add olive oil and chili powder, cumin, salt, and a pinch of cayenne in it.
3. Roast them for half an hour. Shred the chicken pieces and set aside.
4. Take a pot and heat the remaining olive oil. Put garlic and onion, and cook for 5 minutes.

5. Add shredded chicken, beans, oregano, chilies, chile powder, cumin, salt, and cayenne.
6. Add chicken broth.
7. Stir and simmer for 20 minutes on low heat.
8. Remove the pan from heat and set aside for 5 minutes.
9. Add cheese to the pot, and stir in sour cream.
10. Bring the pan back to simmer on low heat.
11. Cook chili for another 15-20 minutes. Add texture by using a masher to mash beans and the chicken.
12. Stir to mix everything.
13. Garnish and serve.

6.6 Mexican Corn and Chorizo Soup

Ingredients

- 1 onion, chopped
- 3/4 pound chorizo or pork sausage
- 1 chopped sweet red pepper
- 3 minced garlic cloves
- 1 chopped poblano pepper
- 1/3 cup flour
- 1/2 tsp. salt
- 1 tsp. ground cumin
- 1/2 tsp. pepper
- 1 1/2 pounds of potatoes
- 1/2 cup of sour cream
- 2 cartons of chicken broth
- 3 cups of frozen corn

Instructions

1. In a pan, cook chorizo over the medium heat for around 4-6 minutes. Crumble it and remove chorizo from pan to paper towels.
2. Put onion, poblano, and red peppers in the pan, and saute over the medium heat for 8-10 minutes.
3. Put garlic in it, and cook for 1 minute.

4. Mix seasonings and flour and cook for 3 minutes.
5. Add broth, and stir constantly.
6. Add corn and potatoes, and bring it to boil.
7. Lower the heat, and cook while keeping it uncovered.
8. When potatoes are cooked, add chorizo and sour cream.
9. Serve with cilantro and cheese.

6.7 Turkey Posole

Ingredients

- 2 yellow onions
- 3 tbsp. olive oil
- 2 poblano chile peppers
- 2 minced cloves garlic
- 4 cups of cooked turkey
- 2 quarts of turkey broth
- 1 can of green chile peppers, chopped
- 2 tbsp. dried oregano
- 1 tbsp. chili powder
- 2 cans cannellini beans
- 2 tbsp. ground cumin
- Salt, to taste
- Pepper, to taste

Instructions

1. Heat the oil over the medium heat.
2. Cook poblano chiles and onions in oil.
3. Put garlic.
4. Mix cumin, chile powder, and oregano.
5. Add cooked turkey, turkey broth, green chile peppers, hominy, and cannellini beans.
6. Add water if needed at this stage.
7. Add salt and pepper. Then bring it to boil.
8. Lower the heat, and simmer while keeping it covered for about one hour.

9. Take out in a bowl and serve.

6.8 Chunky Taco Soup

Ingredients

- 1 chopped medium onion
- 1 1/2 pounds beef
- 1 tbsp. olive oil
- 2 cans diced tomatoes with green chiles
- 2 cans pinto beans
- 2 cups of water
- 1 can of corn
- 1 can of black beans
- 1 envelope of salad dressing mix
- 1/4 cup of minced cilantro
- 1 envelope of taco seasoning

Instructions

1. Take a pan and heat onion and beef and onion in the oil.
2. Put tomatoes, pinto beans, black beans, water, salad dressing mix, corn, and taco seasoning. Then bring it to boil. Lower the heat. Simmer while keeping it covered for about 20-30 minutes.
3. Add cilantro, and serve.

6.9 Mexican Meatball Soup

Ingredients

- 1 chopped red onion
- 1 tbsp. cooking oil
- 2 jalapeño peppers, chopped
- 2 1/4 tsp. dried oregano
- 1 zucchini, diced
- 1/2 tsp. ground cumin
- 2 cups of water

- 1 quart of canned chicken broth
- 1 1/2 cups of canned tomatoes
- 3/4 tsp. black pepper
- 1 3/4 tsp. salt
- 1/2 pound beef, grounded
- 2 1/2 tsp. bread crumbs
- 2 cloves minced garlic
- 1 egg
- 1 tbsp. lime juice
- 1 cup corn kernels

Instructions

1. Heat the oil in the pot over the low heat.
2. Add the onion in it with half of the jalapeños. Cook for about 5 minutes.
3. Put zucchini, cumin, dried oregano, and cook for almost 3 minutes.
4. Then add the water, broth, tomatoes, salt, and black pepper. Then simmer it for about 15 minutes.
5. Take a bowl, mix beef, the remaining jalapeño, garlic, cumin, dried oregano, salt, black pepper, egg, and the bread crumbs. Make meatballs.
6. Put corn and meatballs to the soup, and then simmer for about 5 minutes.
7. Add lime juice and fresh oregano, and serve.

6.10 Mexican Black Bean Soup

Ingredients

- 1 diced red capsicum
- 1 tbsp. olive oil
- 1 finely chopped brown onion
- 1 tsp. ground cumin
- 1 finely chopped garlic clove
- Pinch of chili flakes, dried
- 400g can of diced tomatoes

- 3 cups of vegetable stock
- 1 cup corn kernels, frozen
- 1 tbsp. lime juice
- 425g can o black beans
- 1 packet of corn chips
- 1/2 avocado
- 1/4 cup chopped coriander leaves
- 80g crumbled fetta

Instructions

1. Take a pan and heat the oil.
2. Put onion and capsicum in a pan. Cook for 5 minutes, and stir constantly.
3. Put cumin, garlic, and chili in it.
4. Then add tomatoes, stock, beans, and corn. Bring it to simmer. Then lower the heat.
5. Add lime juice, and season it with pepper and salt.
6. Sprinkle corn chips, avocado, coriander, and fetta.

6.11 Mexican Sweet Potato Soup

Ingredients

- 1 finely chopped onion
- 1 tbsp. of vegetable oil
- 1 tbsp. of chipotle paste
- 750g sweet potato
- 1 cube of vegetable stock
- Coriander leaves
- 4 bread rolls

Instructions

1. Take a pan and heat the oil.
2. Put the onion in it and cook for 4-5 minutes.
3. Add chipotle paste.
4. Add stock cube in boiling water, and then add it to the pan.
5. Add sweet potatoes. Then bring it to boil. Simmer it while keeping it covered for about 10 minutes. Use a blender to make it smooth.
6. Take out in a bowl. Sprinkle coriander leaves and bread rolls, and serve.

Chapter 7: Vegetarian Mexican Recipes

Here are given the most delicious vegetarian Mexican recipes in this chapter. Try these cuisines for having perfect plant-based food in your menu, and enjoy!

7.1 Mexican Fiesta Rice

Ingredients

- 1 finely chopped onion
- 2 tbsp. of olive oil
- 2 peppers, finely chopped
- 1 tsp. of cumin seeds
- 1/2 tsp. of ground cumin
- 4 finely chopped garlic cloves
- 1 tbsp. of tomato purée
- 250g of rice
- Paprika, a small pinch
- 450ml vegetable stock
- Coriander, finely chopped for serving
- Sliced onions, for serving

Instructions

1. Take a skillet, and heat oil, and add the pepper, onion, cumin, and garlic — sizzle for 8-10 minutes.
2. When the vegetables are golden and soft, add tomato purée and paprika, then cook for about 1 min.
3. Add rice.
4. Pour stock in it, then cover. Bring it to boil.
5. Lower the heat, then cook for around 10 minutes.
6. Turn down the heat and keep it covered for another 10 minutes.
7. To serve immediately, add spring onions and coriander.

8. To serve it later, cool down the rice, then refry it before serving. Then add spring onions and coriander.

7.2 Mexican Tomato Rice

Ingredients

- 1 onion, peeled and chopped
- 1 can of peeled tomatoes
- 2 cups chicken broth
- 1/2 tsp. ground cumin
- 1 1/2 tsp. kosher salt
- 1/3 cup cooking oil
- 1 to 2 chile peppers, minced
- 2 cups of white rice
- 4-5 finely chopped cloves garlic
- Juice of 2 limes
- Lime wedges, to serve
- 1/4 cup of finely chopped cilantro

Instructions

1. Place onion and the tomatoes in a blender, and blend it until it is smooth.
2. Add 2 cups of this mixture to a saucepan.
3. Add salt, chicken broth, and cumin. Bring it to boil over the medium heat.
4. On the other hand, toast rice.
5. Over medium heat, heat the oil until shimmering.
6. Put rice and cook, stirring frequently. When it is golden and lightly toasted, put jalapeños in it, and cook for about 2 minutes.
7. Lower the heat. And add garlic, then cook for around 30 seconds.
8. Put boiling tomato puree on the rice and mix thoroughly.

9. Lower the heat. Then cover it and cook. When the liquid is fully absorbed, and rice is cooked, turn off the heat.
10. Set aside for 10 minutes. Put lime juice and cilantro and mix it.
11. Season it with salt if needed, then serve.

7.3 Black Bean Tostadas

Instructions

- 1/2 diced red onion
- 2 cans of black beans
- 1 bell pepper, green
- 1/2 tsp. chili powder
- 3 garlic cloves
- 1/4 tsp. paprika
- Cayenne pepper, a small pinch
- 1/2 tsp. cumin
- Salt, to taste
- 3-4 cup of vegetable stock
- Black pepper, to taste
- 1 tbsp. lime juice

For Tostadas:

2-3 tbsp. of olive oil

8 corn tortillas

For Topping:

- Shredded lettuce
- Avocado, sliced
- Grilled corn
- Cherry tomatoes
- Green onions
- Fresh cilantro
- Cotija cheese, crumbled

- Lime wedges

Instructions

1 Put the onion, black beans, garlic cloves, pepper, paprika, chili powder, cumin, salt, cayenne, and pepper to a pan over medium heat.
2 Mix lime juice and stock in it and stir.
3 Simmer beans while keeping it uncovered, and cook for 10-15 minutes. When the mixture starts to thicken, turn down the heat, and set aside.
4 Remove garlic cloves from it.
5 For making tostadas, fry them in a pan.
6 To do it, heat a pan over the medium heat. Add oil in it.
7 Put the tortilla in it, and cook for 1-2 minutes. Flip and cook the other side.
8 Drain out any excess oil from it, and add salt. Go through the same process for the remaining tortillas.
9 To serve, add some black bean mixture on the top of the tortilla. Add lettuce, pickled avocado onion, tomatoes, grilled corn, cotija cheese, cilantro, and green onions.
10 Sprinkle lime juice, serve, and enjoy!

7.4 Smoky Veggie Nachos

Ingredients

- 4 corn tortillas
- 1 tsp. smoked paprika
- 400g can of black beans
- 2 red peppers
- 1/2 bunch of finely chopped parsley
- 1 finely sliced jalapeño
- 50g of yogurt
- 4 finely sliced spring onions
- 1 avocado, peeled and chopped
- 4 tomatoes, finely chopped

- 1/2 bunch of finely chopped coriander
- 1 lime, juiced
- 1 finely grated garlic clove
- 1 tbsp. of rapeseed oil

Instructions

1 Preheat the oven to 180C.
2 Make pieces of the tortillas, and make triangles. Spread them over two baking sheets.
3 Put oil on it, then add paprika. Bake it for around 7-8 minutes. When it is crisp, leave it to cool down.
4 Heat grill over high heat, then grill peppers for around 7-10 minutes. Leave it to cool down, then peel it off. Toss it with parsley and the beans.
5 Combine all ingredients to make salsa.
6 Put nachos on a plate, and top it with salsa, the bean mix, jalapeño, and yogurt.
7 Pour some paprika, and serve.

7.5 Enchilada Pie

Ingredients

- 1/2 cup onion, diced
- 1 pound of ground beef
- 2 minced cloves garlic
- 1 can of green chilies
- 1 can of Tex Mex-style tomatoes
- 2 tbsp. fresh cilantro, chopped
- 1 can of refried black beans
- 1 packet of taco seasoning mix
- 2 cans of red enchilada sauce
- 1/2 cup of sour cream
- 2 cups of Monterey Jack cheese, shredded
- 2 cups of pepper jack cheese, shredded
- 8 flour tortillas

Instructions

1 Preheat the oven to 200 degrees C.
2 Cook onions and beef in a skillet over the medium heat for about 7-10 minutes.
3 Put garlic in it, and cook for about 30 seconds.
4 Add green chiles, diced tomatoes, taco seasoning mix, and cilantro. Remove it from the heat.
5 Take a bow, and add black beans and red enchilada sauce.
6 Mix Monterey Jack cheese and pepper jack cheese together in a bowl.
7 Heat a skillet over the medium heat, and cook tortillas in it. When they are crisp, take them out.
8 Put a tortilla in a pan, and spread a layer of black bean mixture, then a layer of beef mixture.
9 Add 1 cup of cheese mixture and 1/4 cup of red enchilada sauce on top of it.
10 Repeat this process for all tortillas.
11 Cover the pan with an aluminum foil. Bake in the oven until the enchiladas are cooked, and the cheese is bubbling. It will take around 40 minutes.
12 Cool it down for around 15 minutes.
13 Serve it with sour cream.

7.6 Easy BBQ beans

Ingredients

- 2 cups of Barbecue Sauce
- 15 ounces can of pinto or cannellini beans
- 1 chopped green bell pepper
- 1–2 tsp. of liquid smoke
- 1 chopped yellow onion

Instructions

1 Preheat a saucepan over the medium heat.
2 Then drain and rinse the beans.

3 Put bell pepper, onion, and 2-3 tbsp. of veggie stock or water for cooking.
4 Cook it for about 3-4 minutes.
5 Lower the heat. Then add beans, liquid smoke, and BBQ Sauce.
6 Stir constantly until the beans are coated thoroughly.
7 Simmer it for around 10-15 minutes, then turn off the heat.
8 Serve and enjoy!

7.7 Vegetarian Mushroom Fajitas

Ingredients

- 1 1/2 cups of fresh mushrooms
- 2 bell peppers, red
- 1 sliced onion
- 1/2 tsp. of curry powder
- 1 tbsp. of olive oil
- 1/2 tsp. of chili powder
- 4 flour tortillas
- 1/4 tsp. of cumin
- Sour cream, optional

Instructions

1 Heat mushrooms, the peppers, and the onion in the olive oil for 3-5 minutes.
2 Put spices in it, and cook for about 2 minutes. Make sure the veggies are tender.
3 Put some mixture on a tortilla, the top sour cream over it.
4 Serve and enjoy!

7.8 Grilled Mexican Street Corn

Ingredients

- 1/2 cup of mayonnaise

- 4 ears yellow corn
- 2 tbsp. of finely chopped cilantro
- 1 small pinch of cayenne pepper
- 1 minced clove garlic
- 1 cup of Cotija cheese, finely crumbled
- Lime wedges, to serve
- 1/2 tsp. of chili powder

Instructions

1 Heat a grill over the medium heat.
2 Meanwhile, take a bowl, mix mayonnaise, garlic, cilantro, and cayenne pepper.
3 Put cotija cheese in a dish.
4 When the grill is heated, put corn on the grill. Leave space between corns.
5 Let it cook over grill. Make sure to turn it over to cook from all sides.
6 Brush all corn sides with mayonnaise mixture.
7 Roll it in cheese.
8 Take it out on a baking sheet or platter. Repeat this process with the remaining corn.
9 Add chili powder and cayenne pepper on all sides.
10 Sprinkle with cilantro and use lime wedges to serve.

7.9 Green Tomato Salsa

Ingredients

- ½ diced white onion
- 1 pound green tomatoes
- 1-2 thinly sliced Serrano peppers
- 1/2 cup of chopped cilantro
- 1 tbsp. of lime juice
- 1/2 tsp. of salt

Instructions

1 Cut tomatoes into quarters. Place them on a baking sheet having a foil.
2 Put the baking sheet in the oven. Broil them for 5 minutes.
3 Meanwhile, put the diced onions in a bowl. Fill it with cold water, and soak for 5-10 minutes.
4 Put the broiled tomatoes to a food processor, and break into pieces.
5 Remove water from onion and mix it with peppers, salt, lime juice, and cilantro. Then pulse it again until having the desired texture.
6 Season it with more lime juice and salt if needed.
7 Serve immediately, put it in the fridge for 1-2 hours for additional flavor.

7.10 Mexican Sweet Potatoes

Ingredients

- 2 sweet potatoes
- 1 tbsp. of olive Oil
- 1 diced sweet onion
- 1 chopped bell pepper, red
- 2 minced garlic cloves
- 2 cups of chopped mushrooms
- 1/2 cup of canned black beans
- 2 tbsp. of tomato taste
- 1/2 cup of frozen corn
- 1 tbsp. of chili powder
- Sea salt, to taste
- Black pepper, to taste
- 1 tsp. of ground cumin
- 1 mashed avocado
- Fresh cilantro, for garnishing
- 1 tbsp. sour cream or yogurt

Instructions

1   Preheat the oven to 200 degrees celcius. Prepare a baking sheet with a paper.
2   Make pieces of sweet potatoes, and put them on the baking sheet.
3   Cook them for 15-18 minutes, then take it out of the oven.
4   Meanwhile, take a skillet, and heat the oil.
5   Put onion, garlic, and bell pepper in it. Cook for 4-5 minutes.
6   Add mushrooms. Cook for another 6-7 minutes.
7   Add corn, tomato paste, black beans, chili powder, and chili powder.
8   Put Mexican mixture on the sweet potatoes, and put mashed avocado and yogurt on the top of them.
9   Garnish with cilantro and enjoy!

Chapter 8: Mexican Salad Recipes

Try and enjoy easting some healthy, easy, and tasteful Mexican salad recipes given in this chapter.

8.1 Mexican Salad with Tortilla Croutons

Ingredients

- 1 tbsp. of olive oil
- 3 flour tortillas
- 1 tsp. of Mexican seasoning mix
- 400g can of black bean
- 1 shredded iceberg lettuce,
- 200g pack of cherry tomato
- Juice of 1 lime
- 2 sliced avocados
- 1/2 bunch of coriander leaves

Instructions

1. Heat the oven to 200 degrees Celsius. Put seasoning mix and oil on pieces of tortilla, and put it on the baking tray. Cook for around 10-12 minutes until it is crisped.
2. Take a bowl. Put tomatoes, beans, avocado, lime juice, and the iceberg in it.
3. Drizzle over the dressings and mix it thoroughly.
4. Sprinkle coriander and croutons on it, and serve.

8.2 Spicy Chicken, Jalapeño and Mango Salad

Ingredients

- 2 tbsp. of jalapeños, finely chopped
- 250g pack of sliced cherry tomato
- Small bunch of chopped coriander
- 1 finely chopped red onion

- Juice of 1 lime
- 1 tbsp. of olive oil
- 2 lettuces, cut into pieces
- 4 chicken breasts, cooked and torn into shreds
- 1 sliced red pepper
- A handful of tortilla chips
- 1 ripe diced mango

Instructions

1. Mix jalapeños, cherry tomatoes, lime juice, coriander, oil, and onion in a bowl. Add some seasoning.
2. Top with the remaining ingredients.
3. Mix to coat.
4. Put tortilla chips on the top of it,
5. Serve with lime wedges, and enjoy!

8.3 Mexican Bean Salad

Ingredients

- 1/2 cup red wine vinegar
- 1 can of drained kidney beans
- 1 can of drained black beans
- 1 can of cannellini beans
- 1 package of corn kernels, frozen
- 1 bell pepper, red
- 1 bell pepper, green
- 1 chopped red onion
- 1/2 cup of olive oil
- 2 tbsp. of lime juice
- 1 tbsp. of salt
- 1 tbsp. of lemon juice
- 2 tbsp. of white sugar
- 1 clove garlic, crushed
- 1/2 tbsp. of ground cumin
- 1/4 cup fresh cilantro, chopped

- 1/2 tbsp. of black pepper
- 1/2 tsp. of chili powder
- 1 dash pepper sauce

Instructions

1. Take a bowl, and mix bell peppers, beans, red onion, and frozen corn.
2. Take another bowl, mix red wine vinegar, olive oil, lemon juice, lime juice, salt, sugar, garlic, cumin, cilantro, and black pepper.
3. Season with chili powder and hot sauce.
4. Add olive oil over vegetables, and mix it well.
5. Chill before serving.
6. Enjoy your salad.

8.4 Mexican Corn Salad

Ingredients

- 4 cups corn kernels
- 1 tbsp. of butter
- Salt, to taste
- Pepper, to taste
- 1/4 cup of chopped red onion
- 1 finely chopped bell pepper, red
- 3 tbsp. of lime juice
- 1/2 cup of cilantro leaves, for garnishing
- 1/4 cup of sour cream
- 1/2 tsp. of cumin
- 2 tbsp. mayonnaise
- 1/4 tsp. smoked paprika
- 1/3 cup of finely grated cotija cheese
- 1/2 tsp. of chili powder

Instructions

1. Take a pan and heat butter over medium heat.
2. Put corn in the pan. Cook for around 3-5 minutes.

3. Season with pepper and salt to taste.
4. Cool the corn at room temperature.
5. Put it in a bowl with red bell pepper, jalapeno, onion, and chopped cilantro.
6. Take another bowl, mix cream, lime juice, mayonnaise, smoked paprika, cumin, and chili powder.
7. Put the dressing on the corn mixture.
8. Sprinkle with chili powder, cotija cheese, and cilantro.
9. Serve and Enjoy!

8.5 Mexican Chopped Salad

Ingredients

For Dressing:

- 2 tbsp. of honey
- 1/4 cup of lime juice
- 1/2 tsp. of cumin
- 1/2 tsp. of salt
- 1 finely minced clove garlic
- 2 tbsp. of canola oil
- Black pepper, to taste
- 2 tbsp. olive oil
- Salt, to taste

For Tortilla Strips:

- 1 1/2 tbsp. of canola oil
- 6 corn tortillas (6-inches)
- 1/2 tsp. sea salt

For Salad:

- 4 diced tomatoes
- 1 diced bell pepper, any color
- 1 head lettuce
- 1/2 diced red onion
- 1 diced zucchini
- 1 1/2 cups corn

- 1/2 diced jicama
- 1 1/2 cups of black beans
- 1 1/2 cups corn
- 1/2 cup cilantro, finely chopped

Instructions

1. To prepare the dressing, mix lime juice, cumin, honey, salt, and garlic.
2. Gradually pour the oils while stirring it continuously.
3. Season to taste and put more pepper and salt, if required. Then set it aside.
4. Preheat the oven to 400 degrees F to get it ready for preparing tortilla strips.
5. Put tortillas on the cutting board, and cut them half.
6. Transfer the tortilla strips to a pan, then drizzle them with oil.
7. Add salt, then bake for around 15-20 minutes, while stirring it continuously until it is golden brown. Set aside.
8. To prepare the salad, put corn in the oven, the cook for almost 3 minutes.
9. Cut out the bottom of the corn, then pull back silks and husks and silks.
10. Cut corn kernels from the husks. Set them aside.
11. Mix other ingredients and corn in a bowl. Mix to combine.
12. Pour dressing and stir well.
13. Add cilantro leaves for garnishing.
14. Serve with the tortilla strips on the top.

8.6 Mexican Salad with Lime Dressing

Ingredients

For Salad:

- 1 cup tomatoes, halved
- 1 large head lettuce, chopped

- 1 diced avocado
- 1/2 yellow onion, sliced
- 1/2 sliced cucumber
- l cup peas, whole
- 1/3 bunch of fresh cilantro
- 1/2 cup of corn kernels, freshly cooked or canned

For Lime Dressing:

- 1/3 cup of lime juice
- 1/3 cup of olive oil
- Tabasco sauce, to taste
- 1/8 tsp. of black pepper
- 1/2 tsp. of sea salt

Instructions

1. Mix all ingredients for salad dressing and whisk together.
2. Chop all ingredients of the salad and mix it in a salad bowl.
3. Make sure to shake the dressing before serving.
4. Drizzle as much dressing on the salad as you like, and enjoy!

8.7 Spicy Mexican Salad

Ingredients

- 1 1/2 cups of shredded Monterey and Cheddar cheese
- 1 package of chopped lettuce
- 1 can of pinto beans
- 2 tomatoes, chopped
- 1 can of black beans
- 1 bag of corn chips
- 1 bottle of salad dressing

Instructions

1. Take a bowl, and combine cheese, romaine, pinto beans, tomatoes, and black beans.

2. Add corn chips and dressing, toss it well, and serve.

8.8 Mexican Avocado and Shrimp Salad

Ingredients

- 1 1/3 tbsp. olive oil
- 3/4 pound of shrimp
- 2 tbsp. of lime juice
- Salt, to taste
- Pepper, to taste
- 1/2 tsp. of honey
- 1 tsp.of chili powder
- 1/2 cup of corn kernels
- 1/2 cup of black beans, cooked
- 1 cup tomato, diced
- 1/2 thinly sliced avocado
- 1/3 cup cilantro, chopped
- 4 cups of mixed greens

Instructions

For Dressing:

1. Mix olive oil, lime juice, honey, and chopped cilantro.
2. Add pepper and salt.

For Black Bean Salsa:

1. Take a bowl, mix corn, black beans, tomato, cilantro, and lime juice. Add salt and mix it well.
2. Heat olive oil on the high heat.
3. Add chili powder, pepper, and salt to the shrimp. Cook each side for around 2-3 minutes. Make sure shrimp is opaque and pink.

Assemble the Salad:

Put the greens and dressing in a bowl. Add shrimp, avocado, and black bean salsa on the top, and serve.

8.9 Orange, Avocado, and Jicama Salad

Ingredients

- 2 tbsp. of lime juice
- 3 oranges
- 1 tbsp. cider vinegar
- 1 pinch cayenne pepper
- 2 tbsp. of olive oil
- 1/4 cup cilantro, chopped
- Salt, to taste
- Black pepper, to taste
- 2 thinly sliced avocados
- 1 jicama, peeled and sliced
- 1 cup of feta cheese, crumbled

Instructions

1. Squeeze oranges
2. To extract orange juice. Mix it with lime juice, oil, vinegar, and cayenne.
3. Add jicama, pepper, and salt. Set aside for about 15 minutes.
4. Add orange juice, avocado, cilantro, and feta.
5. Serve, and enjoy!

8.10 Mexican Black Bean and Chicken Salad

Ingredients

- 1 1/2 cups of chicken breast, cooked
- 6 cups of torn lettuce
- 1 can black beans
- 1/2 cup of shredded cheddar cheese
- 1 cup of green pepper, chopped
- 1 cup seeded tomatoes, chopped
- 1/2 cup red onion, sliced
- 1/4 cup seeded tomato, chopped
- 1/4 cup fresh cilantro, minced
- 1 tbsp. cider vinegar
- 1 tbsp. lime juice
- 1/4 tsp. chili powder
- 1 tbsp. olive oil
- 1/2 tsp. lime zest
- 1/4 teaspoon salt
- 1 minced garlic clove
- 1/4 tsp. pepper

Instructions

1. Take a large bowl, mix chicken, lettuce, beans, cheese, green pepper, tomatoes, and onion. Take a blender, and combine the ingredients for the vinaigrette.
2. Then cover it. Make sure it is smooth before pouring over the salad.
3. Serve and enjoy!

Chapter 9: Mexican Desserts

Try this fantastic collection of Mexican dessert recipes given in this chapter, and make your day.

9.1 Tres Leches Cake

Ingredients

- 1 tsp. baking powder
- 1 1/2 cups of flour
- 1/2 cup butter, unsalted
- 5 eggs
- 1 cup of white sugar
- 1/2 tsp. vanilla extract
- 1 can of condensed milk, sweetened
- 2 cups of whole milk
- 1 can of evaporated milk
- 1 cup of white sugar
- 1 1/2 cups of cream
- 1 tsp. of vanilla extract

Instructions

1. Put flour and grease on a baking pan, and preheat the oven to 175 C.
2. Mix baking powder and flour.
3. Mix cream butter and 1 cup of sugar until fluffy.
4. Put eggs and vanilla extract in it and beat well.
5. Gradually pour butter mixture to the flour mixture, mix well.
6. Bake it for around 30 minutes.
7. Mix condensed milk, and whole milk, and evaporated milk.
8. Put on the cake.
9. Mix whipping cream, remaining sugar, and remaining vanilla until it is thick. Pour on the cake.

10. Make sure to keep the cake in the refrigerator, enjoy!

9.2 Dulce de Leche

Ingredients

- 1 1/4 cups of sugar
- 4 cups of milk
- 1/4 tsp. of baking soda
- 1 tsp. of vanilla
- 1 can of sweetened condensed milk

Instructions

1. Mix milk, sugar, and baking soda in a saucepan. Bring it to boil, then lower the heat and keep it uncovered, stir until thickened.
2. Put vanilla into it, and let it cool.
3. Meanwhile, heat the oven to 425 degrees F.
4. Pour the can of sweetened condensed milk in a pie plate. Cover it tightly with a foil.
5. Put the plate in a pan and add hot water. Bake the milk in the oven for about 45 minutes. Regularly see the water level, and continue baking for another 45 minutes.
6. Remove the pie plate from water and let it cool.

9.3 Rumchata Cupcakes

Ingredients

For Cupcakes:

- 1 cup of Rumchata
- 1/2 cup of vegetable oil
- 1 box of vanilla cake mix
- 3 eggs

For Frosting:

- 1 cup of butter

- 4 cups of powdered sugar
- 1/3 cup of Rumchata
- 1 tsp. of cinnamon
- 1 tsp. of vanilla extract
- 1 pinch of kosher salt

Instructions

1. Put the cupcake wrappers on the cupcake pan, and preheat the oven to 350 C.
2. Mix ingredients until smooth.
3. Put batter into the liners, and bake for 25 minutes. Make sure the toothpick comes out clean. When ready, let it cool.
4. Mix 2 cups of powdered sugar with other ingredients. Mix well until creamy.
5. Add powdered sugar in it, and beat until fluffy and light.
6. Pour Rumchata frosting on the cupcakes.
7. Garnish with cinnamon sticks and cinnamon, and serve.

9.4 Churro Apple Pies

Ingredients

For the Apple Pie Filling:

- 2 tbsp. of fresh lemon juice
- 5 apples diced into pieces
- 1 1/4 of cup water
- 1 pinch nutmeg
- 1/2 cup of brown sugar
- 3 tbsp. of cornstarch
- 1 tsp. of ground cinnamon

For the Caramel Sauce:

- 1/4 cup of butter
- 1 cup of brown sugar

- 1/2 cup of thickened cream

Instructions

1. Mix apples with lemon juice in a saucepan.
2. Whisk water and cornstarch until it is lump-free.
3. Put the mixture into a saucepan over the medium heat.
4. Add brown sugar, nutmeg, and cinnamon.
5. Mix to combine it well. Bring it to boil. Whisk continuously.
6. When the mixture starts to thicken, put the diced apple in it.
7. Lower the heat and cover the pan.
8. Let it cook for around 8-10 minutes until soft.
9. Turn down the heat while keeping it covered, and let it cool.
10. Fill each churro bowl with apple pie filling.
11. Drizzle ice cream and caramel sauce.
12. To prepare caramel sauce, mix heavy cream and brown sugar into a saucepan over the medium heat. When sugar just starts to melt, put butter in it.
13. Lower heat and continue cooking until sauce thickens.
14. Let it cool, then pour onto the Apple Pie Churros.
15. Server and enjoy!

9.5 Mexican Hot Chocolate Pie

Ingredients

For the Crust:

- 2 tbsp. of sugar
- 1 1/2 cups of cracker crumbs, divided
- 1 tsp. of ground cinnamon
- 2 tbsp. of egg white
- 1/8 tsp. salt
- 2 tbsp. of butter

For the Filling:

- 2 tbsp. of cornstarch
- 1/2 cup of sugar
- 1 tbsp. of unsweetened cocoa
- 1/8 tsp. salt
- 1/4 tsp. of espresso granules
- 1/8 tsp. of red pepper
- 1 egg yolk
- 1 egg
- 1 3/4 cups of 2% milk
- 1 1/2 cups of frozen topping
- 2 ounces of chopped dark chocolate

Instructions

1. Preheat the oven to 375 degrees C.
2. For preparing the crust. Mix crumbs, sugar, salt, and cinnamon in a bowl.
3. Add butter and egg white. Put crumb mixture in the up and bottom sides of a pie plate, and bake at 375 degrees C for around 9 minutes. Let it cool.
4. For preparing the filling, mix ingredients in a bowl.
5. Put milk in a saucepan over the medium heat. Gradually mix hot milk and egg mixture. Stir constantly.
6. Put milk mixture back to the pan. Cook until it is thick. Stir constantly.
7. Turn off the heat, then put chocolate in it. Stir smoothly.
8. Let it cool, then put filling in the crust. Put plastic wrap to cover it. Chill for 3 hours, then take off the plastic wrap.
9. Pour whipped topping, and sprinkle with cracker crumbs.
10. Serve and enjoy!

9.6 Horchata Cupcakes

Ingredients

For Cake:

- 2 sticks of butter
- 1 tsp. of vanilla extract
- 400 grams of granulated sugar

- 4 egg whites
- 360 grams of flour
- 225 grams of sour cream
- 1/2 tsp. of baking soda
- 2 tsp. of baking powder
- 1 tsp. of salt
- 1 1/4 cup of horchata
- 1 tsp. of ground cinnamon

For Buttercream:

- 115 grams of cream cheese
- 1 stick of butter
- 500 grams of powdered sugar
- 1 tsp. of ground cinnamon
- 1 tsp. of vanilla extract
- 2 tbsp. of horchata

Instructions

1. Preheat the oven to 350 degrees F.
2. Mix flour, baking powder, cinnamon, salt, and baking soda.
3. In a hand mixer, whisk the butter until it is creamy.
4. Mix sugar.
5. Put egg whites in it, and whip until the mixture is fluffy.
6. Put sour cream and vanilla in it.
7. Lower the heat, then mix dry ingredients.

8. Put horchata in it.
9. Fill the cupcake liners, and bake for around 15-18 minutes.
10. Let it cool before icing.
11. To prepare buttercream, whisk cream cheese, and butter.
12. Add powdered sugar.
13. Mix vanilla, cinnamon, and horchata in it. Mix until creamy and smooth.
14. Pour on the cupcakes and serve.

9.7 Traditional Flan Custard

Ingredients

- 6 eggs
- 1 1/2 cups of sugar
- 1 14-ounce can of condensed milk
- 1 tsp. of vanilla
- 1 can of evaporated milk
- 1 pinch of salt

Instructions

1. Preheat the oven to 325 degrees F.
2. To prepare caramel sauce, pour sugar into a pan over the medium heat. Stir constantly.
3. When it is brown and fully melted, it will become caramel.
4. Once the color reaches golden brown, transfer it to the pie plate.
5. To prepare the custard, whisk the eggs for one minute or until they are frothy.
6. Gradually put condensed milk in it, then the evaporated milk. Slowly mix the vanilla and sugar.
7. To bake the flan, put the custard mixture in the caramel pie plate.
8. Put the pie plate in a baking dish.

9. Bake the flan for around 45 minutes. Use a knife to check its status. If it is clean, then your flan is ready.
10. Remove the flan from the baking dish. Let it cool for overnight in the refrigerator for better taste.
11. Serve and enjoy!

9.8 Mexican Churros

Instructions

- 1 cup of water
- 4 cups of vegetable oil
- 1/2 cups of salted butter
- 1/4 tsp. of salt
- 1 tsp. of vanilla extract
- 1 cup flour
- 1 cup of sugar
- 3 eggs
- 1 tsp. of ground cinnamon

Instructions

1. Make the dough by mixing water, vanilla, salt, and butter in a saucepan. When the mixture starts to simmer, turn off the heat.
2. Add eggs one by one, mashing and stirring the dough until it is fully incorporated.
3. Put the mixture to a pastry bag.
4. Put the dough into the hot oil.
5. Cook it until it is puffy. Cook evenly from all sides. It will take 2-4 minutes.
6. Carefully take out churro from the oil, and use a paper towel to drain it.
7. When churros are cooled, put the cinnamon and sugar into a plastic bag.
8. Put churros in it and shake until they are coated.

9.9 Vegan Mexican Chocolate Cake

Ingredients

- 1 cup of sugar
- 1 1/2 cups of flour
- 1/4 cup of cocoa
- 1 1/2 tsp. cinnamon
- 1 tsp. baking soda
- 3/4 tsp. cayenne pepper
- 1 tbsp. white vinegar
- 1 tsp. vanilla
- 5 tbsp. vegetable oil
- 2 tbsp. of powdered sugar
- 1 cup of cold water

Instructions

1. Preheat the oven to 350 degrees F.
2. Grease a cake pan.
3. Take a bowl, and combine sugar, flour, cocoa, cinnamon, baking soda, and cayenne.
4. Mix vanilla, oil, vinegar, and water.
5. Put the mixture in the cake pan, then bake for almost 30 minutes.
6. Sprinkle powdered sugar, and serve.

9.10 Pan de Muerto

Ingredients

- 2 tbsp. of yeast
- 500 grams of flour
- 100 grams of sugar
- 80 grams of butter
- 1 tsp. salt
- 80 grams of unsalted margarine
- 2 oranges

- 4 eggs
- 60 ml. of warm water
- 1 egg
- 1 tsp. of orange essence
- Sugar, for decoration

Instructions

1. Place eggs, margarine, sugar, and salt in a mixer bowl.
2. Add the flour with the water. Then add yeast and mix to combine.
3. Add butter, orange zest, sugar, and orange essence. Mix to make a soft dough.
4. Knead the dough, and transfer it back to the bowl. Cover it with plastic wrap, and set aside for about 45 minutes.
5. Make pieces from the dough, and prepare greased baking sheets.
6. Place these pieces onto baking sheets. And press them slightly.
7. Preheat the oven to 350^0 C.
8. Mix a pinch of salt to the mixture of water and egg.
9. Brush it on the buns.
10. Transfer the buns/pieces to the oven. Bake until it is golden brown.
11. Let it cool at room temperature.
12. When the Pan de Muerto bread is cooled, brush it with butter and sprinkle with sugar.
13. Serve and enjoy!

9.11 Mexican Buñuelos

Ingredients

For Buñuelos:

- 1 1/2 tsp. baking powder
- 2 cups of flour
- 1/2 tsp. salt

- 4 tbsp. oil, for frying
- 3/4 cup of warm water

For Topping:

- 1 tbsp. of ground cinnamon
- 1/2 cup of granulated sugar

Instructions

1. Take a bowl, add salt, baking powder, and flour in it.
2. Add oil and warm water. Mix with your hands.
3. Make the dough and knead it for 8-10 minutes to make it smooth.
4. Cover it and set aside for 30 minutes.
5. Take a pan with frying oil in it and make a topping of cinnamon sugar.
6. Make balls from the dough, then shape them into circles.
7. Heat oil to 350 F, and fry each circle for 60 seconds, until it is golden brown from both sides.
8. Remove any excess oil, and sprinkle cinnamon sugar topping.
9. Serve and Enjoy!

9.12 Mexican Brownies

Ingredients

- 3/4 cup of dark chocolate chips
- 2 tsp. ground cinnamon
- 1 package of fudge brownie mix
- 1 tsp. of ancho chili pepper
- 1/2 cup of canola oil
- 2 eggs
- 1/4 cup of water

Instructions

1. Add brownie mix to spices.
2. Transfer this mixture to a glass jar.

3. Add chocolate chips, then cover it. You can store it in a cool and dry place for up to 3 months.
4. For brownies, preheat the oven to 350 degrees C.
5. Whisk together oil, eggs, and water.
6. Slowly add brownie mix and chocolate chips.
7. Spread it on a baking pan, then bake until or around 20-25 minutes.
8. Let it cool completely, and then serve.

Chapter 10: Most Famous Mexican Recipes

Cook and enjoy some of the most popular Mexican recipes, including tacos, burritos, and quesadillas.

10.1 Tacos Recipes

Marcela's Baja-style Fish Tacos

Ingredients

For Beer Batter:

- 1 cup Mexican beer
- 1 tsp. salt
- 1 cup flour
- 1/2 tsp. black peppe

For Cream Sauce:

- 2/3 cup sour cream
- 1/3 cup of mayonnaise
- 1 tsp. lemon zest
- 2 tbsp. water
- 2 tbsp. fresh lemon juice
- Salt, to taste
- Black pepper, to taste

For Fish Tacos:

- 1 cup flour
- Oil, to fry
- 1 tsp. salt
- Black pepper, to taste
- 2 pounds of skinned halibut
- 4 corn tortillas
- 2 cups of tomatillo salsa, for garnishing
- 2 cups f shredded cabbage
- Pickled jalapenos, optional

Instructions

For Beer Batter:

1. Put salt, pepper, and flour in a bowl.
2. Pour beer and whisk.
3. Set it aside for almost 15 minutes.

For Cream Sauce:

4. Mix crema and mayonnaise in a bowl.
5. Add lemon juice, lemon zest, and water.
6. Add pepper and salt.

For Fish:

7. Take a skillet, heat oil over the medium heat.
8. Take a plate, and combine salt and flour.
9. Cover the fish pieces flour and season with pepper and salt.
10. Dip fillets in beer batter, then cover both sides.
11. Fry until it is golden brown. Cook it thoroughly and put it on paper towels and drain.
12. Combine fish and tortillas.
13. Top with pickled jalapenos, shredded cabbage, cream, and tomatillo salsa.

Tacos Carne Asada

Ingredients

- 2 tbsp. fresh lime juice
- 2 tbsp. soy sauce
- 2 tbsp. canola oil
- 2 tsp. chili powder
- 3 cloves minced garlic
- 1 tsp. ground cumin
- 1 1/2 pounds of skirt steak
- 1 tsp. dried oregano
- 6 flour tortillas
- 1/2 cup of cilantro leaves
- 3/4 cup red onion, diced
- 1 lime

Instructions

1. Take a bowl, mix lime juice, soy sauce, oregano, canola oil, chili powder, garlic, and cumin.
2. Take a bowl, mix steak, and soy sauce mixture. Marinate for 1-4 hours.
3. Heat the remaining canola oil over the medium heat.
4. Put the steak in it and cook until brown.
5. Serve in tortillas and top with cilantro, onion, and lime.

Beef Barbacoa Tacos

Ingredients

- 4 minced cloves garlic
- 3 pounds of beef chuck roast
- 1 chopped white onion
- 1 can of green chiles
- 1/4 cup of lime juice
- 4 bay leaves
- 2 tbsp. of apple cider vinegar
- 1 tbsp. ground cumin
- 2 tsp. sea salt
- 1 tbsp. Mexican oregano, dried
- 1/4 tsp. ground cloves
- 1 tsp. black pepper
- 1/2 cup of beef stock

Instructions

1. In the slow cooker, mix all ingredients.
2. Cook it for 6-8 hours while keeping it covered until beef is cooked.
3. Shred beef into pieces.
4. Season with lemon juice, and cover it. Leave it for 10 minutes.
5. Take out the bay leaves, and serve.

Crispy Chicken Mini Tacos

Ingredients

- 1/2 cup white onion, chopped
- 1 cup tomato, chopped
- 1 jalapeno
- Salt, to taste
- Black pepper, to taste
- 1 tbsp. chopped cilantro leaves
- 1 chicken breast
- Vegetable oil, to fry
- 2 1/2 tbsp. olive oil
- 8 corn tortillas
- 3 tbsp. iceberg lettuce, shredded
- 1/4 cup sour cream
- 3 tbsp. feta or queso fresco cheese

Instructions

1. Mix onion, cilantro, tomato, and jalapeno in a bowl.
2. Add pepper and salt to taste. Then set it aside.
3. Preheat oven to the 350^0 F.
4. Apply olive oil on the chicken breast. Sprinkle with pepper and salt, to taste.
5. Roast the chicken for about 25 minutes.
6. Let it cool, then shred it.
7. Take a skillet and heat vegetable oil.
8. Put shredded chicken in the center of corn tortilla, then roll it.
9. Fry tacos until it is golden brown, then cut into half.
10. Top it with salsa and shredded lettuce.
11. Put queso fresco on it, and serve.

Pork Carnitas Tacos

Ingredients

For Canitas:

- 1 tbsp. lime juice
- 2 1/2 pounds of pork shoulder
- 2 tsp. sea salt
- 1 cup of broth, vegetable, chicken or beef
- 1 tsp. chili powder
- 2 tsp. ground cumin
- 1 tsp. garlic powder
- 1 tsp. onion powder
- 1 tsp. dried oregano
- 1/2 tsp. black pepper

Instructions

For Slow Cooker:

1. Make pieces of pork shoulder, and put them in a slow cooker.
2. Mix chili powder, salt, lime juice, ground cumin, garlic powder, dried oregano, onion powder, and black pepper.
3. Then coat the pork slices with seasonings.
4. Cook while keeping it covered for around 4 hours on medium heat.
5. When it is cooked, take out and shred.
6. Put chopped cilantro in it and serve in tacos.

For Instant Pot:

1. Make pieces of pork shoulder. Put them in an Instant Pot.
2. Mix salt, lime juice, ground cumin, garlic powder, chili powder, dried oregano, onion powder, broth, and black pepper.
3. Then coat the pork slices with seasonings.
4. Cook for around 40 minutes on high pressure.

5. Shred the pieces.
6. Add chopped cilantro, and serve in tacos.

Mushroom, Poblano, and Potato Tacos

Ingredients

- 3 medium potatoes, cut into pieces
- 4 poblano chile peppers
- Kosher salt, to taste
- 1 1/2 tbsp. fresh cilantro finely chopped
- 2 tbsp. olive oil
- 1 1/2 tbsp. fresh parsley, finely chopped
- 1 onion, sliced
- 2 tbsp. unsalted butter
- 12 ounces white mushrooms, sliced
- 1/2 cup of creme fraiche, Mexican crema, or sour cream
- 1 clove minced garlic
- 2 limes, juiced
- Corn tortillas, for serving
- Ground pepper, to taste

Instructions

1. Get a boiler or a gas burner, and roast poblanos for around 10 minutes.
2. Take it out in a bowl, then cover. Let it cool for around 10 minutes.
3. Cut them into strips.
4. Place potatoes in a nonstick skillet; cover them with cold water, and season with the salt.
5. Cook over the medium heat. Cook until they are tender, then drain.
6. Take a skillet and heat oil over the medium heat.
7. Put potatoes in it; cook until they are crisp and golden for 4 minutes.
8. Drain them on paper towels.
9. Sprinkle with salt and herbs.
10. Remove excess oil.

11. Take a skillet and heat butter over the medium heat.
12. Put the onion in it, and cook until it is golden.
13. Put mushrooms in it, and cook until they are golden.
14. Mix garlic and herbs; cook for 1 minute.
15. Put roasted poblanos, lime juice, crema, and some water; stir for 1-2 minutes.
16. Add pepper and salt.
17. Serve mushroom mixture and potatoes in tortillas with toppings.

Chipotle Chicken Meatball Tacos

Ingredients

- 1 egg
- 2 slices of white bread
- 1 finely chopped white onion
- 1/4 cup fresh cilantro, chopped
- 2 cloves minced garlic
- 3/4 pound of ground chicken
- Kosher salt, to taste
- Ground pepper, to taste
- 3 tbsp. olive oil
- 1 chipotle chile pepper, chopped
- 1 jalapeno pepper, chopped
- 1 can of diced tomatoes
- 1/4 tsp. ground cinnamon
- 1/4 tsp. dried thyme
- 3 bay leaves
- Taco shells, for serving

Instructions

1. Put egg and bread in a bowl.
2. Add water and then mash them.
3. Add garlic and onion, then put cilantro, chicken, pepper, and salt. Mix it well.
4. Brush a baking sheet with olive oil.

5. Make meatballs from the mixture and place on baking sheet, then pun in the refrigerator for around 15 minutes.
6. Preheat oven to 475^0 F.
7. Mix the remaining garlic and onion, jalapeno, chipotle, thyme, tomatoes, and cinnamon, and blend until smooth.
8. In the oven, heat olive oil over the medium heat.
9. Add tomato puree, and add bay leaves; cook until sauce thickens.
10. Add 1 1/2 cups of water.
11. Lower the heat and simmer; stir occasionally.
12. Add salt.
13. Bake meatballs until brown for 8 minutes.
14. Put it in the sauce and simmer.
15. Spoon sauce over meatballs, until they are thoroughly cooked
16. Remove bay leaves, and cut meatballs into halves.
17. Serve in tacos with toppings.

Quick Vegetarian Tacos

Ingredients

- 1 cup summer squash, chopped
- 1 Japanese eggplant, cut into pieces
- 1 bell pepper, red
- Olive oil, to drizzle
- 1 cup of cherry tomatoes
- 6 tortillas
- 1 diced avocados
- 1 cup of black beans, cooked
- Chopped cilantro
- Cotija cheese, crumbled, optional
- 1 serrano pepper, optional
- Sea salt, to taste
- Black pepper, to taste

For Sauce:

- 1/4 cup of pepitas
- 1/3 cup of tomatillo salsa
- 1/2 avocado
- 2 tbsp. of olive oil
- 2 tbsp. of spinach
- 1 tbsp. of lime juice
- Sea salt, to taste
- Black pepper, to taste

Instructions

1. Preheat oven to 400 degrees F.
2. Put chopped eggplant, red pepper, tomatoes, and squash in a baking sheet.
3. Add olive oil, pepper, and salt onto it, then roast until it is golden brown.
4. Blend tomatillo salsa, avocado, pepitas, spinach, olive oil, salt, lime juice, and pepper, and set aside.
5. Make tacos with roasted vegetables, black beans, diced avocado, serrano, cilantro, and cotija.
6. Serve with more sauce.

Tex-Mex Taco Pizza

Ingredients

- 1 1 1/2 pounds of pizzeria dough
- 1 cup of jarred salsa
- 1 cup of Cheddar cheese, shredded
- 1 onion, chopped
- 1 tbsp. of olive oil
- 2 tsp. of ground cumin
- 1 tsp. of smoked paprika
- 1 tsp. of garlic powder
- 1 pound of beef sirloin
- 1/4 cup of sour cream
- 1/2 cup pickled jalapeno

- 1 tbsp. of lime juice
- 1 heart thinly sliced romaine lettuce
- 1 tbsp. of milk
- 2 small chopped plum tomatoes

Instruction

1. Preheat the oven to 475^0 F.
2. Pour salsa all over the dough. Put cheddar on it and bake.
3. Take a skillet and heat oil.
4. Add cumin, onion, smoked paprika, and garlic powder, then cook for 3 minutes.
5. Mix beef and salt, and cook for 3 more minutes until brown.
6. Add beef on cheese.
7. Add jalapenos. Then bake for almost 20 minutes.
8. Mix sour cream with milk and lime juice.
9. Put tomatoes and lettuce on top of the pizza.
10. Pour sour cream mixture, and serve.

10.2 Burritos Recipes

Beef and Bean Burritos

Ingredients

- 2 tbsp. taco seasoning
- 1 pound ground beef
- 6 tortillas, flour
- 1 cup Mexican cheese, shredded
- 16 ounces refried bean

Instructions

1. Put beef in a skillet over the high heat; add taco seasoning in it.
2. Cook until it is brown, then drain and set aside.
3. Assemble burritos by putting flour tortilla in the microwave for almost 20 seconds.
4. Put a layer of refried beans, cheese, and then cooked beef on it.
5. Fold the sides and bottom of the tortilla.
6. Wrap it in a parchment paper; if you like to store in the refrigerator for up to 30 days.
7. To serve and eat, wrap it in the paper towel; microwave for around 2-3 minutes, set it aside for almost one minute.
8. Enjoy!

Ultimate Vegan Burrito

Ingredients

- 2 mushroom caps
- 2 cups of Spanish Rice, cooked
- 1/2 red onion
- 2 cans of black beans
- 1 bell pepper, orange
- 2 tbsp. olive oil
- 1 tsp. garlic powder
- 2 tsp. cumin
- 1 tsp. onion powder
- 1 tsp. kosher salt
- 1 tsp. smoked paprika
- 2 tbsp. lime juice
- 4 large tortillas
- 1 avocado

Instructions

1. Remove stems from mushroom caps; cut into slices.
2. Slice bell pepper and red onion.

3. Take a skillet, and heat oil over the medium heat.
4. Cook veggies for almost 6-7 minutes.
5. Put black beans, garlic powder, onion powder, cumin, paprika, lime juice, kosher salt, and some water. Cook until liquid evaporates.
6. Add kosher salt to the mashed avocado.
7. To assemble tortilla, put 1/2 cup of rice on it. Top with the bean mixture, avocado, and vegetable.
8. Fold in all sides of burritos.
9. Cut them, and serve.

Burrito Egg Rolls

Ingredients

- 1/2 cup of black beans
- 1/2 pounds of ground beef
- 1 cup cheddar cheese
- 1/4 cup green pepper
- 1/2 cup of frozen corn
- 1 tsp. taco seasoning
- 14 egg roll wrappers
- 1 tsp. olive oil
- 1 tomato, diced
- Oil, to fry
- Salt, to taste
- Pepper, to taste
- Guacamole, to serve

Instructions

1. Take a skillet, and heat oil over the medium heat.
2. Put taco seasoning and beef in it — season with pepper and salt.
3. Drain fat from beef and put it back to skillet.
4. Put back beans and corn, and cook for 2 minutes.
5. Turn off the heat and take it out in a bowl.
6. Add shredded cheddar, green pepper, and tomato in it.

7. Put the mixture and the egg roll wrapper in the center. Roll it, and continue this process with all burrito mixture and egg roll wrappers.
8. Take a skillet, and heat oil over the medium heat.
9. Fry each side of egg roll until it is golden brown.
10. Turn off the heat; drain the fat.
11. Repeat the process with other egg rolls.
12. Serve immediately with the guacamole.

Cabbage Burritos

Instructions

- 1 tbsp. olive oil
- 8 cabbage leaves
- 1/2 chopped onion
- 2 cloves minced garlic
- 1 pound ground beef
- 1 tbsp. of taco seasoning mix
- Black pepper, to taste
- Kosher salt to taste
- 1 can of black beans
- 1/2 cup shredded cheddar
- 1 cup corn, frozen or canned
- 1 1/2 cup of cherry tomatoes, chopped
- 1 cup of Monterey Jack, shredded

Instructions

1. Preheat the oven to the 350°C.
2. In boiling water, dip cabbage leaves for 30 seconds. Pat them dry.
3. Take a skillet, and heat oil over the medium heat.
4. Put the onion in it and cook for 5 minutes.
5. Add garlic and ground beef. Cook for about 5 minutes.
6. Add taco seasoning mix, pepper, and salt.
7. Add cherry tomatoes, black beans, and corn.
8. Place cabbage leaves on a plate, and put beef mixture with cheese.

9. Fold cabbage leaves, then roll them.
10. Bake them until for around 10 minutes.

Cheesy Baked Burritos

Instructions

- 1 chopped onion
- 1 tbsp. olive oil
- 2 minced garlic cloves
- 1 cup enchilada sauce
- Kosher salt to taste
- 2 cup of rotisserie chicken
- 1 lime, juiced
- Black pepper,
- to taste
- 1 can of black beans
- 1 cup cheddar cheese
- 2 cup of white rice, cooked
- 1 cup cheese, Monterey Jack
- Sour cream, optional
- Chopped cilantro, optional
- 6 flour tortillas
- Hot sauce, optional

Instructions

1. Preheat the oven to 350^0 F.
2. Take a skillet, and heat oil over the medium heat.
3. Put onion and cook until soft.
4. Add garlic for around 30 seconds.
5. Put enchilada sauce and chicken in it.
6. Add lime juice; season with pepper and salt.
7. Put a tortilla on a board. Add beans and rice on top of it.
8. Put in chicken mixture, and top with both kinds of cheese.
9. Roll burrito and put in a dish.
10. Put enchilada sauce on burritos; sprinkle extra cheeses.

11. Cook for around 15 minutes.
12. Add cilantro; serve with hot sauce and sour cream.

Low-Carb Breakfast Burritos

Instructions

- 1 tbsp. of skim milk
- Kosher salt to taste
- 2 eggs
- 1 tbsp. of chopped chives
- Black pepper, to taste
- 1 tbsp. of butter
- 1/2 cup of black beans
- 4 slices bacon, cooked
- 1 avocado, sliced
- Salsa, to serve
- 1/2 cup of shredded cheddar

Instructions

1. Take a bowl, and mix eggs, chives, and milk; season with pepper and salt.
2. Take a skillet, and melt butter in it.
3. Add the egg mixture in it. Cook each side for almost 2 minutes.
4. Place it on a plate; top with black beans, bacon, avocado, salsa, and cheddar.
5. Make a burrito, then serve.

Burrito Avocados

Instructions

- 1/4 finely chopped onion
- 1 tbsp. of olive oil
- 1/2 pounds of ground beef
- 1/2 tsp. of ground cumin
- 1/2 tsp. of chili powder
- 1/2 tsp. of garlic powder
- Black pepper, to taste

- Kosher salt, to taste
- 1/2 cup of frozen corn
- Sliced Cheddar
- 2 avocados
- Monterey Jack, sliced
- 1/4 cup of cherry tomatoes
- 2 tsp. fresh cilantro, for garnishing
- Sour cream, for garnishing

Instructions

1. Take a skillet, and heat oil over the medium heat.
2. Put the onion in it and cook for 5 minutes.
3. Put ground beef and cook for around 6 minutes.
4. Add spices, and season with pepper and salt.
5. Add frozen corn, and cook.
6. Cut slices of avocado.
7. Put avocado on the serving plate.
8. Put cheese slices between cuts, and top with beef mixture.
9. Add sour cream and cilantro.
10. Serve.

Frito Pie Burritos

Ingredients

For Burritos:

- 1 cup of chili con carne
- 4 flour tortillas
- 1 cup of Fritos
- 3/4 cup of refried beans
- 1/2 cup of corn kernels
- 1 cup of cheddar cheese

For Toppings:

- 1/4 cup of minced red onions
- ½ cup of fresh diced tomatoes
- ¼ cup of chopped cilantro

- ½ cup of shredded lettuce
- Lime wedges
- 1 sliced jalapeno
- 1/4 cup of sour cream

Instructions

1. Fill tortillas with corn, chili, Fritos, cheese, and refried beans.
2. Heat a skillet over the medium heat; grease with pan spray.
3. Cook each side of burritos for about 3 minutes until it is golden brown.
4. Serve with toppings.

Steak Burrito

Ingredients

- 2 tsp. of ground cumin
- 1/2 pound of skirt steak
- 2 minced cloves garlic
- 4 tbsp. olive oil
- 2 limes, juiced
- 1 can of black beans
- kosher salt, to taste
- 3 tomatoes, finely diced
- Black pepper, to taste
- 1/3 cup of red onion, minced
- 1 diced avocado
- 5 tbsp. of chopped cilantro
- 1 cup of rice, cooked
- 1 1/2 cups of romaine lettuce, thinly sliced
- Sour cream
- 4 tortillas
- Cheddar cheese, shredded

Instructions

1. Take a bowl, and add steak with garlic clove, cumin, lime juice, and olive oil.
2. Take a skillet, and heat oil over the medium heat.
3. Put remaining garlic and cook for 1 minute.
4. Put black beans in it and cook for 4-5 minutes.
5. Add pepper and salt and mix lime juice.
6. Take a bowl, and stir tomatoes, cilantro, red onion, lime juice, and olive oil, avocado, pepper, and salt.
7. Heat the grill pan over the high heat.
8. Add steak, pepper, and salt; cook for 2-3 minutes.
9. In a bowl, mix rice, cilantro, pepper, and salt.
10. Brush a skillet with olive oil.
11. Put tortillas in it, and crisp each side for 30 seconds.
12. On each tortilla, put rice, beans, pico de gallo, avocado, steak slices, lettuce, cheese, and sour cream.
13. Roll the tortilla. Put burritos back to the skillet, and cook for 30 seconds.
14. Cut in half and serve.

Chicken and Avocado Burritos

Instructions

- 1 package of taco seasoning
- 1 pound chicken
- 1 tbsp. olive oil
- 2 avocados, diced
- 4 flour tortillas
- 1/4 cup of cilantro leaves, chopped
- 1 cup mozzarella cheese, shredded
- 1/4 cup of Ranch dressing
- 1/4 cup of sour cream

Instructions

1. Take a skillet and heat oil over the medium heat.
2. Add taco seasoning to chicken.
3. Cook chicken in the skillet until golden for around 3-4 minutes, then set it aside.

4. Warm the tortillas.
5. Take a tortilla and place chicken, cheese, avocado, sour cream, cilantro, and Ranch. Fold it, and continue this process with all tortillas.
6. Take a pan, and heat it over the medium heat.
7. Put burritos in it; cook each side for around 3 to 4 minutes until it is golden brown.
8. Serve immediately.

10.3 Quesadillas Recipes

BBQ Chicken Quesadillas

Izgredients

- 3 cups of cooked chicken breast
- 10 ounces of rice, cooked
- 1 can of kidney or red beans
- 3 cups Cheddar cheese, shredded
- 1 cup of barbecue sauce
- 6 tortillas

Instructions

1. Take a pan and heat beans and chicken with the BBQ sauce.
2. Add cooked rice, the bean and chicken mixture.
3. Put more sauce if you like.
4. To assemble the quesadillas, sprinkle cheddar cheese.
5. Then add cheese on chicken mixture. Use additional cheese if you like.
6. On each quesadilla, place another tortilla, and set aside.
7. Take a pan and toast quesadillas over the medium heat, then cook them until they are brown.
8. Serve and Enjoy!

Black Bean, Corn, and Wild-rice Quesadillas

Ingredients

- 1 cup of Cheddar cheese, shredded

- 10 ounces of rice, cooked
- 1/2 cup of black beans
- 2 chopped green onions
- 1/2 cup of mild salsa
- 1/2 cup of sweet corn, frozen
- 4 flour tortillas

Instructions

1. Add rice, beans, shredded cheese, green onions, and corn in a bowl.
2. Put 1/4 of this mixture on a tortilla.
3. Add mild salsa on the top. Fold the tortilla.
4. Heat a pan over the medium heat.
5. Put a quesadilla in the pan, and cook until it is golden brown.
6. Cook all the remaining quesadillas.
7. Let them cool, and then cut them in half.
8. Serve with salsa.

Mashed Potato Quesadilla

Ingredients

- 6 slices of bacon, cooked and crumbled
- 2 cups of mashed potatoes
- ¼ cup of green onions, sliced
- 2 cups of Cheddar cheese, shredded
- 1/4 cup of sour cream
- 8 flour tortillas
- 1 cup of salsa
- 2 tbsp. of softened butter

Instructions

1. Mix mashed potatoes, green onions, and bacon.
2. Put this mixture on the tortillas.
3. Add shredded cheese on the top and put remaining tortillas on the top.
4. Put butter on each side of quesadillas.
5. Heat a skillet over the medium heat.

6. Put quesadilla in the pan; cook each side until it is crispy and golden brown.
7. Repeat this process with all quesadillas, then serve with sour cream and salsa.

Shrimp Quesadillas

Ingredients

- 1 sliced onion
- 2 tbsp. of vegetable oil
- 1 bell pepper, red
- 1 tsp. salt
- 1 bell pepper, green
- 1 tsp. ground cumin
- 1 pound shrimp, uncooked
- 1 tsp. chili powder
- 3 cups Mexican cheese, shredded
- 1 jalapeno pepper, minced
- 1 tsp. of vegetable oil
- 1 lime, juiced
- 6 flour tortillas

Instructions

1. Heat oil in a pan over the medium heat.
2. Add onion, green, and red bell pepper; stir frequently. Cook for 6-8 minutes.
3. Add cumin, salt, and chili powder.
4. Add shrimp and cook for 3-5 minutes.
5. Turn off the heat.
6. Add lime juice and jalapeno pepper in shrimp mixture.
7. Heat a pan over the medium heat; brush it with vegetable oil.
8. Put a tortilla in it. Place shrimp filling and cheese blend on it, and then fold the tortilla.
9. Cook each side for around 5 minutes.
10. Repeat the same process with all tortillas.
11. Serve and enjoy!

Peanut Butter Quesadillas

Ingredients

- 2 tbsp. grape jelly
- 1 flour tortilla
- 1 tsp. butter
- 2 tbsp. peanut butter

Instructions

1. Melt butter in a pan over the medium heat.
2. Put peanut butter on tortilla.
3. Fold it in half.
4. Put it in the pan, and heat each side for two minutes, until it is brown.
5. Cut into wedges, then dip it in jelly and serve.

Conclusion

Mexican cuisine has some amazingly loved and popular dishes in the world. It varies by area due to geography, local climate, and ethnic differences. One common thing about Mexican food is its spiciness. Mexican food can easily be recognized as spicy and hot. The use of chiles is the big reason behind it. Its use is more sophisticated in Mexico than in any other place. Many people from other cultures use chiles the way Mexicans use to add texture and flavor in their food. That is the reason, different varieties of chiles are used as each one serves a different purpose. It is used in making salsa. Many Mexican recipes have the use of salsa to add particular flavor.

Vegetables play a crucial part in Mexican food. The use of tomatoes, potatoes, corn, mushrooms, etc. has always been part of traditional Mexican cuisine. The addition of meat makes the Mexican food rich in protein. All ingredients have the unique feature that they brought to the colorful cuisine of Mexican food. So, it is a perfect and healthy combination of proteins and carbs.

Many countries have made slight changes in the Mexican recipes and added a little bit of flavor to their own cultures. You can see it in the famous Mexican food version in the United States named 'Ted-Mex'. But, if you want to try adventure with your taste buds, try at least once the authentic Mexican food. One of the differences between Mexican food and Ted-Mex is the type of cheese used in recipes. In Ted-Mex, yellow cheese is used, while in authentic Mexican recipes, white cheese is used. The other notable differences are in the use of spices, and the type of tortillas. Both versions of the Mexican food offer delicious recipes. It is up to the Mexican food-lovers, whether they want a little bit change, or want to stick to the authentic taste of Mexican food.

The traditional Mexican cooking style is very humble and earthy. So, if you like to cook at home and try delicious Mexican recipes, but feel unsure of your cooking skills, use this 'Mexican Food' cookbook for cooking and enjoying your favorite recipes. Find your favorite recipes for each time of the day in this cookbook. Create a Mexican-style treat at home, from Steak Burrito to Mexican Churros, and some famous Mexican rice, tacos, soups, and fajitas. It is just difficult not to fell in love with authentic as well as modern-day Mexican food. It is not short on flavors at all.

All these Mexican dishes are worth a try. Some dishes are quick to make, but some will take time. When you have the final dish on your table, you will be satisfied with all the effort you put in. Do not hesitate to customize a little bit as per your preferences and health goals.